OXFORD
UNIVERSITY PRESS

Complete

First Language English

for Cambridge IGCSE®

Jane Arredondo

Oxford excellence for Cambridge IGCSE®

OXFORD

OXFORD
UNIVERSITY PRESS

Great Clarendon Street, Oxford OX2 6DP

Oxford University Press is a department of the University of Oxford.
It furthers the University's objective of excellence in research,
scholarship, and education by publishing worldwide in

Oxford New York

Auckland Cape Town Dar es Salaam Hong Kong Karachi
Kuala Lumpur Madrid Melbourne Mexico City Nairobi
New Delhi Shanghai Taipei Toronto

With offices in

Argentina Austria Brazil Chile Czech Republic France Greece
Guatemala Hungary Italy Japan Poland Portugal Singapore
South Korea Switzerland Thailand Turkey Ukraine Vietnam

Oxford is a registered trade mark of Oxford University Press
in the UK and in certain other countries

British Library Cataloguing in Publication Data

Data available

ISBN: 978-0-19-838905-7
10 9 8 7

Printed in China

Acknowledgments

The publisher would like to thank the following for their kind permission to
reproduce photographs and other copyright material.

® IGCSE is the registered trademark of Cambridge International Examinations.

*Past paper questions are reproduced by permission of Cambridge International Examinations.
Cambridge International Examinations bears no responsibility for the example answers to
questions taken from its past question papers which are contained in this publication. The
questions, example answers, marks awarded and/or comments that appear in this book and
CD were written by the author. In examination, the way marks would be awarded to answers
like these may be different.*

tl = top left, tm = top middle, tr = top right, bl = bottom left bm = bottom middle br = bottom right

P2: S.Borisov/Shutterstock; **P5**: SA Team/Foto Natura; **P7**: © Imagebroker/Alamy; **P8**: National Geographic Society/NGS Images; **P8**: Seleznev Oleg/Shutterstock; **P8**: George Green/Shutterstock; **P9**: Sean Gladwell/Shutterstock; **P13**: © Travelbild.Com/Alamy; **P14**: Juniors/Superstock; **P16**: Gary Yim/Shutterstock; **P16**: Volodymyr Goinyk/Shutterstock; **P17**: Khoroshunova Olga/Shutterstock; **P18**: IM_Photo/Shutterstock; **P18**: S.Borisov/Shutterstock; **P19**: Antoni Murcia/Shutterstock; **P20**: Age Fotostock/Robert Harding; **P24**: B.G. Smith/Shutterstock; **P26**: Paul Vinten/Shutterstock; **P28**: Amnartk/Shutterstock; **P32**: Muellek Josef/Shutterstock; **P34**: PRILL/Shutterstock; P37: Sorin Colac/Shutterstock; **P40**: © The Art Archive/Alamy; **P40**: © The Art Archive/Alamy; **P44**: Samot/Shutterstock; **P44**: Pichugin Dmitry/Shutterstock; **P46**: Aodaodaodaod/Shutterstock; **P52**: Przemyslaw Wasilewski/Shutterstock; **P54**: Natursports/Shutterstock.Com; **P56**: Frank B Yuwono/Shutterstock; **P57**: Getty Images; **P59**: Michael Smith | Dreamstime.Com; **P62**: Serghei Starus/Shutterstock; **P63**: City Of London; **P65**: The Art Archive/Alamy; **P69**: Universal History Archive/UIG; **P72**: Jane Cadwallader; **P74**: Zeljko Radojko/Shutterstock; **P80**: F9photos/Shutterstock.Com; **P82**: Zzvet/Shutterstock.Com; **P83**: Posztos/Shutterstock.Com; **P84**: Thor Jorgen Udvang/Shutterstock.Com; **P86**: Trapnest/Shutterstock; **P88**: Copyright © BBC Photo Library; **P92**: Real Deal Photo; **P94**: Arenapal; **P100**: Artem Loskutnikov/Shutterstock; **P101**: Photosani/Shutterstock; **P104**: Bibliotheque Des Arts Decoratifs, Paris, France/Archives Charmet/The Bridgeman Art Library; **P106**: Dubova/Shutterstock; **P108**: © HARISH TYAGI/Epa/Corbis; **P112**: The Ronald Grant Archive; **P113**: Universalimagesgroup/Contributor/Gettyimages; P120: © Photos 12/Alamy; **P121**: Matt Gibson/Shutterstock; **P122**: Edoma/Shutterstock; **P123**: Edoma/Shutterstock; **P129**: Kevdog818/Shutterstock; **P131**: Pavel L Photo And Video/Shutterstock.Com; **P134**: Krystian Konopka/Shutterstock; **P135**: Ralf Siemieniec/Shutterstock; **P136**: Pavel Kapish/Shutterstock; **P137**: Brandon Alms/Shutterstock; **P137**: Hamsterman/Shutterstock; P138: Moviestore/Rex Features; **P142**: Dr. Morley Read/Shutterstock; **P143**: Meunierd/Shutterstock.Com; **P147**: Jacqueline Abromeit/Shutterstock; **P148bl**: Anatolym/Shutterstock; **P148tr**: Serggod/Shutterstock; **P150**: © Splash News/Corbis; **P151**: © Splash News/Corbis; **P152**: British Library/Robana Via Getty Images; **P153**: Girish Menon/Shutterstock; **P153**: Mirec/Shutterstock; P153: Frank Mac/Shutterstock; **P154**: Getty Images; **P154**: © AF Archive/Alamy; **P159**: Mary Evans Picture Library; **P160**: Alamy; **P164**: Ed Kolenovsky/Associated Press; **P167**: Polarise/Eyevine; **P168**: AFP/Gettyimages; **P169**: NI Sydication; **P172**: Matt Craven/Istock; **P173**: Steffen Foerster/Shutterstock; **P175**: Michael Nichols/National Geographic Stock; **P176**: Microstock Man; **P177**: Mares Lucian/Shutterstock; **P181**: Mares Lucian/Shutterstock; **P182**: Andreiuc88/Shutterstock; **P186**: © Per Andersen/Alamy; **P187**: © Chris Hellier/Alamy; **P188tl**: Henri Manuel/Stringer/Gettyimages; **P188br**: Georgios Kollidas/Shutterstock; **P188bl**: Grafissimo/Istock; **P188tr**: Pictorial Press Ltd/Alamy; **P188tm**: Nicoolay/Istock; **P188bm**: © Bettmann/CORBIS; **P189tl**: Vasakkohaline/Shutterstock; **P189tm**: Reeed/Shutterstock; **P189bl**: Photomak/Shutterstock; **P189tr**: Www.Lebrecht.Co.Uk; **P189bm**: Holger W./Shutterstock.Com; **P189br**: Oksana2010/Shutterstock; **P192**: Jaguar PS/Shutterstock; **P193**: © Cugianza84/Dreamstime.Com; **P196tl**: Dmitry Strizhakov/Shutterstock; **P196bl**: Stocker1970/Shutterstock; **P196mr**: Magmarcz/Shutterstock; **P196ml**: Dan Breckwoldt/Shutterstock.Com; **P196tr**: Waj/Shutterstock; **P196br**: Anastasios71/Shutterstock; **P197tl**: Narongsak N./Shutterstock; **P197tr**: Jenifoto/Shutterstock; **P197bl**: Donsimon/Shutterstock; **P197br**: Witr/Istock; **P199**: Wynnter/Istock; **P200**: Karen Gentry/Shutterstock; **P202**: Mogens Trolle/Shutterstock; **P207**: Lebrecht Music And Arts Photo Library/Alamy; **P208**: © Lebrecht Music And Arts Photo Library/Alamy; **P209**: Georgios Kollidas/Shutterstock; **P210**: Science Source/Science Photo Library; **P211**: © Peter Van Evert/Alamy; **P212**: Jeninva/Shutterstock; **P217**: © AF Archive/Alamy; **P220**: © AF Archive/Alamy; **P222**: Dariush M/Shutterstock; **P229**: Barnes Ian/Shutterstock; **P233**: Ruslan M./Shutterstock; **P235**: © Geraint Lewis/Alamy; **P237**: © Photos 12/Alamy; **P246**: Trinity Mirror/Mirrorpix/Alamy; **P247**: National Archive Records Administration; **P248**: David Grigg/Shutterstock; **P249**: Ollirg/Shutterstock; **P250**: OUP.

Cover image courtesy of Kendal (acrylic on card), Powis, Paul (Contemporary Artist)/Private Collection/The Bridgeman Art Library.

Illustrations by Six Red Marbles and Phil Hackett.

The authors and publisher are grateful for permission reprint the following copyright material:

Jean Adams: extract from 'Families and Children: Egyptian Marriage' as written for www.unusualhistoricals.blogspot.com, reprinted by permission of the author.

Patrick Barkham: extract from' What Makes Madame Tussaud's Wax Work?', *The Guardian*, 26.2.2011, copyright © Guardian News & Media Ltd 2011, reprinted by permission of GNM Ltd.

Gemma Bowes: abridged from 'Advice for would-be travel authors', *The Guardian*, guardian.co.uk, 23.9.2011, copyright © Guardian News & Media Ltd 2011, reprinted by permission of GNM Ltd.

Ray Bradbury: 'August 2026: There will come soft rains' from *The Martian Chronicles* (HarperCollins, 2001), copyright © Ray Bradbury 1950, reprinted by permission of Don Congdon Associates.

Elizabeth Brewster: 'Where I Come From' from *Collected Poems of Elizabeth Brewster* (Oberon, 2003), reprinted by permission of Oberon Press.

Bill Bryson: extracts from *A Walk in the Wood: Rediscovering America on the Appalachian Trail* (Doubleday 1997/Black Swan 1998), copyright © Bill Bryson 1997, reprinted by permission of the Random House Publishing Group and Broadway Books, an imprint of the Crown Publishing Group, a division of Random House, LLC; and from *Neither Here nor There* (Secker and Warburg, 1991), copyright © Bill Bryson 1991, reprinted by permission of the Random House Publishing Group and HarperCollins Publishers, Inc.

Alan Butler: 'Plymouth's Drum Theatre Hosts Moving Play *Ivan and the Dogs*', 247 *Magazine* 29.9.2010, reprinted by permission of the publishers, Out of Hand Ltd.

Bruce Chatwin: extract from 'On Yeti tracks', first published in *Esquire* Magazine (1983) from *What Am I Doing Here* (Jonathan Cape, 1989/ Vintage 2005), copyright © The Estate of Bruce Chatwin 1989, reprinted by permission of the Random House Publishing Group, Viking Penguin, a division of Penguin Group (USA) Inc, and Aitken Alexander Associates for the Estate.

Angela Clarence: extracts from 'Children of the Stars', *The Observer*, 5.11.2000, copyright © Guardian News & Media Ltd 2000; and from 'Travelling in the Desert', *The Observer*, 21.5.2000, copyright © Guardian News & Media Ltd 2000, both reprinted by permission of GNM Ltd.

Amy Crawford: 'Who was Cleopatra: Mythology, propaganda, Liz Taylor and the real Queen of the Nile' *Smithsonian Magazine*, 1.4.2007, copyright © 2007, 2013 Smithsonian Institution, reprinted by permission of Smithsonian Enterprises. All rights reserved.

Anita Desai: 'Circus Cat. Alley Cat' first published in *Thought* (New Delhi, 1957), copyright © Anita Desai 1957, reprinted by permission of the author, c/o Rogers Coleridge & White, 20 Powis Mews, London W11 1JN.

Rick Dewsbury: extract from 'Is this final proof the Yeti exists?', *Daily Mail*, 11.10.2011, reprinted by permission of Solo Syndication for Associated Newspapers Ltd.

Chitra Banerjee Divakaruni: extract from *Mistress of Spices* (Black Swan, 2006), copyright © Chitra Banerjee Divarkuni 1997, reprinted by permission of The Random House Publishing Group and Doubleday, an imprint of the Knopf Doubleday Publishing Group, a division of Random House LLC. All rights reserved.

Dorothy Dunnett: extract from *Scales of Gold : Travelling in the Desert in the 15th Century* (Michael Joseph, 1991, Penguin, 2000), copyright © Dorothy Dunnett 1991, reprinted by permission of Penguin Books Ltd.

Fred Ebb: extract from the lyric of 'Money, Money'' (from *Cabaret*), music by John Kander, lyrics by Fred Ebb, copyright © 1972 Alley Music Corp, New York, and Bug Music - Trio Music Co, California, USA, copyright renewed; reprinted by permission of Carlin Music Corp, London NW1 8BD. All rights reserved.

Paul Evans: 'The Crusade for Crusoe's Islands, *Geographical Magazine*, reprinted by permission of the publishers, Syon Publishing Ltd.

Robert Frost: 'Fire and Ice' from *The Poetry of Robert Frost* edited by Edward Connery Lathem (Jonathan Cape, 1971), reprinted by permission of The Random House Publishing Group.

Continued on last page.

Contents

Introduction iv

What's on the CD? v

1 Travellers' tales 2

2 The world of nature 26

3 Points of view 54

4 "All the world's a stage" 80

5 Family and friends 106

6 "Living in a material world" 134

7 "Believe it or not" 160

8 World famous 186

9 Endings 222

10 Exam practice 250

11 Language reference 276

Glossary 309

Index 313

Please note: The Cambridge IGCSE® First Language English (0500) syllabus is known as the Cambridge International Certificate First Language English (0522) in the United Kingdom (UK). In the UK version, Speaking and Listening is compulsory in the L1/L2 assessment.

Introduction

This student book supports the Cambridge IGCSE®
First Language English syllabus. It also aims to
support you in becoming:

- **confident** in working with information and ideas
  (your own and those of others)
- **responsible** for yourself, and responsive to and
  respectful of others
- **reflective** as a learner so you can develop your own
  ability to learn
- **innovative** and equipped for new and future challenges
- **engaged** intellectually and socially.

To this end, and to help you prepare for your
assessments, this book contains:

- a wide range of reading passages with questions
  that ask you to demonstrate your understanding of
  what has been written and to discuss the writer's
  style
- a range of writing tasks where you practise writing
  in various styles for different purposes
- speaking and listening activities where you practise
  giving your opinion, making presentations,
  working with a partner and collaborating in group
  discussions on topical issues.

As you work through the book, you will be developing
your skills and strategies. Units 9 and 10 include
exam-style questions. The Language reference
section (Unit 11) will help you with your grammar,
punctuation and spelling. The Glossary explains
technical words used for Cambridge IGCSE® First
Language English and Cambridge IGCSE® Literature
(English).

Cambridge IGCSE® First Language English exams include:

Reading Paper 1 (Core) – two reading passages
and three questions testing reading comprehension,
understanding of the writer's craft and summary skills

or

Reading Paper 2 (Extended) – two reading passages
and three questions testing reading comprehension,
understanding of the writer's craft and summary skills

and

Writing Paper 3 (Core and Extended) – two sections
that test candidates' ability in directed writing and
creative writing.

or

Component 4 Coursework Portfolio – three
assignments of between 500 and 800 words, written in
different styles.

Schools may also enter candidates for:

Component 5 Speaking and Listening tests, which
demonstrate individual speaking and listening skills

or

Component 6 Speaking and Listening Coursework,
which demonstrates candidates' speaking and listening
skills in individual, pair-based and group discussions.

Apart from helping you to improve the English
language skills you need in all your lessons, it will also
help you to develop the language skills you need in
your future studies and when you leave school. Each
unit contains reading passages where you need to skim
read or scan the text to get the idea of what it is about
and locate specific information. You will also find texts
where you must look closely at how a writer has used
language to create a particular effect. One of the most
important reading skills you will practise is inference.
This is where you have to read between the lines to
identify themes, ideas and unspoken meanings.

Many of the writing styles, such as summaries and
reports, have real-life applications; you need to know
how to write in various styles for different purposes for
your further education and your future employment.
Writing panels set out advice or guidelines on how to
plan and present different types of essay.

Talking points and speaking and listening topics are
designed to help you improve your communication
skills and practise speaking in different ways for
different purposes. There are discussion topics, issues
for debates and guidelines for giving speeches or
presentations. For the last of these you will learn how
to address an audience and, when relevant, persuade
them to your way of thinking.

You can also use or adapt many of the topics for your
portfolio or assessments if you are doing Component 4
Coursework Portfolio and/or Component 6 Speaking and
Listening Coursework.

Above all, however, this book should help you to
develop your thinking skills. Throughout your studies,
you need to think about what you are reading, writing
or saying, and demonstrate your reasoning. This book
will help you to learn how to do this – but only you can
do the thinking and answer the questions!

What's on the CD?

The material on the CD-ROM has been specially written to support your learning. Below is an outline of what you will find on the CD–ROM, followed by two sample pages. Everything in the book and on the CD-ROM has been designed to help you develop your language skills and achieve your best. Sample pages from the CD-ROM follow on the next two pages.

Help yourself!

This section will help you think about where, when and how you study and how to cope.

Interactive activities

These interactive activities are designed to test your spelling and grammar and help you to improve your use of English.

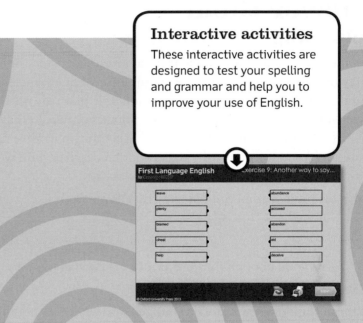

Exam-style questions

Here you will find useful advice and information with exam-style questions to help you improve the skills needed for Reading questions, Directed Writing and Compositions.

Skills practice

Specially written exam-style questions and specimen Cambridge IGCSE® First Language English Reading Passages papers give you more practice and help you revise.

Sample pages from CD-ROM

Exam-style questions and how to answer them
Paraphrasing

When we are talking about a passage from a novel, short story or scene from a play in lessons, we re-phrase or paraphrase what characters say and/or think. We say what a character has said or explain narrative details in our own words. You need to do the same thing and then go that little bit further by re-phrasing direct speech and explaining narrative detail to show you understand how and why the author has used certain words and that you understand what a character is *really* saying.

Look at this example from *A Suitable Boy* by Vikram Seth.

"What is good enough for your brother is good enough for you."

"Yes, Baoji," said Maan, smiling.

Mr Mahesh Kapoor frowned. His younger son, while succeeding to his own habit of fine dress, had not succeeded to his obsession with hard work. Nor did he have any ambition to speak of.

"It is no use being a good-looking young wastrel forever," said (Maan's) father. "And marriage will force you to settle down and take things seriously. I have written to the Banaras people and I expect a favourable answer any day."

Questions

1. Why does Mr Kapoor despair of his son Maan and how does he propose to remedy his character? (3 marks)

Before you answer this, identify the keywords in the question to be sure you understand what you are being asked to do and therefore answer correctly.

This question has two parts. Identify what you are being asked to do.

a. Why does Mr Kapoor despair of his younger son, Maan? (1 mark)

b. How does Mr Kapoor propose to remedy Maan's character? (2 marks)

Remember:

a. You need to explain why Mr Kapoor despairs of his son.

b. You need to say what Mr Kapoor proposes to do and why.

To answer the question appropriately, you now need to annotate the text for each part of question to identify the relevant information.

> Explain what is wrong with Maan's character.

> 1 mark suggests there is only one part to this question.

> 2 marks suggest there are two elements or details needed to answer this question.

> What is Mr Kapoor going to do/already doing to 'improve' his son?

Help yourself!

This section of the CD is to help you think about where, when and how you study.

How can I improve my language skills by myself?

There is one simple answer as to where and how to get help for English – books!

Every time we read we learn something new or consolidate what we already know.

Now you have learned to read, make time for reading to learn.

Reading novels (hardback, paperback or ebook), newspapers, magazines and online blogs will improve your vocabulary and help you with every aspect of your English. It will also help you to prepare for life after school.

Reading for success

Reading is necessary to learn and share information in every aspect of our lives.

Reading is the very first building block in any kind of learning [...]

A poor reader will not be able to reach a high level of education. This, in turn, will severely limit the choices of occupation. The poor reader that grew up with very few job opportunities will inevitably become part of the lower socio-economic population. Earning potential, if any, will be low.

Barbara Nuzum, 30 January 2010

From: http://www.helium.com/items/1726560-reading-for-success-and-economic-and-social-implications

1 Travellers' tales

In this unit you will:

→ **Visit** Ancient Greece, Antarctica, the British Isles, Canada, Chile, Guiana, Indonesia, Italy, Spain, the USA, Venezuela and Xanadu

→ **Read** autobiography, holiday advertisements and travel articles, modern and pre-20th century poems

→ **Write** to inform, entertain and persuade.

Asclepius and the two travellers

Many centuries ago in Greece, Asclepius the doctor was walking in the dry, rugged countryside outside Athens. At noon, with the sun high in the sky, Asclepius, who had been walking since dawn and was very hot and thirsty, heard a most welcome sound; trickling water. He followed the sound to its source, a small stream running over smooth rocks, and sat down thankfully to rinse his hands and take a drink. At this point, where the stream rose out of the ground, the water was refreshingly cold.   5

As Asclepius cupped his hands to gather water, he noticed a stranger approaching him.

"Excuse me," said the man, "I'm going to Athens and I've never been there before. Can you tell me what it's like?"

"Where have you come from?" asked Asclepius.

"Piraeus," said the man.   10

"Well, what's it like in Piraeus?" asked Asclepius.

"Oh dreadful!" said the man. "It's full of noisy, dirty, unfriendly people – a horrible place."

"Well I'm afraid you are probably going to find Athens is the same," said Asclepius.

"Oh dear," sighed the man, and shaking his head with disappointment he continued slowly on his way.

Asclepius also shook his head, but then he felt and heard his stomach rumble, so he unpacked the   15
food he had brought with him. There was a hunk of sweet-smelling bread, some sharp, white goat's cheese and a handful of delicious fat, black olives.

He was just about to take his first bite of bread when another traveller appeared.

"Good day, sir," said this traveller. "Forgive me for disturbing you, but I'm on my way to Athens, do you know it? Can you tell me what it's like?"   20

"Where have you come from?" asked Asclepius.

"Piraeus," said the man.

"Well, what's it like in Piraeus?" asked Asclepius.

"Oh it's a charming place!" said the man. "Clean and colourful, full of friendly, generous people – a charming place."   25

"Ah, then I think you are going to find Athens is very similar, if not just the same."

"Excellent, excellent! Thank you, sir. Enjoy your meal. I must say that bread smells very appetizing." And with that the second traveller waved his staff in farewell and strode off with a spring in his step towards Athens.

Asclepius watched him go then, smiling to himself, he bit into his crusty bread. It was delicious.

Based on *In Your Hands*,
by Jane Revell and Susan Norman (1997)

Talking points

- What do you think the first traveller will find in Athens? Explain why you believe this.
- How do you think the second traveller will feel about Athens? Explain why you believe this.
- What was Asclepius trying to tell us through this tale?

Travel writing

In this unit you will read various types of travel writing, including extracts from travel books from different times. Look carefully at how each writer makes his or her description of a place interesting or exciting.

Charles Waterton

The author and adventurer Charles Waterton was a British naturalist, who was literally wandering (often barefoot) in South America during the early part of the 19th century. Waterton is known for bringing a sample of *wourali* – a poison – back to Europe, where it was modified, called *curare* and used in surgical operations as a muscle relaxant. In the passage opposite Waterton describes how the Macoushi Indians of Guiana make *wourali*.

Practising summary skills

Charles Waterton describes how the Macoushi Indians of Guiana make a poison to kill their prey. The properties of the poison prevent the dead bird or animal from putrefying (rotting) before the Macoushi can eat it.

Read the passage again. Make notes and then summarise how Macoushi Indians made *wourali*. Include:

a. the ingredients

b. the method.

Write between 100 and 150 words.

Summary skills
Summarising a text

1. Read the passage twice.

2. Read the question and keyword it.

3. Find relevant information in the text and underline it. Colour code your underlining by using different coloured pencils. Using two different coloured pencils for different types of information helps you to identify two parts of a task. For the activity on this page, you would need one colour for the ingredients and another for the method.

4. Number and/or letter the separate points you have underlined according to the task so you can write them out in order. Using numbers and letters helps you locate and organise your material before you write it out in your own words. In more difficult tasks, number and/or letter the points according to how you are going to use them in your summary. In the activity on this page, which has two parts, you need to number the ingredients that are used for the poison (1, 2, 3 ...) and use letters to label the stages of making the poison (a, b, c ...).

5. Make brief notes before you write your summary.

6. Write your summary in your own words as far as possible. Never copy or "lift" from the text. Think of synonyms (words with similar meanings) or new ways to make essential points. Synonyms can be used to avoid copying the writer's words, but don't go to extremes! Water is *water*, not a tasteless, colourless liquid; a tree is a *tree*, not a tall, wooden-stemmed, long-lived plant.

7. Edit your summary. Proofread it, correcting any spelling, grammar or punctuation mistakes.

Wanderings in South America

In the month of April, 1812, I [Charles Waterton] left the town of Stabroek to travel through the wilds of Demerara and Essequibo, a part of Dutch Guiana, in South America. The chief objects in view were to collect a quantity of the strongest Wourali 5 poison and to reach the inland frontier fort of Portuguese Guiana.

Wourali

A day or two before the Macoushi Indian prepares his poison, he goes into the forest in quest of the 10 ingredients. A vine grows in these wilds, which is called Wourali. It is from this that the poison takes its name, and it is the principle ingredient. When he has procured enough of this, he digs up a root of a very bitter taste, ties them together, and then looks 15 about for two kinds of bulbous plants, which contain a green and glutinous juice. He fills a little quake, which he carries on his back, with the stalks of these; and lastly, ranges up and down till he finds two species of ants. One of them is large and black, 20 and so venomous, that its sting produces a fever; it is most commonly to be met with on the ground. The other is a little red ant, which stings like a nettle, and generally has its nest under the leaf of a shrub.

A quantity of the strongest Indian pepper is used; 25 but this he has already planted round his hut.

The pounded fangs of the Labarri snake, and those of the Counacouchi, are likewise added. These he commonly has in store; for when he kills a snake he generally extracts the fangs, and keeps 30 them by him.

Having thus found the necessary ingredients, he scrapes the wourali vine and bitter root into thin shavings, and puts them into a kind of colander made of leaves: this he holds over an earthen pot, 35 and pours water on the shavings: the liquor which comes through has the appearance of coffee. When a sufficient quantity has been procured, the shavings are thrown aside. He then bruises the bulbous stalks, and squeezes a proportionate quantity of their juice 40 through his hands into the pot. Lastly the snakes' fangs, ants and pepper are bruised and thrown into it. It is then placed on a slow fire, and as it boils, more of the juice of the wourali is added, according as it may be found necessary, and the scum is taken 45 off with a leaf: it remains on the fire till reduced to a thick syrup of a deep brown colour. As soon as it has arrived at this state, a few arrows are poisoned with it, to try its strength.

By Charles Waterton (1825)

Labarri (n): a very deadly snake, of Guiana and eastern Brazil. Its greyish-brown colouring and darker markings harmonise with dead leaves and fallen branches.

REMINDER – annotating

To annotate means to add notes, explanations or comments to a written text.

Reading

In the article "Children of the Stars" opposite find:

a. facts (historical and geographical)

b. examples of personal impression or opinion.

REMINDER – quoting

The SQuEE technique

In many language tasks you need to identify, analyse and discuss a writer's style or choice of words. Use the SQuEE technique to help you.

State the facts or what you believe.

Quote a relevant word or phrase to support the point.

Explain the choice of words.

Effect – describe the effect created.

Reading skills
Reading to identify information

In most school subjects you have to read and locate information before you can answer a question. As you go through school you acquire the habit of reading with different levels of concentration, perhaps without even realising it. When you are preparing for your exams, however, you need to develop your reading skills so that you can understand exactly what a question is asking you to do in a given time limit.

Keywording

The first and perhaps most important skill is **keywording**: finding the key words in a question or task. In English, it is as important to annotate the question you have been set as it is to make notes on the text you have been given to read. This will help you to identify the root of a question and understand how to answer it – what exactly the question is calling for. Always underline or circle the key words in a question.

Skimming

Skimming is reading a text quickly to get an idea of what it is about. We often skim the headlines on the front page of a newspaper and then quickly read the subheadings and first paragraphs to gain an idea of what the reports are about and see which are of interest to us.

Scanning

Scanning means reading in order to locate information. We sometimes scan the information sheets that come with medicines to find out what quantity of the medication should be taken, how it should be consumed and how frequently.

Remember

In English exams you need to **keyword** the question and then **skim** the text to get a clear idea of what it is about before you scan it in order to locate specific items of information.

The writer's craft – description

Look at the ways that the writer of the article opposite makes Los Roques sound like an inviting and interesting holiday location. Explain how she makes the following descriptions effective:

- the location (its history and geography)
- the people who live or do not live there
- animal and bird life.

Children of the Stars

Walking the soft white beaches of Los Roques it is rare to see another human being. There are empty conch shells, coral sculptures, scuttling hermit crabs, shiny lizards and long-legged sandpipers, a watching heron, a fluffy white chick sitting in 5 its nest amidst the green sea-purslane. When I took to the warm turquoise waters, jumping jacks flopped in the shallows; frigate birds with sharply angled wings floated above; curious terns looked me in the eye; and pelicans dive-bombed for 10 breakfast. Below the surface, designer fish played hide and seek in the corals: angelfish, butterfly fish, parrotfish, blueheads, snappers, baby damsels and a fleeing turtle, to mention but a few.

Los Roques is a coral archipelago 150 km off 15 the coast of Venezuela consisting of 42 small islands surrounding a huge lagoon. Here, in this paradisiacal playground, hurricanes hardly happen. The days are hot and the nights are cool. Venezuelans visit at weekends to snorkel, 20 scuba dive and watch the sunset, returning to Gran Roque, the only inhabited island, for dinner and a comfortable night in one of the many delightful posadas.

Following in the wake of Christopher Columbus 25 and Walter Raleigh, we took a boat up the Orinoco River. Our guides encouraged us to take a dip in the river at sunset. It looked inviting – the wide dark waters tinged with pink, parrots winging their way home above a wall of green jungle. A 30 young Belgian couple took the plunge. But are there crocodiles? And piranha fish? Yes! But there are also electric-blue morph butterflies with wings as large as your hand, noisy families of red howler monkeys and the part-reptile guacharacca bird, a 35 hang-over from pre-historic times.

There was also plenty of wildlife activity at the jungle camp. A magnificent puma, brought in as a baby by the Indians, paced the length of its enclosure. In the rafters of the dining room an 40 ocelot* and a racoon played together while a family of otters honked noisily for scraps at our table. A huge tarantula sitting on an adjacent banana plant caused a stir. The young Belgian

took it on the back of his hand but his mosquito 45 repellent irritated the spider which slowly "hunched up", a sign that it was ready to deliver its poison. Our guide gently coaxed it back to its leaf – no harm done!

The Orinoco Delta is home to the Warao Indians. 50 The river is their highway and the canoe their only mode of transport. Made from a single tree, the hollowed out trunk is heated over fire which causes it to unfurl like a flower and seals the wood at the same time. A father crafts a canoe for his 55 child before it can walk and when a member of the family dies he or she is placed in a canoe covered with flowers and carried far into the jungle. The family then moves to another part of the river and builds a new house to avoid the spirit of death. 60

The Warao believe they came from the stars and their god brought them to the Orinoco Delta, to paradise, where the Mareche, the "tree of life", grow in abundance. The Mareche produces an orange fruit which, when softened for several days, 65 makes a palatable juice – or wine, if fermented. The young tree yields a string from which hammocks and baskets are made. When the tree rots it is home to a large, yellow grub, an excellent source of protein – eaten live. I was offered a chance to try 70 this wriggling delicacy – I just wasn't hungry! For the most part the Warao still live in the old way, at one with the jungle in their riverside houses on stilts – the dwellings that caused Columbus to christen the country Little Venice –Venezuela. 75

By Angela Clarence, *The Observer*
(5 November 2000)

Speaking and listening

Travel and tourism

People have been on the move since the end of the Ice Age when they had to follow the animals they were hunting in order to survive. Nowadays, most people live in one place, but many still make long journeys for work, obligations or leisure.

Discuss the following questions with a partner.

- Do you think that travelling is part of human nature?
- Why do so many people like visiting places they will never live in or return to?
- If you had the opportunity to go anywhere in the world for two weeks, where would you go? Why would you choose that place?

Coursework idea

Use the activity above in pairs and/or groups to practise for your Speaking and Listening Coursework.

Expedition (n.): a journey or voyage for a particular purpose.

(*Oxford Study Dictionary*)

Travel writing informs, describes and entertains. Voyage narratives were very popular in the 17th and 18th centuries, but most were written by travellers, not writers. The narrator of *A New Voyage Round the World* by William Dampier says, "[A] seaman, when he comes to the press, is pretty much out of his element, and a very good sailor may make but a very indifferent author."

Daniel Defoe

Defoe (*c*.1660–1731) was a great traveller with a journalist's curiosity and an eye for detail. He is best known for writing *Robinson Crusoe*, but his other stories also include long ocean voyages. His descriptive narratives are based on information obtained from men and women who had made expeditions to exotic places.

Apart from fiction, Defoe wrote numerous volumes of what we now call travel writing. He said each book contained a "diverting account of whatever is curious and worth observation".

Defoe's use of English looks and sounds very old-fashioned to us, but his narrative technique is not that different to modern travel writing, which is characterised by:

- a detailed description of people and places
- the inclusion of the writer's thoughts and feelings
- a descriptive, imaginative use of language
- being written in the first person.

" He never heard a sound more dismal than their parting oars."—p. 8.

Tour Thro' the Whole Island of Great Britain

The author's preface to the first volume

By Daniel Defoe

[...] In every county something of the people is said, as well as of the place, of their customs, speech, employments, the product of their labour, and the manner of their living, the circumstances as well as situation of the towns, their trade and government; of the rarities of art, or nature; the rivers, of the inland, and river navigation; also of the lakes and medicinal springs, not forgetting the general dependance of the whole country upon the city of London, as well for the consumption of its produce, as the circulation of its trade.

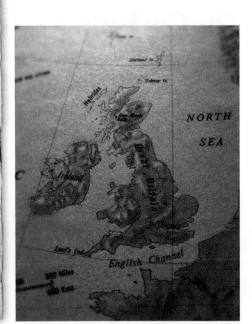

Tour Thro' the Whole Island of Great Britain

The author's preface to the second volume

By Daniel Defoe

[...] Our manner is plain, and suited to the nature of familiar letters; [...] we keep close to the first design of giving, as near as possible, such an account of things, as may entertain the reader, and give him a view of our country, such as may tempt him to travel over it himself, in which case it will be not a little assisting to him, or qualify him to discourse of it, as one that had a tolerable knowledge of it, tho' he stay'd at home.

Now read an extract from Defoe's *Tour* about the county of Cornwall in the south-west of England. Is Defoe giving an objective or subjective account of the place he is visiting?

On Cornwall

We have nothing more of note in this county, that I could see, or hear of, but a set of monumental stones, called The Hurlers, of which the country, nor all the writers of the country, can give us no good account; so I must leave them as I found them.   5

The game called the Hurlers, is a thing the Cornish men value themselves much upon; I confess, I see nothing in it, but that it is a rude violent play among the boors, or country people; brutish and furious, and a sort of an evidence,   10 that they were, once, a kind of barbarians: It seems, to me, something to resemble the old way of play, as it was then called, with whirle-bats, with which Hercules slew the gyant [...] The wrestling in Cornwall, is, indeed, a much more manly and   15 generous exercise, and that closure, which they call the Cornish Hug, has made them eminent in the wrestling rings all over England.

By Daniel Defoe

Hurlers (n.): the game may have been similar to Gaelic shinty or Irish hurling, both old forms of modern hockey.

Whirle-bat (n.): perhaps like a hockey stick.

Now read some advice on how to write modern travel articles.

How To Write the Perfect Travel Article

Travel writing is part reporting, part diary and part providing traveller information. Travel writers create their art using a multitude of different styles and techniques but the best stories generally share certain characteristics, notably:

1) Clear writing style used by a writer who knows the point of the story, gets to it quickly and gets it across to the reader strongly and with brevity and clarity. 5

2) Strong sense of the writer's personality, ideally demonstrating intelligence, wit and style.

3) Use of the writer's personal experiences, other anecdotes and quotations to add life to the piece. 10

4) Vivid reporting – the ability of the writer to convey to readers, using as many of the senses as possible, the travel experience through the use of words alone.

5) High literary quality and the accurate use of grammar and syntax. 15

6) Meaty, practical and accurate information that is useful to the reader.

Be Fresh: Give your story a fresh point of view and, if at all possible, cover some out-of-the-ordinary subject matter. Be creative in your writing. Strive for the best and strongest use of English and the most original and powerful metaphors and similes. 20

Be Personal: Take your own approach to a location you've visited, an activity you've tried or an adventure that thrilled you. What was it that really excited or inspired you? Identify it and get it across to your readers. To stand out from the crowd, your story must have a personal voice and point of view. Remember that most places you write about will already have been written about before. Your challenge is to find something new and original to say. 25 30

Be Funny: Travel writing should mostly have a light, bright, lively and fun tone. Travel, the process of leaving the familiar to go to the foreign and unfamiliar, is often rich in comedy and comical events. Also, don't be afraid to incorporate mishaps into your pieces. These can be just as worth reading about, maybe more so, particularly if they also incorporate an element of comedy. 35

Be Surprising: Give the reader something out of the ordinary; something that only someone who has been to the location would know. 40

Be Balanced: Travel writing must blend your personal observations, descriptions and commentary with practical information that is useful to your readers. The precise balance depends on the outlet you are aiming your story at but rarely should a good travel piece comprise more facts than description. Two-thirds or even three-quarters' colorful description to one-third or one-quarter facts would be a reasonable guideline to start from. 45 50

Be a Quoter: Work in quotes from visitors to locations, or participants in activities. Let them express their thoughts about how they feel about a place or activity. Quotes lift stories.

The Big Picture (What is the main point you want to get across to your reader?): Decide at the outset what main point about a location or activity you want to convey. This is the "big picture" and you then work your impressions and facts around it. 55

From "The Insider Secrets of Freelance Travel Writing," by Martin Li, www.transitionsabroad.com (13 January 2012)

Here is some more advice for would-be travel authors from Gemma Bowes and other writers for *The Guardian*, a daily newspaper published in Britain.

Tips for travel writing

Check out these handy tips from *The Guardian* Travel team.

- Write in the first person, past tense (or present if the action really justifies it), and make your story a personal account, interwoven with facts, description and observation.

- Many writers start their piece with a strong – but brief – anecdote that introduces the general feeling, tone and point of the trip and story. Something that grabs the reader's attention and makes them want to read on. Don't start with the journey to the airport – start with something interesting, not what happened first. [5] [10]

- Early on you need to get across the point of the story and trip – where you were, what were you doing there and why. If there is a hook – a new trend, discovery or angle – make that clear within the first few paragraphs. [15]

- Try to come up with a narrative thread that will run throughout the piece, linking the beginning and end; a point you are making. The piece should flow, but don't tell the entire trip chronologically, cherry pick the best bits, anecdotes and descriptions, that will tell the story for you. [20]

- Quotes from people you met can bring the piece to life, give the locals a voice and make a point it would take longer to explain yourself. Quote [25] people accurately and identify them: Who are they? Where did you meet them?

- Avoid clichés. Try to come up with original descriptions that mean something. Our pet hates include: "bustling markets" ... "azure/cobalt sea" ... "nestling among" ... "hearty fare" ... "a smorgasbord of ... ". [30]

- Don't use phrases and words you wouldn't use in speech (such as "eateries" or "abodes"), and don't try to be too clever or formal; the best writing sounds natural and has personality. [35]

- Check your facts! It's good to work in some interesting nuggets of information, perhaps things you've learned from talking to people, or in books or other research, but use reliable sources and double-check they are correct. [40]

- Write economically – don't waste words on sentences that could be condensed. E.g., say "there was a ... " not "it became apparent to me that in fact there existed a ... ". [45]

- Moments that affected you personally don't necessarily make interesting reading. Avoid tales of personal mishaps – missed buses, diarrhoea, rain – unless pertinent to the story. [50]

By Gemma Bowes *et al.*,
www.guardian.co.uk (23 September 2011)

REMINDER – chronological order

Chronological order refers to the order in which things happen. It derives from the Greek *chronos* = time.

Tips and techniques

1. Where do Li and Bowes *et al.* agree and disagree in their travel writing tips? Make two lists: one list for points on which they agree, the other for points on which they disagree.

2. Look back at the article "Children of the Stars" (page 7) by Angela Clarence. Referring back to the guidelines for travel writers, what recommended techniques has the author used to make this article so readable?

Writing to inform and entertain

Using the travel writing guidelines, create your own piece of travel writing. Choose one of the following titles and add the location:

- On the beach in ...
- At a market in ...
- Downtown in ...

Write between 350 and 450 words.

REMINDER – planning

Before you start writing, think about the location and what makes it special or memorable. Do a mind map or a spidergram and make notes on its distinctive features. Try to use the five senses in your description.

The crusade for Crusoe's islands

Chile's remote Juan Fernández Islands inspired the story of Robinson Crusoe. Paul Evans flies in to see if tourism can help to protect the islands' unique, diverse but threatened ecosystems.

The Juan Fernández Islands, located 600 kilometres 5 off the coast of Chile, were named after the 16th-century Spanish explorer who stumbled across them while trying to find a new trade route between Peru and Valparaiso in 1574, but are more famous for a Scotsman called Alexander Selkirk, who, 10 in 1704, marooned himself here, and became the inspiration for Daniel Defoe's famous novel *Robinson Crusoe*.

Endemics at risk

The Juan Fernández archipelago is full of castaways – plants and animals that somehow 15 ended up on these remote outcrops and evolved into species that occur nowhere else on Earth. "This is one of the global jewels of biodiversity," says Peter Hodum, an ecologist from the University of Puget Sound in Washington State. 20 "Although it doesn't have the cachet of the Galápagos, it's just as important."

The islands have more than 130 endemic plant species – nearly two thirds of its flora – including

the white-flowering Luma trees and the Juan Bueno, a purple-tube-flowered shrub that has co-evolved with the astonishingly beautiful but critically endangered Juan Fernández firecrown hummingbird. Then there are the ferns – from huge tree ferns to tiny delicate fronds on dripping cliffs – not to mention the red-backed hawk and the Juan Fernández subspecies of the American kestrel, and 400 beetle species. [25] [30]

Because of this unique biodiversity and spectacular scenery, the islands were designated a Chilean national park during the 1930s, and a UNESCO [United Nations Educational, Scientific, and Cultural Organization] biosphere reserve in 1977. However, a visitor with an ecological eye will soon pick up trouble in paradise. The problems started in 1540, when the archipelago's discoverer, Juan Fernández, dropped off four goats to provide food for future mariners. They were a godsend for castaways such as Selkirk, but a nightmare for the island's flora – their [35] [40] [45]

numbers have since swelled to around 3,500 and their voracious appetites have wreaked havoc on the native vegetation.

Unlike Selkirk, who was eager to be rescued, many of those who came later decided to stay: pirates, political prisoners and, during the 19th century, colonists. The island's population has always been small – there are currently around 750 islanders, 600 of whom live in San Juan Bautista sustained by lobster fishing, cattle farming and government subsidies. Like Juan Fernández, those who followed brought the seeds of the islands' destruction with them, often literally. [50] [55]

Overgrazing by livestock, including rabbits and those goats, has led to irreversible erosion. Rats and mice jumped ship to become predators of endemic birds and gnawers of rare plants. Domestic cats and the introduced coati also preyed on ground-nesting birds. Ornamental plants skipped over garden fences to colonise; a [60] [65]

Coati (n.): a mammal related to the raccoon, with a narrow snout and a striped tail.

European blackberry hedge went mad and started smothering hectares of pristine forest. A dense-thicket-forming South American shrub called the maqui has had the same effect. The spread of introduced plants is aided and abetted by one of the locals, the Magellan thrush, which disperses non-native seeds far and wide. 70

Limited tourism

The Chilean government has worked to keep tourism in the archipelago low key. "Chile 75 values the unique flora and fauna of the Juan Fernández Islands as heritage for the world," says Miguel Schottlander, the head of the natural resources protection department. "Even special-interest tourism, restricted to 80 small groups, could damage the ecology if it's left uncontrolled. However, tourism is very important for the local people; they would like to see more. At present, there is a stable population, and we are afraid that the island 85 can't sustain a larger population."

Aaron Cavieres of Chile's National Commission for the Environment, who is the executive secretary of the Biodiversity Conservancy Programme for the Juan Fernández Islands, 90 believes that tourism has played an important role in creating a strong local interest in biodiversity. "This is because islanders have come to realise what a treasure their archipelago is," he says. "And because they do not depend so 95 much on the land [for agriculture] as they did in the past, tourism is an important source of income. Tourism is becoming more important.

The sustainability problem, in my view, comes from bad practices of the past – overgrazing, felling trees 100 and invasive species. I would say tourism could play a role in the sustainability of the islanders by reducing dependence on government subsidies."

"If it's done sensitively and on an appropriate scale, tourism could be helpful," says Hodum. "It would 105 raise awareness and benefit the local economy if tourism was thoughtfully focused on the endemic species and their uniqueness. But people should also understand the threats and see the destruction of cloud forests invaded by non-native plants. This 110 would build a commitment for conservation."

Until recently, tourists numbered a steady 1,500–2,000 a year, coming to dive, snorkel, hike, watch wildlife and eat lobster. Infrastructure is currently pretty basic, with a hotel, a few hostels 115 and campsites, and a couple of bars and restaurants catering to the intrepid few.

To the rescue

On Robinson Crusoe Island, 500 metres above the harbour at San Juan Bautista, is a knife-edge ridge; a 120 windy look-out where Alexander Selkirk would come to scan the horizon for ships. Conservationists dream of rescue too. As Ivan Julio Leiva Silva, director of the Juan Fernández National Park, says: "The important thing about this biodiversity is that it has a meaning 125 for itself, but it's up to us to take care of it."

By Paul Evans, *Geographical* online magazine, www.geographical.co.uk

Writing an article

Using information from the article on the Juan Fernández Islands, write an article for a blog or magazine about the advantages and disadvantages of encouraging tourism in this location and similar environments.

Write between 250 and 350 words.

Holiday brochures

Coursework idea

You could use holiday brochures for a Speaking and Listening activity.

Petrel (n.): seabird.

Speaking and listening

The holiday of a lifetime

The next few pages feature descriptions of four very different holidays. Which one is for you?

Read the information and make notes on where you would like to go in order of preference.

1. *I would most like to go to …*
2. *I would love to go to …*
3. *I wouldn't really enjoy going to …*
4. *I wouldn't want to go to …*

Tell your partner where you would most like to go.

Use the content of the advertisements to explain your reasons.

Tell your partner which holiday you believe you would least enjoy and why.

Antarctica expedition

The adventure of an Antarctic expedition is the ultimate holiday experience. The 7th continent, Antarctica, is for many the ultimate wilderness destination – a pristine area navigable only by small specially ice-strengthened vessels.

Until recently, Antarctica was accessible only to the men and women of meticulously planned pioneering expeditions. However, following strict environmental guidelines, small groups on expedition vessels can now follow in the footsteps of those explorers and navigate through sea-sculpted bergs and groaning, crumbling glaciers to discover sights rarely seen by humanity.

During the short summer months the vast pack ice opens and this often harsh and inhospitable environment plays host to one of the greatest wildlife spectacles on earth. Millions of penguins, petrels and albatrosses breed here, seals laze languidly on ice floes, and whales indulge Zodiacs benignly under virtual 24 hour daylight.

Some choose the Peninsula, others further afield to the Circle and those with more time may visit the wildlife strongholds of the Falklands and especially South Georgia. Whatever the decision, this wilderness, seen from a small expedition vessel, not a monstrous cruise ship, will attract and enchant like no other.

INDONESIAN ADVENTURE

Rainforest and orang-utans, culture, volcanoes and beaches

Discover orang-utans in the primal jungles of Sumatra and relax by Lake Toba in an immense volcanic crater, the cultural centre of the Batak people. Gaze at volcanoes and see Mt Bromo at sunset before relaxing on the beach in Bali. Java's temples and enigmatic ruins are exemplified in Yogyakarta where we visit the World Heritage site of Borobudur. Indonesia's islands are all different, and we offer a comprehensive trip showcasing its diversity from the vast areas of wilderness that support the world's second highest level of biodiversity, to its exotic golden beaches, all encompassed in a cultural melting pot where gods, demons and magic still define daily life.

Sample itinerary: Start Medan (Sumatra).

Day 2: Drive to Bukit Lawang; free afternoon to swim or tube in the river (optional).

Day 3: Walk in Gunung Leuser N.P. [National Park], home to gibbons, orang-utans, elephants and hundreds of different bird species; visit Bohorok Orang-utan Rehabilitation Centre.

Day 4: Drive to picturesque hill town of Berastagi with views over two active volcanoes.

Day 5: Visit the royal village of the Batak Simalungun people and Si Piso waterfall; on to Samosir island on Lake Toba, the largest volcanic lake in the world ...

Home   Holidays   City breaks   Cruise   Florida   Ski   Worldwide   UK   Adventure   Hotels   Flights   Extras

amsterdam   barcelona   dublin   krakow   new york   paris   venice

New York, New York!

New York City is a heady blend of iconic images, eclectic neighbourhoods and community spirit and no other place in the world will give you such a strong feeling of déjà vu.

Yellow cabs, steaming vents and towering buildings provide a continuous reminder of where you are and the unique personality of a typical New Yorker has got to be experienced first-hand.

No matter whether you're taking a stroll through Central Park, marvelling at the money monuments on Wall Street or simply enjoying a lazy brunch at one of the easy-going diners, New York City really does have something for everyone.

The layout of the city makes navigation straight forward and all the major suburbs can be visited via bus, cab or on foot. From Manhattan to China Town, Little Italy to Brooklyn, New York is one destination that you'll want to visit time and time again.

Eats and drinks

There are thousands of restaurants in this city representing every type of cooking possible. 21 Club is a New York institute, as is Diner, a converted dining car with a loyal clientele. Chat 'n' Chew, just off Union Square, is a heartland eatery where people chat as they wait to chew on gooey, piping hot macaroni cheese or a mountainous burger!

Historic Venice

Mists and masked balls in palace and piazza, romance, pageant and splendour. Take a step out of reality and enjoy five unforgettable days in romantic, historic Venice.

Perhaps you think you know it already. You've seen the Bond movies, the ads featuring gondoliers steering enraptured tourists along the Grand Canal. But Venice is far more than picturesque bridges. Come and discover its hidden corners. Take a turn through historic streets, see its architecture and experience its other-worldly atmosphere. Wander the City of Water with a loved one or join a group walk with an experienced guide, who'll tell you about Canaletto and the peccadilloes of the wicked Lord Byron.

Stop to listen to a string quartet, drink the best espresso as you wait for your vaporetto, take a trip to Murano or wander through colourful street markets. And then, when you've found the real Venice, see the Bridge of Sighs, the Doge's Palace, the Piazza San Marco and the Rialto Bridge. And make sure to visit an original Venetian glass factory to choose a keepsake for ever – for this is a holiday to remember – for ever.

Once a powerful state, home to bankers and speculators, Venice was an influential player in world politics. It is now a UNESCO World Heritage Site and the most delightful car-free zone in Europe. But Venice is under threat from rising water levels. Be sure to see this enchanting City of Light, before it's too late!

Combine your Venice break with a beach holiday in Lido di Jesola. Culture and relaxation – the perfect combination for that holiday of a lifetime.

Writing to persuade

Working on your own or with a partner, create an advertisement for your perfect holiday destination.

Include the following information:

- location – with a focus on what makes it special
- what you can do there – sample itinerary, trips and local attractions
- accommodation – where holiday-makers stay
- food and drink – including local delicacies
- the best time of year to go and what to pack (special clothing and equipment).

REMINDER – persuasive advertisements

Persuasive advertisements should look interesting and appealing and should combine facts with persuasive details.

- Use short paragraphs.
- Use subheadings.
- Include images and captions.
- Use colours.
- Use different font sizes.

Banff & Lake Louise

Adventure is calling you to Banff, Lake Louise and Banff National Park! As a UNESCO World Heritage Site, Banff offers rugged beauty, unspoiled landscapes and pristine mountain ranges. Experience an unrivaled alpine escape at "The World's Finest National Park". You can also drink in nature's wonder at Lake Louise – one of the Canadian Rockies' most beloved destinations, with turquoise waters sparkling underneath the towering Victoria Glacier.

The Lake Louise area provides essential habitat for female grizzly bears, who must raise their young successfully to ensure the future of this threatened species. The group of four hiking rule is one way we can increase public safety and decrease disturbance to grizzlies during the important summer feeding season. A "tight" group of four is less likely to surprise a bear, or be attacked by a bear, than an individual hiker. For this to work, stay within easy speaking range of each other throughout the hike. Ecologically speaking, it is less disruptive for a bear to encounter one tight group versus individual hikers strung out along the trail. Come as a group or join up with other hikers at trailheads where this requirement is in place.

▼ *More than any species, grizzlies represent wilderness. If the grizzly bear, with its wide ranging habits, can survive, then many other species will survive.*

Black bears rarely attack. But here's the thing. Sometimes they do. All bears are agile, cunning and immensely strong, and they are always hungry. If they want to kill you and eat you, they can, and pretty much whenever they want. That doesn't happen often, but – and here is the absolutely salient point – once would be enough.

Bill Bryson discussing a very real danger when you take *A Walk in the Woods*.

Talking point

Do you think people should be encouraged to travel to remote areas for holidays where they may disrupt the natural eco-system? Look at the advertisement for Banff and Lake Louise in Canada and discuss the negative impact that tourists may have on the local environment.

A writer's choice of words

Writers and poets often choose words very carefully to create a wide range of specific effects.

In the passage below, the British author and poet Laurie Lee makes his description vivid through the use of paradox and oxymoron. Here, Lee is writing about the royal palace and gardens of La Granja, in the sierra of Madrid, Spain. During the 18th century, La Granja (meaning farm in Spanish) was the Spanish royal family's rural retreat.

> **Paradox (n.):** an apparently contradictory statement or a statement that conflicts with logic or common sense but which contains a truth, for example, "more haste less speed". From Greek: beside opinion.
>
> **Oxymoron (n.):** putting together words which seem to contradict one another, for example, "bitter-sweet", "the living dead" and "organised chaos".

A few miles south of Segovia, at the foot of the Sierras, I came on the royal gardens of La Granja – acres of writhing statues, walks, and fountains rising from the dust like a mirage. It was a grandiose folly, as large as Versailles and even more extravagant, and I found it   5
in the peak of bloom and entirely deserted except for a few old gardeners with brooms.

A hundred fountains were playing, filling the sky with rainbows and creating an extraordinary dreamlike clamour. Marble gods and wood-nymphs, dolphins   10
and dragons, their anatomies studded with pipes and nozzles, directed complex cascades at one another or shot them high above the flowering trees. Everything that could be done with water seemed to be going on here, almost to the point of   15
hydromania. Lakes, pools, jets, and falls, flooded grottoes and exotic canals, all throbbed and surged at different levels, reflecting classical arbours, paths, and terraces, or running like cooling milk down the statuary.   20

Yet there was nobody to see it. Nobody but me – except, of course, for the gardeners, who went shuffling about as though under some timeless instruction, preparing for the return of some long-dead queen.

I stayed in the gardens for an hour or more, furtively   25
paddling among the trickling leaves. The fountains,

I learned later, played only on rare occasions, and I don't know why they played that day. It was like the winding-up of some monarch's toy, of which the owner had rapidly tired, and which now lay   30
abandoned at the foot of the mountain together with its aged keepers. The fact was that La Granja, when looked at closely, was more than a little vulgar – a royal inflation of a suburban mind, a costly exercise with gnomes and toadstools.   35

From *As I Walked Out One Midsummer Morning*, by Laurie Lee (1971)

The writer's craft

Explain what you think Lee means by "writhing statues" (line 3) and "paddling among the trickling leaves" (line 26).

Can you find other paradoxical statements or oxymorons in the extract?

Think about the closing sentence. Why do you think Lee found the royal palace and gardens of La Granja "more than a little vulgar"?

A poet's choice of words

Although there are no poems in the exams, reading poetry helps you to understand how writers choose words to create a specific effect. Read, on this and the next page, one of the most famous poems in the English language. How has the poet created the mythical setting of Xanadu?

Kubla Khan

By Samuel Taylor Coleridge (1772–1834)

In Xanadu did Kubla Khan
  A stately pleasure-dome decree:
Where Alph, the sacred river, ran
Through caverns measureless to man
  Down to a sunless sea.   5
So twice five miles of fertile ground
With walls and towers were girdled round:
And there were gardens bright with sinuous rills,
Where blossomed many an incense-bearing tree;
And here were forests ancient as the hills,   10
Enfolding sunny spots of greenery.

But oh! that deep romantic chasm which slanted
Down the green hill athwart a cedarn cover!
A savage place! as holy and enchanted
As e'er beneath a waning moon was haunted   15
By woman wailing for her demon-lover!
And from this chasm, with ceaseless turmoil seething,
As if this earth in fast thick pants were breathing,
A mighty fountain momently was forced:
Amid whose swift half-intermitted burst   20

Huge fragments vaulted like rebounding hail,
Or chaffy grain beneath the thresher's flail:
And 'mid these dancing rocks at once and ever
It flung up momently the sacred river.
Five miles meandering with a mazy motion   25
Through wood and dale the sacred river ran,
Then reached the caverns measureless to man,
And sank in tumult to a lifeless ocean:
And 'mid this tumult Kubla heard from far
Ancestral voices prophesying war!   30

    The shadow of the dome of pleasure
    Floated midway on the waves;
    Where was heard the mingled measure
    From the fountain and the caves.
It was a miracle of rare device,   35
A sunny pleasure-dome with caves of ice!

    A damsel with a dulcimer
    In a vision once I saw:
    It was an Abyssinian maid,
    And on her dulcimer she played,   40
    Singing of Mount Abora.
    Could I revive within me
    Her symphony and song,
    To such a deep delight 'twould win me
That with music loud and long   45
I would build that dome in air,
That sunny dome! those caves of ice!
And all who heard should see them there,
And all should cry, Beware! Beware!
His flashing eyes, his floating hair!   50
    Weave a circle round him thrice,
    And close your eyes with holy dread,
    For he on honey-dew hath fed
    And drunk the milk of Paradise.

Writing

Explore the ways that Coleridge describes Xanadu and discuss how he creates setting and atmosphere in his poem "Kubla Khan".

This poem was written by a Scotsman who as a young boy yearned to travel. After leaving school, Stevenson began to study Engineering, then changed to Law. At the age of 25, he left Scotland to see the world. He died in Samoa in 1894.

Drumlie (adj.): gloomy.

Travel

I should like to rise and go
Where the golden apples grow;—
Where below another sky
Parrot islands anchored lie,
And, watched by cockatoos and goats,   5

Lonely Crusoes building boats;—
Where in sunshine reaching out
Eastern cities, miles about,
Are with mosque and minaret
Among sandy gardens set,   10

And the rich goods from near and far
Hang for sale in the bazaar,—
Where the Great Wall round China goes,
And on one side the desert blows,
And with bell and voice and drum   15

Cities on the other hum;—
Where are forests, hot as fire,
Wide as England, tall as a spire,
Full of apes and cocoa-nuts
And the negro hunters' huts;—   20

Where the knotty crocodile
Lies and blinks in the Nile,
And the red flamingo flies
Hunting fish before his eyes;—
Where in jungles, near and far,   25

Man-devouring tigers are,
Lying close and giving ear
Lest the hunt be drawing near,
Or a comer-by be seen
Swinging in a palanquin;—   30

Where among the desert sands
Some deserted city stands,
All its children, sweep and prince,
Grown to manhood ages since,
Not a foot in street or house,   35

Not a stir of child or mouse,
And when kindly falls the night,
In all the town no spark of light.
There I'll come when I'm a man
With a camel caravan;   40

Light a fire in the gloom
Of some dusty dining-room;
See the pictures on the walls,
Heroes, fights and festivals;
And in a corner find the toys   45
Of the old Egyptian boys.

By Robert Louis Stevenson (1885)

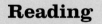

Reading

Make a list of all the places Stevenson says he would like to see.

Writing

Imagine you have travelled to some of the places Stevenson would like to see. Now you are an old person and all you have left are your memories and the "pictures on the walls" of "heroes, fights and festivals". Create a memory based on one part of this poem and tell your story. Include the following:

* where you went
* your thoughts and impressions about what you saw
* why you still remember this place.

Write between 500 and 800 words.

Writing – descriptive writing

Choose one of the following:

* Describe a wild or lonely place you know.
* Describe a popular tourist attraction you have visited.

Write between 350 and 450 words.

Remember that in descriptive writing you should not tell a story. Focus on the description only.

Unit 1: Self-assessment

In this unit we have read autobiography, travel writing, holiday advertisements, newspaper and magazine articles, and poems.

Two key skills we have looked at are: annotating texts (prose and poetry) and summary writing.

1. What is the difference between skimming and scanning?

2. What steps do you need to follow when writing a summary?

Make notes about Unit 1

Consider the work you have done in this unit, then copy and complete the chart.

Two texts (poetry or prose) I remember in Unit 1 are:
Two new skills I learned are:
Two things I'm not sure about are:
I enjoyed doing:
Something I would like to do again is:
I would like to do this again because:

Where I Come From

People are made of places. They carry with them
hints of jungles or mountains, a tropic grace
or the cool eyes of sea-gazers. Atmosphere of cities
how different drops from them, like the smell of smog
or the almost-not-smell of tulips in the spring,   5
nature tidily plotted in little squares
with a fountain in the centre; museum smell,
art also tidily plotted with a guidebook;
or the smell of work, glue factories maybe,
chromium-plated offices; smell of subways   10
crowded at rush hours.

Where I come from, people
carry woods in their minds, acres of pine woods;
blueberry patches in the burned-out bush;
wooden farmhouses, old, in need of paint,   15
with yards where hens and chickens circle about,
clucking aimlessly; battered schoolhouses
behind which violets grow. Spring and winter
are the mind's chief seasons: ice and the breaking of ice.

A door in the mind blows open, and there blows   20
a frosty wind from fields of snow.

By Elizabeth Brewster

Writing

Write two or three paragraphs about where you come from. Say whether the place (its geography, climate and customs) has affected the way you think and feel. If so, say how and why.

2 The world of nature

In this unit you will:

→ **Visit** Britain, China, Ethiopia, France, Germany, Greece, India, Italy, Mali, North America, Switzerland, Thailand and Tibet

→ **Read** classical literature, folk tales, information texts, myths, newspaper articles and poetry

→ **Write** to inform, entertain, argue and persuade

Myths

Most cultures have stories that explain such matters as how the universe came into being, how and why the sun crosses the sky, and how humans acquired fire to keep them warm. We call these stories myths. It was the old way of explaining the inexplicable. Below are two versions of how our world began.

Nature (n.): the world with all its features and living things; the physical power that produces these; this power personified. (From Latin *natus* = born.)

(*Oxford Study Dictionary*)

Metamorphoses, Book 1

By the Roman poet Ovid (between years 2 and 8 CE); translated by Mary M. Innes (1955)

Before there was any earth or sea, before the canopy of heaven stretched overhead, Nature presented the same aspect the world over, that to which men have given the name of Chaos. This was a shapeless uncoordinated mass, nothing but a weight of lifeless matter, whose ill-assorted elements were indiscriminately heaped together in one place. There was no sun, in those days, to provide the world with light, no crescent moon; the earth was not poised in the enveloping air, balancing there by its own weight, nor did the sea stretch out its arms along the margins of the shores. Although the elements of land and air and sea were there the earth had no firmness, the water no fluidity, there was no brightness in the sky. Nothing had any lasting shape, but everything got in the way of everything else; for, within that one body, cold warred with hot, moist with dry, soft with hard, and light with heavy.

Ginnungagap – from Norse mythology

According to the ancient tales of the great North, at the dawn of time, there existed only ice and snow. There was no land we know, only a yawning emptiness, the Great Abyss of Ginnungagap. Ice and snow fell into the Great Abyss but never filled it. In the South, in the land of fire and heat, burning rivers flowed from mountains down to the Deep.

After an eternity of time, the land of ice and snow and the land of heat and fire moved together. The warm air of the South met the chill air of the North and little by little the ice in Ginnungagap melted. From this moisture emerged Ymir the Frost Giant, although some say it was Surt, the great Fire Giant. It was Surt, they say, who struck sparks against the ice and brought Audumla the cow into being.

One day, as Audumla licked ice to quench her thirst, a man emerged from the salt rock her warm tongue had touched. The man's name was Bore, the Born One ...

Talking points

In the poem "In Memoriam", written in 1833, the British poet Alfred, Lord Tennyson speaks of "Nature, red in tooth and claw" – an expression we still use today.

- What do you think Tennyson was referring to?
- Is Nature, *by nature*, cruel?
- What do we mean when we say "by nature"?
- Do you think people should try to tame or change Nature?
- In what ways does Nature defeat humanity and constantly prove its power?
- List three ways that people try to change the natural world for their personal benefit. (Examples of this are fish-farming, irrigation canals and training elephants to work in forests.)

The elements

In the olden days earth, air, fire and water were regarded as the fundamental elements or constituents of the universe. Read the articles, stories and poems on the following pages about the elements and do the activities that go with them.

Earth

An important natural substance, salt is also known as white gold. Merchants in 12th-century Timbuktu, the seat of scholars, valued salt as highly as books and gold. By the 14th century, Timbuktu in Mali had become a world-renowned focal point for the gold–salt trade. Merchants from all over Europe and North Africa came to the city to obtain salt, bringing with them gold and scholars. The Tuareg people gained control of the city in 1433, but they ruled from the desert and, although they plundered periodically, trade and learning continued to flourish. By the 15th century Timbuktu had become an intellectual and spiritual centre for the propagation of Islam throughout Africa; this continued through the 15th and 16th centuries. Three great mosques, Djingareyber, Sankore and Sidi Yahia, are testimony to Timbuktu's golden age, but despite continuous restoration these monuments are under threat from desertification.

Facts about salt

Here are ten interesting historical facts about salt. Arrange the information into chronological order. Note that some items do not have dates; you should put them in the order that you think makes most sense.

1. Marco Polo, a Venetian traveller to the court of Kublai Khan, who is said to have lived from 1254 to 1324, noted that in Tibet tiny cakes of salt were pressed with images of the Grand Khan and used as coins.

2. The belief that spilling salt brings bad luck dates back to the 16th century.

3. Greek slave traders often bartered salt for slaves, hence the expression someone "is not worth his/her salt".

4. To be "above/below the salt" refers to the seating arrangement at the long table in a manor house or palace in medieval times. Rank and honour were signified by where people sat in relation to the salt. A large salt-cellar was placed in the centre of the dining table and those who sat nearer to the host were "above the salt" with inferiors, seated further away, being "below the salt".

5. The expression to take something "with a pinch of salt" has been in use since the 17th century.

6. Protesting against British rule in 1930, Mahatma Gandhi led a 200-mile march to the Arabian Ocean to collect untaxed salt for India's poor.

7. The word *salary*, which we use to refer to what a person earns, was derived from the word "salt". Roman legionnaires were paid in *salarium* – meaning "salt" – the Latin origin of the word *salary*.

8. Salt is still used as money among the nomads of Ethiopia's Danakil Plains.

9. It is said that the first ever recorded war, in Essalt on the Jordan River, was fought over precious salt supplies.

10. In 2200 BC, the Chinese emperor Hsia Yu levied one of the first known taxes. He taxed salt.

Air

Windmills and other wind turbines have provided people with power for more than 7,000 years. Now, with concern about fossil fuels, many countries are once again considering the efficiency and reliability of this age-old technology.

Wind Turbines (two poems)

A whoosh, a whirl
Blades slice through air,
Spinning invisible sparks

Pointed petals
Blossom on a stiff white stem –
Windflower

By Elaine Magliaro

REMINDER – personification

Personification is a type of metaphor in which something non-human (such as an object or idea) is described as if it were a person; for example "the angry sea".

Read the following poem and the short extract from *King Lear*. Look at how wind is personified in each. Choose either the poem or the lines from *King Lear*, and say why you think the writer personified wind. Then explain the effect this has on you as the reader.

Pain

All was quiet in this park
Until the wind, like a gasping messenger, announced
The tyrant's coming.
Then did the branches talk in agony.
You remember that raging storm?   5

In their fear despairing flowers nevertheless held
Bouquets to the grim king;
Meteors were the tassels of his crown
While like branches that only spoke when the storm menaced
We cried in agony as we fell   10
Slashed by the cold blade of an invisible sword.

Mutilated our limbs were swept away by the rain
But not our blood;
Indelible it stuck on the walls
Like wild gum on tree trunks.   15

By Mbella Sonne Dopoko

King Lear

By: William Shakespeare (1605)

Blow, winds, and crack your
    cheeks! rage! blow!
You cataracts and hurricanes,
    spout
Till you have drench'd our
    steeples, drown'd the cocks!
You sulphurous and thought-
    executing fires,
Vaunt-couriers to oak-cleaving
    thunderbolts,
Singe my white head! And thou,
    all-shaking thunder,
Smite flat the thick rotundity o'
    the world!
Crack nature's moulds, and
    germens spill at once,
That make ingrateful man!

Fire

It is probable that the myths and legends about fire we still hear today originated in the oral tradition of storytelling around a campfire. Long before people could read or write they told stories to explain strange events and celebrate great feats of bravery. As they sat around the fire these people must have wondered how the flames they watched had come into being. Fire gave them warmth and cooked their food, but that same campfire could burn and consume. So it is that in most fire myths fire appears as a creative blessing, a useful source for the good of humankind, and yet also a destructive power, which no person can fully control.

Fire and anger come together in the famous Greek myth about Prometheus. Zeus, the chief of the older Greek gods, had hidden fire away, but the Titan Prometheus stole fire and gave it to humankind. Zeus was furious; Prometheus was chained to a rock and every day an eagle ate his liver. Fortunately, or unfortunately, Prometheus was immortal so every night his liver grew again. And that is how the great god Zeus punished the thief of fire.

Read a fire myth from North America and do the activities that follow.

How Coyote Gave Fire to the People

A Native American Story

Long ago, when man first walked on the Earth, the chill of autumn and the bitter cold of winter were difficult times, especially for the very young and the very old among them. Coyote, like the rest of the animals, had a fine fur coat to keep him warm, so 5 he did not worry when the days grew shorter and the sun's rays weakened. But one spring day, as he approached a human village, he could hear the laments for those who had been lost during the harsh winter months. 10

"Our children, holders of our future, have been lost," cried one old woman.

"Our grandparents, holders of our past, have been lost," cried one young man.

Coyote felt great pity in his heart, and he decided 15 to do something to help these men and women. He had traveled far and wide and had seen the mountaintop where the Three Fire Protectors lived. These Protectors selfishly hoarded their fire, afraid that man might become as powerful as they were 20 if he could somehow gain control over fire. So Coyote loped up the mountain of the Fire Protectors and crept close to the area where the Protectors guarded their precious fire. When they heard someone approaching, the Fire Protectors sprang to their feet, 25 ready to attack.

"Who goes there?" one shouted.

"Show yourself, thief!" hissed the second.

"You cannot hide from us," announced the third.

When the Fire Protectors saw an ordinary coyote 30 making its way through the trees, they relaxed.

"It is only a gray coyote," said the first Fire Protector, greatly relieved.

Coyote ignored the Fire Protectors, and they paid no more attention to him. Coyote watched the Fire 35 Protectors for three days and three nights to learn how he might get past the guard they kept around the clock. He noticed that the fire was unguarded for a very few moments in the morning as the Fire Protector who sat next to the fire entered the tepee to awaken 40 the Protector who was to take her place. Coyote had a plan, but he needed the help of the other animals, so he crept down the mountain and gathered some of his friends together. He explained the pain and misery that human beings were suffering, and he told them of the Fire Protectors who would never share their gift with humans. The other animals spoke among themselves and soon agreed to help Coyote.

Coyote returned to the top of the mountain, and once more the Fire Protectors reacted angrily when they heard his approach.

"Who goes there? Show yourself, thief," one shouted.

But, as before, they relaxed when they recognized the coyote.

Coyote slept the entire day, and awoke as the sun set. He watched as two of the Protectors entered the tepee to sleep while the third settled down to watch the fire. As dawn approached, the Protector next to the fire rose to call her sister to replace her. She entered the tepee, and for a very brief moment no one sat to guard the fire.

"Wake up!" Coyote heard her call. "It is your turn to watch the fire."

Coyote's moment had come! Coyote raced to the fire, grasped a portion of the flame between his teeth, and began his escape down the mountainside.

The Fire Protectors screamed frantically, but they wasted no time in the confusion and began to chase Coyote within moments. Despite his speed, the Protectors overcame Coyote just as he reached the foot of the mountain. The Fire Protector closest to Coyote reached out to grab his tail. Her touch turned the tip of his tail white, and you can see that the tips of coyotes' tails are white today.

Coyote realized that he would soon be within the grasp of the Fire Protectors. He saw his friend Squirrel standing nearby, ready to help him, and he tossed the flame to Squirrel, who began to run as quickly as he could. The Fire Protectors shifted their pursuit, and now chased Squirrel. One of the Fire Protectors reached Squirrel and laid her hand on his back. The pain caused Squirrel to curl his tail up and back, and you can see that the tails of squirrels are curled today. Squirrel did not let the pain stop him from passing the flame to Chipmunk, who stood ready to continue the escape. As Chipmunk raced along, one of the Fire Protectors veered off

to pursue him. As he sped along, she reached out with one of her claws and scratched Chipmunk's back, leaving three stripes that you can see on chipmunks today.

Chipmunk knew that he could not outlast the Fire Protectors. He glanced around and decided to throw the flame to Wood, who lay on the ground, ready to help. Wood swallowed the flame, and the Fire Protectors were helpless. They could not get back the flame which had been stolen from them. They tried flattery, threats, and bribery, but Wood would not give up the flame which he had swallowed. At last, the Fire Protectors left, admitting that they had been defeated.

After they were gone, Coyote brought Wood to the people and showed them how to get the flame out of Wood by rubbing two sticks together. From that time on, man was warm and comfortable through the winter months.

Retold by Marie Swiston, *Houston Chronicle* (2010)

Reading

1. Many Native American myths show why humans should respect the environment in which they live and live in harmony with the creatures around them. How does the folk tale on pages 30–31 illustrate why people should respect the natural world?

2. As with ancient myths, folk tales were a means of explaining the natural world. This is a story that tells how people in North America first acquired fire. It also explains how some animals acquired their physical appearance. How does this story explain the characteristics of these animals?

Coursework ideas

Choose one of the tasks below. Write between 500 and 800 words.

- What other stories from different cultures that tell how humans first acquired fire do you know? Re-tell a myth in your own words.

- Write a short "folk tale" to explain how a certain animal acquired its special features. For example, you could write about the jaw of a crocodile, the stripes of a zebra, the mane of a horse, or the whiskers of a cat.

Water

Now read two articles about the Yangtze River in China. The first was written before the Three Gorges Project to dam the river was completed. The second article describes what is happening now the river has the huge dam. After you have read the first article, do the activity below.

Reading

The article opposite about the Three Gorges Project in China contains a number of hard facts, but it is written in such a way as to maintain the reader's interest.

1. Find three facts.

2. Find two examples of what people believe.

3. Find one example of what people say.

4. Does the writer give her opinion? If so, where and how (give line references).

5. Explain in your own words what the writer means in lines 68–9: "they will sail over thousands of years of China's heritage."

6. Explain in your own words how people living along the Yangtze River should benefit from the Three Gorges Project.

7. Describe the less welcome effects the damn will have on:

   a. the river

   b. the people who live by the river.

The Yangtze River Three Gorges Project

Formed from melting Tibetan ice and snow, the Yangtze River journeys over 6,000 miles to the Pacific Ocean. From a silent alpine world it flows a tortuous 4,000 miles to the teeming metropolis of Shanghai, population 13 million, and then on and on to empty itself into the sea.

Defying all the obstacles nature can put in its way the "Long River" plunges through tight gorges, transforming into angry rapids and then dangerous shallows and traitorous shoals. At some points it slows and laps gently on fertile plains; at others it becomes a water serpent, snaking through sheer cliffs and jagged mountains. In its lower reaches it creates vast inland lakes full of fish and colourful water birds.

For nearly three millennia, the Yangtze River has been the principal bearer and sustainer of Chinese life and culture. Where people lived along its banks marked their identity. Even now, in an age of efficient rapid transport, people still divide themselves into those who live on the north bank of the river and those who belong on the south. The river creates a natural social and political divide.

Around 300 million people live in the Yangtze valley and along its main tributaries – more than the entire population of the United States. Its middle and lower reaches produce nearly one quarter of China's industrial and agricultural output. They call the Yangtze the "golden waterway" for good reasons.

But the golden waterway is a taker as well as a giver of life. During the 20th century alone there have been three catastrophic floods: in 1931, 1935, and 1954. Each year summer brings the prospect of excellent harvests in fertile Yangtze valleys, but also fear: fear that too much Tibetan ice will melt or heavy rain will swell the river until it bursts its banks and destroys crops, homes and livelihoods. The decision to build a dam and start the Three Gorges Project was made in response to the terrible floods of 1954.

There is a strain of Chinese philosophy that teaches people "to go with the flow", that is, to respect and conform to nature because we humans are part of it. Another school of thought, however, one which is more Western and utilitarian in approach, encourages humans to transform nature, to make it more manageable and more productive. It is this modern perception that has led to the Three Gorges Project. Chinese people no longer see themselves as servants or slaves to the river; they plan to halt its flow and transform its appearance in order to control its surges, navigate its upper reaches and use it to drive the turbines essential for new industrial growth.

The Three Gorges Project will commence at Sandouping and alter but not ruin the stunning scenery of water, mountains and sky that makes the gorges what they are. However, when the dam is built and the rapids are swallowed into what will become the world's largest reservoir, the rising water level will claim the ancient site of Fengdu with its 4,000-year-old tombs and Palace of the Nether World Monarch. Vessels as large as 10,000 tonnes will sail upriver as far as Chungking, China's largest, most important inland city, but they will sail over thousands of years of China's heritage.

Life along the river banks is going to change forever; over one million people will have to move to higher ground. These migrants (or refugees) have been told there will be new job opportunities in their new locations, which may be true. But those with a less optimistic outlook argue that upstream and downstream marine life will be destroyed. The 400 billion tonnes of silt yielded by the Yangzte each year – silt that is so important to farmland – might become trapped disastrously behind the dam. They fear their "Long River", their "golden waterway", will not be content to remain within its new confines for long. Water, they say, is stronger than stone.

By Joan Gir Ling, *The New European*
(27 September 1994)

http://www.guardian.co.uk/news/world/asia/

Home | World | UK | England | N. Ireland | Scotland | Wales | Business | Politics | Health | Education | Arts
Africa | Asia | Europe | US | M. East | Canada

China warns of "urgent problems" facing Three Gorges Dam

The Three Gorges dam, the flagship of China's massive hydro-engineering ambitions, faces "urgent problems", the government has warned.

In a statement approved by prime minister Wen Jiabao, the state council said the dam had pressing geological, human and ecological problems. The report also acknowledged for the first time the negative impact the dam has had on downstream river transport and water supplies.

Since the start of construction in 1992 about 16m tonnes of concrete have been poured into the giant barrier across the Yangtze River, creating a reservoir that stretches almost the length of Britain and drives 26 giant turbines.

The world's biggest hydropower plant boasts a total generating capacity of 18,200MW and the ability to help tame the floods that threaten the Yangtze delta each summer.

But it has proved expensive and controversial due to the rehousing of 1.4 million people and the flooding of more than 1,000 towns and villages. Pollution, silt and landslides have plagued the reservoir area. [...]

"Problems emerged at various stages of project planning and construction but could not be solved immediately, and some arose because of increased demands brought on by economic and social development," the statement said.

Since the 1.5 mile barrier was completed in 2006 the reservoir has been plagued by algae and pollution that would previously have been flushed away. The weight of the extra water has also been blamed for tremors, landslides and erosion of slopes.

To ease these threats the government said last year many more people may have to be relocated. This week it promised to establish disaster warning systems, reinforce riverbanks, boost funding for environmental protection and improve benefits for the displaced.

This is not the first warning. Four years ago the state media quoted government experts who said: "There are many new and old hidden ecological and environmental dangers concerning the Three Gorges dam. If preventive measures are not taken the project could lead to a catastrophe." Last year, site engineers recommended an additional movement of hundreds of thousands of nearby residents and more investment in restoring the ecosystem.

The government has already raised its budget for water treatment plants but opponents of the dam say this is not enough. "The government built a dam but destroyed a river," said Dai Qing, a longtime critic of the project. [...]

The frank assessment of the challenges posed and benefits offered by the dam came amid growing concerns about a drought on the middle stretches of the Yangtze. This has left 1,392 reservoirs in Hubei with only "dead water" and has affected the drinking supplies of more than 300,000 people.

Chinese media reported this month that the Yangtze water levels near Wuhan hit their lowest point since the dam went into operation in 2003. Long stretches have apparently been closed to water traffic after hundreds of boats ran aground in the shallows.

By Jonathan Watts, *The Guardian* (20 May 2011)

Speaking and listening

Advantages and disadvantages of the project

- How has the Three Gorges Project made the Yangtze River "more manageable and more productive"?

- Were the fears and potential negative impact on the river's natural course outlined in the first article on the Three Gorges Project justified?

- If you lived in a rural area beside the Yangtze River, how would you feel about the Three Gorges Project?

- If you were a worker living in an industrial area, would you feel the same way?

The writer's craft – using data and statistics

"Since the start of construction in 1992 about 16m tonnes of concrete have been poured into the giant barrier across the Yangtze River, creating a reservoir that stretches almost the length of Britain and drives 26 giant turbines" (Jonathan Watts, *The Guardian*, 20 May 2011).

The author of the article opposite has had to combine a significant number of dates with statistics and other numerical data.

1. Make a list of phrases that involve numbers.

2. When has the author spelled out numbers as words and when has he used figures?

3. Why has he used data and numbers in different ways?

Reading – developing your skills

1. Look back at the passages you have read in this unit so far. Find an example for each of the following:

   a. a hard fact

   b. something that suggests or implies someone's attitude(s) or belief(s)

   c. information that has led you to form an opinion or given you a new idea about something.

2. Make notes on where you found each piece of information (give the title, author and line reference).

Coursework ideas

In pairs or groups, talk about how your country uses energy for industry and agriculture.

- Has it made changes to "harness the environment" in recent years?

- How did people create energy in the past?

You could discuss wind turbines and old-fashioned windmills, irrigation canals and water wheels, solar panels and central heating.

Talk about the problems of creating and supplying energy that future generations may experience.

Ice cold in Alaska

Treacherous currents, icebergs and hungry grizzlies ... Eowyn Ivey finds danger – and romance – round every bend as she and her husband raft down the Copper River.

The Copper River flows cold and fast out of the heart of Alaska, 300 miles through rocky canyons and past 5 calving glaciers until it branches into a broad delta of wetlands and into the Gulf of Alaska. It is a river of wild salmon and seals and drowning men, and my imagination has been swirling in those waters. Now, on a sunny July day, I set afloat in its current. 10 My husband Sam and I will spend the next five days alone, rafting the most remote 80-mile stretch of the Copper River. We are armed with a tent, camera, maps, freeze-dried food, chest waders and a rifle for bear protection. There will be no mobile-phone 15 reception or contact with civilisation. We will be completely on our own. The prospect both thrills and terrifies me.

"We don't want to end up against those rocks," Sam says. He gestures downstream to Salmon Point, a 20 rocky outcropping where people catch salmon with long-handled nets. Three weeks ago a fisherman fell from the rocks not far from here and drowned, his body swept away by the river.

The raft is pushed and pulled towards the rocks 25 by the merging currents of the Chitina and Copper rivers, and Sam rows harder, beads of sweat forming on his brow. The 14ft raft has only one rowing seat, so all I can do is sit and watch.

With Salmon Point quickly approaching, Sam 30 wonders aloud if we've made a mistake. He strains at the oars and puts us into a ferry position, with the nose of the raft at an angle away from the shore, in an attempt to keep us from being crushed into the outcropping or drawn into the dangerous eddy. The 35 fishermen on the rocks watch us, and time seems to slow. We are near enough that I can see their eyes. And then the current sweeps us past and spits us out the other side towards Woods Canyon. Back at home, on our kitchen counter, we'd left a hastily typed note: "In 40 the event of both of our deaths, Samuel Service Ivey and Eowyn LeMay Ivey ... "

In late afternoon we pitch our tent on the sandy bank and unroll our sleeping bags.

"There's a lot of bear sign," I say, looking towards the 45 willow bushes and cottonwood trees.

"Yep."

More than anyone I've known, Sam is at home in the Alaskan wilderness. He awoke in a tent once with a black bear nosing him in the shoulder. Years ago, 50 when a sow grizzly bear with three cubs charged at us, he calmly took out his pistol and shot into the ground to frighten her away. But even he is wary here. We passed up a previous campsite because the ground was riddled with bear tracks. We start a campfire and 55 heat water to make our dinner.

The next morning, a dozen people on two larger rafts float past. They call out to us, asking where we intend to camp next. "Dewey Creek", Sam answers. "Watch out for the bears," one of the women shouts. 60 We all wave cheerfully at each other. They are the last people we will see for four days.

The float is easy now. When the river braids, Sam rows us into the larger channel, but mostly he leaves the oars at rest. The land changes, leaving behind the stunted 65 shrubs and rolling hills of interior Alaska for the snow-capped mountains and tall evergreen trees of the coast. As we float, Sam and I talk – about jobs, family, my book, our plans for the future. When we stop talking, it is so quiet we notice a strange, slithering 70 sound that we realise comes from the tiny grains of silt in the river gliding along the bottom of the raft.

On the third day, we spot a brown bear with two small cubs on shore. At first the animals are so far away I can barely see them. As the raft draws closer I watch 75 the sow pause mid-stride to look back for her cubs, and my heart quakes.

How can I come to know this wild river? By following its current and sleeping with its roar in my ears? Or is it revealed through facts? The Copper River 80 discharges 1m gallons of water a second. More than 2m wild salmon swim upstream each year. Even in summer, the temperature of the river barely rises above freezing and, with the fast current and heavy silt

load, those who fall in without a life jacket are likely 85
to drown and their bodies never be found.

But maybe the Copper is more intimately known
by its afternoon sand storms, or the icy fog that
settles along the bends in the early mornings. Or
the harbour seals bobbing and splashing as they 90
chase salmon; the beaver, coyote, fox and wolves
that wander down its valleys; the silver willow
and fireweed thriving on its muddy banks. Or is
the river simply this cold, gritty water at the tips
of my fingers as I let my hand trail off the edge of 95
the raft?

The river carries us down through the mountains and
spills us into Miles Lake, cradled between two
glaciers. We have been warned that the three-mile lake
is sometimes blocked by ice dams even in the middle 100
of summer, so we are relieved to find the water empty
of icebergs. On the far side, we can see the bridge
leading back to civilisation. Tomorrow, we'll row
across the lake.

On the sandy shore, we sit outside our tent [...] 105
and watch small pieces of ice float on the water. Our
adventure is winding to an end. But in the dark of
night we are startled awake by a splitting boom, like

dynamite being detonated. We sit up in our sleeping bags. Miles Glacier is calving, great chunks of ice falling from its side and crashing into the lake. Again, and again – all through the night. We can't sleep, not just because of the noise, but because of what it might mean.

When we stick our heads out of the tent the next morning, our fears are confirmed. The passageway across the lake is filled with house-sized chunks of glacier ice. "Maybe we can make it through there," I say, pointing. Just then the huge shards of ice grind and shift, and what looked like a small berg overturns with a deep "sploosh," revealing its blue underside that now towers 20ft into the air. "We could get crushed in that," Sam says. We decide to wait another night to see if the ice floats away, but in the meantime, the glacier continues to calve.

Just after noon, we spot a narrow open channel along the shore and around the ice jam. We get in the raft, and Sam studies the currents to see which way the ice will move when it does. As he cautiously rows us between the icebergs, I feel the cold radiating off their glistening sides. We are tired and weather-beaten when we arrive at the far side of the lake. We haven't bathed in nearly a week and we smell of wood smoke. At the bridge, a massive brown bear lumbers down the dirt road. Just before it reaches us it stops, paces, and turns to disappear into the forest.

But we have one last night on the Copper River. We camp near the bridge. As I lie in the dark with Sam, the brown bear is a shadow at the edge of my consciousness. Just downstream, a chunk of blue-white ice the size of a 10-storey building falls from the side of Child's Glacier into the river. The crash roars like thunder, and the ground trembles beneath me. I reach over to squeeze Sam's hand.

110
115
120
125
130
135
140

By Eowyn Ivey, *The Observer*
(29 January 2012)

REMINDER – news and feature articles

Newspapers print two types of article: news articles and feature articles. News articles are time-dependent and written as soon as possible after a newsworthy event. Feature articles are about interesting, newsworthy topics, but they are more general in nature and written to be read at any time.

Ice cold in Alaska by Eowyn Ivey on pages 36–38 is a feature article.

Speaking and listening

Giving a talk on a trip

Working with a partner, prepare a talk on the Copper River. You and your partner are Eowyn and Sam Ivey. You have returned home safely after your raft trip. Prepare a talk on your experiences to be given at your children's school.

Include the following:

- where you went
- how you travelled
- what you saw
- the dangers you encountered.

Be sure to comment on the "calving glaciers" and the bears.

Try to predict probable questions from the audience and prepare answers.

Writing skills
Writing to argue and persuade

Writing to argue and persuade presents a case and promotes the writer's/speaker's point of view.

In argumentative writing, you explain a situation or problem, give your opinion and persuade readers to your way of thinking.

What you say needs to be logical and convincing.

Think about the topic carefully and examine different points of view.

Planning strategies

- Use an essay planning strategy suitable for the task, such as a spider-gram, a mind map or simply a list of the relevant points.

- Number the points in the order you want to make them.

- Check that you have included both sides of the argument.

- Consider opposing points of view and prepare a well-reasoned argument.

Before you start writing

- Decide what your standpoint is and check your argument. Imagine you are a lawyer presenting a case in court. What evidence do you need to convince the judge or jury?

When you start writing

- Begin with a clear opening statement. Do not indent the first paragraph.

- Start a new paragraph for each main point.

- Each paragraph must have a clear topic sentence taken from your plan.

- Link paragraphs in a logical manner.

- Lead your reader to your conclusion.

- Show that you are justified in thinking the way you do.

Use of English

- Use emotive language to persuade your audience.

- Beware of open-ended or rhetorical questions that could get the wrong answer!

- Use interesting linking phrases: *Nonetheless ... Furthermore ... In spite of this ...*

- Use polite phrases when making counter-arguments: *While many see this as ... This is not a convincing argument because ...*

- You should not be rude: *... which is rubbish ... It's nonsense to think ...*

- Do not use too many rhetorical questions: *So how do we define a weapon/uniform?*

- Do not make sweeping statements such as: *It's a well-known fact that ... Everyone thinks ...*

- Avoid words like *normal* and *ordinary*. What may seem normal to one person might seem very strange to someone else.

Writing to argue and persuade

Choose one of the options below.

- Humans should not alter the environment in which they live.

- Training animals to work for humans is cruel and unnecessary.

Write between 500 and 800 words.

Bestiaries

A bestiary is an illuminated medieval manuscript with illustrations of real and imaginary birds and animals. Each "beast" was assigned certain values. For example, lions were associated with strength and nobility. Written in Latin, bestiaries were used extensively in the 12th and 13th centuries by the Christian Church to teach moral values. By 1500, the meaning of animal symbols was well known by the general population across Europe.

The nature of lions

The extract (left) is from the 13th-century Arundel Manuscript, a bestiary written in Middle English. A literal translation in modern English reads: "The lion stands on a hill, and when he hears a man hunting or through his sense of smell scents a man approaching, by whatever way he will go down to the valley."

According to the medieval bestiary:

[T]he lion has three natures: when a lion walking in the mountains sees that it is being hunted, it erases its tracks with its tail; it always sleeps with its eyes open; and its cubs are born dead and are brought to life on the third day when the mother breathes in their faces or the father roars over them. A lion only kills out of great hunger; it will not attack a prostrate man; it allows captive men to depart; it is not easily angered; the lioness first has five cubs, then one less each year.

*The leun stant on hille,
and he man hunten here,*

*Other thurg his nese smel
smake that he negge,*

*Bi wilc weie so he wile to
dele nither wenden.*

From the British Library
Arundel Manuscript 292

Animals in folklore

In the Middle Ages, animal stories were immensely popular throughout Europe, North Africa and the Middle East. At that time everyone was dependent on wild and domestic animals for their survival so they had a keen interest in the animals around them. A great deal of popular folk-lore was based on animal behaviour, and even today we still use expressions like "as stubborn as a mule". People in those days, however, were interested in more than just their local environment and the animals around them; they were fascinated by tales of strange and wonderful creatures in distant lands.

Animals in holy texts

During the medieval period people were very religious and superstitious. In Western Europe, the religion was Christianity; in North Africa and the Middle East it was primarily Islam. Jews who practised their religion lived among Christians and Muslims in many different countries. Occasionally, there was tension and violence between the three religions, but generally people seem to have lived in harmony, possibly because they shared similar values. Those who could read, read from many of the same spiritual and historical texts. Each religion still considers all or most of the Hebrew Bible (called the Old Testament by Christians) to be sacred and the Hebrew Bible contains many references to animals.

Weird and wonderful beasts

The lavish illustrations in the bestiaries served as visual information for the illiterate public. However, medieval animal illustrations were rarely accurate: crocodiles looked like long dogs; whales were depicted as large fish with scales; many serpents were given feet and wings, and now look rather like the modern idea of dragons. These "mistakes" were probably due to the fact that the illustrators may never have seen the beasts they were drawing. They relied on written descriptions, which may have been embellished or exaggerated in order to seem more exotic. As bestiaries became more popular, one illustrator might copy another, and so on for generations. In this way, one small oddity in an ancient document, such as the hooves of the ostrich bird, could become a common feature of later bestiaries!

Some manuscripts might have strange-looking creatures in them simply because the illustrator wasn't very good or because an illustration might have been started by one monk but finished by another. Whatever the cause, it is highly unlikely that the elaborate drawings we see today were executed by anyone who had actually seen the creatures with their own eyes. Most monks spent their entire lives in a secluded environment and had little idea about the animals beyond the monastery garden: standing at their *scriptoria*, mixing colours and painting wings on beasts we now call mammals – all they could do was dream. Nevertheless, fanciful or true to life, each bestiary is magnificent in its own way.

Moral tales and human nature

As well as tales of the habits and peculiarities of birds and animals, a bestiary contained a collection of allegorical fables and each fable included a moral. Over time the animals became symbols for certain human traits. When Chaucer and Shakespeare mentioned specific animals in relation to the characters in their works, their readers or audiences would have understood the references immediately. Some animals were believed to have certain characteristics that were examples for "proper conduct". For example, the way the young hoopoe bird was said to care for its parents showed how human children should care for theirs.

Animal imagery

Imagery is not something you only find in literature; we use imagery all the time. Look at the following examples:

- to ape = to mimic
- to duck = to dip down
- to ferret out = to search out
- mousy = timid and quiet; fair-haired
- to ram = to drive at something.

1. Which of the above is the odd one out?

2. What do you think the following verbs mean?
   ➤ to fox
   ➤ to hound
   ➤ to wolf

3. Can you explain the following expressions?
   ➤ a snake in the grass
   ➤ a wolf in sheep's clothing

   Example: *a dark horse = someone who does not draw attention to himself/herself and may have something to hide (not necessarily something bad).*

Animal adjectives

The following adjectives used in English come from Latin. Match each adjective to the appropriate picture.

| Equine | Feline | Vulpine | Canine | Asinine | Aquiline | Leonine |

Bearing in mind that Shakespeare lived in England during the late 16th century and the early 17th, does anything strike you as odd about his choice of animals and birds?

Shakespeare's animal imagery

If you are studying Shakespeare or any other pre-20th-century text, it is interesting to remember what the world was like in the writer's time. In Shakespeare's time there were no large industrial cities. There was no electricity, so workers typically started their day at sunrise and finished at sunset. People used to live much closer to nature and were more familiar with the wildlife around them than many of us are now. This means that audiences would have understood references or allusions to the natural world. People in just about every part of Britain would have heard and seen owls and foxes, deer and snakes. Birds of prey lived right in the heart of London and kites scavenged in the streets.

In his plays, Shakespeare often uses metaphors, similes and other figures of speech to compare people to animals.

These are some of the creatures Shakespeare compares people to in *King Lear*:

- a kite – a bird of prey that feeds on small animals, fish and carrion

- a vulture – a scavenger that feeds primarily on carcasses

- a serpent – a large snake such as a python or boa constrictor

- a pelican – a bird with a large, capacious beak that feeds on fish in warm waters

- a tiger – the largest member of the cat family.

The writer's craft – animal and bird imagery in *Macbeth*

The play *Macbeth* is the story of a loyal, noble and brave soldier who falls prey to ambition and murders his cousin, the King of Scotland, and his best friend, Banquo. He makes himself King of Scotland and becomes a blood-thirsty tyrant.

Read the three passages below from the play *Macbeth*. They are in the order spoken in the play.

1. Find and underline examples of how Shakespeare compares humans to animals and birds.

2. Rewrite the comparisons and the metaphors in modern English.

3. Explain what you think Shakespeare was trying to convey to his audience through these references to birds and animals.

Passage 1

SERGEANT: (*reporting how bravely Macbeth has fought against the invading Norwegian army*)

    ... But the Norweyan lord surveying vantage,
    With furbish'd arms and new supplies of men
    Began a fresh assault.   5

DUNCAN:
    Dismay'd not this
    Our captains, Macbeth and Banquo?

SERGEANT:
                     Yes;
    As sparrows eagles, or the hare the lion.   10
    If I say sooth, I must report they were
    As cannons overcharged with double cracks;
    So they doubly redoubled strokes upon the foe

Passage 2

BANQUO (*Macbeth's friend Banquo is speaking to King Duncan and Lady Macbeth before they go into Macbeth's castle*)
                This guest of summer,
    The temple-haunting martlet, does approve,
    By his lov'd mansionry, that the heaven's breath   5
    Smells wooingly here: no jutty, frieze,
    Buttress, nor coign of vantage, but this bird
    Hath made her pendent bed and procreant cradle:
    Where they most breed and haunt, I have observed,
    The air is delicate.   10

Passage 3

LADY MACDUFF: (*talking to Ross about her husband, who suspects Macbeth's crime and has gone to England to raise an army*)
                   He loves us not;
    He wants the natural touch: for the poor wren,
    The most diminutive of birds, will fight   5
    Her young ones in her nest, against the owl.

Martlet (n.): house martin. Only seen in Scotland during the warm summer months. Often builds nests against church (temple) walls.

Animals and people

You are going to read about two different animals and their relationships with people. Before you start reading, quickly make a list of the animals that people use for work purposes and those they look after as pets. Do not include the animals that people eat. In pairs, compare your lists.

Taming the wolf: domesticating the dog

The first evidence for domesticated dogs has just got earlier with the recent dating of a dog's skull and teeth from Kesslerloch Cave in Switzerland. That puts the transition from wolf to dog to over 14,000 years ago. Previously, the earliest date was from a single jawbone that was found in a human grave at Oberkassel in Germany, dating to about 13,000 years ago. [...]

The finds from Switzerland were uncovered in 1873 but it was only last year that archaeologists at Tübingen University in Germany recognised that the remains came from a dog rather than a wolf. The dating carried out on a tooth has revealed the animal died between 14,000 and 14,600 BP (before present).

These early dates are curious, as hunting strategies at that time would not necessarily require the assistance of dogs. Studies from northern France show that hunting was ambush-based with animals speared as they passed through natural bottlenecks in the landscape, such as the Ahrensburg Valley. Here, the use of a spear-thrower increased the effectiveness of the weapon and the migrating reindeer died in great numbers. Interestingly, some people engraved their spear-throwers with scenes of the hunt but none shows the appearance of dogs. Indeed, in such a massacre, it is difficult to see how dogs would fit in at all and, yet, the remains from Switzerland suggest that they existed by this time.

Stalking, the hunting method where a dog might have proved invaluable, came later. The warming climate at the end of the Ice Age caused large game animals to either die-out or move north and it was red deer and wild boar that took advantage of the advancing tree cover to expand their range. The people of the time changed their hunting strategy accordingly and the bow and arrow now became the weapon of choice. Dogs would have proved invaluable for stalking, flushing and tracking dying animals. This is the time that we might expect people to have actively sought to domesticate the dog but, from the evidence in Switzerland, it had already happened, presumably without any human intervention. The change from wolf to dog requires a different explanation.

It is likely that wolves had always been aware of humans in the landscape. Scavenging human

44

kill sites would have been a sure way of obtaining food and it is likely that this became the main survival strategy for a few packs. Over time, they may have ventured closer to human camps and even started to forage leftovers or eat any excrement that lay nearby. The people at the camp may have welcomed this cleaning service and tolerated the presence of the wolves. They may have even kept other, more dangerous predators at a safe distance. 50 55

Over time, it is likely that animals that chose to live with humans bred with other animals that adopted a similar lifestyle, replicating the traits that made the animal tolerant of humans. Slowly, the camp-wolves became the camp-dogs. In effect, the dog domesticated itself. 60

It is likely that the dogs did not remain in packs for long but divided themselves between the family groups of the hunters. Evidence from modern hunter-gatherer villages where semi-tame dogs roam, shows that these animals do not necessarily form packs but tend to organise themselves into groups of no more than three, which then adopt a particular dwelling (and its occupants) as their own. In the past, perhaps this was the reason that people began to interact with dogs on an individual basis and the first relationships, with which we are now so familiar, began. 65 70

By Mike Williams, *The Independent*
(27 September 2010)

Reading

1. Explain in your own words how the dog may have "domesticated itself".

2. Using paragraph 3 only, explain how early man used to hunt animals.

3. Explain how men could have used dogs to survive at the end of the Ice Age.

4. In your own words, give three ways people may have benefited from the company of dogs in the distant past.

5. How do dogs organise themselves in modern hunter-gatherer societies?

6. According to the writer, how has "evidence for domesticated dogs" (line 1) got earlier?

7. When, according to the writer, did the transition from wolf to dog probably occur?

Practising scanning and note-making

1. Scan the article "Taming the wolf" and make a list of suitable subheadings, one for each paragraph, using your own words.

2. Check that your subheadings suggest the contents of the article.

3. Write out your subheadings in full sentences to form a piece of continuous writing.

Read this article about working with elephants and then do the Directed Writing task that follows.

Working Elephants in Thailand

A Thai working elephant is considered to come into its prime at age twenty and is expected to have a further working life of approximately thirty five years, with retirement at sixty. A man who wishes to be a mahout must master a number of skills involved with his elephant's work, such as knowledge of a proper diet, complex knot tying, the fabrication of various kinds of tack for his elephant, and the like. His primary task, however, it to learn to understand and manage his animal.

In the past, to become a mahout was like acquiring mastery of artisan skills, through a long apprenticeship. A would be mahout would join a logging team, consisting of approximately five to six elephants and fifteen men, in the teak forests.

An apprentice who showed skill in working with the animals might be promoted to foot mahout, but several more years of learning and absorbing knowledge from the senior mahouts was needed before the apprentice mahout graduated to being a neck mahout. The rough logging camps were ideal learning environments as the range of possible activities was limited to conversation and work. The apprentice mahout could absorb the wealth of technical details which were necessary knowledge for handling the elephant and working in the forest through conversations with the senior mahouts and watching them in action during the three to five months of uninterrupted work in the forest.

The forest apprenticeship system produced mahouts who were skilled workers and controllers

Writing to inform

Write an informative passage on how elephants are trained to work in teak forests in Thailand for a book called "Working Animals".

Use the information in the article on this page and the guidelines in Writing skills panel on page 50 to help you.

Write between 250 and 350 words.

of their animals, but that is a thing of the past. Once there were several small elephant training centers in North Thailand, but in 1969 they were shut down and consolidated at the Center for Training Baby Elephants, located on a fifteen rai plot of land south of the city of Lampang. The center was intended to nurture baby elephants and successfully wean them so their mothers could be returned to work, protect them and provide them with veterinary care, as well as to train mahouts.

A baby elephant born at the center nurses at first and is gradually weaned to an elephant's natural diet. At age three it is corralled for a period of seven days with other babies to wean it from dependence on its mother. It is then introduced to its two mahouts and all three begin an arduous seven year training period.

Mahouts control elephants by three methods: commands given by voice; those given using an elephant prod, a stick ending in a blunt hook; and by applying pressure with the feet and legs. The prod might be to tap parts of the animal's body to indicate the angle of work, the desired direction to move indicated with the feet, and the action begun with a voice command.

When training begins the foot mahout accustoms the animal to the various tack used in working and applies permanent leg chains which can be used to hobble it. The first order of training is to teach the elephant to lift either of its front legs so the mahout can step up to mount it, and to lower its head to facilitate mounting. This action is taught by prodding the animal's legs with sharp sticks.

The next skill taught is for the elephant to pick up objects with its trunk and give them to the mounted neck mahout. The animal is allowed to eat several pieces of sugar cane and then a piece with a cord attached is thrown down. When the

elephant moves to eat it, the mahout jerks the cord, elevating the animal's trunk over the forehead. The action is repeated until the elephant is habituated to offer objects picked up with its trunk to the mahout before consuming them.

The next step in training is to accustom the animal to commands given with pressure from the feet or legs, used to guide it. Mahouts must shove or tug on the animals to get them to get them go in the proper direction in the beginning. But they eventually learn which way to go from pressure applied in the sensitive area behind their ears. Pressure administered behind the animal's right ear, for example, indicates the elephant should turn left. Directional training provides a good example of the closeness of the mahout-elephant bond. Accustomed to its mahout's voice, odour, and technique of applying pressure commands, the elephant will refuse to respond to commands given by a strange mahout.

Once the initial obedience training is complete, the elephant and mahouts enter into a four–five year course in log handling and other specialized tasks. The animal is taught to drag logs on a chain, beginning with small logs with the size gradually increased. The second skill introduced is to teach the animal to lower its head and push a log along the ground with its tusks. It is also trained to lift logs using the tusks instead of obeying its instinct to lift it with its trunk. A mature elephant is capable of lifting up to a 400 kg. log with its tusks and dragging a load of 1.5 tons. Logging training will also include habituating the animals to noisy machinery, such as saws and trucks, which they might encounter while working.

From *Weclome to Chiangmai and Chiangria* magazine, www.chiangmai-chiangrai.com (16 June 2010)

Writing skills
Writing to inform

An information text describes people, places, products or events and then tells the reader more about the subject.

Writers use an impersonal writing style.

This style is used in academic projects, information leaflets, brochures, textbooks and encyclopaedias. It is also used and adapted for news media reports.

Here is a list of 12 features of informative writing:

- clear and factual
- impersonal and objective
- may include data, diagrams, illustrations, tables or maps
- does not have to be chronological
- opens with a general statement and introduction
- may use subheadings or divide information into categories
- may include references and citations
- sentences are short and clear
- vocabulary is precise
- written in the third person
- mixes active and passive verbs
- mixes present and past tenses.

Writing – narrative writing

Choose one of the following.

- Write an episode of a story where the main character is in a dangerous situation.
- "The Rescue". Write the end of a story that involves a rescue.

Write between 350 and 450 words.

Remember to keyword the question. Neither of these options asks you to tell a complete story.

Unit 2: Self-assessment

In this unit we have read fiction, non-fiction and poetry.

Three writing skills we have looked at are: writing to inform and writing to argue and persuade.

1. Name two forms in which writing to inform can be used.

2. What do you need to consider when you are writing or speaking to argue and persuade?

Make notes about Unit 2

Consider the work you have done in this unit. Then copy and complete the chart.

Two texts (poetry or prose) I remember in Unit 2 are:
Two new skills I learned are:
Two things I'm not sure about are:
I enjoyed doing:
Something I would like to do again is:
I would like to do this again because:

REMINDER – Writing episodes in narrative

When you are asked to write the beginning, the end or an episode from a story you only have to write one scene. However, you need to plan where that scene occurs in a complete story and decide who is in it. Start your planning by creating a rough outline for the whole story, then select which part you are going to write. This will help you know more about the events and to make what your characters say and do more believable.

Coursework idea

Invent a title and write an exciting episode from a story for your Coursework Portfolio. Add an introduction to explain where the episode occurs in the whole the story. Write between 500 and 800 words.

Unit 2: Literature extension

Read two poems about creatures that many people find unpleasant or dangerous
and think about why the poets chose to write about them.

Snake

A snake came to my water-trough
On a hot, hot day, and I in pyjamas for the heat,
To drink there.

In the deep, strange-scented shade of the great dark
   carob-tree
I came down the steps with my pitcher   5
And must wait, must stand and wait, for there he
   was at the trough before me.

He reached down from a fissure in the earth-wall in
   the gloom
And trailed his yellow-brown slackness soft-bellied
   down, over the edge of the stone trough

And rested his throat upon the stone bottom,
And where the water had dripped from the tap, in   10
   a small clearness,
He sipped with his straight mouth,
Softly drank through his straight gums, into
   his slack long body,
Silently.

Someone was before me at my water-trough,
And I, like a second comer, waiting.   15

He lifted his head from his drinking, as cattle do,
And looked at me vaguely, as drinking cattle do,
And flickered his two-forked tongue from his lips,
   and mused a moment,
And stooped and drank a little more,
Being earth-brown, earth-golden from the burning
   bowels of the earth   20
On the day of Sicilian July, with Etna smoking.

The voice of my education said to me
He must be killed,
For in Sicily the black, black snakes are innocent,
   the gold are venomous.

And voices in me said, If you were a man   25
You would take a stick and break him now, and
   finish him off.

But must I confess how I liked him,
How glad I was he had come like a guest in quiet,
   to drink at my water-trough

And depart peaceful, pacified, and thankless,
Into the burning bowels of this earth?   30

Was it cowardice, that I dared not kill him?
Was it perversity, that I longed to talk to him?
Was it humility, to feel so honoured?
I felt so honoured.

And yet those voices: 35
If you were not afraid, you would kill him!
And truly I was afraid, I was most afraid,
But even so, honoured still more
That he should seek my hospitality
From out the dark door of the secret earth.   40

He drank enough
And lifted his head, dreamily, as one who has drunken,

And flickered his tongue like a forked night on the
air, so black,
Seeming to lick his lips,
And looked around like a god, unseeing, into the air, 45
And slowly turned his head,
And slowly, very slowly, as if thrice a dream,
Proceeded to draw his slow length curving round
And climb again the broken bank of my wall-face.

And as he put his head into that dreadful hole, 50
And as he slowly drew up, snake-easing his shoulders,
and entered farther,
A sort of horror, a sort of protest against his
withdrawing into that horrid black hole,
Deliberately going into the blackness, and slowly
drawing himself after,
Overcame me now his back was turned.

I looked round, I put down my pitcher, 55
I picked up a clumsy log
And threw it at the water-trough with a clatter.

I think it did not hit him,
But suddenly that part of him that was left behind
convulsed in undignified haste,

Writhed like lightning, and was gone 60
Into the black hole, the earth-lipped fissure in the
wall-front,
At which, in the intense still noon, I stared with
fascination.

And immediately I regretted it.
I thought how paltry, how vulgar, what a mean act!
I despised myself and the voices of my accursed
human education. 65

And I thought of the albatross,
And I wished he would come back, my snake.
For he seemed to me again like a king,
Like a king in exile, uncrowned in the underworld,
Now due to be crowned again. 70

And so, I missed my chance with one of the lords
Of life.
And I have something to expiate;
A pettiness.

By D.H. Lawrence (1920)

The writer's craft – tone and imagery

The snake in this poem is an ordinary Sicilian snake, but D.H.
Lawrence describes it as a mythical lord of the underworld. The
poem is as much about the poet's attitude and reaction to the snake
as it is about the creature itself.

1. How would you describe the tone of the poem?
2. Think about the poet's imagery. How does he use images that are
familiar to him when he is describing the snake?
3. When does Lawrence use more formal, dignified language?
4. What words and phrases in the poem suggest the god-like
qualities of the snake?
5. Look at lines 16–34 and 55–62, and try to explain the conflict
Lawrence experiences as he watches the snake.

Carob-tree (n.): red-flowered
evergreen common to the
Mediterranean.

Etna (n.): a volcanic mountain
in Sicily.

Paltry (adj.): mean-spirited.

Albatross (n.): a very large
oceanic bird.

Expiate (v.): make amends for.

Pike

Pike, three inches long, perfect
Pike in all parts, green tigering the gold.
Killers from the egg: the malevolent aged grin.
They dance on the surface among the flies.

Or move, stunned by their own grandeur,   5
Over a bed of emerald, silhouette
Of submarine delicacy and horror.
A hundred feet long in their world.

In ponds, under the heat-struck lily pads –
Gloom of their stillness: 10
Logged on last year's black leaves, watching upwards.
Or hung in an amber cavern of weeds

The jaws' hooked clamp and fangs
Not to be changed at this date:
A life subdued to its instrument;   15
The gills kneading quietly, and the pectorals.

Three we kept behind glass,
Jungled in weed: three inches, four,
And four and a half: red fry to them –
Suddenly there were two. Finally one   20

With a sag belly and the grin it was born with.
And indeed they spare nobody.
Two, six pounds each, over two feet long
High and dry and dead in the willow-herb –

One jammed past its gills down the other's gullet: 25
The outside eye stared: as a vice locks–
The same iron in this eye
Though its film shrank in death.

A pond I fished, fifty yards across,
Whose lilies and muscular tench   30
Had outlasted every visible stone
Of the monastery that planted them –

Stilled legendary depth:
It was as deep as England. It held
Pike too immense to stir, so immense and old   35
That past nightfall I dared not cast

But silently cast and fished
With the hair frozen on my head
For what might move, for what eye might move.
The still splashes on the dark pond,   40

Owls hushing the floating woods
Frail on my ear against the dream
Darkness beneath night's darkness had freed,
That rose slowly toward me, watching.

By Ted Hughes (1959)

Understanding poetry

Diction is the word given to a poet's choice of words.

1. "Killers from the egg" (line 3): look at the diction in this poem and discuss the different ways Hughes tries to convey the aggressive nature of the pike.

2. "Delicacy and horror" (line 7): find two more examples of how the the poet combines opposites to describe the fish.

3. Find two more examples of how the poet combines paradoxical words and opposites, such as "delicacy and horror" (line 7), in different stanzas.

Speaking and listening

Discussing poets' descriptions

Ted Hughes and D.H. Lawrence both write about creatures many people find unattractive or dangerous.

Discuss how the poets describe the fish and the snake and how they feel about the creatures they are describing.

REMINDER – talking about poets and authors

Give the poet or author's full name in the introduction and then refer to them only by their last name.

Examples:

The British poet, David Herbert Lawrence, wrote "Snake" while he was in Sicily in 1920. I think this poem shows Lawrence's conflicting feelings about the snake. On the one hand, he dislikes the creature because

Or

Pike was written by the British Poet Laureate Ted Hughes. Many of Hughes' poems are about birds and animals. In this poem Hughes talks about a pike that …

REMINDER – imagery

Imagery makes all forms of description more effective.

Imagery helps the reader or listener to imagine.

Imagery can use any of the five senses.

Imagery uses:

- comparisons
- impressions
- similes
- metaphors.

REMINDER – simile and metaphor

simile: a way of comparing two things in an interesting or unusual way using the word *like* or the word *as*.

metaphor: gives one thing the quality or the nature of another without explicitly drawing the comparison; a person, creature, plant or object is described as though it is something else.

3 Points of view

In this unit you will:

→ **Visit** the Balkans, England, Kenya, New Zealand, Northern Ireland, Sri Lanka, Uganda, the USA, Wales and Zimbabwe

→ **Read** autobiographies, fiction, poetry and radio broadcast transcripts

→ **Write** to describe, inform and entertain.

Memories

To reminisce (v.): to think or talk about past events and experiences.

(*Oxford Study Dictionary*)

Read the beginning of the award-winning novel *The Tiger's Wife* by Teá Obreht. It is about a young doctor in a Balkan country and her memories of her grandfather, who was also a doctor.

Teá Obreht grew up in Belgrade; she currently lives in the USA.

Now read what happens at the zoo. The zoo is located in an ancient castle.

In my earliest memories, my grandfather is bald as a stone and he takes me to see the tigers. He puts on his hat, his big-buttoned raincoat, and I wear my lacquered shoes and a velvet dress. It is autumn and I am four years old …

The tigers live in the outer moat of the fortress. We climb the castle stairs, past the waterbirds and the sweating windows of the monkey house, past the wolf growing his winter coat. We pass the bearded vultures and then the bears, asleep all day, smelling 5 of damp earth and the death of something. My grandfather picks me up and props my feet against the handrail so I can look down and see the tigers in the moat.

My grandfather never refers to the tiger's wife 10 by name. His arm is around me and my feet are on the handrail, and my grandfather might say, "I once knew a girl who loved tigers so much she almost became one herself." Because I am little, and my love of tigers comes directly from him, I 15 believe he is talking about me, offering me a fairy tale in which I can imagine myself – and will, for years and years.

The cages face a courtyard, and we go down the stairs and walk slowly from cage to cage. There is a 20 panther, too, ghost spots paling his oil-slick coat; a sleepy, bloated lion from Africa. But the tigers are awake and livid, bright with rancor. Stripe-lashed shoulders rolling, they flank one another up and down the narrow causeway of rock, and the smell 25

Reading

This scene is written from the point of view of an adult woman looking back on her childhood; however, we see this incident through the eyes of a child.

Answer the following questions in full sentences.

Quote from the extract to support your views.

1. How has Obreht told the reader about the child's age – directly or indirectly, or both?

2. Look at how the author describes the other people in this scene. What does this suggest about the age of the child?

3. Look at the last three sentences starting: "My grandfather has not turned away … " In your opinion, why did the grandfather not try to prevent the child witnessing the incident with the tiger?

---

of them is sour and warm and fills everything. It will stay with me the whole day, even after I have had my bath and gone to bed, and will return at random times: at school, at a friend's birthday party, even years later, at the pathology lab, or on the 30 drive home from Galina.

I remember this, too: an altercation. A small group of people stand clustered around the tigers' cage. Among them: a boy with a parrot-shaped balloon, a woman in a purple coat, and a bearded 35 man who is wearing the brown uniform of a zookeeper. The man has a broom and a dustpan on a long handle, and he is sweeping the area between the cage and the outer railing. He walks up and down, sweeping up juice boxes and candy 40 wrappers, bits of popcorn people have tried to throw at the tigers. The tigers walk up and down with him. The woman in purple is saying something and smiling, and he smiles back at her. She has brown hair. The dustpan keeper stops and 45 leans against the handle of his broom, and as he does so, the big tiger sweeps by, rubbing against the bars of the cage, rumbling, and the keeper puts a hand through the bars and touches its flank. For a moment, nothing. And then pandemonium. 50

The tiger rounds on him and the woman shrieks, and suddenly the dustpan keeper's shoulder is between the bars, and he is twisting, twisting his head away and trying to reach for the outer railing so that he has something to hold on to. The tiger 55 has the dustpan keeper's arm the way a dog holds a large bone: upright between his paws, gnawing on the top. Two men who have been standing by with children jump over the railing and grab the dustpan keeper's waist and flailing arm and try to pull him 60 away. A third man jams his umbrella through the bars and pushes it over and over again into the tiger's ribs. An outraged scream from the tiger, and then it stands up on its hind legs and hugs the dustpan keeper's arm and shakes its head from 65 side to side, like it's pulling on rope. Its ears are flattened, and it is making a noise like a locomotive. The dustpan keeper's face is white, and this entire time he hasn't made a sound.

Then suddenly, it's no longer worth it, and the 70 tiger lets go. The three men fall away, and there is a splatter of blood. The tiger is lashing its tail, and the dustpan keeper is crawling under the outer railing and standing up. The woman in purple has vanished. My grandfather has not turned away. I 75 am four years old, but he has not turned me away either. I see it all, and, later, there is the fact that he wants me to have seen.

From *The Tiger's Wife*, by Téa Obreht (2011)

Read the following passage from a radio transcript written by the famous Welsh poet and author Dylan Thomas. It is about his memories of Christmas in Wales during the Second World War.

After you have read the passage, do the activities in the box.

The writer's craft

1. Look at the first paragraph. What do you notice about the punctuation? What effect does this have when you are reading?
2. Look at the second paragraph and make a list of what Dylan Thomas remembers.
3. Write which of the five senses he is using next to each item. For example: *mouth organs = sound – auditory*.
4. Choose a paragraph and read it aloud to a partner. What do you notice about:
    a. the sound and tone of the words?
    b. the effect of the punctuation?

12:43 PM   99% 🔋

𝕸emories of Christmas (1)

A CHILD'S CHRISTMAS IN WALES

One Christmas was so much like another, in those years, around the sea-town corner now, and out of all sound except the distant speaking of the voices I sometimes hear a moment before sleep, that I can never remember whether it snowed for six days and six nights when I was twelve or whether it snowed for twelve days and twelve
5   nights when I was six; or whether the ice broke and the skating grocer vanished like a snowman through a white trap-door on that same Christmas Day that the mince-pies finished Uncle Arnold and we tobogganed down the seaward hill, all the afternoon, on the best tea-tray, and Mrs Griffiths complained, and we threw a snowball at her niece, and my hands burned so, with the heat and the cold, when I
10 held them in front of the fire, that I cried for twenty minutes and then had some jelly.

All the Christmases roll down the hill towards the Welsh-speaking sea, like a snowball growing whiter and bigger and rounder, like a cold and headlong moon bundling down the sky that was our street; and they stop at the rim of the ice-edged, fish-freezing waves, and I plunge my hands in the snow and bring out whatever I can find; holly or
15 robins or pudding, squabbles and carols and oranges and tin whistles, and the fire in the front room, and bang go the crackers, and holy, holy, holy, ring the bells, and the glass bells shaking on the tree … mouth-organs, tin-soldiers, blancmange, and Auntie Bessie playing "Pop Goes the Weasel" and "Nuts in May" and "Oranges and Lemons" on the untuned piano in the parlour all through the thimble-hiding musical-chairing
20 blind-man's-buffing party at the end of the-never-to-be-forgotten day at the end of the unremembered year.

From *Quite Early One Morning*,
by Dylan Thomas (1954)

Memories of Christmas (2)

It was on the afternoon of the day of Christmas Eve, and I was in Mrs Prothero's garden, waiting for cats, with her son Jim. It was snowing. It was always snowing at Christmas; December, in my memory, is white as Lapland, though there were no reindeers. But there were cats. Patient, cold, and callous, our hands wrapped in socks, we waited to snowball the cats. Sleek and long as jaguars and terrible-whiskered, spitting and snarling they would slink and sidle over the white back-garden walls, and the lynx-eyed hunters, Jim and I, fur-capped and moccasined trappers from Hudson's Bay off Eversley Road, would hurl our deadly snowballs at the green of their eyes. The wise cats never appeared. We were so still, Eskimo-footed arctic marksmen in the muffling silence of the eternal snows – eternal, ever since Wednesday – that we never heard Mrs Prothero's first cry from her igloo at the bottom of the garden. Or, if we heard it at all, it was, to us, like the far-off challenge of our enemy and prey, the neighbour's Polar Cat. But soon the voice grew louder. "Fire!" cried Mrs Prothero, and she beat the dinner-gong. And we ran down the garden, with the snowballs in our arms, towards the house, and smoke, indeed, was pouring out of the dining-room, and the gong was bombilating, and Mrs Prothero was announcing ruin like a town-crier in Pompeii. This was better than all the cats in Wales standing on the wall in a row. We bounded into the house, laden with snowballs, and stopped at the open door of the smoke-filled room. Something was burning all right; perhaps it was Mr Prothero, who always slept there after midday dinner with a newspaper over his face; but he was standing in the middle of the room, saying 'A fine Christmas!' and smacking at the smoke with a slipper.

"Call the fire-brigade," cried Mrs Prothero as she beat the gong.

"They won't be there," said Mr Prothero, "it's Christmas."

There was no fire to be seen, only clouds of smoke and Mr Prothero standing in the middle of them, waving his slipper as though he were conducting.

"Do something," he said.

And we threw all our snowballs into the smoke – I think we missed Mr Prothero – and ran out of the house to the telephone-box.

"Let's call the police as well," Jim said.

"And the ambulance."

"And Ernie Jenkins, he likes fires."

But we only called the fire-brigade, and soon the fire engine came and three tall men in helmets brought a hose into the house and Mr Prothero got out just in time before they turned it on. Nobody could have had a noisier Christmas Eve. And when the firemen turned off the hose and were standing in the wet and smoky room, Jim's aunt, Miss Prothero, came downstairs and peered in at them. Jim and I waited, very quietly, to hear what she would say to them. She said the right thing, always. She looked at the three tall firemen in their shining helmets, standing among the smoke and cinders and dissolving snowballs, and she said: "Would you like something to read?"

From *Quite Early One Morning*,
by Dylan Thomas (1954)

Reading

1. Why did the writer go into the Protheros' house? (Do this seem odd?)

2. Who was with the writer when he went into the hous

3. Why do the boys go into the Protheros' garden and w were they doing there?

4. Look at the first paragraph. Find two similes (where something is described as being *like* or *as* something e What effect does the writer create with these similes?

5. Explain in your own words why the writer says that t cats were "terrible-whiskered, spitting and snarling".

6. What was Mrs Prothero doing before the boys ran in the house?

7. Compare what Mrs Prothero says and does with what Mr Prothero says and does before the firemen arrive. Ho do their attitudes differ?

8. Imagine you were playing in the snow with Dylan Thomas and Jim Prothero. Describe in your own wor what happened on the afternoon of the fire. Write between 100 and 150 words.

An unforgettable character

Read this passage from *Running in the Family* by Michael Ondaatje.

Ondaatje is describing his youth in Sri Lanka and memories of his maternal grandmother, Lalla.

Lalla

For years Palm Lodge attracted a constant group – first as children, then teenagers, and then young adults. For most of her life children flocked to Lalla, for she was the most casual and irresponsible of chaperones, being far too busy   5 with her own life to oversee them all. Behind Palm Lodge was a paddy field which separated her house from "Royden," where the Daniels lived. When there were complaints that hordes of children ran into Royden with muddy feet, Lalla   10 bought ten pairs of stilts and taught them to walk across the paddy fields on these "borukakuls" or "lying legs." Lalla would say "yes" to any request if she was busy at bridge so they knew when to ask her for permission to do the most outrageous   15 things. Every child had to be part of the group. She particularly objected to children being sent for extra tuition on Saturdays and would hire a Wallace Carriage and go searching for children like Peggy Peiris. She swept into the school at noon   20 yelling "PEGGY!!!," fluttering down the halls in her long black clothes loose at the edges like a rooster dragging its tail, and Peggy's friends would lean over the banisters and say "Look, look, your mad aunt has arrived."   25

As these children grew older they discovered that Lalla had very little money. She would take groups out for meals and be refused service as she hadn't paid her previous bills. Everyone went with her anyway, though they could never be sure of   30 eating. It was the same with adults. During one of her grand dinner parties she asked Lionel Wendt who was very shy to carve the meat. A big pot was placed in front of him. As he removed the lid a baby goat jumped out and skittered down the   35 table. Lalla had been so involved with the joke – buying the kid that morning and finding a big enough pot – that she had forgotten about the real dinner and there was nothing to eat once the shock and laughter had subsided.   40

From *Running in the Family*,
by Michael Ondaatje

Chaperone (n.): (in this context) an older woman in charge of a younger, unmarried girl on social occasions.

Bridge (n.): a card game.

Reading

1. What does the writer remember about Lalla's character (personality)?

2. What did Lalla do, and/or not do, that has stayed in the author's memory?

3. Using information in the passage, describe Lalla in your own words. Include:

   a. her clothes

   b. her personality

   c. why young people liked her.

Writing a radio transcript

Read the extract from Michael Ondaatje's memories of staying at his grandmother's house in Sri Lanka. Using details from the passage, write a radio transcript of an interview with Michael Ondaatje. Use the Writing skills panel opposite to help you.

Before you start writing:

- Plan what you are going to say using the interview writing frame.

- Remember that you can use summary writing strategies in directed writing.

- Identify the points you need and number them.

- Organise these points in your plan so the script sounds natural.

Start like this:

Interviewer (I): I'd like to welcome the author Michael Ondaatje to our programme this evening.
Michael Ondaatje (M.O.): Thank you, it is a pleasure to be here.
I: I believe your family is from Sri Lanka and you spent a lot of time there. Tell us about your childhood. Do you have any special memories of anything in particular?

REMINDER – Directed Writing

Directed Writing tests your reading and your writing skills. Remember to pay attention to your style and technical accuracy (grammar and spelling).

Writing skills
Writing an interview script

Introduction by I

I'd like to welcome the author Mr Michael Ondaatje to our programme this evening.

Response by interviewee (M.O.)

Thank you, it is a pleasure to be here.

I: Topic 1

Mr Ondaatje, I believe your family is from Sri Lanka and you spent a lot of time there. Tell us about your childhood. Do you have any special memories of anything in particular?

M.O. (Number points for what M.O. will say.)

1.

2.

3.

I: Second question to encourage Michael Ondaatje to say more about his memories

M.O. (Use your reading skills to interpret Ondaatje's thoughts and feelings from the passage.)

I: (Bring interview to a close and thank guest.)

M.O.

REMINDER – scriptwriting

When you write a play script, radio or television transcript, think about the way each person speaks and their mannerisms.

- Use different "voices" for different people.

- Write the dialogue as if the people are really talking.

- Do not punctuate speech (" ") in a script.

Mood and tone in fiction

Mood and tone in any writing are created through the writer's diction or choice of words. In fiction, and many types of non-fiction, the images the writer describes also contribute to how the reader perceives mood and tone.

Mood and tone are created through a combination of:

- diction
- the rhythm of the language used
- the sound effects created by words, using alliteration (words beginning with the same/similar consonants) or sibilance (consonants that are pronounced with a long "s" sound)
- imagery.

Many poets and authors use Nature to convey their feelings. If the narrator is sad, the weather is often described as gloomy. If the writer is happy and feeling positive, everything is bright and beautiful. The attribution of human emotions to natural elements or surroundings is a form of metaphor.

Read the following two passages and think about how the writers have created a mood or atmosphere through their choice of words and imagery.

Passage A

The air and the sky darkened and through them the sun shone redly, and there was a sting in the air. During the night the wind raced faster over the land, dug cunningly among the rootlets of the corn and the corn fought the wind with its weakened leaves until the roots were freed by the prying wind and then each stalk settled   5
wearily sideways toward the earth and pointed the direction of the wind.

The dawn came at last, but no day. In the grey sky a red sun appeared, a dim red circle that gave a little light, like dusk; and as the day advanced, the dusk slipped toward darkness, and the wind   10
cried and whimpered over the fallen corn.

From *The Grapes of Wrath*, by John Steinbeck (1939)

The writer's craft – metaphor and personification

Answer the following questions in full sentences.

1. What human and/or animal qualities does Steinbeck give the corn, the sun and the wind in Passage A?

2. Why do you think the narrator says, "the wind cried and whimpered over the fallen corn" in lines 10–11?

The following passage is from the novel *Bleak House* by Charles Dickens, published in 1853. The story is told by a third-person narrator. In this scene, which is right at the beginning of the story, the narrator is describing the city of London on a foggy day. What atmosphere or mood is Dickens trying to create with his words in this passage?

Blinkers (n.): a pair of leather flaps attached to a horse's bridle to prevent the horse seeing sideways.

Greenwich (n.): an area of London.

'prentice boy (n.): an apprentice; a young boy or girl learning a trade.

Passage B

Smoke lowering down from chimney-pots, making a soft black drizzle, with flakes of soot in it as big as full-grown snow-flakes – gone into mourning, one might imagine, for the death of the sun. Dogs, undistinguishable in mire.   5
Horses, scarcely better; splashed to their very blinkers. Foot passengers, jostling one another's umbrellas in a general infection of ill-temper, and losing their foot-hold at street-corners, where tens of thousands of other foot passengers have   10
been slipping and sliding since the day broke (if the day ever broke), adding new deposits to the crust upon crust of mud, sticking at those points tenaciously to the pavement […] Fog everywhere. Fog up the river, where it flows   15
among green meadows; fog down the river, where it rolls defiled among the tiers of shipping and the waterside pollutions of a great (and dirty) city. […] Fog lying out on the yards, and hovering in the rigging of great ships; fog drooping on   20
the gunwales of barges and small boats. Fog in the eyes and throats of ancient Greenwich pensioners … ; fog in the stem and bowl of the afternoon pipe of the wrathful skipper, down in his close cabin; fog cruelly pinching the toes   25
and fingers of his shivering little 'prentice boy on deck. Chance people on the bridges peeping over the parapets into a nether sky of fog, with fog all round them, as if they were up in a balloon, and hanging in the misty clouds.   30

From *Bleak House*, by Charles Dickens (1885)

Mood and tone in poetry

Fifty years before Dickens wrote *Bleak House*, the poet William Wordsworth (1770–1850) saw London and the River Thames in a very different light.

Composed Upon Westminster Bridge, September 3, 1802

(*Written on the roof of a coach, on my way to France.*)
Earth has not any thing to show more fair:
Dull would he be of soul who could pass by
A sight so touching in its majesty:
This City now doth, like a garment, wear
The beauty of the morning; silent, bare,   5
Ships, towers, domes, theatres, and temples lie
Open unto the fields, and to the sky;
All bright and glittering in the smokeless air.
Never did sun more beautifully steep
In his first splendour, valley, rock, or hill;   10
Ne'er saw I, never felt, a calm so deep!
The river glideth at his own sweet will:
Dear God! the very houses seem asleep;
And all that mighty heart is lying still!

By William Wordsworth (1807)

The writer's craft – mood and tone

1. Copy the table below and add words and phrases from Dickens' description of London in Passage B and Wordsworth's sonnet "Composed on Westminster Bridge" on page 63. Some examples have been done for you.

2. Look at the words and phrases for Dickens and Wordsworth. What tone or mood does each writer create? Find a word or phrase of your own to summarise each writer's tone or mood.

3. How might the time of day mentioned in each text influence what the writer says?

4. How might the date when these two works were written affect the writers' choices of imagery?

	Dickens	Wordsworth
Nouns	*smoke*	*splendour*
Adjectives	*defiled*	*fair*
Images	*waterside pollutions of a great (and dirty) city*	*The river glideth at his own sweet will*

Read this famous poem by Seamus Heaney and do the writing activity that follows.

Death of a Naturalist

All year the flax-dam festered in the heart
Of the townland; green and heavy headed
Flax had rotted there, weighted down by huge sods.
Daily it sweltered in the punishing sun.
Bubbles gargled delicately, bluebottles   5
Wove a strong gauze of sound around the smell.
There were dragon-flies, spotted butterflies,
But best of all was the warm thick slobber
Of frogspawn that grew like clotted water
In the shade of the banks. Here, every spring   10
I would fill jampotfuls of the jellied
Specks to range on window-sills at home,
On shelves at school, and wait and watch until
The fattening dots burst into nimble-
Swimming tadpoles. Miss Walls would tell us how 15
The daddy frog was called a bullfrog
And how he croaked and how the mammy frog
Laid hundreds of little eggs and this was
Frogspawn. You could tell the weather by frogs too
For they were yellow in the sun and brown   20
In rain.

Then one hot day when fields were rank
With cowdung in the grass the angry frogs
Invaded the flax-dam; I ducked through hedges
To a coarse croaking that I had not heard   25
Before. The air was thick with a bass chorus.
Right down the dam gross-bellied frogs were cocked
On sods; their loose necks pulsed like sails. Some hopped:
The slap and plop were obscene threats. Some sat
Poised like mud grenades, their blunt heads farting. 30
I sickened, turned, and ran. The great slime kings
Were gathered there for vengeance and I knew
That if I dipped my hand the spawn would clutch it.

By Seamus Heaney (1966)

The writer's craft

How does Heaney convey two points of view in this poem? Explore the words and images, and think about how and why the speaker changes his opinion.

Quote from the poem to justify your interpretation and ideas.

Points of view in a short story

Read the first part of a short story by Katherine Mansfield. The story is set in New Zealand at the beginning of the 20th century. Leila, who lives in a country area, is visiting her cousins in town. Think about how the author presents Leila's point of view.

Twig? (colloquial): Do you understand?

Her first ball

EXACTLY when the ball began Leila would have found it hard to say. Perhaps her first real partner was the cab. It did not matter that she shared the cab with the Sheridan girls and their brother. She sat back in her own little corner of it, and 5 the bolster on which her hand rested felt like the sleeve of an unknown young man's dress suit; and away they bowled, past waltzing lamp-posts and houses and fences and trees.

"Have you really never been to a ball before, 10 Leila? But, my child, how too weird –" cried the Sheridan girls.

"Our nearest neighbour was fifteen miles," said Leila softly, gently opening and shutting her fan.

Oh dear, how hard it was to be indifferent like 15 the others! She tried not to smile too much; she tried not to care. But every single thing was so new and exciting … Meg's tuberoses, Jose's long loop of amber, Laura's little dark head, pushing above her white fur like a flower through snow. 20 She would remember for ever. It even gave her a pang to see her cousin Laurie throw away the wisps of tissue paper he pulled from the fastenings of his new gloves. She would like to have kept those wisps as a keepsake, as a remembrance. 25 Laurie leaned forward and put his hand on Laura's knee.

"Look here, darling," he said. "The third and the ninth as usual. Twig?"

Oh, how marvellous to have a brother! In her 30 excitement Leila felt that if there had been time, if it hadn't been impossible, she couldn't have helped crying because she was an only child and no brother had ever said 'Twig?' to her; no sister would ever say, as Meg said to Jose that 35 moment, "I've never known your hair go up more successfully than it has to-night!"

But, of course, there was no time. They were at the drill hall already; there were cabs in front of them and cabs behind. The road was bright on 40 either side with moving fan-like lights, and on the pavement gay couples seemed to float through the air; little satin shoes chased each other like birds.

"Hold on to me, Leila; you'll get lost," said Laura. 45

"Come on, girls, let's make a dash for it," said Laurie.

Leila put two fingers on Laura's pink velvet cloak, and they were somehow lifted past the big golden lantern, carried along the passage, and 50 pushed into the little room marked "Ladies." Here the crowd was so great there was hardly space to take off their things; the noise was deafening. Two benches on either side were stacked high with wraps. Two old women in white aprons ran up 55 and down tossing fresh armfuls. And everybody was pressing forward trying to get at the little dressing-table and mirror at the far end.

A great quivering jet of gas lighted the ladies' room. It couldn't wait; it was dancing already. 60 When the door opened again and there came a

burst of tuning from the drill hall, it leaped almost to the ceiling.

Dark girls, fair girls were patting their hair, tying ribbons again, tucking handkerchiefs down the fronts of their bodices, smoothing marble-white gloves. And because they were all laughing it seemed to Leila that they were all lovely. 65

"Aren't there any invisible hair-pins?" cried a voice. "How most extraordinary! I can't see a single invisible hair-pin." 70

"Powder my back, there's a darling," cried someone else.

"But I must have a needle and cotton. I've torn simply miles and miles of the frill," wailed a third. 75

Then, "Pass them along, pass them along!" The straw basket of programmes was tossed from arm to arm. Darling little pink-and-silver programmes, with pink pencils and fluffy tassels. Leila's fingers shook as she took one out of the basket. She 80 wanted to ask someone, "Am I meant to have one too?" but she had just time to read: "Waltz 3. *Two, Two in a Canoe*. Polka 4. *Making the Feathers Fly*," when Meg cried, "Ready, Leila?" and they pressed their way through the crush in the passage 85 towards the big double doors of the drill hall.

Dancing had not begun yet, but the band had stopped tuning, and the noise was so great it seemed that when it did begin to play it would never be heard. Leila, pressing close to Meg, 90 looking over Meg's shoulder, felt that even the little quivering coloured flags strung across the ceiling were talking. She quite forgot to be shy; she forgot how in the middle of dressing she had sat down on the bed with one shoe off and one 95 shoe on and begged her mother to ring up her cousins and say she couldn't go after all. And the rush of longing she had had to be sitting on the veranda of their forsaken up-country home, listening to the baby owls crying [...] in the 100 moonlight, was changed to a rush of joy so sweet that it was hard to bear alone. She clutched her fan, and, gazing at the gleaming, golden floor, the azaleas, the lanterns, the stage at one end with its red carpet and gilt chairs and the band in a 105 corner, she thought breathlessly, "How heavenly; how simply heavenly!"

All the girls stood grouped together at one side of the doors, the men at the other, and the chaperones in dark dresses, smiling rather 110 foolishly, walked with little careful steps over the polished floor towards the stage.

"This is my little country cousin Leila. Be nice to her. Find her partners; she's under my wing," said Meg, going up to one girl after another. 115

Strange faces smiled at Leila – sweetly, vaguely. Strange voices answered, "Of course, my dear." But Leila felt the girls didn't really see her. They were looking towards the men. Why didn't the men begin? What were they waiting for? 120 There they stood, smoothing their gloves, patting their glossy hair and smiling among themselves. Then, quite suddenly, as if they had only just made up their minds that that was what they had to do, the men came gliding over the parquet. 125 There was a joyful flutter among the girls. A tall, fair man flew up to Meg, seized her programme, scribbled something; Meg passed him on to Leila. "May I have the pleasure?" He ducked and smiled. There came a dark man wearing an 130 eyeglass, then cousin Laurie with a friend, and Laura with a little freckled fellow whose tie was crooked. Then quite an old man – fat, with a big bald patch on his head – took her programme and murmured, "Let me see, let me see!" And 135 he was a long time comparing his programme, which looked black with names, with hers. It seemed to give him so much trouble that Leila was ashamed. "Oh, please don't bother," she said eagerly. But instead of replying the fat man 140 wrote something, glanced at her again. "Do I remember this bright little face?" he said softly. "Is it known to me of yore?" At that moment the band began playing; the fat man disappeared. He was tossed away on a great wave of music that 145 came flying over the gleaming floor, breaking the groups up into couples, scattering them, sending them spinning …

Leila had learned to dance at boarding school. Every Saturday afternoon the boarders 150 were hurried off to a little corrugated iron mission hall where Miss Eccles (of London) held her "select" classes. But the difference between that dusty-smelling hall – with calico texts on the walls, the poor, terrified little woman in a brown velvet toque with rabbit's ears thumping the cold piano, Miss Eccles poking the girls' feet with her long white wand – and this was so tremendous that Leila was sure if her partner didn't come and she had to listen to that marvellous music and to watch the others sliding, gliding over the golden floor, she would die at least, or faint, or lift her arms and fly out of one of those dark windows that showed the stars. 155 160

"Ours, I think –" Someone bowed, smiled, and offered her his arm; she hadn't to die after all. Someone's hand pressed her waist, and she floated away like a flower that is tossed into a pool. 165

"Quite a good floor, isn't it?" drawled a faint voice close to her ear. 170

"I think it's most beautifully slippery," said Leila.

From *The Garden Party, and Other Stories*, by Katherine Mansfield (1922)

Tuberoses (n.): white funnel-shaped flowers.
Programmes (n.): men wrote their names in little books called programmes to reserve dances with the girls; the programmes were carried by the girls.
Parquet (n.): wooden floor.

Reading

1. What does the scene in the carriage in "Her First Ball" tell the reader about Leila?

2. Leila is very excited. Do other people feel the same way about the ball?

3. Imagine you are Meg or Laurie, Leila's girl and boy cousins. You are writing your diary after the ball. Describe Leila and how she behaved at the ball. Say what you thought of the ball (you have been to many). Include your thoughts on:
   - your cousin Leila
   - the other people at the ball
   - the venue and its decoration.

The writer's craft – mood and tone

1. Choose words and phrases that convey how Leila feels at the ball. Quote from the text.

2. How does Mansfield create a sense of movement through her words?

Use the SQuEE method to write your answers.

Remember to use quotation marks when you use an author's words.

School in the past and present

Read this 19th-century poem written to help American school children of the time improve their English.

The Nine Parts of Speech

Three little words you often see,

Are articles – a, an, and the.

A noun's the name of anything

As school, garden, hoop, or swing.

An adjective tells the kind of noun –

Great, small, pretty, white, or brown.

Instead of nouns the pronouns stand –

Her head, his face, your arm, my hand.

Verbs tell of something to be done,

To read, sing, jump, or run.

How things are done the adverbs tell,

As slowly, quickly, ill, or well.

Conjunctions join words together,

As men and women, wind or weather.

The prepositions stands before

A noun, as at or through the door.

The interjection shows surprise,

As ah! how pretty – Oh! how wise.

The whole are called nine parts of speech,

Which reading, writing, speaking teach.

Speaking and listening

Working with a partner, talk about how your school life differs to what pupils were doing 150 years ago.

1. Discuss:

   a. how you think the education pupils received in one-room schoolhouses or 'dame schools' differed to the way you learn today

   b. a subject that you do at school which pupils would not have studied then.

2. Working together, write out a timetable for a one-room schoolhouse teacher for one day of the week.

The poem *The Nine Parts of Speech* is believed to have been written by Green Baker in 1865 or 1866.

One hundred and fifty years ago, many children in rural areas of America and Great Britain went to a one-room schoolhouse or a "dame school" in order to learn to read, write and do basic arithmetic. Class work was done on black slates with white chalk. Pupils stayed in the same school room from the age of 6 or 7 to 12 or 14. The older pupils taught the younger pupils what they had already learned. There was no school caretaker or janitor, so teachers and pupils had to clean up each afternoon ready for the following day.

Teachers sometimes lived in or above the schoolroom, but in some areas of America they were expected to "board around". That meant living in the homes of each of the pupils for a few weeks or months at a time. While boarding in someone else's home, the teacher was expected to help out with the domestic chores and tutor the children.

In big cities, schools were more crowded, but the style of teaching and learning was not very different from in country schools.

Look at the illustration opposite of a London "ragged school" in 1853. Parents in England who could spare a few pennies a week sent their children to this type of school.

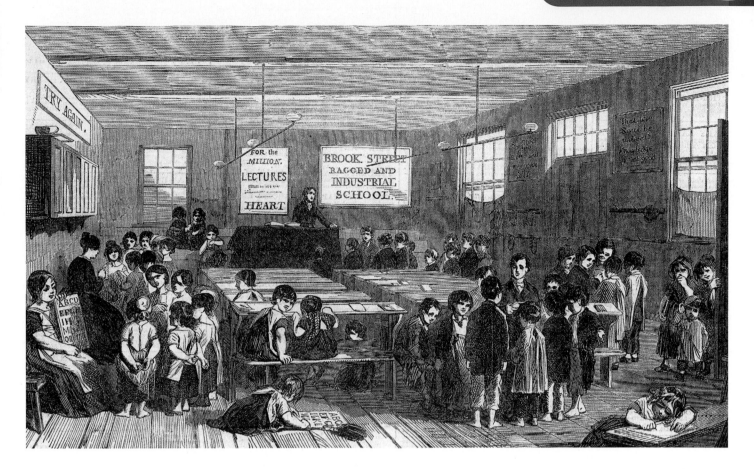

Writing to inform and entertain

You have just finished your first day as a new teacher at Brook Street Ragged and Industrial School in London in 1853. Write a letter to your parents telling them about it. Write about what happened during the day and what you feel about the school and the pupils. Use the Writing skills box on page 70 to help you.

Include the following points:

- why you are working in this school
- what your pupils are like
- what equipment you have to teach them
- what you expect your pupils to learn.

Use the information on account writing to help you.

Write between 500 and 800 words.

Start like this:

Dear Parents,

I have just finished my first day at Brook Street School ...

Writing skills

Writing an account of an incident or experience

Accounts retell past events and are used to inform and sometimes to entertain. You find this style of writing in letters, autobiographies, biographies, diaries, travel writing, feature articles and magazine articles.

When you write an account of a past experience:

- Start by setting the scene: where, when.
- Retell the events in chronological order – what happened, when.
- Use the past tense and first-person active voice.
- Use time connectives: *meanwhile, after that, much later, almost immediately*, etc.

- Focus on specific events objects or people.
- Use interesting words to engage the reader.
- Use imagery and metaphors so the reader understands what you saw, felt, heard ….
- Start with a short sentence to grab the readers' attention and then set the scene.
- Use sentences with many clauses to create a sense of movement or confusion.
- Remember that the final paragraph can link back to the opening lines.

Now read about a student's first day at school. Njoroge lives with his family in a rural area of Kenya. He is excited because he is beginning school. Going to school was a privilege for poor Kenyan boys in 1950. Unfortunately, Njoroge's first day at school is not what he was expecting.

First Day at School

On Monday, Njoroge went to school. He did not quite know where it was. He had never gone there, though he knew the direction to it. Mwihaki took him and showed him the way. Mwihaki was a young girl. Njoroge had always admired her. Once, some herd- 5 boys had quarrelled with Mwihaki's brothers. They had thrown stones and one had struck her. Then the boys had run away followed by her brothers. She had been left alone crying. Njoroge who had been watching the scene from a distance now approached 10 and felt like soothing the weeping child. Now she, the more experienced, was taking him to school. […]

The other boys were rough. They laughed at him and made coarse jokes that shocked him. His former high regard of schoolboys was shaken. He 15 thought that he would never like to make such jokes. Nyokabi, his mother, would be angry if he did.

One boy told him, "You are a Njuka."

"No! I'm not a *Nju-u-ka*," he said.

"What are you?" 20

"I am Njoroge."

They laughed heartily. He felt annoyed. Had he said anything funny? Another boy commanded him, "Carry this bag. You're a *Njuka*."

He was going to take it. But Mwihaki came to 25 his rescue.

"He is my *Njuka*. You cannot touch him."

Some laughed. Others sneered.

"Leave Mwihaki's *Njuka* alone."

"He is Mwihaki's boy." 30

"He'll make a good husband. A *Njuka* to be a husband of Mwihaki."

"A *Njuka* is a *Njuka*. He must carry my bag for me."

All this talk embarrassed and confused Njoroge. He did not know what to do. Mwihaki was annoyed. 35 She burst out. "Yes, he is my *Njuka*. Let any of you touch him."

Silence followed. Njoroge was grateful. Apparently the boys feared her because her sister was a teacher and Mwihaki might report them. 40

The school looked a strange place. But fascinating. The church, huge and hollow, attracted him. It looked haunted. He knew it was the House of God. But some boys shouted while they were in there. This too shocked him. He had been brought 45 up to respect all holy places, like graveyards and the bush around fig trees.

The teacher wore a white blouse and a green skirt. Njoroge liked the white and green because it was like a blooming white flower on a green plant. 50 Grass in this country was green in wet weather and flowers bloomed white all over the land. Especially in Njahi season. Njoroge, however, feared her when two days later she beat a boy, whack! whack! ("Bring the other hand") whack! whack! whack! The stick broke 55 into bits. Njoroge could almost feel the pain. It was as if it was being communicated to him without physical contact. The teacher looked ugly while she punished. Njoroge hated seeing anybody being thrashed and he was sorry for the boy. But he should not have bullied 60 a *Njuka*. It was on that day that Njoroge learnt that *Njuka* was the name given to a new-comer.

From *Weep Not, Child*,
by Ngugi Wa Thiongo (1964)

Reading

Answer the following questions in full sentences.

1. Why does Mwihaki help and defend Njoroge on his first day at school?

2. In your opinion, why do the boys at school make fun of Njoroge?

3. Why does Njoroge deny being a *Njuka* without knowing what *Njuka* means?

4. Suggest two reasons that the boys "feared" Mwihaki.

5. Explain Njoroge's conflicting feelings about his new teacher.

The writer's craft

1. What do you notice about the writer's use of sentences and punctuation?

2. Find an example of a simple sentence with only one verb.

3. What effect do these short, simple sentences have when you are reading?

4. Why do you think the author, Ngugi Wa Thiongo, used this style in this passage?

Writing a fictional first-person account

Read the passage from *Weep Not, Child* by Ngugi Wa Thiongo again and write the scene from Mwihaki's point of view.

Try to write in the same style as the author, using short, simple sentences where you can.

Write between 250 and 350 words.

The picture above shows a rural village school in Rwebigaga, Kibaale District, Uganda.

The children at the Rwebigaga school are aged from three to nine years of age. Some pupils have to walk four kilometres to get to school each morning and then four kilometres to get home in the afternoon.

The school is made of mud and palm tree poles. The roof is corrugated iron.

Pupils follow the Ugandan curriculum, doing typical school subjects such as Maths, Social Sciences and English. At exam time, the older students stay in class to do their test papers while the younger ones play outside and sing.

The children's parents are mainly subsistence farmers who grow matoke (green bananas), maize, ground nuts and cassava for their own use.

There are schools like this all over the world. Different countries try to help the children of poorer families in different ways. Governments basically have two options:

- to encourage overseas charities and non-governmental organisations (NGOs) to send money, clothes, books, teachers and doctors

- to stimulate the country's economy and improve export trade so everyone in the country becomes richer. This enables poorer farmers to sell their crops and raise more money so their children have a better future.

Talking point

In pairs, discuss what you would do to help the children of poorer families in rural areas if you were a member of the government.

1. Write down your ideas.

2. Try to create a "policy plan".

Points of view in poetry

Little Boy Crying

Your mouth contorting in brief spite and
Hurt, your laughter metamorphosed into howls,
Your frame so recently relaxed now tight
With three-year-old frustration, your bright eyes
Swimming tears, splashing your bare feet,   5

You stand there angling for a moment's hint
Of guilt or sorrow for the quick slap struck.
The ogre towers above you, that grim giant,
Empty of feeling, a colossal cruel,
Soon victim of the tale's conclusion, dead   10

At last. You hate him, you imagine
Chopping clean the tree he's scrambling down
Or plotting deeper pits to trap him in.
You cannot understand, not yet,
The hurt your easy tears can scald him with,   15
Nor guess the wavering hidden behind that mask.

This fierce man longs to lift you, curb your sadness
With piggy-back or bull-fight, anything,
But dare not ruin the lessons you should learn.

You must not make a plaything of the rain.   20

By Mervyn Morris (1979)

Speaking and listening

Explaining thoughts and exchanging ideas

Although poems are not used in oral assessments, you could use the poem above to practise your speaking and listening skills.

Poets often use a narrator to describe an event or a scene, or to tell a story. Sometimes the voice we hear is that of the poet; sometimes it is a fictitious persona.

In "Little Boy Crying" there are two points of view, but whose voice do you hear?

Do a *wh-* analysis of the poem (who, what, where, when, why and how) and annotate it. Include:

- where the poem is set (if this is relevant)
- when the scene or event takes place
- whose voice you hear as you read the poem

- who the narrator is speaking to
- what the speaker is talking about and his/her point of view
- how we hear what the child is thinking or feeling
- what you feel about the poem.

Tell your partner about the poem. Include the following points:

- who is in the poem and whose voice you hear
- the age of the child (approximately)
- how you think the narrator feels.

Now listen to what your partner thinks about the poem. Are your ideas similar or different?

Reading

Working with a partner, do a *wh-* analysis of "Before the Sun" by the Zimbabwean poet Charles Mungoshi.

Whose voice do you hear in "Before the Sun"?

Before the Sun

Intense blue morning
promising early heat
and later in the afternoon,
heavy rain.

The bright chips   5
fly from the sharp axe
for some distance through the air,
arc,
and eternities later;
settle down in showers   10
on the dewy grass.

It is a big log:
but when you are fourteen
big logs
are what you want.   15

The wood gives off
a sweet nose-cleansing odour
which (unlike sawdust)
doesn't make one sneeze.

It sends up a thin spiral   20
of smoke which later straightens
and flutes out
to the distant sky: a signal
of some sort,
or a sacrificial prayer.   25

The wood hisses,
The sparks fly.

And when the sun
finally shows up
in the East like some   30
latecomer to a feast
I have got two cobs of maize
ready for it.

I tell the sun to come share
with me the roasted maize   35
and the sun just winks
like a grown-up.

So I go ahead, taking big
alternate bites:
one for the sun,   40
one for me.
This one for the sun,
this one for me:
till the cobs
are just two little skeletons   45
in the sun.

By Charles Mungoshi (1981)

Writing – descriptive and narrative writing

Choose one of the following.

- Children often keep a box of special things. Describe the contents of such a box.

- "Accused". Write a story in which a person is mistakenly accused of doing something wrong.

Write between 350 and 450 words.

Remember to check the activity before you start. Do not confuse the descriptive writing question with the narrative writing question.

Coursework idea

Remember to include a narrative or descriptive composition of between 500 and 800 words in your written Coursework Portfolio.

Unit 3: Self-assessment

In this unit we have read extracts from novels, autobiographies and short stories.

Two writing skills we have looked at in Unit 3 are: writing an interview and writing an account to inform, describe and entertain.

Name two ways of writing an account to inform, describe and entertain can be used.

Write down what you remember about:

- metaphors
- similes
- point of view
- narrative voice

Make notes about Unit 3

Consider the work you have done in this unit. Then copy and complete the chart.

Two texts (poetry or prose) I remember in Unit 3 are:
Two new skills I learned are:
Two things I'm not sure about are:
I enjoyed doing:
Something I would like to do again is:
I would like to do this again because:

Unit 3: Literature extension

This is a short story by Doris Lessing, who grew up in Zimbabwe, Africa.
While you are reading, think about how the author presents different points of view.

Flight

Above the old man's head was the dovecote, a tall wire-netted shelf on stilts, full of strutting, preening birds. The sunlight broke on their grey breasts into small rainbows. His ears were lulled by their crooning, his hands stretched up towards the favourite, a homing pigeon, a young plump-bodied bird which stood still when it saw him and cocked a shrewd bright eye. 5

'Pretty, pretty, pretty,' he said, as he grasped the bird and drew it down, feeling the cold coral claws tighten around his finger. Content, he rested the bird lightly on his chest, and leaned against a tree, gazing out beyond the dovecote into the landscape of a late afternoon. In folds and hollows of sunlight and shade, the dark red soil, which was broken into great dusty clods, stretched wide to a tall horizon. Trees marked the course of the valley; a stream of rich green grass the road. 10 15

His eyes travelled homewards along this road until he saw his granddaughter swinging on the gate underneath a frangipani tree. Her hair fell down her back in a wave of sunlight, and her long bare legs repeated the angles of the frangipani stems, bare, shining-brown stems among patterns of pale blossoms. 20 25

She was gazing past the pink flowers, past the railway cottage where they lived, along the road to the village.

His mood shifted. He deliberately held out his wrist for the bird to take flight, and caught it again at the moment it spread its wings. He felt the plump shape strive and strain under his fingers; and, in a sudden access of troubled spite, shut the bird into a small box and fastened the bolt. "Now you stay there," he muttered; and turned his back on the shelf of birds. He moved warily along the hedge, stalking his granddaughter, who was now looped over the gate, her head loose on her arms, singing. The light happy sound mingled with the crooning of the birds, and his anger mounted. 30 35 40

"Hey!" he shouted; saw her jump, look back, and abandon the gate. Her eyes veiled themselves, and she said in a pert neutral voice: "Hullo, Grandad." Politely she moved towards him, after a lingering backward glance at the road. 45

"Waiting for Steven, hey?" he said, his fingers curling like claws into his palm.

"Any objection?" she asked lightly, refusing to look at him. 50

He confronted her, his eyes narrowed, shoulders hunched, tight in a hard knot of pain which included the preening birds, the sunlight, the flowers. He said: "Think you're old enough to go courting, hey?" 55

The girl tossed her head at the old-fashioned phrase and sulked, "Oh, Grandad!"

"Think you want to leave home, hey? Think you can go running around the fields at night?"

Her smile made him see her, as he had every evening of this warm end-of-summer month, swinging hand in hand along the road to the village with that red-handed, red-throated, violent-bodied youth, the son of the postmaster. Misery went to his head and he shouted angrily: "I'll tell your mother!" 60 65

"Tell away!" she said, laughing, and went back to the gate. He heard her singing, for him to hear:

"I've got you under my skin,

I've got you deep in the heart of … " 70

"Rubbish," he shouted. "Rubbish. Impudent little bit of rubbish!"

Growling under his breath he turned towards the dovecote, which was his refuge from the house he shared with his daughter and her husband and their children. But now the house would be empty. Gone all the young girls with their laughter and their squabbling and their teasing. He would be left, uncherished and alone, with that square-fronted, calm-eyed woman, his daughter. 75 80

He stooped, muttering, before the dovecote, resenting the absorbed cooing birds. From the gate the girl shouted: "Go and tell! Go on, what are you waiting for?"

Obstinately he made his way to the house, with quick, pathetic persistent glances of appeal back at her. But she never looked around. Her defiant but anxious young body stung him into love and repentance. He stopped, "But I never meant … " he muttered, waiting for her to turn and run to him. "I didn't mean … "

She did not turn. She had forgotten him. Along the road came the young man Steven, with something in his hand. A present for her? The old man stiffened as he watched the gate swing back, and the couple embrace. In the brittle shadows of the frangipani tree his granddaughter, his darling, lay in the arms of the postmaster's son, and her hair flowed back over his shoulder.

"I see you!" shouted the old man spitefully. They did not move. He stumped into the little whitewashed house, hearing the wooden veranda creak angrily under his feet. His daughter was sewing in the front room, threading a needle held to the light.

He stopped again, looking back into the garden. The couple were now sauntering among the bushes, laughing. As he watched he saw the girl escape from the youth with a sudden mischievous movement, and run off through the flowers with him in pursuit. He heard shouts, laughter, a scream, silence.

"But it's not like that at all," he muttered miserably. "It's not like that. Why can't you see? Running and giggling, and kissing and kissing. You'll come to something quite different."

He looked at his daughter with sardonic hatred, hating himself. They were caught and finished, both of them, but the girl was still running free.

"Can't you see?" he demanded of his invisible granddaughter, who was at that moment lying in the thick green grass with the postmaster's son.

His daughter looked at him and her eyebrows went up in tired forbearance.

"Put your birds to bed?" she asked, humouring him. 130

"Lucy," he said urgently, "Lucy … "

"Well, what is it now?"

"She's in the garden with Steven."

"Now you just sit down and have your tea."

He stumped his feet alternately, thump, 135 thump, on the hollow wooden floor and shouted: "She'll marry him. I'm telling you, she'll be marrying him next!"

His daughter rose swiftly, brought him a cup, set him a plate. 140

"I don't want any tea. I don't want it, I tell you."

"Now, now," she crooned. "What's wrong with it? Why not?"

"She's eighteen. Eighteen!" 145

"I was married at seventeen and I never regretted it."

"Liar," he said. "Liar. Then you should regret it. Why do you make your girls marry? It's you who do it. What do you do it for? Why?" 150

"The other three have done fine. They've three fine husbands. Why not Alice?"

"She's the last," he mourned. "Can't we keep her a bit longer?"

"Come, now, Dad. She'll be down the road, 155 that's all. She'll be here every day to see you."

"But it's not the same." He thought of the other three girls, transformed inside a few months from charming petulant spoiled children into serious young matrons. 160

"You never did like it when we married," she said. "Why not? Every time, it's the same. When I got married you made me feel like it was something wrong. And my girls the same. You get them all crying and miserable the way you go on. 165 Leave Alice alone. She's happy." She sighed, letting her eyes linger on the sunlit garden. "She'll marry next month. There's no reason to wait."

"You've said they can marry?" he said incredulously. 170

"Yes, Dad, why not?" she said coldly, and took up her sewing.

His eyes stung, and he went out on to the veranda. Wet spread down over his chin and he took out a handkerchief and mopped his whole 175 face. The garden was empty.

From around the corner came the young couple; but their faces were no longer set against him. On the wrist of the postmaster's son balanced a young pigeon, the light gleaming on its breast. 180

"For me?" said the old man, letting the drops shake off his chin. "For me?"

"Do you like it?" The girl grabbed his hand and swung on it. "It's for you, Grandad. Steven brought it for you." They hung about him, affectionate, 185 concerned, trying to charm away his wet eyes and his misery. They took his arms and directed him to the shelf of birds, one on each side, enclosing him, petting him, saying wordlessly that nothing would be changed, nothing could change, and that they 190 would be with him always. The bird was proof of it, they said, from their lying happy eyes, as they thrust it on him. "There, Grandad, it's yours. It's for you."

They watched him as he held it on his wrist, 195 stroking its soft, sun-warmed back, watching the wings lift and balance.

"You must shut it up for a bit," said the girl intimately. "Until it knows this is its home."

"Teach your grandmother to suck eggs," 200 growled the old man.

Released by his half-deliberate anger, they fell back, laughing at him. "We're glad you like it." They moved off, now serious and full of purpose, to the gate, where they hung, backs to him, talking 205 quietly. More than anything could, their grown-up seriousness shut him out, making him alone; also, it quietened him, took the sting out of their tumbling like puppies on the grass. They had forgotten him again. Well, so they should, the old man reassured 210 himself, feeling his throat clotted with tears, his lips trembling. He held the new bird to his face, for the caress of its silken feathers. Then he shut it in a box and took out his favourite.

"Now you can go," he said aloud. He held 215
it poised, ready for flight, while he looked down the garden towards the boy and the girl. Then, clenched in the pain of loss, he lifted the bird on his wrist, and watched it soar. A whirr and a spatter of wings, and a cloud of birds rose 220
into the evening from the dovecote.

At the gate Alice and Steven forgot their talk and watched the birds.

On the veranda, that woman, his daughter, stood gazing, her eyes shaded with a hand 225
that still held her sewing.

It seemed to the old man that the whole afternoon had stilled to watch his gesture of self-command, that even the leaves of the trees had stopped shaking. 230

Dry-eyed and calm, he let his hands fall to his sides and stood erect, staring up into the sky.

The cloud of shining silver birds flew up and up, with a shrill cleaving of wings, over the dark ploughed land and the darker belts 235
of trees and the bright folds of grass, until they floated high in the sunlight, like a cloud of motes of dust.

They wheeled in a wide circle, tilting their wings so there was flash after flash of 240
light, and one after another they dropped from the sunshine of the upper sky to shadow, one after another, returning to the shadowed earth over trees and grass and field, returning to the valley and the 245
shelter of night.

The garden was all a fluster and a flurry of returning birds. Then silence, and the sky was empty.

The old man turned, slowly, taking his 250
time; he lifted his eyes to smile proudly down the garden at his granddaughter. She was staring at him. She did not smile. She was wide-eyed and pale in the cold shadow, and he saw the tears run shivering off her face. 255

From *African Stories*,
by Doris Lessing (1965)

This story could be set in Zimbabwe or anywhere else because where the story takes place is less important than what happens to the characters.

The central character is an elderly man: we are not told his name. The reader is told that he is Lucy's father and Alice's grandfather. Does it matter that we do not know the grandfather's name?

The reader sees most of this story through the old man's eyes. Does the author let us see any other character's points of view? If so, how and why? Does the grandfather's age affect his point of view?

Writing

Do you think Lessing wants the reader to feel sorry for the grandfather in "Flight"?

Support your ideas with details from the story.

4 "All the world's a stage"

In this unit you will:

→ **Visit** Ancient Greece, England, India, Italy, Japan, Scotland and Russia

→ **Read** drama scripts and the history of different forms of theatre

→ **Write** to inform, discuss and entertain.

Talking points

In the play *As You Like It* by William Shakespeare, first performed in 1599, the character Jaques, a melancholy philosopher, says:

> All the world's a stage,
> And all the men and women merely players
> They have their exits and entrances;
> And one man in his time plays many parts,
> His acts being seven ages ...

- What do you think Jaques means by "All the world's a stage"?
- Do we generally perform what is expected of us at different stages of our lives?
- If you divide a person's life into seven acts, what would be in each act?

Stage (n.): 1. a platform on which plays, etc. are performed before an audience. 2. theatrical work, the profession of actors and actresses. 3. To stage (v.) to present a play, etc. on the stage.

(*Oxford Study Dictionary*)

Writing

Make notes on the seven different roles or parts you expect to play in your life.

Start like this:

1. *Helpless but adorable baby.*
2. *Innocent/naughty/reluctant/keen schoolboy/girl...*

Write out how you see your past, present and future as one of the following:

- a poem: write seven stanzas – one for each act
- a first-person account.

Theatre language

Look at the words below and explain what they mean. What other theatre or drama words do you know?

1. Scenery
2. Proscenium arch
3. Backdrop
4. Prompt
5. Auditorium
6. Soliloquy
7. Monologue
8. Stage left/stage right
9. Orchestra pit
10. Dénouement

Pathos (n.): the effect in literature or drama that provokes a sense of sadness or pity.

Read about different forms of theatre in India and Japan on the next few pages and do the activities that follow.

http://www.worlddance.com/styles/performance/asia/

| Cinema | Circus | Comedy | Dance | Drama | Mime | Music | Opera | Poetry |

KATHAKALI dance-drama

Kathakali, which literally means "story play", is an elaborate dance-drama that tells stories from the great Hindu epics, the *Ramayana* and the *Mahabharatha*. It is the classical theatre of Kerala in southern India. Kathakali began in the 17th century as a form of ritual dance performed in temples during religious ceremonies.

Nowadays, Kathakali reaches a broad audience as a popular entertainment, but it is still a highly stylised combination of literature, music, painting, acting and dance that serves to do more than merely entertain. Kathakali dramas encourage people to think about what is important in life. The plots evoke a sense of nostalgia or pathos. In this respect, Indian Kathakali can be compared to Ancient Greek theatre, where skilled dramatists created plots and characters that required an audience to think about human nature. The principal theme in Kathakali is the victory of truth over falsehood.

Kathakali performers wear specific costumes and headgear to denote character; they also use colourful masks, flowing scarves, padded jackets and wide, swirling skirts. It is all larger than life, emphasising that they are super-beings from another world. Each performance is accompanied by powerful vocal music with drummers creating rhythmic, atmospheric background music for the dance movements.

Performers use hand signals, known as the *mudras*, and facial expressions as a form of sign language to convey their emotions and attitudes. Actors need immense powers of concentration and physical stamina, which is why much of their training is based on *Kalaripayattu*, the ancient martial art of Kerala. Studying to become a performer

begins around the age of ten and lasts eight to ten years. Students have to learn the complete language of Kathakali, memorising the combinations of facial expressions, body movements and hand gestures. There are special lessons on how to control eye movements.

Apart from the dance-drama training, the eye movements and the *mudras*, performers also have to learn how to mix the "paint" for their make-up and how to apply it. Some trainee performers choose to become make-up artists instead of actors, but they still have to undergo an apprenticeship of several years.

Actors start preparing for a Kathakali performance many hours before it is due to begin. Mixing the coconut oil-based make-up alone can take up to four hours. While it is being applied, performers meditate upon the characters they are to portray. Kathakali performances generally start at 10 o'clock in the evening and go on all night, which is why everyone involved has to be focused, fit and strong.

The spectacle aspect of Kathakali has contributed a great deal to its survival as an art form and its continuing popularity in modern times. Performances are no longer restricted to sacred temple grounds or palaces, making it accessible to ordinary people. During the 20th century, Kathakali attracted the interest of Western audiences and performing troupes now regularly visit Europe and the USA.

Reading

1. Number the paragraphs in the article on Kathakali and write a subheading for each one.

2. In paragraph 2 the writer says, "Kathakali dramas encourage people to think about what is important in life." What is the connection to the drama of Ancient Greece?

3. In your opinion, do all forms of drama, or only some, encourage people to think about their lives? Write down your thoughts on this.

Noh theatre

Noh is the classical theatre of Japan. Plays are performed on a square stage raised slightly above the ground. To one side there is a balcony for six to eight singers who form the chorus; at the back there is a smaller stage occupied by four musicians and two stage-hands. Actors make their entrances along slanting catwalks wearing masks and elaborate costumes that create a larger-than-life presence on stage. The stage has no scenery: outdoor locations are indicated by pebbles and small pine trees; buildings are intimated by the use of frameworks. The audience sits on two sides of the main stage.

In Noh theatre there are two main actors who wear masks and elaborate costumes. These performers are always men. The principal actor performs scenes from a story; the second actor is the storyteller. The other actors use their visual appearance and body movements to suggest aspects of the story rather than act it out. The name "Noh" comes from the Japanese word for talent or skill.

Noh is believed to be one of the oldest forms of performance theatre. It developed during the 14th century out of a combination of Chinese performing arts known as *sarugaku* and traditional Japanese dance called *dengaku*. Acting troupes originally belonged to shrines and temples and performed dramas that conveyed moral values. In those days Noh theatre was for the aristocracy; ordinary folk were actually forbidden to learn the music or dances. By the end of the 19th century, however, Noh became increasingly popular among working people.

Today Noh is still considered a highbrow form of entertainment, perhaps because of the heroic theme, the chorus and the stylised action. While modern audiences may attend plays for the entertainment value of the spectacle – every Noh performance is a combination of song, dialogue, music and dance – the content of each drama requires an audience to reflect on human values. Noh theatre still represents many aspects of the Buddhist way of life.

| Cinema | Circus | Comedy | Dance | Drama | Mime |

KABUKI

Kabuki is another popular Japanese entertainment that combines music, dance and mime. The word itself is written using three Japanese characters: *ka* = song, *bu* = dance and *ki* = skill. It dates from the beginning of the 17th century, when it developed out of the nobility's more serious Noh theatre to become an entertainment for townspeople. Most Kabuki dramas are based on popular myths and legends – stories with gods, heroes and animals with magic powers. Actors are not masked as in Noh theatre, but wear heavily conventionalised make-up for the classical and female roles, which are always performed by men specialising in female impersonation.

Kabuki is said to have been created by a woman named O Kuni in the 17th century. In its early years Kabuki had a bad reputation; actors and actresses were so notorious that the authorities forbade women and young boys to perform on stage. This meant that men had to take female roles. Kabuki is still performed by an all-male cast. Despite efforts to control the more provocative aspects of Kabuki, however, and even after women were banished from the stage, audiences continued to get out of hand so the authorities tightened control further: troupes consisting entirely of older actors were required to perform very formal, stylised dramas that eliminated opportunities for audience interaction. Changes were made to the Kabuki stage to separate actors from their audiences and curtains were used. Nevertheless, actors found a way to make contact with their audiences via the *hanamichi*, a sort of catwalk extending through the audience. Nowadays, the highly melodramatic Kabuki is performed on a large, revolving platform using elaborate stage devices such as trapdoors for surprise exits and entrances.

Reading – finding and using information

Using the information given on the last few pages, copy the grid onto a large sheet of paper and complete it to show what traditional Indian and Japanese dance-dramas have in common.

	Kathakali	Noh	Kabuki
Origin: where, when, why and how the dance-dramas began			
Audience and popularity: past and present			
Spectacle: costumes, make-up, special effects and music			
Performers: who performs and how they are trained			
Style of acting: how performers convey the stories			
Other points			

Writing – Directed Writing

Read the information on traditional Japanese theatre on pages 83–4 again. Write an informative article for an entertainment blog on traditional Japanese Noh and Kabuki theatre.

Include the following points:

- how each type of theatre began
- what an audience can expect to see in performances
- why, in your opinion, Noh and Kabuki are still popular.

Write between 350 and 450 words.

REMINDER - audience

The term "audience" means the people who watch a play or film, but also the people expected to read a written text of any type. Audiences include the readers of novels and newspapers, radio listeners, television viewers, film-goers and Internet users.

When an author, scriptwriter, journalist or blogger targets an audience, he/she has to consider not just their intended purpose (for example, to inform or entertain), but also some or all of the following factors about the audience: age, social class, educational background, cultural background, religion, gender.

Aristotle's analysis of theatre and tragedy

In about 334–335 BC, the Greek philosopher Aristotle (384–322 BC) wrote a series of essays on drama known as *The Poetics*. Some time later his writings were separated onto two scrolls of papyrus; the first scroll was about the nature of tragedy and the second about comedy. Regrettably, only the first part of his writing on theatre survived.

Taking the plays of Sophocles as examples, Aristotle set out six theoretical criteria in order of importance to explain how a play is performed and how an audience reacts to it. He examined:

- plot
- character
- diction (in those days this was known as "rhythmic language")
- thought
- spectacle
- song.

The importance of plot

Much of what Aristotle wrote about theatre in Ancient Greece still applies today and many scriptwriters for long-running soap operas go back to the plays of Ancient Greece for their plots.

Plot, according to Aristotle, is the most important part of any drama. Plot determines what

characters do, whether they will be successful in their aims or whether they will fail. Plot determines whether the play (or episode) should have a happy or sad ending.

The plot of a tragedy, Aristotle said, should involve a reversal of fortune from good to bad and the main character should suffer. This will arouse fear and pity in the audience. In the sequence of three Acts (beginning, middle and end) a tragedy takes its hero from a peaceful existence to despair. A comedy does the opposite, taking its hero from ill-fortune and complications to an ending where everything is resolved and everyone lives "happy ever after".

Flawed characters

Tragedy in Ancient Greece focused on character, especially human weakness: the hero is brought down by a fatal flaw in his/her character, the hero meets with a "tragical accident" or a mistake is made with devastating repercussions. If the hero knowingly does wrong, the audience can sympathise with them; if he/she unknowingly does wrong, the audience can empathise with them.

Effective diction

While a good plot and a complex main character are essential to successful, meaningful drama, what the protagonist and other characters say on stage (dialogue) and how they convey their characters' thoughts are also very important. Actors must have good speaking voices and know how to vary the pace and pitch of their diction (how they speak their words) in order to get a response from the audience.

Memorable spectacle

Dramatists in Ancient Greece used a chorus to tell the audience what was happening and provide what is nowadays called "back-story". In Aristotle's analysis of theatre, the chorus' chant or song formed part of the overall spectacle; it helped the audience interpret the plot, empathise with the tragic characters or enjoy a comedy. Spectacle includes all aspects of a performance that contribute to its overall effect: costumes, music, scenery, the gestures of the actors and the resonance of their voices. After the plot, spectacle is perhaps what an audience remembers most when a play has ended.

Reading – sympathy and empathy

The plots of Greek tragedies include sequences that arouse "fear and pity" in the audience. Think about how authors, dramatists and script writers try to make an audience fear for what will happen to their main character or feel pity for that character when something tragic does happen. Using the information on these two pages to help you, answer the following questions.

1. How and when, according to the writer, does an audience:

    a. sympathise with a hero?

    b. empathise with a hero?

2. Tragedy in Ancient Greece focused on character.

    a. What, in your opinion, is a "fatal flaw"?

    b. How might this "fatal flaw" lead to a tragic ending in a play or film? (Give examples from a television programme, film or play if you can.)

Talking point

Look at what Aristotle said about drama and think about current theatre productions, film releases and television programmes.

Does anything in Aristotle's analysis of drama apply to modern plays, films and television soap opera?

12:43 PM   99% 🔋

'Enders reveals Greek tragedy influence

EastEnders' series story producer Dominic Treadwell-Collins has revealed that the soap's team often draws on Greek tragedy when devising storylines.

Speaking on a special Radio 4 arts programme called *Oedipus Enders*, Treadwell-Collins named Ronnie Mitchell's (Samantha Womack) secret

5   daughter plotline with Danielle Jones (Lauren Crace) as one plot which was heavily influenced by ancient legends.

Treadwell-Collins explained: "Going back to the origins of storytelling – going back to Greek tragedy is a great way to start, and then of course take it in different directions.

10   "I think the biggest story we've done in my time that reflects that is Ronnie's story with Danielle. We went back and made it Greek."

The producer went on to describe the plot as a "variation" on the tale of the mythical Greek King Oedipus, who was unaware of the identity of his real parents.

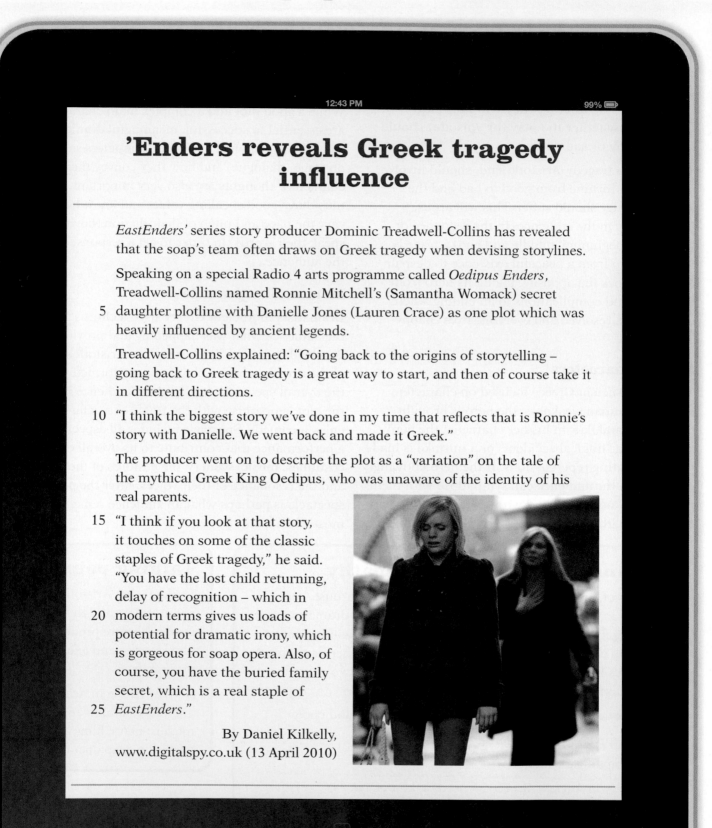

15   "I think if you look at that story, it touches on some of the classic staples of Greek tragedy," he said. "You have the lost child returning, delay of recognition – which in

20   modern terms gives us loads of potential for dramatic irony, which is gorgeous for soap opera. Also, of course, you have the buried family secret, which is a real staple of

25   *EastEnders*."

By Daniel Kilkelly,
www.digitalspy.co.uk (13 April 2010)

What do soap operas have in common with Greek tragedies?

When I was first approached about making a documentary on the links between Greek tragedy and soap, I was sceptical. The differences between them seemed far greater to me than their similarities – soap is ongoing, a Sophocles play can be performed in about 90 minutes; soap is prose, tragedy is verse; the tragedies have endured for millennia, soap is generally forgotten 5
the week after it airs. Also, there is a quality distinction. Much as I like plenty of the writers on *EastEnders*, I don't think they're in the same league as the men who wrote *Medea* and *Oedipus the King*.

But when we started doing the research, I realised that soap and tragedy had far more in common than I had ever noticed. I spoke to a writer who 10
cheerfully admitted that he had based storylines in *EastEnders* on Aeschylus's *Oresteia* … I discovered from John Yorke – the man who brought the Slaters to Albert Square – that he designed his soap characters to have a fatal flaw, exactly like tragic heroes. And the BBC Writers' Academy – which trains future generations of soap writers – apparently uses Aristotle's *Poetics* to 15
teach its writers about unity of time and place.

So I started watching *EastEnders* with a different attitude: looking for similarities, instead of ticking off differences. The storylines are full of tragic archetypes – suffering women, siblings at war, children battling parents, buried family secrets. Soap may have started out as gritty urban realism or 20
an everyday story of country folk, but it certainly hasn't stayed that way.

By Natalie Haynes, www.guardian.co.uk (12 April 2010)

Speaking and listening

In pairs, choose a television programme or film you have both seen. Talk about the plot and what makes the characters seem real. Discuss:

a. why you sympathise with, or feel sympathy for, what is happening to the characters

b. whether it is possible to identify personally with any of the characters; whether you understand or empathise with their feelings.

You can discuss a programme or film like this for Speaking and Listening Coursework.

Scripts and register

Radio and television series, news programmes and documentaries all require prepared scripts. Scripts written for films are called screenplays; television series use teleplays.

Appropriate dialogue and register

The dialogue in any script has to be appropriate for the person saying the words. The register (vocabulary and tone) must fit the person speaking and the particular situation that the character is in at the time. We all use different registers at different times in our lives. Most adults in positions of responsibility do not speak like primary school pupils in a playground. Boys and girls speak in a different manner with their close friends to the way they do when they are with their parents or teachers. A newsreader or presenter on television will probably use a different vocabulary and style of voice to how they might speak with their family.

In drama (on stage, television or film) characters speak in different ways depending on setting and with whom they are speaking. A playwright or scriptwriter provides this dialogue; it is then up to the director and actor to decide how those words should be spoken.

Audience reaction

Scriptwriters have to think about more than just what their characters say. They also need to consider how an audience will interpret and react to the actors' words. Five centuries ago Shakespeare was very aware of this. However, in those days everyone who could went to the theatre, so Shakespeare couldn't just write for a specifically noble audience or a poor audience of uneducated people because both extremes of society were present in the audience. In the late 16th century, theatre was an immensely popular form of entertainment for all sorts of people with different attitudes and beliefs: aristocrats and bakers; doctors and butchers; royalty and street-cleaners.

The secret of Shakespeare's success

Examine any of Shakespeare's plays closely and you will see that he involves a wide range of characters, all of whom speak in different registers. Shakespeare's success lay largely in knowing his audience. Being a good businessman as well as a playwright, he represented the people in his audience on stage. His histories and tragedies contain kings, nobles and humble folk, and much of the humour in his comedies comes about through the sometimes absurd interaction between members of different social groups, who rarely seem to understand one another.

This may not be obvious when you first start reading a Shakespeare play because there are virtually no stage directions apart from entrances and exits. Actors and directors have to read the dialogue very carefully before they decide how characters should speak and behave on stage.

Writing skills
Writing a script

A script is set out so it is easy for the actor to read what he/she has to say and do on stage. The name of the person speaking is put in the left-hand margin and what they say follows. For each new person speaking, start a new line.

Stage directions such as *stands up/sits down/crosses to front of stage* are written after the character's name and usually before the dialogue. Stage directions are sometimes put in brackets.

Scenes often start with information necessary for the stage manager: set, scenery, props, etc.

The features of writing a script are:

- clear, easy to read layout
- direct speech
- no speech marks
- scenes begin with information needed by directors and stage managers
- statements, questions and responses may be very short
- dialogue/use of language is designed to affect the audience
- written like real-life conversations using personal and emotive language
- stage directions are included (usually in brackets) to tell actors when to enter and exit or what to do on stage.

Stage directions

Shakespeare's tragedy *Macbeth* was written in about 1605–6. Shakespeare does not give stage directions to help actors know how to speak their lines.

1. Read the passage on page 93 by yourself and make notes on the following points:
    - how the witches speak
    - how Macbeth and Banquo speak.

2. The scene takes place on a "blasted heath" and there is thunder. If you were directing this scene, what sound or special effects would you use to make this scene more dramatic?

3. How would these sound effects have been made in the 17th century?

Practising your speaking skills

There is no drama in oral assessments, but you can use this activity to improve your speaking skills.

In groups of five, act out the scene from *Macbeth* opposite.

Before you begin, look at how Macbeth and Banquo react to the witches. Think about how they speak and how their words suggest their different reactions.

Macbeth

Act 1 Scene 3 – A blasted heath. Thunder. Enter
three witches.

THIRD WITCH
A drum, a drum!
Macbeth doth come.   5

ALL:
The weird sisters, hand in hand,
Posters of the sea and land,
Thus do go about, about:
Thrice to thine and thrice to mine   10
And thrice again, to make up nine.
Peace! the charm's wound up.

     Enter MACBETH and BANQUO.

MACBETH:
So foul and fair a day I have not seen.   15

BANQUO:
How far is't call'd to Forres? – What are these
So wither'd and so wild in their attire,
That look not like the inhabitants o' the earth,
And yet are on't? Live you? or are you aught   20
That man may question? You seem to understand me,
By each at once her choppy finger laying
Upon her skinny lips: you should be women,
And yet your beards forbid me to interpret
That you are so.   25

MACBETH:
Speak, if you can: what are you?

FIRST WITCH:
All hail, Macbeth! hail to thee, Thane of Glamis!

SECOND WITCH: 30
All hail, Macbeth, hail to thee, Thane of Cawdor!

THIRD WITCH:
All hail, Macbeth, thou shalt be king hereafter!

BANQUO:
Good sir, why do you start, and seem to fear   35
Things that do sound so fair? – I' the name of truth,
Are ye fantastical, or that indeed
Which outwardly ye show? My noble partner
You greet with present grace and great prediction
Of noble having and of royal hope,   40

That he seems rapt withal; to me you speak not.
If you can look into the seeds of time,
And say which grain will grow and which will not,
Speak then to me, who neither beg nor fear
Your favours nor your hate.   45

FIRST WITCH:
Hail!

SECOND WITCH:
Hail!

THIRD WITCH: 50
Hail!

FIRST WITCH:
Lesser than Macbeth, and greater.

SECOND WITCH:
Not so happy, yet much happier.   55

THIRD WITCH:
Thou shalt get kings, though thou be none:
So all hail, Macbeth and Banquo!

FIRST WITCH:
Banquo and Macbeth, all hail!   60

MACBETH:
Stay, you imperfect speakers, tell me more:
By Sinel's death I know I am Thane of Glamis;
But how of Cawdor? The Thane of Cawdor lives,
A prosperous gentleman; and to be king   65
Stands not within the prospect of belief,
No more than to be Cawdor. Say from whence
You owe this strange intelligence, or why
Upon this blasted heath you stop our way
With such prophetic greeting? Speak, I charge you. 70

Witches vanish.

BANQUO:
The earth hath bubbles, as the water has,
And these are of them. Whither are they vanish'd?

MACBETH: 75
Into the air; and what seem'd corporal melted
As breath into the wind. Would they had stay'd!

    By William Shakespeare

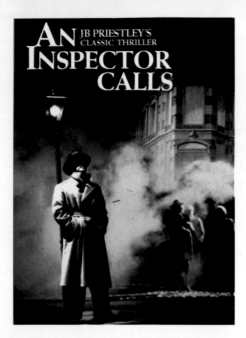

JB PRIESTLEY'S CLASSIC THRILLER

AN Inspector CALLS

Classic British drama

An Inspector Calls is a three-act drama by J.B. Priestley that takes place on a single night in 1912. It is set in the middle-class home of the Birling family who live in Brumley, an industrial town in the British north midlands. During a family dinner to celebrate the engagement between Celia Birling and Gerald Croft, a man calling himself Inspector Goole calls. He questions the family about a young working-class woman, Eva Smith (also known as Daisy Renton). The Inspector says that Eva Smith has just died in hospital after drinking disinfectant and he is looking for information.

At first the Birlings and Gerald Croft deny knowing the young woman, but the Inspector persists with his questioning and gradually shows them how they have each contributed to Eva Smith's death.

An Inspector Calls

(Gerald *and* Eric *exchange uneasy glances. The* Inspector *ignores them.*)

GERALD:
I'd like to have a look at that photograph now, Inspector.   5

INSPECTOR:
All in good time.

GERALD:
I don't see why –

INSPECTOR: 10
(*cutting in, massively*) You heard what I said before, Mr Croft. One line of inquiry at a time. Otherwise we'll all be talking at once and won't know where we are. If you've anything to tell me, you'll have an opportunity of doing it soon.   15

GERALD:
(*rather uneasily*) Well, I don't suppose I have –

ERIC:
(*suddenly bursting out*) Look here, I've had enough of this.   20

INSPECTOR:
(*dryly*) I dare say.

ERIC:
(*uneasily*) I'm sorry – but you see – we were having a little party [...] and I've got a headache –   25

and as I'm only in the way here – I think I'd better turn in.

INSPECTOR:
And I think you'd better stay here.

ERIC: 30
Why should I?

INSPECTOR:
It might be less trouble. If you turn in, you might have to turn out again soon.

GERALD: 35
Getting a bit heavy-handed, aren't you, Inspector?

INSPECTOR:
Possibly. But if you're easy with me, I'm easy with you.

GERALD: 40
After all, y'know, we're respectable citizens and not criminals.

INSPECTOR:
Sometimes there isn't as much of a difference as you might think. Often, if it was left to me, I   45
wouldn't know where to draw the line.

GERALD:
Fortunately, it isn't left to you, is it?

INSPECTOR:
No, it isn't. But some things are left to me.   50
Inquiries of this sort, for instance.

(*Enter* SHEILA, *who looks as if she's been crying.*)

Well, Miss Birling?

SHEILA:

(*coming in, closing the door*) You knew it was me 55
all the time, didn't you?

INSPECTOR:

I had an idea it might be – from something the girl
herself wrote.

SHEILA: 60

I've told my father – he didn't seem to think it
amounted to much – but I felt rotten about it at
the time and now I feel a lot worse. Did it make
much difference to her?

INSPECTOR: 65

Yes, I'm afraid it did. It was the last real steady job
she had. When she lost it – for no reason that she
could discover – she decided she might as well try
another kind of life.

SHEILA: 70

(*miserably*) So I'm really responsible?

INSPECTOR:

No, not entirely. A good deal happened to her
after that. But you're partly to blame. Just as your
father is. 75

ERIC:

But what did Sheila do?

SHEILA:

(*distressed*) I went to the manager at Milwards and
I told him that if they didn't get rid of that girl, 80
I'd never go near the place again and I'd persuade
mother to close our account with them.

INSPECTOR:

And why did you do that?

SHEILA: 85

Because I was in a furious temper.

INSPECTOR:

And what had this girl done to make you lose
your temper?

SHEILA: 90

When I was looking at myself in the mirror I
caught sight of her smiling at the assistant, and
I was furious with her. I'd been in a bad temper
anyhow.

INSPECTOR: 95

And was it the girl's fault?

SHEILA:

No, not really. It was my own fault. (*Suddenly, to*
GERALD). All right, Gerald, you needn't look at
me like that. At least, I'm trying to tell the truth. I 100
expect you've done things you're ashamed of too.

GERALD:

(*surprised*) Well, I never said I hadn't.
I don't see why –

INSPECTOR: 105

(*cutting in*) Never mind about that. You can settle
that between yourselves afterwards. (*To* SHEILA.)
What happened?

SHEILA:

I'd gone in to try something on. It was an idea of 110
my own – mother had been against it, and
so had the assistant – but I insisted. As soon as I
tried it on, I knew they'd been right. It just didn't
suit me at all. I looked silly in the thing. Well, this
girl had brought the dress up from the workroom, 115
and when the assistant – Miss Francis – had asked
her something about it, this girl, to show us what
she meant, had held the dress up, as if she was
wearing it. And it just suited her. She was the right
type for it, just as I was the wrong type. She was a 120
very pretty girl too – with big dark eyes – and that
didn't make it any better. Well, when I tried the
thing on and looked at myself and knew that it was
all wrong, I caught sight of this girl smiling at Miss
Francis – as if to say: 'Doesn't she look awful' – and 125
I was absolutely furious. I was very rude to both of
them, and then I went to the manager and told him
that this girl had been very impertinent – and –
and – (*She almost breaks down, but just controls
herself*.) How could I know what would happen 130
afterwards? If she'd been some miserable plain
little creature, I don't suppose I'd have done it. But
she was very pretty and looked as if she could take
care of herself. I couldn't be sorry for her.

INSPECTOR: 135

In fact, in a kind of way, you might be said to have
been jealous of her.

SHEILA:

Yes, I suppose so.

INSPECTOR: 140

And so you used the power you had, as a daughter of a good customer and also of a man well known in the town, to punish the girl just because she made you feel like that?

SHEILA: 145

Yes, but it didn't seem to be anything very terrible at the time. Don't you understand? And if I could help her now, I would –

INSPECTOR:

(*harshly*) Yes, but you can't. It's too late. She's dead. 150

ERIC:

My God, it's a bit thick, when you come to think of it –

SHEILA:

(*stormily*) Oh shut up, Eric. I know, I know. It's 155 the only time I've ever done anything like that, and I'll never, never do it again to anybody. I've noticed them giving me a sort of look sometimes at Milwards – I noticed it even this afternoon – and I suppose some of them remember. I feel now I can 160 never go there again. Oh – why had this to happen?

INSPECTOR:

(*sternly*) That's what I asked myself tonight when I was looking at that dead girl. And then I said to myself: 'Well, we'll try to understand why it had to 165 happen.' And that's why I'm here, and why I'm not going until I know all that happened. Eva Smith lost her job with Birling and Company because the strike failed and they were determined not to have another one. At last she found another job – 170 under what name I don't know – in a big shop, and had to leave there because you were annoyed with yourself and passed the annoyance on to her. Now she had to try something else. So first she changed her name to Daisy Renton – 175

GERALD:

(*startled*) What?

INSPECTOR:

(*steadily*) I said she changed her name to Daisy Renton. 180

GERALD:

(*pulling himself together*) D'you mind if I give myself a drink, Sheila?

(SHEILA *merely nods, still staring at him* [...])

INSPECTOR: 185

Where is your father, Miss Birling?

SHEILA:

He went into the drawing-room, to tell my mother what was happening here. Eric, take the Inspector along to the drawing-room. 190

(As ERIC *moves, the* INSPECTOR *looks from* SHEILA *to* GERALD, *then goes out with* ERIC.)

Well, Gerald?

GERALD:

(*trying to smile*) Well what, Sheila? 195

SHEILA:

How did you come to know this girl – Eva Smith?

GERALD:

I didn't.

SHEILA: 200

Daisy Renton then – it's the same thing.

GERALD:

Why should I have known her?

SHEILA:

Oh don't be stupid. We haven't much time. You 205 gave yourself away as soon as he mentioned her other name.

GERALD:

All right. I knew her. Let's leave it at that.

SHEILA: 210

We can't leave it at that.

GERALD:

(*approaching her*) Now listen, darling –

SHEILA:

No, that's no use. You not only knew her but 215 you knew her very well. Otherwise, you wouldn't look so guilty about it. When did you first get to know her?

(*He does not reply*.)

Was it after she left Milwards? When she changed 220 her name, as he said, and began to lead a different sort of life? Were you seeing her last spring and summer, during that time when you hardly came near me and said you were so busy? Were you?

(*He does not reply but looks at her*.) 225

Yes, of course you were.

GERALD:

I'm sorry, Sheila. But it was all over and done with, last summer. I hadn't set eyes on the girl for at least six months. I don't come into this suicide business. 230

SHEILA:
I thought I didn't, half an hour ago.

GERALD:
You don't. Neither of us does. So – for God's sake – don't say anything to the Inspector.   235

SHEILA:
About you and this girl?

GERALD:
Yes. We can keep it from him.

SHEILA:
(laughs rather hysterically) Why – you fool – he   240
knows. Of course he knows. And I hate to think how much he knows that we don't know yet. You'll see. You'll see.

(She looks at him almost in triumph. He   245
looks crushed. The door slowly opens and the
INSPECTOR appears, looking steadily and
searchingly at them.)

INSPECTOR:
Well?   250

(The INSPECTOR remains at the door for a
few moments looking at SHEILA and GERALD.
Then he comes forward, leaving the door open
behind him.)

SHEILA: 255
(with hysterical laugh, to GERALD) You see? What
did I tell you?

INSPECTOR:
What did you tell him?

GERALD: 260
(with an effort) Inspector, I think Miss Birling
ought to be excused any more of this questioning.
She's nothing more to tell you. She's had a long,
exciting and tiring day – we were celebrating
our engagement, you know – and now she's   265
obviously had about as much as she can stand.
You heard her.

SHEILA:
He means that I'm getting hysterical now.

INSPECTOR: 270
And are you?

SHEILA:
Probably.

INSPECTOR:
Well, I don't want to keep you here. I've no more   275
questions to ask you.

SHEILA:
No, but you haven't finished asking questions – have you?

INSPECTOR: 280
No.

SHEILA:
(to GERALD) You see? (To INSPECTOR) Then I'm
staying.

GERALD: 285
Why should you? It's bound to be unpleasant and
disturbing.

INSPECTOR:
And you think young women ought to be protected
against unpleasant and disturbing things?   290

GERALD:
If possible – yes.

INSPECTOR:
Well, we know one young woman who wasn't,
don't we?   295

GERALD:
I suppose I asked for that.

SHEILA:
Be careful you don't ask for any more, Gerald.

GERALD: 300
I only meant to say to you – Why stay when you'll
hate it?

SHEILA:
It can't be any worse for me than it has been. And
it might be better.   305

GERALD:
(bitterly) I see.

SHEILA:
What do you see?

GERALD: 310
You've been through it – and now you want to see
someone else put through it.

SHEILA:
(bitterly) So that's what you think I'm really like.
I'm glad I realised it in time, Gerald.   315

GERALD:
No, no, I didn't mean –

SHEILA:
(cutting in) Yes, you did. And if you'd really loved
me, you couldn't have said that. You listened to   320
that nice story about me. I got that girl sacked

from Milwards. And now you've made up your mind I must obviously be a selfish, vindictive creature.

GERALD: 325

I never said that nor even suggested it.

SHEILA:

Then why say I want to see someone else put through it? That's not what I meant at all.

GERALD: 330

All right then, I'm sorry.

SHEILA:

Yes, but you don't believe me. And this is just the wrong time not to believe me.

INSPECTOR: 335

(*massively taking charge*) Allow me, Miss Birling. (To Gerald) I can tell you why Miss Birling wants to stay on and why she says it might be better for her if she did. A girl died tonight. A pretty, lively sort of girl, who never did anybody any harm. But   340 she died in misery and agony – hating life –

SHEILA:

(*distressed*) Don't please – I know, I know – and I can't stop thinking about it –

INSPECTOR: 345

(*ignoring this*) Now Miss Birling has just been made to understand what she did to this girl.

She feels responsible. And if she leaves us now, and doesn't hear any more, then she'll feel she's entirely to blame, she'll be alone with her   350 responsibility, the rest of tonight, all tomorrow, all the next night –

SHEILA:

(*eagerly*) Yes, that's it. And I know I'm to blame – and I'm desperately sorry – but I can't believe – I   355 won't believe – it's simply my fault that in the end she – she committed suicide. That would be too horrible –

INSPECTOR:

(*sternly to them both*) You see, we have to share   360 something. If there's nothing else, we'll have to share our guilt.

SHEILA:

(*staring at him*) Yes, that's true. You know. (*She goes close to him, wonderingly.*) I don't understand   365 about you.

INSPECTOR:

(*calmly*) There's no reason why you should.

(*He regards her calmly while she stares at him wonderingly and dubiously.*)   370

By J.B. Priestley

Discussing the setting of a play

An Inspector Calls was written in English by a British playwright, but it was first performed in Moscow. The action of the play takes place in the Birlings' house in the British north midlands. Could this play be set in New York (America), Kolkata (India), Beijing (China), Mexico City (Mexico) or Oslo (Norway) without significant changes? Discuss how a theatre director might have to adapt the play for another country.

Writing a review

Write a review of a film or television programme that relies heavily on elaborate special effects such as a Harry Potter or Pirates of the Caribbean film, or an episode in a science fiction series. Give your opinion on what the special effects add to the film or programme as a whole. Include the following:

- a brief summary of the plot
- how and why special effects are used in the storyline
- an example of how one or two special effects are used, including how the actors are involved
- what these special effects bring to the film or programme.

Plan your review carefully before you start. The focus of the task is on special effects, so it is not necessary to re-tell the entire plot. Just summarise it in a few words.

Adverbs in stage directions

Modern playwrights often provide stage directions that tell actors what to do and how to say their lines on stage. These stage directions are usually included in brackets after the characters' names.

Look at the stage directions in J.B. Priestley's script for *An Inspector Calls*.

Make a list of all the adverbs that tell the actors how to speak.

Examples: *uneasily, dryly*.

Coursework idea

There is no drama in the exams, but you could talk about a play or film you have seen for your Speaking and Listening Coursework.

Writing

You have been asked to rewrite *An Inspector Calls* as a film script. The film is to be set in another country (not England). Write a letter to the film company. Describe the new setting and say how you would adapt the scene you have read from the play for the film script.

Include the following points:

- Setting: where you would set this play and why.
- Adaption: how you would change the script if necessary and, if you had to translate the play, how the dialogue would be adapted. How else would the change of country affect the script apart from the dialogue?

Modern drama: *Ivan and the Dogs*

Originally written for the radio, the play *Ivan and the Dogs* by Hattie Naylor has now been adapted and performed on both sides of the Atlantic. The play opens in the 1990s in Moscow, where an economic recession is having a serious effect on family life. In the following passages we hear the voice of Ivan Mishukov, who walked out of his mother's Moscow apartment when he was four and spent two years living on the city streets with a pack of dogs.

Passage 1

Author's note: *The dialogue in Soundscapes is spoken in Russian.*

IVAN:

So. All the money went and there was nothing
to buy food with.
Mothers and fathers couldn't feed their children or
their animals.   5

Mothers and fathers tried all sorts of things to find
  money to
buy food, but there wasn't any
because all the money was gone.
So mothers and fathers tried to find things they   10
could get rid of, things that ate, things that drank
or things that needed to be kept warm.
They looked about their apartments for these things.

The dogs went first.

They took them in their cars and drove them to   15
the other side of the city and left them there.

But still there was no money.
So mothers and fathers looked for other things,
other things that ate, and drank and needed to be
kept warm.   20

And some
children
were taken to the other side of the city
and left.

Then I was four.   25

Four.

So I can't remember everything because I was very
Little but I can tell you as much as I can.

Passage 2

Author's note: *In this scene Ivan is trying to befriend a white female dog he calls Belka.*

IVAN:

I lay my hand open for her to take it.

(*Referring to hand.*) Potato in my hand.
I wait.
We wait together.   5
But she won't take it.
She just looks down on the ground with big hungry
sad eyes and I am not frightened of her any more.
I think very sad eyes.
So I put the potato on the ground.   10
I move away.
Now she comes near to the potato, very near.
And then snaps it up.
Now she eats it.
I stand as far away as I was from the Bombzi   15
so I cannot hurt her.
I would never hurt her.
I eat the rest of my potato – giving her two
  more bits.
She waits for me.   20
She sighs. I sigh.
I close my eyes.
Then I sleep. I sleep knowing she is watching me –
knowing the white dog watches me.

Bombzi (n.): homeless people.

Passage 3

IVAN:

In the morning the white dog has gone.
I take the picture of my mother out of my
pocket but I still can't make the lines go.
One day my mother will be kind and   5
beautiful again and she will be happy when
I come home.
And we will live on our own in a place with a
garden. And when I go home I will bring
her lots of packets of crisps.   10
[...]

I am at the back of the factory.
It is a large building made of metal
And everything smells burnt and dirty.
And nothing is tidy.

And now the men are coming to work.   15
So I hide.

Then I see her again. The white dog.
She knows I'm there. Though the men don't.
She is careful not to get near them and then
I see her disappear underneath the building.   20
This is her den.
There are other dogs that live in her den.

Passage 4

IVAN:

I am begging much further down the street
than where I go.
Today has been no good and no one has given
me any money to buy biscuits or drink with.   5
I think people have less again.

Some of the shops have nothing inside.
I think things are very bad.

It is dangerous to beg here as I know it
belongs to the other children. But I'm   10
  not worried.
And then there is shouting.

Soundscape. Boy.
  – *Hey you, what are you doing here?*

It's the bully boy, that made the children   15
have nothing in their eyes.

Soundscape. Boy.
  – *What are you doing here? This is my territory.*

But I am not scared.

Soundscape. Boy.   20
  – *Hey, you deaf or something?*

He comes closer.

Soundscape. Boy.
  – *I'm talking to YOU.*

Come close, I think. Come very close.   25

Soundscape. Boy.
  – *This is my territory. You listening?*

And then he runs towards me to push me.
But then I bark.

Soundscape. Dogs growling and snapping.   30

All my dogs are there.
They circle him.
They are very angry with him
For trying to hurt me.
And then he starts to cry.   35
He is crying and crying.

We go.

Passage 5

IVAN:

It's a full moon. The summer is going.
We go to the hills at the top of Moscow and look
Over the city, my dogs and me.
And we howl.

From *Ivan and the Dogs*, by Hattie Naylor (2010)

Plymouth's Drum Theatre hosts moving play Ivan and the Dogs

Audiences of the Drum Theatre in Plymouth are being invited to experience the very different real life childhood of Ivan Mishukov. At four years of age, Ivan walked out of his Moscow apartment and spent the following two years living on the streets where he was adopted by a pack of wild dogs. 5

247 spoke to the show's writer, Hattie Naylor, about how influences from her background, in painting, mime and radio drama, equipped her to deal with the challenge of conveying Ivan's story to a theatre audience. 10

Hi Hattie, *Ivan and the Dogs* is not the first time that Ivan's story has been presented on The Drum stage. In October 2009, the NIE Company dealt with the same story in *My Life with the Dogs*. Are you familiar with the piece? 15

Not really, no I'm afraid; I haven't managed to see it yet but my understanding of the piece is that it's very physical theatre with members of the company playing dogs while one takes the role of Ivan. It's very different to the way in which I approached the story. 20

Was your approach determined more by your diverse background? Mime and radio writing seem to provide you with quite a range of approaches that you could adopt – allowing for either the physical or the textual depending on what you feel would work best. 25

Definitely, when working on this story I kept going back in my mind to the story of Mowgli in Kipling's *The Jungle Book* and how that story worked because Kipling could provide us with the narrative that was going on inside Mowgli's head. It seemed to me that 30 physical theatre could only show you some aspects of Ivan's life but couldn't show you what that really meant to him or how it affected him. This became particularly clear when considering the story for a radio play. That genre only contains text and, if you 35

really want to allow the audience inside, a monologue can be the most effective means.

So this story is presented in the form of a monologue?

Yes, the play is spoken by Ivan to the audience. I felt the only way for us to understand what the 40 experience meant to Ivan was to put him in a position where he could tell us. So, an actor takes the part of Ivan later in his lifetime. Looking back on his time with the dogs and relating to the audience how that shaped him. It seemed to me to be the only logical 45 way to present the audience with whole story.

And Plymouth and the Drum are providing the official launch for the tour?

Yes I'm so excited about it. We've been working with an incredible composer and sound designer to create 50 a really filmic feel to the piece. The words will be really supplemented through the music and also the stage itself. We've a wonderful set designer who's come up with really special ways of incorporating projections into the action to really make the story 55 come alive for the audience – particularly those who are used to this type of medium.

So you feel the subject matter is something that will connect with a younger audience of theatre goers?

I really do. Ivan's crazy childhood gives us all a 60 different way of looking at our own childhood and it really connects the audience to their own experiences. It's not been unusual up to now to find members of the audience crying and I'm really touched that people are finding it that relevant to 65 their own lives. I can't wait to see how it's received by the Drum audience. ∎

By Alan Butler, *247 Magazine*
(29 September 2010)

Reading

1. How many times has the story of Ivan Mishukov been staged at the Drum Theatre?

2. How does Hattie Naylor's play differ to the NIE production of *My Life with the Dogs*?

3. What problem did Hattie Naylor have to overcome in her version of Ivan's story?

4. How did she solve the problem?

5. Explain in your own words what a monologue is.

6. How has Hattie Naylor's radio play been adapted for the stage?

7. How has Hattie Naylor's own background helped her to convert a radio monologue into a stage show?

8. Beginning at line 49 from: "Yes I'm so excited … " to line 57 " … this type of medium", explain in your own words how there is now a "filmic feel to the piece".

9. Why do you think audiences are so moved by the story of Ivan Mishukov?

10. Why, and in what ways, might younger audiences (lines 58–61) "connect" with the subject and/or performance of this play?

Comedy

What makes people laugh in one country does not always work in another. The same goes for jokes and age. What you may have found very funny when you were small might now seem just plain silly. Read about Italian comedy in the Middle Ages and decide whether this type of humour and entertainment still works today.

Comedy (n.): 1. a light amusing play. 2. humour. (From Greek *komos* = merry-making and *oide* = song.)

(*Oxford Study Dictionary*)

Commedia dell'Arte

Commedia dell'Arte was improvised Italian street theatre performed for passers-by on market days or in a town *piazza*. It began during the 14th century and lasted as a hugely popular entertainment for at least 400 years. Originally, *Commedia dell'Arte* was pure entertainment, not what a modern audience would call drama or a play. There was no script, little dialogue and, more often than not, no stage.

Early improvisation

Performances were organised to suit the crowd present. After a brief consultation between the performers, a sketch was developed on the spot through a combination of skilled teamwork, knockabout comedy and inspiration. The players chose their subjects and characters, decided on their relationships and then set up a situation. This was acted out in what we would call slapstick fashion. (The word *slapstick* in fact comes from the *Commedia dell'Arte* stock character *l'arlecchino* or Harlequin, who always carried a stick that made a tremendous clacking noise when he slapped someone with it.)

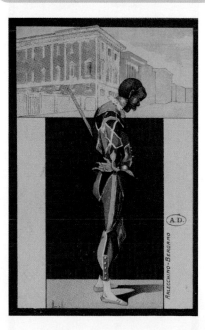

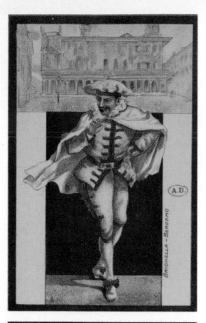

As *Commedia dell'Arte* developed as recognised street theatre, plays became longer. Having decided on their topic, the players now devised acts and scenes starting with a prologue so there was a clear beginning, middle and end to their dramatic nonsense. Situations were established and the outcome of each scene was planned as before, but once they had begun, the actors did everything they could to heighten, vary and embellish their parts for maximum entertainment.

Improvising

Gradually, however, street audiences grew over-familiar with the simple plots and standard characters so there was a constant need for surprise, clarity and wit. This meant that performers needed excellent histrionic skills. If a scene demanded the audience's sympathy or empathy, they had to find the proper words to make the tears flow. If a scene was designed to make people laugh, they got up to every trick to be original and because there was no script to follow, they had to be very focused, aware of what their fellow actors were saying and doing all the time.

Typical plots

Initially plots were simple, even predictable. They revolved around disgraceful intrigues, clever traps to get money out of a miser or efforts to outwit a simpleton. There were long-lost children stolen by pirates, gossiping maids, servants dressed up as their masters, bragging captains, aged fathers and clever widows. There were the usual incidents, such as night scenes when the hero was mistaken for the villain, and there were fires, fireworks and shipwrecks – anything that provided an excuse for a pretty actress to go into hysterics on stage. It was outrageous, riotous fun, but *Commedia dell'Arte* served to introduce the professional actor into Europe.

Setting new standards

In its later years, *Commedia dell'Arte* developed from being just a common street entertainment into a much more sophisticated drama form with stock characters played by performers who made a serious study of their parts. Actors took pride in their achievements and willingly accepted the discipline which all professional art demands. The groups of uneducated travelling performers of the Middle Ages had become professional, highly skilled acting troupes, setting new standards for theatre as a performing art.

Commedia dell'Arte clearly influenced Shakespeare's comedies and is even present in two of his tragedies as comic relief; the troupe of actors in *Hamlet* and the gatekeeper in *Macbeth* owe their origins to inventive, often very naughty, Italian street comedians.

Reading

Answer the following questions in full sentences.

1. Explain in your own words how *Commedia dell'Arte* began.

2. Using only the third paragraph, from the top of page 104, explain how performers devised their plays.

3. Why do you think *Commedia dell'Arte* lasted for so long?

4. What aspects of *Commedia dell'Arte* are still popular in modern comedy?

5. Does slapstick humour make you laugh? Explain why or why not.

Unit 4: Self-assessment

In this unit we have been looking at different types of drama.

1. Explain in your own words the difference between plot and theme.

2. What are stage directions?

3. Write down what you remember about the following:
   a. Kathakali
   b. Noh
   c. Kabuki
   d. *Commedia dell'Arte*
   e. Greek theatre
   f. monologue
   g. the way that different characters speak in *Macbeth*.

Make notes about Unit 4

Consider the work you have done in this unit. Then copy and complete the chart.

Two plays I remember in Unit 4 are:
Two new skills I learned are:
Two things I'm not sure about are:
I enjoyed doing:
Something I would like to do again is:
I would like to do this again because:

5 Family and friends

In this unit you will:

→ **Visit** Ancient Egypt, Bhutan, China, England, India, Northern Ireland, Scotland and the USA

→ **Read** blogs, passages from drama, novels, short stories, poetry and news reports

→ **Write** to summarise, inform, entertain, explore, analyse and discuss.

Speaking and listening

Love and friendship

The following quotations describe aspects of love and friendship.

Work with a partner. Choose one quotation and explain to your partner why you agree or disagree with it.

A friend in need is a friend indeed.

> A Latin saying *Amicus certus in re incerta cernitur* meaning: a sure friend is made known when one is in difficulty.

Two is company, three is none.

> An old proverb.

Fate chooses our relatives, we choose our friends.

> Jacques Delille (1738–1813)

Only one being is missing, and your whole world is bereft of people.

> Lamartine (1790–1869)

Friendship often ends in love; but love in friendship – never.

> Charles Caleb Colton (1803–82)

We flatter those we scarcely know,
We please the fleeting guest,
And deal many a thoughtless blow
To those who love us best.

> Ella Wheeler Wilcox (1850–1919)

Experience shows us that love is not looking into one another's eyes but looking together in the same direction.

> Antoine de Saint-Expury (1900–4)

Talking point

"Fairweather friends"

1. What is the difference between a friend and a "true friend"?

2. What qualities does a true friend possess?

3. When does a good friend become a best friend?

The writer's craft – chronological order

Read the report on the next page of a wedding in Bhutan, a kingdom in the Himalayas.

Make notes on how the writer has organised the account to include the past and the present.

1. When does the reporter use the present tense and why?

2. When does she use the past tense and why?

Happiness in Bhutan

Read two articles about the small kingdom of Bhutan in the Himalayas and do the activities that follow.

Royal Wedding in Bhutan: Dragon King Marries Commoner Sweetheart in Spectacular Buddhist Ceremony

His majesty King Jigme Khesar Namgyel Wangchuck, 31, and Queen Jetsun Pema, 21, wearing traditional costume during their wedding ceremony, in ancient Punakha Dzong on 13 October 2011 in Punakha, Bhutan.

The Himalayan country of Bhutan, known for its policy of Gross National Happiness, celebrated today as King Jigme Khesar Namgyel Wangchuck married his long-time girlfriend Jetsun Pema at 8:20 in the morning – a time set by royal astrologers. 5

Bhutan's Dragon King, who studied in the USA and at Oxford University, wore a fancy yellow sash over a flowered golden robe and a crown with a raven's head. He sipped from a from a ceremonial cup of a special drink symbolising eternal life, in a 10 sumptuous Buddhist ceremony in Punakha Dzong, an ancient monastic fortress. He then placed an embroidered silk crown on the head of his 21-year-old commoner bride, Jetsun Pema, while monks chanted their blessings in front of a massive statue 15 of Buddha. After the ceremony, musicians beat drums and sounded ceremonial trumpets as well-wishers outside admired decorated baby elephants guarding the fortress. Thousands of Bhutanese villagers joined the royal couple for their wedding 20

reception in a fairground and dancers performed traditional routines.

Jetsuna Pema, daughter of an airline pilot, comes from an elite Bhutanese family. She and the king started dating three years ago. Their engagement in May 25 was described as a true love match. On announcing his decision to marry to the country's parliament, Wangchuck said that he had been seeking a woman with a strong character, who was willing to dedicate her life to Bhutan and its people. "I have found such 30 a person, and her name is Jetsun Pema," he told parliament. "While she is young, she is warm and kind in heart and character. These qualities, together with the wisdom that will come with age and experience, will make her a great servant to the nation." 35

Wangchuck has a reputation for being down-to-earth and is a keen basketball player and Elvis fan. His more austere father, who believed development should not damage the environment or traditional culture, introduced the policy of Gross National Happiness. 40 Its framework ties the nation to the Buddhist values of spiritual fulfilment and mental well-being, which are seen as more important than money. In 2006, Wangchuck's father abdicated in favour of his son, bringing democracy to his reluctant subjects. 45

The new king has had a lot to live up to, but he has personally overseen rebuilding following earthquakes and floods in 2009, and handed out land to farmers throughout Bhutan. While his father was known for his power, King Wangchuck has dropped the family's 50 elitist behaviour and likes to keep it more free and easy. When asked by a reporter what it felt like to be married, he answered with a huge smile, "It's great! You should try it yourself."

By Juana D'Arlon, *The New European*, (13 October 2011)

Bhutan's 'Gross National Happiness' index

The tiny, remote Himalayan kingdom of Bhutan first invented the idea of using happiness as a measure of good governance – an idea its superpower neighbour China has now borrowed. 5

It was first proposed in 1972 by Jigme Singye Wangchuck, the country's former king.

King Wangchuck said that instead of relying on Gross Domestic Product as the best indicator of Bhutan's progress, it should instead consider its 10 "Gross National Happiness."

That was to be measured by its people's sense of being well-governed, their relationship with the environment, satisfaction with the pace of economic development and a sense of cultural and national belonging. 15

Pavan K. Verma, India's ambassador to Bhutan and a leading social commentator, said the spread of the idea from remote Bhutan reflects the inadequacy of economic activity as a measurement of success.

"There are limits to the satisfaction economic 20 growth by itself provides," he said. "There's a search to look beyond material fulfilment. There are many aspects of social life in countries as diverse as China and the United Kingdom which are falling apart, like family relations and community life. It is becoming 25 an atomised, individualistic world. The Gross National Happiness looks at the quality of life, how much leisure time you have, what's happening in your community and how integrated you feel with your culture."

By Dean Nelson, *The Telegraph* (2 March 2011)

The writer's craft – tone and register

The two news reporters writing about Bhutan use English in different ways to inform their readers.

How do the articles differ in tone and register?

Write a paragraph to compare and contrast the articles. Include the following:

- register and word choice
- tone and its effect.

REMINDER – tone

The tone of a piece of writing or poem is achieved through the combination of diction (word choice), register (formal, neutral or informal) and syntax (sentence structure).

Speaking and listening

Discussing family relationships

"There are many aspects of social life in countries as diverse as China and the United Kingdom which are falling apart, like family relations and community life."

By Dean Nelson, *The Daily Telegraph*

Working with a partner, discuss the following:

- Do you think your grandparents had closer family relationships with their parents and extended families than you do?
- Do you think modern technology has had any effect on family life?

REMINDER – register

Register is the style of language used to suit a particular situation.

Families in Ancient Egypt

Read about marriage customs in the distant past.

Families and Children: Ancient Egyptian Marriage

The Ancient Egyptians held marriage sacred. The family was broken down into roles that each would play in order for things to run smoothly. The father would work all day while, in smaller households, the mother was in charge of all things pertaining to the house. Cooking, cleaning and watching the children were all her responsibilities. Marriage and a close family played an integral role in Egyptian life. A bride would be young, about 14 or 15, and her husband could be anywhere from 17 to 20 – older if he was divorced or a widower. The Ancient Egyptians were encouraged to marry young, considering that the life span was relatively short. 5 10

Many marriages were arranged with parental consent, as they have been in all societies, especially among the upper classes. But the abundance of love poetry between young people signifies that many couples did fall in love and choose each other as mates. Women played a large role in arranging a marriage. A suitor sometimes used a female go-between to approach the girl's mother – not her father. 15 20

It's interesting that one of the most affectionate titles you could call your love was "brother" or "sister". This had nothing to do with sibling relations, but led many archaeologists and scholars to assume, wrongly, that most ancient Egyptians married their siblings. This usually occurred only among royalty and was not common. 25

The day of the marriage was simple. The bride merely moved her belongings into the home of her husband. He might be living alone or with his parents. The bride wore a long dress or tunic made of linen, which was probably covered with bead-net. If she owned any gold, silver or lapis lazuli, she would adorn herself with those. There was no official ceremony, 30 35 but knowing how much the ancient Egyptians loved music, dance and food, there were usually family celebrations in honor of the couple.

Most marriages had a contract drawn up between the two parties. Marriage settlements were drawn up between a woman's father and her prospective husband, although many times the woman herself was part of the contract. The sole purpose of the contract was to establish the rights of both parties to maintenance and possessions during the marriage and after divorce, if it should occur. 40 45

A man could marry as soon as he was physically mature and had reached a point in his chosen career that ensured his ability to provide for his wife and for the children they could expect. Most Egyptians were content to have only one wife. Marriage was an expensive matter for the man, and the whole contract provided such far-reaching safeguards for the material rights of wives and children that most men could only afford one wife at a time. 50 55

Marriages were mostly between people of the same social class, but there seems to have been little regard given to race or even nationality. It was not unusual for a northern Egyptian to marry a Nubian or someone even from another country. 60

[...]

There are many indications that husbands and wives in Ancient Egypt were often happy and in love. There are many touching portraits and statues of families including spouses and their children that reveal marital delight and warmth within the family. 65

By Jean Adams, http://unusualhistoricals.blogspot.com (26 February 2012)

pertaining to: relating or belonging to something

an integral role: an essential or necessary part

lapis lazuli: a blue gemstone

marriage settlements: financial arrangements

safeguards: ways of protecting (in this case, clauses in the contract)

The writer's craft – *would* + infinitive

When we write to inform and explain, we sometimes use the auxiliary verb would + infinitive to express what used to happen in the past instead of *used to*, as in "The father would work all day ... "

1. Find another example of how the author of the blog on page 110 has used *would* + infinitive to talk about life in Ancient Egypt.

2. Rephrase the following sentence in your own words:

    "A man could marry as soon as he was physically mature and had reached a point in his chosen career that ensured his ability to provide for his wife and for the children they could expect." (lines 47–50)

3. Find another word or words for the following:

    *   sibling (lines 24 and 27)

    *   spouse (line 64).

Writing a summary – Core

Using the information from "Families and Children: Ancient Egyptian Marriage", make notes on when a boy from a humble family could marry in Ancient Egypt. Although the passage is longer than you will encounter in assessments, you do not need to use it all. Find the paragraphs you need before you start to annotate the text. In your notes, include:

*   his age and circumstances

*   how his bride was chosen

*   what arrangements he was expected to make for his bride.

Write your notes out as a summary.

Write between 100 and 150 words.

Writing a summary – Extended

Using information from the blog article "Families and Children: Ancient Egyptian Marriage", make notes on how weddings were arranged in Ancient Egypt. Include:

*   when young people married

*   how marriages were arranged

*   what was in a marriage contract.

Write your notes out as a summary.

Write about 200 words.

Read the following article about Cleopatra and make notes on how she turned herself into an iconic pharaoh.

Who Was Cleopatra?

Mythology, propaganda, Liz Taylor and the real Queen of the Nile

The struggle with her teenage brother over the throne of Egypt was not going as well as Cleopatra VII had hoped. In 49 BC, Pharaoh Ptolemy XIII – also her husband and, by the terms of their father's will, her co-ruler – had driven his sister from the palace at Alexandria after Cleopatra attempted to make herself the sole sovereign. The queen, then in her early twenties, fled to Syria and returned with a mercenary army, setting up camp just outside the capital. 10

Meanwhile, pursuing a military rival who had fled to Egypt, the Roman general Julius Caesar arrived at Alexandria in the summer of 48 BC, and found himself drawn into 15 the Egyptian family feud. For decades Egypt had been a subservient ally to Rome and preserving the stability of the Nile Valley, with its great agricultural wealth, was in Rome's economic interest. Caesar took up 20 residence at Alexandria's royal palace and summoned the warring siblings for a peace conference, which he planned to arbitrate. But Ptolemy XIII's forces barred the return of the king's sister to Alexandria. Aware that 25 Caesar's diplomatic intervention could help her regain the throne, Cleopatra hatched a scheme to sneak herself into the palace for an audience with Caesar. She persuaded her servant Apollodoros to wrap her in a 30 carpet (or, according to some sources, a sack used for storing bedclothes), which he then presented to the 52-year old Roman.

The image of young Cleopatra tumbling out of an unfurled carpet has been dramatized 35 in nearly every film about her, from the silent era to a 1999 TV miniseries, but it was also a key scene in the real Cleopatra's staging of her own life. "She was clearly using all her talents from the moment she arrived on the 40 world stage before Caesar," says Egyptologist Joann Fletcher, author of a forthcoming biography, *Cleopatra the Great*.

Like most monarchs of her time, Cleopatra saw herself as divine; from birth she and 45 other members of her family were declared to be gods and goddesses. Highly image-conscious, Cleopatra maintained her mystique through shows of splendor, identifying herself with the deities Isis and Aphrodite, 50 and in effect creating much of the mythology that surrounds her to this day. Though Hollywood versions of her story are jam-packed with anachronisms, embellishments, exaggerations and inaccuracies, the Cleopatras 55 of Elizabeth Taylor, Vivien Leigh and Claudette Colbert do share with the real queen a love of pageantry. "Cleopatra was a mistress of disguise and costume," says Fletcher. "She could reinvent herself to suit the occasion, and I think that's 60 a mark of the consummate politician."

When Cleopatra emerged from the carpet – probably somewhat disheveled, but dressed in her best finery – and begged Caesar for aid, the gesture won over Rome's future 65

dictator – for life. With his help Cleopatra regained Egypt's throne. Ptolemy XIII rebelled against the armistice that Caesar had imposed, but in the ensuing civil war he drowned in the Nile, leaving Cleopatra safely in power. 70

Though Cleopatra bore him a son, Caesar was already married and Egyptian custom decreed that Cleopatra marry her remaining brother, Ptolemy XIV. Caesar 75 was assassinated in 44 BC, and with her ally gone Cleopatra had Ptolemy XIV killed to prevent any challenges to her son's succession. To solidify her grip on the throne, she dispatched her rebellious 80 sister Arsinoe as well. Such ruthlessness was not only a common feature of Egyptian dynastic politics in Cleopatra's day, it was necessary to ensure her own survival and that of her son. With all 85 domestic threats removed, Cleopatra set about the business of ruling Egypt, the richest nation in the Mediterranean world and the last to remain independent of Rome. 90

What kind of pharaoh was Cleopatra? The few remaining contemporary Egyptian sources suggest that she was very popular among her own people. Egypt's Alexandria-based rulers, 95 including Cleopatra, were ethnically Greek, descended from Alexander the Great's general Ptolemy I Soter. They would have spoken Greek and observed Greek customs, separating themselves 100 from the ethnically Egyptian majority. But unlike her forebears, Cleopatra actually bothered to learn the Egyptian language. For Egyptian audiences, she commissioned portraits of herself in the 105 traditional Egyptian style. In one papyrus dated to 35 BC Cleopatra is called *Philopatris*, "she who loves her country."

By identifying herself as a truly Egyptian pharaoh, Cleopatra used patriotism to 110 cement her position.

Cleopatra's foreign policy goal, in addition to preserving her personal power, was to maintain Egypt's independence from the rapidly expanding Roman Empire. 115 By trading with Eastern nations – Arabia and possibly as far away as India – she built up Egypt's economy, bolstering her country's status as a world power.

By Amy Crawford, www.smithsonianmag.com/ history-archaeology/biography/cleopatra.html (1 April 2007)

Subservient ally (n.): a friendly nation.

Disheveled (adj.): untidy, with ruffled hair.

The writer's craft – past tenses and modern idioms

When we write to inform and explain, we often have to talk about events that happened in the distant and more recent past, but not always in chronological order. To clarify the order of events or make it clear when something happened, we use different forms of the past tense: the past perfect, the past simple and the past continuous.

Look at how past tense verbs are used in the short passage to the right, taken from the article on Cleopatra.

"In 49 BC, Pharaoh Ptolemy XIII [...] had driven his sister from the palace at Alexandria after Cleopatra attempted to make herself the sole sovereign. The queen, then in her early twenties, fled to Syria and returned with a mercenary army, setting up camp just outside the capital." (lines 3–11)

The past perfect tense *had driven* gives the idea that Cleopatra was forced to leave before she returned (past simple) and set up camp outside the capital.

- Cleopatra set up camp outside Alexandria with her mercenary army.

- Cleopatra fled to Syria.

- 49 BC: Ptolemy XIII had driven Cleopatra from the palace in Alexandria after she attempted to make herself sole sovereign.

- Cleopatra returned to Alexandria.

1. Find another example of the past perfect (*had* + past participle) in the article and explain in your own words why the author uses it.

2. Although the author is writing about events in the distant past, she also uses the present tense, the present perfect (*has/have* + past participle) and the present continuous. Here is an example:

    "The image of young Cleopatra tumbling out of an unfurled carpet has been dramatized in nearly every film about her, from the silent era to a 1999 TV miniseries ... " (lines 34–7)

    Why does the author use the present tense here?

3. Although the subject matter of the article is the distant past, the author uses a number of modern colloquial idioms or figures of speech. For example:

    "Cleopatra hatched a scheme ... " (lines 27–8)

    Find two more examples of modern figures of speech.

4. The author uses idiomatic language and links events in Cleopatra's time to modern international politics. The use of phrases we are familiar with from current media coverage of news events makes the article more relevant to modern readers.

    Add to the chart below by finding one more example in the text of the modern use of English and one more example of familiar, newsworthy events.

Modern use of English	Familiar, newsworthy events
"Cleopatra set about the business of ruling Egypt." (lines 86–7)	"Caesar [...] summoned the warring siblings for a peace conference." (lines 20–3)

5. Rewrite the following in your own words:

- "Though Hollywood versions of her story are jam-packed with anachronisms, embellishments, exaggerations and inaccuracies ... " (lines 52–5)

- "She could reinvent herself to suit the occasion ... " (lines 59–60)

6. Cleopatra "built up Egypt's economy, bolstering her country's status as a world power" (lines 118–19).

7. Using your own words as far as possible, write a paragraph to explain why Cleopatra is called "*Philopatris*" on a papyrus dated 35 BC.

Writing skills
Writing to inform and entertain

As we have seen in previous units, an information text or account describes events or people and then tells the reader more about the subject. This impersonal writing style is used in academic projects, informative leaflets, textbooks and encyclopaedias. To make articles or essays more entertaining for the modern mass media and Internet web pages, however, writers include modern references and use less formal language.

Features of writing to inform and entertain in blogs, web pages, newspapers and magazines

- clear and factual about the subject with topical references

- objective but given a more personal twist

- historical references linked to modern readers' lives

- historically accurate but does not have to be chronological

- opens with an attention-grabbing statement and an introduction to the topic

- may include quotations, historical references and citations

- the language is clear and neutral to informal; it may include modern figures of speech

- vocabulary is precise where necessary

- mixes active and passive verbs

- written in the present and/or past tense.

Writing to inform and entertain

Choose a famous person or event from your country's history and write an informative but entertaining article for a web page dedicated to that person or event.

Write between 350 and 450 words.

REMINDER – biography

A biography is an account of a person's life written in the third person.

A biography:

- informs readers about a person

- describes events in the person's life and what the person did

- entertains the reader and makes him/her want to know more.

Family and loyalty

In this scene from the play *Macbeth* the audience sees Macbeth alone on stage before the murder of King Duncan.

Make a list of the reasons Macbeth gives for not killing the king.

Act 1 sc vii – Inverness. Macbeth's castle.

MACBETH:

If it were done when 'tis done, then 'twere well

It were done quickly: if the assassination

Could trammel up the consequence, and catch

With his surcease success; that but this blow | 5

Might be the be-all and the end-all here,

But here, upon this bank and shoal of time,

We'd jump the life to come. But in these cases

We still have judgment here, that we but teach

Bloody instructions, which, being taught, return | 10

To plague the inventor: this even-handed justice

Commends the ingredients of our poison'd chalice

To our own lips. He's here in double trust;

First, as I am his kinsman and his subject,

Strong both against the deed; then, as his host, | 15

Who should against his murderer shut the door,

Not bear the knife myself. Besides, this Duncan

Hath borne his faculties so meek, hath been

So clear in his great office, that his virtues

Will plead like angels, trumpet-tongued, against | 20

The deep damnation of his taking-off;

And pity, like a naked new-born babe,

Striding the blast, or heaven's cherubim, horsed

Upon the sightless couriers of the air,

Shall blow the horrid deed in every eye, | 25

That tears shall drown the wind. I have no spur

To prick the sides of my intent, but only

Vaulting ambition, which o'erleaps itself

And falls on the other.

Surcease (n): death.

Kinsman (n): a relative such as an uncle or cousin.

Follower

By Seamus Heaney (1939 –)

My father worked with a horse plough,
His shoulders globed like a full sail strung
Between the shafts and the furrow.
The horses strained at his clicking tongue.

An expert. He would set the wing   5
And fit the bright-pointed sock.
The sod rolled over without breaking.
At the headrig, with a single pluck.

Of reins, the sweating team turned round
And back into the land. His eye   10
Narrowed and angled at the ground,
Mapping the furrow exactly.

I stumbled in his hobnailed wake,
Fell sometimes on the polished sod;
Sometimes he rode me on his back   15
Dipping and rising to his plod.

I wanted to grow up and plough,
To close one eye, stiffen my arm.
All I ever did was follow
In his broad shadow around the farm.   20

I was a nuisance, tripping, falling,
Yapping always. But today
It is my father who keeps stumbling
Behind me, and will not go away.

Reading

1. What do we learn about the father in this poem?

   Include:

   - his appearance
   - his skill as a farmer
   - his character.

2. Choose two words or phrases from the poem to show why the boy admired his father.

3. Why, in your opinion, does the speaker say "I was a nuisance" (line 21)?

4. Explain in your own words what you think the speaker means in the last two lines.

Sock (n.): the detachable part of a plough that cuts into the soil.

Headrig (n.): a strip left unploughed in a field where the horse-plough turns.

Different forms of love

Romantic love is just one form of love. Copy the chart below and add to it where you can.

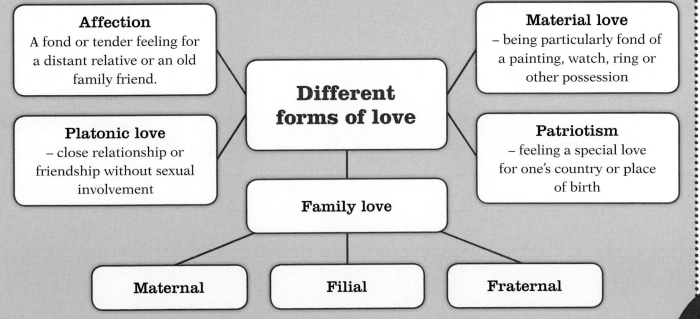

Affection
A fond or tender feeling for a distant relative or an old family friend.

Platonic love
– close relationship or friendship without sexual involvement

Different forms of love

Material love
– being particularly fond of a painting, watch, ring or other possession

Patriotism
– feeling a special love for one's country or place of birth

Family love

Maternal   **Filial**   **Fraternal**

Human emotions

Here are three poems from different epochs (17th, 18th and 20th century; note each poet's dates) about human relationships and personal feelings. Working with a partner, read the poems through carefully and make notes on the relationships and/or personal feelings expressed by each poet.

Which is the odd one out?

To Anthea, Who May Command Him Anything

By Robert Herrick (1591–1674)

Bid me to live, and I will live
　Thy Protestant to be,
Or bid me love, and I will give
　A loving heart to thee.

A heart as soft, a heart as kind,　　5
　A heart as sound and free
As in the whole world thou canst find,
　That heart I'll give to thee.

Bid that heart stay, and it will stay
　To honour thy decree:　　10
Or bid it languish quite away,
　And't shall do so for thee.

Bid me to weep and I will weep
　While I have eyes to see:
And having none, yet will I keep　　15
　A heart to weep for thee.

Bid me despair, and I'll despair
　Under that cypress tree.
Or bid me die, and I will dare
　E'en death to die for thee.　　20

Thou art my life, my love, my heart,
　The very eyes of me,
And hast command of every part,
　To live and die for thee.

A Poison Tree

By William Blake (1757–1827)

I was angry with my friend:

I told my wrath, my wrath did end.

I was angry with my foe:

I told it not, my wrath did grow.

And I watered it in fears,　　5

Night and morning with my tears;

And I sunned it with smiles,

And with soft deceitful wiles.

And it grew both day and night,

Till it bore an apple bright.　　10

And my foe beheld it shine.

And he knew that it was mine,

And into my garden stole

When the night had veiled the pole;

In the morning glad I see　　15

My foe outstretched beneath the tree.

In the next poem, Little Frieda is the poet's young daughter.

Full Moon and Little Frieda

By Ted Hughes (1930–98)

A cool small evening shrunk to a dog bark and the
    clank of a bucket –
And you listening.
A spider's web, tense for the dew's touch.
A pail lifted, still and brimming – mirror
To tempt a first star to a tremor.   5

Cows are going home in the lane there, looping the
hedges with their warm wreaths of breath –
A dark river of blood, many boulders,
Balancing unspilled milk.
"Moon!" you cry suddenly, "Moon! Moon!"   10

The moon has stepped back like an artist gazing
    amazed at a work
That points at him amazed.

Synonyms for love and hate

Using a thesaurus, write down nouns for *love* and for *hate*.

Copy the diagram and put the nouns in the appropriate triangle according to the strength of the emotion: stronger emotions go in the wider parts of the triangles; weaker emotions go in the narrower parts. Write the nouns in red.

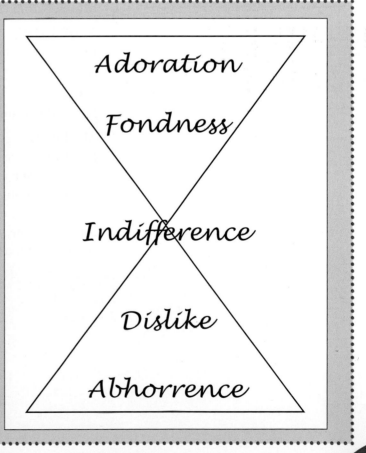

Adoration

Fondness

Indifference

Dislike

Abhorrence

The proposal

Read this scene from *The Importance of Being Earnest*, a comedy by the British playwright, author and poet Oscar Wilde.

Then, working with a partner, do the Speaking and listening activity.

Speaking and listening

Discussing romance

Do you agree with Algernon when he says; "The very essence of romance is uncertainty"?

Explain your reasons for agreeing or disagreeing.

JACK:
[...] Who is coming to tea?

Algernon:
Oh! merely Aunt Augusta and Gwendolen.

JACK:
How perfectly delightful!   5

ALGERNON:
Yes, that is all very well; but I am afraid Aunt Augusta won't
quite approve of your being here.

JACK.   10
May I ask why?

ALGERNON:
My dear fellow, the way you flirt with Gwendolen
is perfectly disgraceful. It is almost as bad as the way
Gwendolen flirts with you.   15

JACK:
I am in love with Gwendolen. I have come up to town
expressly to propose to her.

ALGERNON:
I thought you had come up for pleasure? ... I call   20
that business.

JACK:
How utterly unromantic you are!

ALGERNON:
I really don't see anything romantic in proposing.   25
It is very romantic to be in love. But there is nothing
romantic about a definite proposal. Why, one may be
accepted. One usually is, I believe. Then the excitement
is all over. The very essence of romance is uncertainty.
If ever I get married, I'll certainly try to forget the fact.   30

From *The Importance of Being Earnest*,
by Oscar Wilde (1895)

Happy ever after

Read the following poem about marriage as a long-term partnership.
What is the poet saying about the woman in the poem?

Marrysong

He never learned her, quite. Year after year
that territory, without seasons, shifted
under his eye. An hour he could be lost
in the walled anger of her quarried hurt
or turning, see cool water laughing where   5
the day before there were stones in her voice.
He charted. She made wilderness again.
Roads disappeared. The map was never true.
Wind brought him rain sometimes, tasting of sea –
and suddenly she would change the shape of shores   10
faultlessly calm. All, all was each day new:
the shadows of her love shortened or grew
like trees seen from an unexpected hill,
new country at each jaunty, helpless journey.
So he accepted that geography, constantly strange.   15
Wondered. Stayed home increasingly to find
his way among the landscapes of her mind.

By Dennis Scott (1939–91)

Reading

1. "He never learned her, quite." (line 1)
    Does the verb "to learn" surprise you in a poem about a
    relationship?

2. How does the poet of "Marrysong" make the reader feel the hurt,
    the anger and the joy in his marriage?
    (Look at the imagery and the sound of the lines.)

3. What metaphor is Scott using in this text:

    "Year after year / that territory, without seasons, shifted /
    under his eye." (lines 1–3)

4. How does the poet use imagery in lines 8–15? Why do you think
    he chose this imagery?

5. Do you think the imagery Scott uses is suitable for a poem about
    marriage?

6. Read lines 7 and 8 aloud. What is the effect of using short
    sentences here?

Family values

Read part a short story by the American author William Saroyan, who was the son of Armenian immigrants living in California. Think about the relationship between the two boys in the story and the importance of the extended family and family values.

The Summer of the Beautiful White Horse

One day back there in the good old days when I was nine and the world was full of every imaginable kind of magnificence, and life was still a delightful and mysterious dream, my cousin Mourad, who was considered crazy by everybody who knew him except me, came to my house at four in the morning and woke me up by tapping on the window of my room. 5

Aram, he said.

I jumped out of bed and looked out the window. I couldn't believe what I saw. 10

It wasn't morning yet, but it was summer and with daybreak not many minutes around the corner of the world it was light enough for me to know I wasn't dreaming.

My cousin Mourad was sitting on a beautiful 15
white horse. I stuck my head out of the window and rubbed my eyes. Yes, he said in Armenian. It's a horse. You're not dreaming. Make it quick if you want to ride.

I knew my cousin Mourad enjoyed being alive 20
more than anybody else who had ever fallen into the world by mistake, but this was more than even I could believe.

In the first place, my earliest memories had been memories of horses and my first longings had been 25
longings to ride.

This was the wonderful part.

In the second place, we were poor.

This was the part that wouldn't permit me to believe what I saw. 30

We were poor. We had no money. Our whole tribe was poverty-stricken. Every branch of the Garoghlanian family was living in the most amazing and comical poverty in the world. Nobody could understand where we ever got money enough to 35
keep us with food in our bellies, not even the old men of the family. Most important of all, though, we were famous for our honesty. We had been famous for our honesty for something like eleven centuries, even when we had been the wealthiest 40
family in what we liked to think was the world. We were proud first, honest next, and after that we believed in right and wrong. None of us would take advantage of anybody in the world, let alone steal.

Consequently, even though I could *see* the horse, 45
so magnificent; even though I could *smell* it, so lovely; even though I could *hear* it breathing, so exciting; I couldn't *believe* the horse had anything to do with my cousin Mourad or with me or with any of the other members of our family, asleep 50
or awake, because *I knew* my cousin Mourad couldn't have *bought* the horse, and if he couldn't have bought it he must have *stolen* it, and I refused to believe he had stolen it.

No member of the Garoghlanian family could be 55
a thief.

I stared first at my cousin and then at the horse. There was a pious stillness and humor in each of them which on the one hand delighted me and on the other frightened me. 60

Mourad, I said, where did you steal this horse?

Leap out of the window, he said, if you want to ride.

It was true, then. He *had* stolen the horse. There was no question about it. He had come to invite me to ride or not, as I chose.   65

Well, it seemed to me stealing a horse for a ride was not the same thing as stealing something else, such as money. For all I knew, maybe it wasn't stealing at all. If you were crazy about horses the way my cousin Mourad and I were, it wasn't   70 stealing. It wouldn't become stealing until we offered to sell the horse, which of course I knew we would never do.

Let me put on some clothes, I said.

All right, he said, but hurry. I leaped into my   75 clothes.

I jumped down to the yard from the window and leaped up onto the horse behind my cousin Mourad.

That year we lived at the edge of town, on Walnut Avenue. Behind our house was the country: 80 vineyards, orchards, irrigation ditches, and country roads. In less than three minutes we were on Olive

Avenue, and then the horse began to trot. The air was new and lovely to breathe. The feel of the horse running was wonderful. My cousin Mourad who   85 was considered one of the craziest members of our family began to sing ...

From *My Name is Aram*,
by William Saroyan (1940)

Writing to explore and entertain

We are told that all the members of the Garoghlanian family are very poor but they are famous for their honesty.

Read the passage from *The Summer of the Beautiful White Horse* again. Try to decide what sort of personality each boy has.

What do you think happens to the two boys and the horse? Finish the story in your own words.

Use the information on writing to entertain in a short story on page 124 to help you.

Write between 350 and 450 words.

REMINDER – writing dialogue

Remember to indent the first line of dialogue like a new paragraph.

Start a new (indented) line for each new person speaking.

Don't forget to use speech marks.

End pieces of dialogue with a comma, full stop, question mark, exclamation mark or ellipsis *before* you close the speech marks.
For example:

"Do it like this," said the expert.

"All right, if you say so," I replied.

Writing skills
Writing to entertain in a short story

1. A story worth writing is worth writing well. So think before you write!

   Before you even start making a plan, decide on these points.

   - Who you are writing for? Who is your audience?

   - What you are writing about? What is the subject of your story?

   - Where and when is the story set?

   - Who is in the story?

   - How you are going to write – in first or third person?

2. Make notes.

   - Make decisions about the plot – plan what is going to happen.

   - Decide how the story ends.

   - Keep the number of characters to a minimum to avoid confusing the reader.

   - Choose names that are not similar.

   - Make each person interesting. Very few people are all good or all bad. Give your main character (hero/heroine/villain/ detective) a weak spot or a flaw that will make him/her more believable and add to the story.

   - Decide on the narrator. Who is telling the story?

   - Are you in the story, writing subjectively in the first person? If so, remember that you can only speculate on what other characters are thinking and the reader needs to know something about your personality.

   - Are you in the story, writing in the first person, but objectively? If so, let the reader know why you are telling the story.

   - Are you telling the story from a third-person all-knowing (omniscient) point of view? If so, consider the relationship between the characters and how they behave. A third-person omniscient narrator knows what everyone is doing, thinking and feeling.

3. Don't lose the plot!

   - A short story needn't have a beginning, a middle and an end. You don't have to tell the whole story. You can focus on one event and leave it open-ended or create a cliffhanger ending. However, as the writer, you need a clear idea about what finally happens, even if you don't write it.

4. Start writing, but think about your style.

   - A short story needs to get to the point very quickly so only include description that is totally relevant to setting, character and plot.

   - Use the five senses in your description so readers can see and feel what is happening.

5. Now finish the story and then read what you have written!

6. You have now reached the proofreading stage. Professional writers spend hours choosing words, improving descriptive detail and correcting mistakes. You may not have hours, but you must spend time checking and correcting spelling and grammar before you can ask anyone to read what you have written.

Matchmaking

Read this passage from *The Joy Luck Club* by the Chinese American writer
Amy Tan.

The Matchmaker

[T]he village matchmaker came to my family when
I was just two years old. No, nobody told me this, I
remember it all. It was summertime, very hot and
dusty outside, and I could hear cicadas crying in
the yard. We were under some trees in our orchard. 5
The servants and my brothers were picking pears
high above me. And I was sitting in my mother's
hot sticky arms. I was waving my hand this way
and that, because in front of me floated a small
bird with horns and colorful paper-thin wings. And 10
then the paper bird flew away and in front of me
were two ladies. I remember them because one lady
made watery "shrrhh, shrrhh" sounds. When I was
older, I came to recognize this as a Peking accent,
which sounds quite strange to Taiyuan people's ears. 15

The two ladies were looking at my face without
talking. The lady with the watery voice had a
painted face that was melting. The other lady had
the dry face of an old tree trunk. She looked first at
me, then at the painted lady. 20

Of course, now I know the tree-trunk lady was
the old village matchmaker, and the other was
Huang Taitai, the mother of the boy I would be
forced to marry. No, it's not true what some Chinese
say about girl babies being worthless. It depends on 25
what kind of girl baby you are. In my case, people
could see my value. I looked and smelled like a
precious buncake, sweet with a good clean color.

The matchmaker bragged about me: "An earth
horse for an earth sheep. This is the best marriage 30
combination." She patted my arm and I pushed her
hand away. Huang Taitai whispered in her shrrhh-
shrrhh voice that perhaps I had an unusually bad
pichi, a bad temper. But the matchmaker laughed
and said, "Not so, not so. She is a strong horse. She 35
will grow up to be a hard worker who serves you
well in your old age."

And this is when Huang Taitai looked down at me
with a cloudy face as though she could penetrate my
thoughts and see my future intentions. I will never 40
forget her look. Her eyes opened wide, she searched
my face carefully and then she smiled. I could see a
large gold tooth staring at me like the blinding sun
and then the rest of her teeth opened wide as if she
were going to swallow me down in one piece. 45

This is how I became betrothed to Huang
Taitai's son, who I later discovered was just a baby,
one year younger than I. His name was Tyan-yu-
ryan for "sky," because he was so important, and
yu, meaning "leftovers," because when he was born 50
his father was very sick and his family thought
he might die. Tyan-yu would be the leftover of
his father's spirit. But his father lived and his
grandmother was scared the ghosts would turn
their attention to this baby boy and take him 55
instead. So they watched him carefully, made all
his decisions, and he became very spoiled.

But even if I had known I was getting such a bad
husband, I had no choice, now or later. That was
how backward families in the country were. We 60
were always the last to give up stupid old fashioned
customs. In other cities already, a man could choose
his own wife, with his parents' permission of course.
But we were cut off from this type of new thought. You
never heard if ideas were better in another city, only 65
if they were worse. We were told stories of sons who
were so influenced by bad wives that they threw their
old, crying parents out into the street. So, Taiyuanese
mothers continued to choose their daughters-in-law,
ones who would raise proper sons, care for the old 70
people, and faithfully sweep the family burial grounds
long after the old ladies had gone to their graves.

Because I was promised to the Huangs' son for
marriage, my own family began treating me as if I
belonged to somebody else. My mother would say 75
to me when the rice bowl went up to my face
too many times, "Look how much Huang Taitai's
daughter can eat."

My mother did not treat me this way because
she didn't love me. She would say this biting back 80
her tongue, so she wouldn't wish for something that
was no longer hers.

From *The Joy Luck Club*, by Amy Tan (2006)

Reading – Core

1. Answer these questions in full sentences and give examples to support your views. Use the SQuEE method (see page 7).

   a. Whose voice do you hear when you read the passage?

   b. How old is the girl at this point in the story?

   c. Who is Huang Taitai?

   d. What does the matchmaker say to convince Huang Taitai she is making a good choice?

   e. Why do the people in country areas continue with the old customs?

   f. What do you think the "small bird with horns colorful and paper-thin wings" (lines 9–10) is and why does the author use this description?

   g. How does the marriage arranged for the baby girl work out for her as an adult?

   h. Find examples in the passage that suggest the narrator's character.

2. You are one of the baby girl's parents. Describe in your own words what happened the day the matchmaker brought the baby's future mother-in-law to see her. Include what happened on the day, and your thoughts and feelings about your daughter going to live with her husband's family.

Reading – Extended

1. You are a reporter for a Chinese city newspaper. Using information from "The Matchmaker", write an article about the practice of matchmaking in rural areas. Include:

   a. the role of the matchmaker in rural marriages

   b. what the custom involves

   c. why the custom has not died out in rural areas.

2. Re-read the first three paragraphs of the passage where the narrator gives her first impressions of the matchmaker and her future mother-in-law. Explain how the author has used two of the five senses to describe these impressions. Include:

   a. what is being described

   b. which sense the author is using

   c. how the author has used imagery.

Writing a discursive essay

"Parents know what is best for their children. Caring parents will obviously choose good marriage partners for their sons and daughters."

Use the framework on how to write a discursive essay on page 127 and write your views on the subject of arranged marriage.

Writing skills
Writing a discursive essay

Introduction: the topic to be discussed

Thesis statement: the principal aspect of the topic you are discussing and your opinion

Give a general overview and define your terms.

Objective outline of what the topic involves: who, what, where, when, why ...

Example 1 – advantages

Example 2 – disadvantages

Transition

A different aspect of the subject: looking at same topic from another perspective

Example 1 – positive outcome

Example 2 – negative outcome

Transition

Other thoughts on the topic and/or people involved (individuals and/or community)

Example 1 – evidence with example(s)

Example 2 – opposing evidence with example(s)

Conclusion – brief summary of points made and your views based on the evidence above

Saving Richard Parker

The narrator's family run a zoo. In this scene they are transporting some of their animals in a ship when there is a terrible storm.

Read the extract and make notes on how and why the narrator tries to save a tiger called Richard Parker. Ravi is the narrator's brother.

The ship sank. It made a sound like a monstrous metallic burp. Things bubbled at the surface and then vanished. Everything was screaming: the sea, the wind, my heart. From the lifeboat I saw something in the water. 5

I cried, "Richard Parker, is that you? It is so hard to see. Oh, that this rain would stop! Richard Parker? Richard Parker? Yes, it is you!"

I could see his head. He was struggling to stay at the surface of the water. 10

"[...] Don't give up, please. Come to the lifeboat. Do you hear this whistle? *TREEEEEE! TREEEEEE! TREEEEEE!* You heard right. Swim, swim! You're a strong swimmer. It's not a hundred feet."

He had seen me. He looked panic-stricken. He 15 started swimming my way. The water about him was shifting wildly. He looked small and helpless.

"Richard Parker, can you believe what has happened to us? Tell me it's a bad dream. Tell me it's not real. Tell me I'm still in my bunk on the *Tsimtsum* 20 and I'm tossing and turning and soon I'll wake up from this nightmare. Tell me I'm still happy. Mother, my tender guardian angel of wisdom, where are you? And you, Father, my loving worrywart? And you, Ravi, dazzling hero of my childhood? [...] *TREEEEEE!* 25 *TREEEEEE! TREEEEEE!*

I was not wounded in any part of my body, but I had never experienced such intense pain, such a ripping of the nerves, such an ache of the heart.

He would not make it. He would drown. He was 30 hardly moving forward and his movements were weak. His nose and mouth kept dipping underwater. Only his eyes were steadily on me.

"What are you doing, Richard Parker? Don't you love life? Keep swimming then! *TREEEEEE!* 35 *TREEEEEE! TREEEEEE!* Kick with your legs. Kick! Kick! Kick!"

He stirred in the water and made to swim.

"And what of my extended family – birds, beasts and reptiles? They too have drowned. Every single thing I 40 value in life has been destroyed.

[...] His head was barely above water. He was looking up, taking in the sky one last time. There was a lifebuoy in the boat with a rope tied to it. I took hold of it and waved it in the air. 45

"Do you see this lifebuoy, Richard Parker? Do you see it? Catch hold of it. *HUMPF!* I'll try again. *HUMPF!*

He was too far. But the sight of the lifebuoy flying his way gave him hope. He revived and started beating the water with vigorous, desperate strokes. 50

"That's right! One, two. One, two. One, two. Breathe when you can. Watch for the waves.

[...] Look how close you are! *TREEEEEE! TREEEEEE! TREEEEEE!* Hurrah, hurrah! You've made it, Richard Parker, you've made it. Catch! *HUMPF!*" 55

I threw the lifebuoy mightily. It fell in the water right in front of him. With his last energies he stretched forward and took hold of it.

"Hold on tight, I'll pull you in. Don't let go. Pull with your eyes while I pull with my hands. In a few seconds 60 you'll be aboard and we'll be together. Wait a second. Together? We'll be *together*? Have I gone mad?"

I woke up to what I was doing. I yanked on the rope.

"Let go of that lifebuoy, Richard Parker! Let go, I 65 said. I don't want you here, do you understand? Go somewhere else. Leave me alone. Get lost. Drown! Drown!"

He was kicking vigorously with his legs. I grabbed an oar. I thrust it at him, meaning to push him away. 70 I missed and lost hold of the oar.

I grabbed another oar. I dropped it in an oarlock and pulled as hard as I could, meaning to move the lifeboat away. All I accomplished was to turn the lifeboat a little. Bringing one end closer to Richard 75 Parker.

I would hit him on the head! I lifted the oar in the air.

He was too fast. He reached up and pulled himself aboard. 80

[...] I had a wet, trembling, half-drowned, heaving and coughing three-year-old adult Bengal tiger in my lifeboat. Richard Parker rose unsteadily to his feet on the tarpaulin, eyes blazing as they met mine, ears laid tight to his head, all weapons drawn. His head was the 85 size and the colour of the lifebuoy, with teeth.

From *Life of Pi*, by Yann Martel

Reading – comprehension

Write two or three paragraphs about how and why the boy in this extract from *Life of Pi* tried to save Richard Parker. Explain your reasons fully and quote from the passage to support your ideas where necessary.

Unit 5: Self-assessment

In this unit we have read newspaper reports, online magazine articles, scenes from plays and poems from different times.

Three key skills we have looked at are: writing to inform, analyse and discuss, and writing to entertain.

1. Explain in your own words what we mean by:

    a. style

    b. tone

    c. register.

2. Explain in your own words how writers use the past tenses and present tenses in news reports and articles to make information interesting and easy to understand.

Make notes about Unit 5

Consider the work you have done in this unit. Then copy and complete the chart.

Two texts I remember in Unit 5 are:
Two new skills I learned are:
Two things I'm not sure about are:
I enjoyed doing:
Something I would like to do again is:
I would like to do this again because:

Unit 5: Literature extension

Read this story by the Indian writer Anita Desai and do the activity that follows.

Circus Cat, Alley Cat

I first saw Anna, the new "nanny" of the English children who lived next door, in a pink stucco house, late one evening when she came to hound us out of the shrubbery where we were playing hide-and-seek, a game which, as anyone knows, grows exciting only at dinnertime. I crept behind a screen of bamboos and peered out at her through the polished bars of the bamboo stalks. She was large and heavily built, with very black bright eyes and a lot of wiry black hair. She bent down to pick up a neam switch and slapped it against her thigh as she called to us in a loud, sharp voice. And through the cage of bamboos, in that blue twilight, I saw the lawn turn to a sawdust covered stage floor and Nanny's white uniform into spangled pink tights and the switch in her hand to a long, whistling whip that cracked in the air which was filled no longer with the talking of mynah birds and the barks of pet dogs, but with the roars of tigers and the gibbering of apes. Sick with terror, I found I could scarcely breathe and preferred to creep over the manure pit to my own home than on to the lawn and face to face with Nanny.

My imagination was fired, no doubt, as much by the fact that I had only that morning heard that Nanny came from a circus where she had worked as cat-trainer, as by the cracking of the switch in her hand and her hefty shoulders and authoritative voice. How the staid, plain, and entirely unimaginative family of Bates could choose a circus performer to be a Nanny for their children is an eternal mystery, though they endeavoured to explain it to us as an act of charity. Anna, they told us (her real name, or stage name, was Shakti – Strength! Power! – but the Bateses preferred to call her by the more tame and domestic name of Anna) was a Malabar girl who had been born into the circus, and had trained the big cats since she was thirteen. Her special "breath-taking, death-defying, terror-striking" act was to drape a tiger over her shoulders and stand on the backs of two lions whom she would then order to emit great, rumbling roars that made her large frame tremble all over and the tiger snarl. Dressed in parrot-green tights and a lilac shirt with silver spangles, her free mane of hair standing on end, she must have looked a sight. Then she married the boy who fed the cats. The boy was ambitious. In no time, he had taught her that a woman's place is her home and was straddling the lions himself and wrapping the tiger round his

5

10

15

20

25

30

35

own neck. Anna, in a spurt of cat-like temper, left. By that time she
had a baby, and when Mrs Bates found her, she and the child were
near starvation, begging on a Daryaganj Street. Mrs Bates gave her   40
a white uniform and put bath-salts in her tub in order to wash off
that special circus odour of elephant manure and cat sweat; she was
installed as the children's Nanny, and her baby put in a cradle on the
back verandah and fed on milk and oranges.

All this played real havoc on our imagination, as nothing had   45
ever done before. She had only to rattle the knobs of the windows
and doors as she banged them shut against the summer heat, to make us
feel we were being shut into our cages. We would no longer walk, or run,

but prowl. We would not hop or skip, but spring and leap. Even our voices changed. Anna had only to come into the room with a tricycle or our skipping-ropes, and we would feel the trainer had arrived, wooden chair in hand, to practise the act and in this spirit we would play the games she ordered us to play. Anna had only to sit down at the breakfast table and cut the bread into slices for us, to make us think of it as a great hunk of fresh meat, dripping with scarlet blood, and we would shudder as we gnawed at it. A cooking-spoon in Anna's hand would become a biting, snapping, snaky whip. A plain brooch pinned in her lapel would change the plain white uniform to a gaudy, satin stage costume. When the lights were switched on at night, the brightness of Anna's eyes was the brightness of a stage-performer's eyes in the glare of white-hot arc lamps. No matter how hard Mrs Bates tried to domesticate her and turn her into a tame alleycat, a nice, motherly pussy cat, Anna remained to us the "breath-taking, death-defying, terror-striking" Anna of the circus. Poor Anna herself played no part in this. No matter how hard we tried, and how cleverly, she never spoke of the circus once. Yet the very house, with its Rangoon creeper, its worn rugs and nursery pictures, became the Big Top for us, the dinner-bell, the big drums, the lights, the spotlights of the stage. We lived in a constant quiver of thrill upon thrill. I dreamt of cats all the night, long-striped cats leaping in the air, great cats shaking their manes as they roared, their muscles rippling under the smooth skin, the shining hair. They sprang soundlessly from dream to dream, landing softly on my eyelids, and from strangers of the jungle they became companions of the long nights of excitement.

And then Anna's baby vanished. I came across Anna in the garden one day, her hair more disordered than ever, her eyes red from weeping. "My baby's gone!" she cried theatrically, "My baby's been taken away. Oh God, oh God, give my baby back to me – but I'll never see her again – she's been taken away from me." And I joined whole-heartedly in the weeping to think that God had taken the child at such a tender age and left poor Anna all alone. As I ran back to the house to tell my mother, I wondered if the baby had suddenly been taken ill, because she had seemed very healthy and well only the previous day. My mother was, for this reason, equally shocked and immediately went to see Anna.

Anna wept on her shoulders, looking quite thin and pathetic in her sorrow. My mother pressed her hand and soothed her, "What God decrees we must accept Anna. It is sad but it must be, Anna." On her way out, she looked in on Mrs Bates, and asked, "When is the funeral to be?"

"The funeral?" Mrs Bates jumped. "What funeral?"

"Why, of poor Anna's baby!"

"Anna's baby? Why, is it dead?"

We were nonplussed that the mistress of the house should not   95
have heard of the tragedy yet. My mother and I interrupted each
other in trying to tell her what had happened and were horrified
when the kind old missionary's wife chortled and clapped her hand
over her mouth to stop her laughter.

"The baby dead!" she cried. "Whatever gave you the idea? It's only   100
that Anna's husband and his family came and took it away. We're
trying to get it back, only the circus has moved to Bombay now so it
will be a bit difficult. We're sending Anna off to try though."

That was the last we saw of Anna for a long time. The next time
was several years later when we went to see a circus and found   105
Shakti's name on the handbill, and a picture of Anna with a snarling
tiger on her shoulders. She was smiling hugely.

We could scarcely wait till she appeared and then were so
excited we could not even applaud. We watched out for her
baby and wondered if it had grown into the little girl who was   110
somersaulting in the sawdust and tumbling around with a deeply
preoccupied expression on her thin face. But throughout the
performance, the thought uppermost in my mind was: where
is Anna's husband? And I had a vivid picture of Anna in a great
cage, gnawing, gnawing upon a great, bleeding hunk of flesh,   115
Anna snarling at the people who carne to snatch it from her, Anna
throwing back her mane and giving a great roar of triumph, Anna
the queen of the circus cats, Anna the circus cat ...

By Anita Desai (1980)

Exploring the passage

1. Write a paragraph or draw a diagram to explain the relationships between the people in this story. For example:

   The narrator is friends with the children next door.

   The children's nanny is ...

2. Do you think the author wants the reader to see the Bates as typical "colonials"? Give your reasons.

3. What is your personal opinion of Mrs Bates? Give your reasons.

4. Discuss the different ways the narrator sees Anna/Shakti.

6 "Living in a material world"

In this unit you will:

→ **Visit** Ancient Turkey, Australia, Britain, China, France, Peru, South America, Sweden and the USA

→ **Read** a fable, a feature article, press releases, passages from a novel and a play, and poems

→ **Write** to persuade, inform and complain.

A mark, a yen, a buck, or a pound
A buck or a pound
A buck or a pound
Is all that makes the world go around,
That clinking clanking sound
Can make the world go round.

"The Money Song" in *Cabaret*

Lyrics by Fred Ebb; music by John Kander

Material (adj.): 1. of matter; consisting of matter; of the physical (as opposed to spiritual) world. From Latin *material* = matter.

(*Oxford Study Dictionary*)

Talking points

- Is it possible to live without money in the modern world?

- There is an expression that says "football moves a lot of money". Do you think football is now more of a financial business than a recreational sport?

Hard cash and flexible finance

Categorising information

Working with a partner, read through the following information. There are 20 points: 10 points on the history of money and 10 on the history of credit (flexible finance). Separate the information into these two categories.

a. *Wampum* is an Algonquian word for cylindrical beads threaded together to form short strings, necklaces or belts.

b. Notes for less than £50 were not available in 1696. Since the average income in Britain during the 17th century was well under £20 a year, very few people needed banknotes.

c. Paper money evolved into "representative money". This meant the money itself was not made of anything that was actually of any value; it only *represented* value.

d. *Wampum* was firmly established as a currency of exchange when Europeans established colonial settlements in North America.

e. In the 16th century goldsmith-bankers accepted deposits, made loans and transferred funds. They also gave receipts for cash known as "running cash notes".

f. The Banque Générale in Paris issued bank notes from January 1719, but a government decree in May 1720 halved the value of this paper currency so people lost faith in the system.

g. *Wampum* was so well respected that a *wampum* belt formed sealed agreements and solemnised formal speeches and meetings.

h. In 118 BC leather money was being used in China. It was made from deerskin and had colourful borders. It could be considered as the first form of banknote.

i. Indians and old-established colonisers tried to pass off inferior shells as fraudulent *wampum* to new arrivals. Legislation was introduced to prevent this.

j. Representative money was backed by a government's or bank's promise to exchange it for a certain quantity of silver or gold. The British pound, known as the "pound sterling", was the equivalent of a pound of sterling silver.

k. Barter is the exchange of goods or services: a sack of rice for a sack of salt; a day working in a field for a day building an irrigation canal.

l. Paper money was first printed in the USA on 10 March 1862.

m. Sometimes people could not agree on the equal value of goods or services. Commodity money was used to solve this problem. Commodity money is a basic item used or of value to everyone.

n. Metal objects were used as money around 5000 BC. Metal is used because it is easy to work, durable and can be recycled.

o. The first recorded use of paper money was in 7th-century China.

p. Different coins were given different values so people could know or negotiate the price of what they wanted to buy.

q. In 1656 John Palmstruch established a private bank in Stockholm. In 1661 he issued credit notes that could be exchanged in his bank for a stated number of silver coins. Palmstruch issued more notes than his bank could afford to redeem with silver. In 1667 he was imprisoned for fraud.

r. As far back as 1200 BC cowrie shells from the Pacific and Indian Oceans were being used by many societies as currency. The cowrie shell is the most widely used and longstanding form of currency in the world.

s. The feature that made Bank of England notes a means of exchange was the "promise to pay the bearer on demand" the sum indicated on the note. This meant that whoever presented the note at the Bank could redeem it for gold or coins.

t. *Wampum* was the standard legal tender of Indians and New England colonists until the end of the 17th century.

Speaking and listening

Giving a talk on money

1. In pairs, each choose one list and organise it into chronological order as far as possible.

2. Prepare your information for a talk on the history of money and credit.

3. Take turns giving your talk. Listen to your partner and suggest ways he/she can make the talk more interesting.

Wampum (n.): small cylindrical beads made by North American Indians from shells strung together and worn as decoration or used as money strings. (From Algonquian *wampumpeag*; from *wap* = white + *umpe* = string + the plural suffix *ag*.)

(*Oxford Dictionaries Online*)

Wealth

The following passage is about a wealthy man in New York. Read it carefully and do the questions that follow.

In the extract below, from a novel called *The Great Gatsby*, the narrator describes Gatsby's lavish parties. The story takes place in the 1920s.

The Great Gatsby

At high tide in the afternoon I watched his guests diving from the tower of his raft, or taking the sun on the hot sand of his beach while his two motor-boats slit the waters of the Sound, drawing aquaplanes over cataracts of foam. On week-ends his Rolls-Royce became an omnibus, bearing parties to and from the city between nine in the morning and long past midnight, while his station wagon scampered like a brisk yellow bug to meet all trains. And on Mondays eight servants, including an extra gardener, toiled all day with mops and scrubbing-brushes and hammers and garden-shears, repairing the ravages of the night before. 5 10

Every Friday five crates of oranges and lemons arrived from a fruiterer in New York – every Monday these same oranges and lemons left his back door in a pyramid of pulpless halves. There was a machine in the kitchen which could extract the juice of two hundred oranges in half an hour if a little button was pressed two hundred times by a butler's thumb. 15 20

At least once a fortnight a corps of caterers came down with several hundred feet of canvas and enough colored lights to make a Christmas tree of Gatsby's enormous garden. [...] 25

By seven o'clock the orchestra has arrived, no thin five-piece affair, but a whole pitful of oboes and trombones and saxophones and viols and cornets and piccolos, and low and high drums. The last swimmers have come in from the beach now and are dressing up-stairs; the cars from New York are parked five deep in the drive, and already the halls and salons and verandas are gaudy with primary colors, and hair shorn in strange new ways, and shawls beyond the dreams of Castile. The [...] air is alive with chatter and laughter, and casual innuendo and introductions forgotten on the spot, and enthusiastic meetings between women who never knew each other's names. 30 35 40

The lights grow brighter as the earth lurches away from the sun, and now the orchestra is playing yellow cocktail music, and the opera of 45

voices pitches a key higher. Laughter is easier
minute by minute, spilled with prodigality, tipped
out at a cheerful word. The groups change more
swiftly, swell with new arrivals, dissolve and form
in the same breath; already there are wanderers,   50
confident girls who weave here and there among
the stouter and more stable, become for a sharp,
joyous moment the centre of a group, and then,
excited with triumph, glide on through the sea-
change of faces and voices and color under the   55
constantly changing light.

Suddenly one of the gypsies [...] dances out
alone on the canvas platform. A momentary hush;
the orchestra leader varies his rhythm obligingly
for her, and there is a burst of chatter as the   60
erroneous news goes around that she is Gilda
Gray's understudy from the Follies. The party
has begun.

By F. Scott Fitzgerald (1925)

Reading – Core

1. Answer the following questions in full
   sentences.

   a. Describe two ways people arrive at Jay
   Gatsby's parties.

   b. What do his guests do in the afternoon?

   c. Explain in your own words who and
   what is involved in "repairing the
   ravages of the night before" (line 13).

   d. What is the narrator referring to when
   he says Jay Gatsby's garden is like a
   Christmas tree in lines 24–27?

2. You are one of Jay Gatsby's eight servants
   mentioned in line 10. Write a letter to your
   friend describing one of his parties. Give
   your opinion of:

   • the food

   • the music

   • what you are expected to do.

   Write between 200 and 300 words.

Reading – Extended

1. Imagine that you live near to Gatsby's
   house where the parties take place. You
   object to the parties for several reasons,
   including the lavish display of wealth.

   Write a letter to Mr Gatsby setting out your
   various objections and justifying each one by
   developing ideas and details from the passage.

   Use the information on how to write a
   letter of complaint on page 141 to help you.

   Write between 250 and 350 words.

2. Re-read paragraphs 3–5, which describe the
   lights, colours and sounds of the party.

   By referring closely to the language used
   by the writer, explain how Scott Fitzgerald
   makes these descriptions effective.

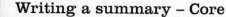

REMINDER – using complex sentences in summaries

A complex sentence has a main clause and one or more subordinate clauses.

Using complex sentences is a good way to combine information concisely in a summary.

The main clause is the most important aspect of the sentence.

Summary

Writing a summary – Core

1. Make notes on the different ways Gatsby spends his money.

2. Using your notes to help you, summarise how Gatsby spends his money. Write no more than 150 words.

Summary

Writing a summary – Extended

1. Make notes on the different ways Gatsby spends his time and how he uses his money.

2. Using your notes to help you, summarise the main features of Gatsby's lifestyle. Write about 250 words.

Letter of complaint

Below is a student's response to the Extended Reading question on page 139, which asks for a letter to Mr Gatsby.

1. Read the student's letter carefully. There are a number of mistakes. Identify as many as you can.

2. What advice would you give this student to help him improve?

Dear Mr Gatsby,

I am one of your neighbours. I live opposite your house. We have two children aged seven and four. I'm writing to you on behalf of the residents in this area to complain about the noise you make every weekend. My wife and I, in particular, find your parties very disturbing. The behaviour of your guests is very anti-social and often offensive. We are very worried about the image you are giving to our peaceful community. You are a very bad example for our children.

The large amount of food consumed at your parties is a matter of concern because it is enough to feed everyone in this street. Outside your gates people make too much noise and someone has even been sick in our garden. We worry about the way people drive: it's dangerous. Last weekend there was a fight. We could hear everything that was happening. This is not the sort of behaviour we like in this area. My wife has to keep our children indoors every weekend so they cannot witness what is happening.

This brings me to the matter of cars, parking and dangerous driving. If you must have parties, can't you organise transport for your guests? Next time

someone backs into my gates or blocks our drive I am going to call the police.

Last but not least, I want to complain about all the noise. You have whole orchestras in your garden! It's too much and not fair on those of us who like a quiet life. Also all the lights keep us awake at night. This weekend the music went on all day and night. We're exhausted, we can't sleep. Please have some consideration for families with young children. Sometimes your guests come to our door and ring the bell because they can't move their cars and they need to get a taxi. This must stop.

I ask you, in the name of all the residents of this tranquil and small community, to please show some consideration. We are not all as young and rich as you. We don't all want to have a party every weekend. If you do not stop causing so much disturbance, we shall go to a lawyer because it seems to me you are bribing the police to stay away!

Yours sincerely,

Lipton Masterson

(380 words)

Writing skills
Writing a letter of complaint

Most people have to complain about unsatisfactory goods, poor service, bad conditions or other types of problem at some point in their lives.

A letter of complaint should be written using a formal to neutral register; it should be set out clearly and concisely, should explain the nature of the problem(s) and should request an answer and/or solution to the problem(s).

Here are a few "dos" and "don'ts" to help you write a letter of complaint.

Do:

- collect all the relevant details together before you start writing the letter
- say where and when the goods were purchased: provide the invoice number, the date of purchase, the time of purchase, the price and the form of payment (recorded on the receipt)
- mention any previous communication with the company concerned, giving dates
- get straight to the point and explain the nature of your complaint concisely
- give all the relevant information in a clear and logical sequence
- state what action you want the recipient of the letter to take and by when
- enclose copies of relevant documents and receipts to support your case.

Don't:

- be rude or use abusive language in any way
- allow yourself to get sidetracked
- criticise the company as a whole or be negative about all of its products and/or services
- send your letter without checking it carefully for grammar or spelling mistakes.

Salutation

Start your letter with *Dear Mr/Mrs/Ms/Miss*…

If you don't know the name of the person to whom you are writing, begin *Dear Sir/Madam.*

Content

Open with a heading alerting the reader to the subject of the letter.

The first sentence should state clearly the matter you wish to discuss. For example:

I wish to express my dissatisfaction with …
I wish to draw your attention to …

I have purchased a bicycle from your company that is faulty …

Introduce your main point immediately and state your reason for writing.

Provide relevant details to justify your complaint.

Provide relevant background information as necessary, but stick to the point.

Conclude by saying how you want the matter rectified. If relevant, set a deadline.

Finish by saying:

Please inform me as soon as possible what action you propose to take …

I look forward to hearing from you (within the next … *days).*

Closing a letter

The wording at the end of a formal letter follows a standard format.

- If you are writing to someone you know, end with *Yours sincerely* + your signature.
- If your letter begins with *Dear Sir/Madam* end with *Yours faithfully* + your signature.

Type your full name under your signature.

Gold and the Midas touch

Read this feature article about gold miners in Peru and do the questions that follow.

The Devastating Costs of the Amazon Gold Rush

Spurred by rising global demand for the metal, miners are destroying invaluable rainforest in Peru's Amazon basin.

It's a few hours before dawn in the Peruvian rainforest, and five bare light bulbs hang from a wire 5 above a 40-foot-deep pit. Gold miners, operating illegally, have worked in this chasm since 11 a.m. yesterday. Standing waist-deep in muddy water, they chew coca leaves to stave off exhaustion and hunger.

In the pit a minivan-size gasoline engine, set on a 10 wooden cargo pallet, powers a pump, which siphons water from a nearby river. A man holding a flexible ribbed-plastic hose aims the water jet at the walls, tearing away chunks of earth and enlarging the pit every minute until it's now about the size of six football 15 fields laid side by side. The engine also drives an industrial vacuum pump. Another hose suctions the gold-fleck-laced soil torn loose by the water cannon.

At first light, workers hefting huge Stihl chain saws roar into action, cutting down trees that may 20 be 1,200 years old. Red macaws and brilliant-feathered toucans take off, heading deeper into the rainforest. The chain saw crews also set fires, making way for more pits.

This gaping cavity is one of thousands being 25 gouged today in the state of Madre de Dios at the base of the Andes – a region that is among the most biodiverse and, until recently, pristine environments in the world. All told, the Amazon River basin holds perhaps a quarter of the world's 30 terrestrial species; its trees are the engine of perhaps 15 percent of photosynthesis occurring on landmasses; and countless species, including plants and insects, have yet to be identified.

In Peru alone, while no one knows for certain 35 the total acreage that has been ravaged at least 64,000 acres – possibly much more – have been razed. The destruction is more absolute than that caused by ranching or logging, which accounts, at least for now, for vastly more rainforest loss. Not only 40 are gold miners burning the forest, they are stripping away the surface of the earth, perhaps 50 feet down. At the same time, miners are contaminating rivers and streams, as mercury, used in separating gold, leaches into the watershed. Ultimately, the potent 45 toxin, taken up by fish, enters the food chain.

Gold today commands a staggering $1,700 an ounce, more than six times the price of a decade ago. The surge is attributable to demand by individual and institutional investors seeking a hedge against losses 50 and also the insatiable appetite for luxury goods made from the precious metal. "Who is going to stop a poor man from Cuzco or Juliaca or Puno who earns $30 a month from going to Madre de Dios and starting to dig?" asks Antonio Brack Egg, formerly 55 Peru's minister of the environment. "Because if he gets two grams a day" – Brack Egg pauses and shrugs. "That's the theme here."

Engineering specs (n.): specifications for engineering works.

The new Peruvian gold-mining operations are expanding. The most recent data show that the rate of deforestation has increased sixfold from 2003 to 2009. "It's relatively easy to get a permit to explore for gold," says the Peruvian biologist Enrique Ortiz, an authority on rainforest management. "But once you find a suitable site for mining gold, then you have to get the actual permits. These require engineering specs, statements of environmental protection programs, plans for protection of indigenous people and for environmental remediation." "Miners circumvent this," he adds, "by claiming they're in the permitting process." Because of this evasion, Ortiz says, "They have a claim to the land but not much responsibility to it. Most of the mines here – estimates are between 90 or 98 percent of them in Madre de Dios state – are illegal."

The Peruvian government has taken initial steps to shut down mining, targeting more than 100 relatively accessible operations along the region's riverbanks. "There are strong signals from the government that they are serious about this," says Ortiz. But the task is enormous: There may be as many as 30,000 illegal gold miners in Madre de Dios.

The pit that we visited that day is not far from Puerto Maldonado (pop. 25,000), capital of Madre de Dios, a center of Peru's gold mining because of its proximity to the rainforest. In a supreme irony, the city has also become a locus of Peru's thriving ecotourism industry, with inviting hotels, restaurants and guesthouses in the forest, at the threshold of a paradise where howler monkeys leap in tall hardwood trees and clouds of metallic blue morpho butterflies float in the breeze.

On our first morning in Puerto Maldonado, photographer Ron Haviv, Ortiz and I board a small wooden boat, or barca, and head up the nearby Madre de Dios River. For a few miles upstream, wood-frame houses can be glimpsed along heavily forested bluffs. Birds dart through the trees. Mist burns away on the tranquil, muddy-brown river.

Suddenly, as we round a bend, the trees are gone.

Barren stretches of rock and cobblestone line the shore. Jungle is visible only in the distance.

"We are coming to the mining," says Ortiz.

Ahead of us, nosed against the stony banks, countless dredge barges are anchored. Each is fitted with a roof for shade, a large motor on deck and a huge suction pipe running from the stern into the water. Silt and stones extracted from the river bottom are sprayed into a sluice positioned on the bow and angled onto shore. The sluice is lined with heavy synthetic matting, similar to indoor-outdoor carpet. As silt (the source of gold) is trapped in the matting, stones hurtle down the incline, crashing in great mounds on the banks. Thousands of rocky hillocks litter the shoreline.

As we pass one barge, its blue-painted steel hull faded by the intense sun, the crew members wave. We beach our *barca* and clamber over the stone-strewn shore toward the barge, moored along the bank. A man who appears to be in his 30s tells us that he has mined along the river for several years. He and his family own the barge. The entire clan, originally from Puerto Maldonado, lives aboard much of the time, bunking in handmade beds on deck beneath mosquito nets and eating from a galley kitchen run by his mother. The din from the dredging engine is deafening, as is the thunder of rocks tumbling into the sluice.

"Do you get a lot of gold?" I ask.

From *Smithsonian* magazine,
by Donovan Webter (February 2012)

Reading

1. Answer the following questions in full sentences. Give line references where relevant.

    a. Explain in your own words the meaning of "gold rush".

    b. Where is this gold rush taking place?

    c. In paragraph 5 the writer tells us that thousands of gold-mining cavities are being dug in the state of Madre de Dios. Why is this area ecologically important? Give three reasons.

    d. In paragraph 6 the writer says, "The destruction is more absolute than that caused by ranching or logging". Explain in your own words what the writer means by "more absolute" in this context.

    e. Explain three ways the mining described in this article damages the environment and say how this may have long-term effects.

    f. Explain the following in your own words:
    - surge (line 49) (in this context)
    - a hedge against losses (line 50) (in the context of gold)
    - the insatiable appetite for luxury goods made from the precious metal.

    g. Why is obtaining a licence to mine legally difficult?

    h. Give two reasons why tourists might want to visit this area of Peru.

2. You are an illegal miner working in the Madre de Dios area. Writing in the first person, give an account of a typical day. Include:

    a. where you are working and why

    b. what you like and/or dislike about this work.

    Write no more than 200 words.

Speeches

You are now going to write a persuasive speech about gold mining in Peru. Read the guidelines for speech writing in the Writing skills box opposite before you start.

Coursework idea

You could write a persuasive speech on something you feel strongly about for your Coursework Portfolio.

Writing a speech

Write a persuasive speech on one of the following topics.

- You believe that gold mining in Peru is damaging the environment. Write a speech to persuade your audience that gold mining in the state of Madre de Dios should be halted.

- You believe that gold mining in Peru will benefit the country's economy and help improve conditions for the poor. Write a speech to persuade your audience that gold mining in the state of Madre de Dios should be encouraged.

Write between 500 and 800 words.

Writing skills
Writing a persuasive speech

Use the following points to help you write an effective persuasive speech.

1. **Artistotle's strands of persuasion**

   When you are persuading someone to change their behaviour, think about Aristotle's three strands of persuasion.

   - The logical strand explains the situation now and shows how the recommended course of action will bring about a positive outcome in the future. Listeners should start to think about what they can do to help.

   - The personal or emotional strand affects listeners' emotions to help them feel that they ought to help – because if they don't, the future will be worse not better.

   - The social strand makes it clear that society will benefit from what each member of the audience can do. Listeners should start asking themselves: "What could happen if everyone does this?" or "What will happen if we stop this?"

2. **Ideas**

   Look at your topic from different angles.

   - To show your audience that what you are saying is right or justifiable, you need to destroy opposing arguments.

   - Ask someone to play "the devil's advocate" so you can find good answers to difficult questions.

3. **Data and quotations** (ammunition)

   - List the points as you will make them.

   - Provide data where possible.

   - Choose a few powerful, relevant quotations from people your audience will know.

4. **Style and technique**

   Read and/or listen to speeches made by good orators.

   - Write the speech as if you are speaking it.

   - Open with a memorable image that will stick in the audience's mind.

   - Use short paragraphs and make sure that each one addresses a specific point.

   - Each paragraph should lead to a logical outcome – your desired outcome.

   - Use linking phrases that show how you are building your argument.

   - Use tripling to reinforce your message – say the same thing in three different ways.

   - Use figurative language but keep your vocabulary appropriate to your audience.

   - Use emotive language and imagery that will affect the audience's emotions.

   - Use rhetorical questions and the pronoun *you* to address the audience directly.

   - Do not use fancy rhetorical devices or meaningless flowery expressions.

   - Never use words like *wanna, gotcha*; they spoil the power of your argument.

   - Use dynamic verbs; avoid passive sentences.

   - Keep sentences short; this makes the speech easier for the audience to remember.

   - Bring your audience into the speech – use *we* not *they*, *us* not *them* – uniting you as the speaker with your audience.

   - Add humour or dramatic points to prevent listeners getting bored.

   - Do not finish with a question that could prompt a negative response.

5. **Desired response or effect**

   This speech is to persuade your audience to either do something or to stop doing something.

   - If you want to persuade someone to do something, end with a pleasant image to show what you are striving for or aspiring to.

   - If you want to persuade someone to stop doing something, end with a terrible "worst case scenario" image to show what will happen if we don't stop.

Midas and the River Pactolus

The myth of King Midas and his golden touch has been told and retold as a fairy tale for centuries on end. However, it is not commonly known that this tale is really an etiological myth, i.e. a myth that explains a real-world phenomenon. In this case, they say the actions of King Midas account for the rich alluvial deposits of the Pactolus river. [5]

According to the myth, King Midas earned the gratitude of the Greek god Dionysus for hosting the god's mentor. As thanks, Dionysus agreed to grant Midas any wish he desired. Midas wished that whatever he touched would turn to gold. However, he soon realized his blessing was a curse when the food he tried to eat turned to gold and hugging his daughter resulted in the same. [10] [15]

Saddened and starving, Midas prayed to Dionysus to remove his golden touch. Dionysus answered and said that if Midas would wash his body in the River Pactolus, he would wash away his curse. When Midas did this his powers washed away from him into the river. [20]

The Pactolus, which flows near Sardis, the capital of ancient Lydia, was known for its rich deposits of electrum. The river was so rich in fact, that Lydia based its economy on it. In addition, the Lydians are credited with inventing the first gold coins in or around 7th century bc. All thanks (mythically) to King Midas. [25]

From www.mgsrefining.com, Precious Metals Refining Blog (5 March 2012)

> **Alluvial deposit (n.):** soil and sand deposited on land by flowing water.
>
> **Mentor (n.):** an advisor or teacher.
>
> **Electrum (n.):** a mix of gold and silver.

Metamorphoses

The story of King Midas is thought by some to be a "fairy tale". Much of what we know about the mythical King Midas, however, comes from *Metamorphoses* by the Roman poet Ovid (43 BC–17 AD).

In Ovid's version, the Roman god Bacchus rewards Midas for the kindness he showed to Silenius. The god offers to grant Midas any wish and the king requests that everything he touches turn into gold. Midas then finds that he cannot eat or drink because food becomes gold as it passes through his lips. Midas begs Bacchus to free him of this curse.

The god instructs the king to bathe in the source of the River Pactolus, which is now in modern Turkey. As Midas immerses himself in the water, his fatal gift is taken away.

The various different versions of the fable by both Greek and Roman authors demonstrate that Midas was greedier than he was wise. The legend may have started as a way to explain the real King Midas' great wealth. The gold specks people still see in the river, which have been identified as electrum, were said to be there because Midas washed himself in the water to get rid of the curse.

(*Metamorphoses*, 11.136–141)

Writing to inform

Using the article on King Midas and the information on Ovid's version of the story, write a short article for a student magazine on the possible truth behind the ancient fable of King Midas and the gold in the River Pactolus.

Write between 350 and 450 words.

Selecting a diamond

When selecting a diamond, the following 4C's criteria is used: Nature dictates the characteristics of *colour*, *clarity* and *carat* whilst *cut* is directly influenced by humans.

Carat

Carat is a standard unit of weight for diamonds. 1 carat = 0.2 grams and 100 points = 1 carat. The price of diamonds does not increase linearly with weight. There are various weights above which there is a steep increase in value. The most notable transition is at 1 carat where the highest quality diamond will cost significantly more than an equivalent diamond quality weighing 0.95 carats.

Clarity

Clarity relates to a diamond's relative freedom from inclusions and blemishes. These inclusions can comprise of cracks, carbon spots, minerals and bubbles and originate when the diamond is forming in the earth. When light enters a diamond it is reflected and refracted out. If there is anything disrupting the flow of light in the diamond, such as a crack, a proportion of the light reflected will be lost. The highest grading is FL (flawless), followed by IF (internally flawless), then VVS (very very slightly included), VS (very slightly included), SI (slightly included) and P (piqué, or included – often visible to the naked eye).

Colour

This refers to the intensity of colour or lack of colour in a diamond. Colourless diamonds are graded alphabetically from D while descending alphabetical letters to Z are assigned to increasing amounts of grey or brown colouration. D colour diamonds are the most valuable in the white range. Colours that fall beyond Z enter into the category of fancy colours. They are assigned descriptive names, such as "fancy intense yellow" or "fancy vivid purplish pink". With fancy coloured diamonds, the more intense the colour, the greater the value. An intense coloured stone is of much greater value than a D colourless diamond because of its relative scarcity.

Cut

The cut refers to the overall proportions and symmetry in transforming a rough diamond to a polished diamond. These factors affect the brilliance and scintillation (fire) of a diamond. A well cut diamond will reflect light internally from one mirror-like facet to another, dispersing it through the top of the stone. Cuts that are too deep or too shallow lose or leak light through the side or bottom, affecting the diamond's brilliance. The most common cut for a diamond is round brilliant, for which specific proportions and facet arrangements have been accepted by the diamond industry.

There are various shapes of diamonds and jewellery designs, including: baguette, emerald, heart, marquise, oval, pear, princess, radiant, triangle, round single-cut and round brilliant.

Rio Tinto (2009)

In 2010 some very rare pink diamonds were discovered in Australia. The company that sold them sent press releases to the media around the world to announce the results of their auction.

First, read about press releases in the Reading skills box below. Then read the actual press releases on the pink diamonds on pages 150 and 151. (Note that they are quite a bit longer than Directed Writing passages.) Then do the related activites below and on page 152.

Reading skills
Media and press releases

A press or media release is a carefully worded statement written to announce something new or newsworthy. It is sent to all news media and may be included in a news report or used in a documentary programme or magazine article. A news release will be faxed or emailed to the appropriate editors of newspapers, magazines, journals, radio and/or television network programme-makers.

A media release is concise, just one or two pages, and is usually written in short, simple sentences.

Paragraph 1 starts with the most important detail and explains what is new.

Paragraph 2 and subsequent paragraphs provide more information about the subject.

The conclusion contains contact details, including full name, email, phone number and web address, or uniform resource locator (URL).

The finished press release is proofread and carefully edited. Then it is adapted or changed for different interest groups or the interests of the person/people to whom it is being sent.

The writer's craft

1. In pairs and using a dictionary, find the contextual meaning for the following words from the Press release 1 on page 150.

   a. "tender" (line 7)

   b. "lot" (line 27)

   c. "investors" (line 20)

   d. "bidders" (and "bids") (line 27)

   e. "captivated" (line 27).

2. Rephrase the following phrases in your own words (in the context of Rio Tinto diamonds):

   a. "the most exclusive diamond sale in the world" (lines 6–7)

   b. "notable for its unparalleled depth of colour" (lines 11–12)

   c. "mature and emerging markets" (line 23)

   d. "from a certifiable source" (lines 16–17)

   e. "keenly sought after" (line 30)

Press release 1

Rio Tinto's rare pink diamonds set new records and enter new markets

Perth, November 4, 2010 – Rio Tinto is delighted to announce an exceptional result for its 2010 Argyle Pink Diamonds Tender. 5

Known as the most exclusive diamond sale in the world, this year's Tender collection comprised 55 of the rarest and the best pink diamonds from Rio Tinto's Argyle Diamond Mine in the remote east Kimberley region of Western Australia. The 10 collection, titled Earth Magic, was notable for its unparalleled depth of colour across all lots and was showcased around the world, including for the first time ever, mainland China.

The Argyle Diamond Mine produces virtually the 15 entire supply of the world's pink diamonds. From a certifiable source and of a depth and range of colour never seen before, they command the attention of the world's diamond connoisseurs, collectors and investors. 20

All 55 diamonds in the 2010 Argyle Pink Diamonds Tender were sold into a broad representation of mature and emerging markets. This year's Tender confirmed the very strong interest from new markets that was observed in 2009, with India 25 and China based customers performing very well again. Bidders were particularly captivated by Lot Number 1, a magnificent 2.02 carat round brilliant fancy vivid purplish pink diamond named Argyle

Mystra TM that was keenly sought after for its 30 depth of colour and unparalleled beauty.

Josephine Archer, Business Manager for Argyle Pink Diamonds, commented on the 2010 collection, "This exquisite suite of Argyle pink diamonds has set new benchmarks that are a testament to all 35 those who were a part of their journey from the mine to the market. We are delighted with the result and look forward to hearing of the next stage in their journey – of the heirloom pieces and the beautiful jewellery that will be created with these 40 truly limited edition gems."

ENDS

For further information please contact:
Robyn.Ellison@riotinto.com

Notes to editors

About Rio Tinto's Argyle Diamond Mine 45

Rio Tinto's Argyle Diamond mine (100% owned by Rio Tinto), in Australia, is the world's only consistent supplier of rare pink diamonds and provides a large proportion of the world's coloured diamonds. Production commenced in 1983 and at 50 its peak the mine produced more than 40 million carats per annum.

The discovery of the Argyle diamond deposit is one of innovation, patience, foresight and meticulous attention to detail in an area that is remote, even 55 for Australians. The search for diamonds in the Kimberley region began in 1972 with a number of exciting finds proving uneconomic. However, in October 1979 diamonds were found embedded in an ant hill in the East Kimberley region of 60 Western Australia.

In a classic exploration exercise these discoveries were followed up along a creek bed and led to what is known as the AK1 pipe, the remnant of an ancient volcano and the site of the vast 65 Argyle deposit. Today the Argyle Diamond mine is currently transitioning from an open pit mine to an underground mine, which on current estimates will extend its life to at least 2019.

Media release 2

Rio Tinto discovers Australia's biggest rough pink diamond at Argyle

21 February 2012

Australia's biggest pink rough diamond has been discovered at Rio Tinto's Argyle mine, the world's largest producer of rare pink diamonds.

The 12.76 carat diamond was unearthed at the Argyle open pit in the East Kimberley region of Western Australia.

The diamond will be known as The Argyle Pink Jubilee.

The Argyle Pink Jubilee is a light pink diamond, similar in colour to The Williamson Pink, which is the diamond that Her Majesty The Queen received as a wedding gift and was subsequently set into a brooch for her Coronation.

Expert diamond polisher Richard How Kim Kam, who has worked for Argyle for 25 years, started work on polishing the amazing pink diamond in Perth today.

After two months of careful assessment and planning, it will take about 10 days to cut and polish the diamond as a single stone. Richard said "I'm going to take it very carefully. I know the world will be watching."

When the diamond has been cut and polished it will be graded by a team of international experts and showcased to the world before being sold as part of the iconic Argyle Pink Diamonds Tender later this year.

Argyle Pink Diamonds Manager Josephine Johnson said "This rare diamond is generating incredible excitement. A diamond of this calibre is unprecedented – it has taken 26 years of Argyle production to unearth this stone and we may never see one like this again. The individual who gets to wear this remarkable pink diamond will be incredibly lucky indeed."

More than 90 per cent of the world's pink diamonds come from the Argyle mine.

Large pink diamonds tend to go to museums, are gifted to royalty or end up at auction houses like Christie's auctions. Christie's has only auctioned 18 polished pink diamonds over 10 carats in its 244 year history.

Email: media.enquiries@riotinto.com
High resolution photographs and media pack available at: www.riotinto.com/media

Writing a report

You are a purchasing manager (buyer) for an important jewellery firm in your country. Write a report for your managing director advising him/her to purchase some of the Rio Tinto pink diamonds to be made into jewellery by your firm. Include the following:

- a brief description of Rio Tinto pink diamonds
- how your company will benefit from turning these rare diamonds into jewellery.

Use the information on diamonds and the two Rio Tinto press releases for information. Use the Writing skills box below to help you set out the information appropriately.

Write between 350 and 450 words.

Writing skills
Writing a report

1. Before you start, think about who will be reading the report.

   - Gather your information or data.
   - Check that the information you are going to include is relevant to the task set.
   - Create subheadings for the relevant information.

2. Plan your report carefully.

   - Number the points as they should be included.
   - Plan the report so the contents follow a logical sequence.

3. Write the report in a formal to neutral style.

   - Use plain English and passive verbs.
   - Do not use colloquial expressions, informal phrasal verbs or contractions (e.g. *can't*, *won't*).
   - Clarify points under subheadings.
   - Use bullet points as required.
   - Ensure the conclusion clearly states your findings and/or purpose.

4. Edit and proofread your report for maximum impact and clarity.

Fair Trade goods

Read about Fair Trade shops and gold on the web pages opposite. Then do the activity below.

Writing a blog article

Find out more about Fair Trade goods. Write a blog article about why young people should check labels to see whether they are purchasing Fair Trade goods before they hand over their money. Include the following:

- what Fair Trade goods are
- how Fair Trade can benefit workers, producers and the environment
- why young people should help to improve conditions for the workers and producers.

Join BAFTS | About Fair Trade | Organisations and campaigns | Find Fair Trade Shops | Resources

The British Association of Fair Trade Shops

Fair Trade in Europe started as a grassroots movement about 40 years ago. The aim was to alleviate poverty in the "Global South" – Africa, Asia, Latin America, the Caribbean – by building direct, sustainable relationships with disadvantaged producers and providing fair access to markets in the developed "North". The aims are the same now, but Fair Trade has developed into a powerful force, symbolised by a high level of European co-operation.

Fair Trade is a trading partnership, based on dialogue, transparency and respect, which seeks greater equity in international trade. It contributes to sustainable development by offering better trading conditions to, and securing the rights of, marginalised producers and workers – especially in the South.

Fair Trade organisations (backed by consumers) are engaged actively in supporting producers, raising awareness and campaigning for changes in the rules and practices of conventional international trade.

All involved in Fair Trade accept that it has to include: paying fair prices to producers which reflect the true cost of production, supporting producer organisations in their social and environmental projects, promoting gender equality in pay and working conditions, advising on product development to increase access to markets, committing to long-term relationships to provide stability and security, and campaigning to highlight the unequal system of world trade which places profit above human rights and threatens our environment.

From http://www.bafts.org.uk

Home | About | Miners | Businesses

Gold: every piece tells a story

Fairtrade gold, the world's first independent ethical certification system for gold, ensures that a product has been responsibly mined.

It's important to know how your most treasured pair of earrings or your showpiece necklace started their journey. Important because all Fairtrade gold is mined from small-scale and artisanal mines in a way that seeks to reduce dependence on harmful chemicals. Good news for mining communities in South America and good news for the people who live and mine there. Look carefully and you'll find the Fairtrade stamp on the inside of every piece.

"I think that Fairtrade is going to help us to sell our gold at the right price and we will be better paid. It will also help the environment." Gina Dávila, mineral sorter, Sotrami Mine.

From http://www.fairtrade.org.uk/gold

Money and matrimony

The following scene from Oscar Wilde's comedy *The Importance of Being Earnest* has a very serious theme. The upper-class audiences who first saw this play being performed in London in the final years of the 19th century would have understood the implications of what was going on very clearly. Do you?

GWENDOLEN:
I am engaged to Mr. Worthing, mamma. [*They (Gwendolen and Jack Worthington) rise together.*]

LADY BRACKNELL:
Pardon me, you are not engaged to any one. When you do become engaged to some one, I, or your father, should his health permit him, will inform you of the fact. An engagement should come on a young girl as a surprise, pleasant or unpleasant, as the case may be. It is hardly a matter that she could be allowed to arrange for herself … And now I have a few questions to put to you, Mr. Worthing. While I am making these inquiries, you, Gwendolen, will wait for me below in the carriage.

GWENDOLEN:
[*Reproachfully.*] Mamma!

LADY BRACKNELL:
In the carriage, Gwendolen! [*GWENDOLEN goes to the door. She and JACK blow kisses to each other behind LADY BRACKNELL'S back. LADY BRACKNELL looks vaguely about as if she could not understand what the noise was. Finally turns round.*] Gwendolen, the carriage!

GWENDOLEN:
Yes, mamma. [*Goes out, looking back at JACK.*]

LADY BRACKNELL:
[*Sitting down.*] You can take a seat, Mr. Worthing.

[*Looks in her pocket for note-book and pencil.*]

JACK:
Thank you, Lady Bracknell, I prefer standing.

LADY BRACKNELL:
[*Pencil and note-book in hand.*] I feel bound to tell you that you are not down on my list of eligible young men, although I have the same list as the dear Duchess of Bolton has. We work together, in fact. However, I am quite ready to enter your name, should your answers be what a really affectionate mother requires. Do you smoke?

JACK:
Well, yes, I must admit I smoke.

5

10

15

20

25

30

35

LADY BRACKNELL:
I am glad to hear it. A man should always have an occupation
of some kind. There are far too many idle men in London as it is.
How old are you?

JACK: 40
Twenty-nine.

LADY BRACKNELL:
A very good age to be married at. I have always been of opinion
that a man who desires to get married should know either
everything or nothing. Which do you know?   45

JACK:
[*After some hesitation*.] I know nothing, Lady Bracknell.

LADY BRACKNELL:
I am pleased to hear it. I do not approve of anything that tampers
with natural ignorance. Ignorance is like a delicate exotic fruit;   50
touch it and the bloom is gone. The whole theory of modern
education is radically unsound. Fortunately in England, at any
rate, education produces no effect whatsoever. If it did, it would
prove a serious danger to the upper classes, and probably lead to
acts of violence in Grosvenor Square. What is your income?   55

JACK:
Between seven and eight thousand a year.

LADY BRACKNELL:
[*Makes a note in her book*.] In land, or in investments?

JACK: 60
In investments, chiefly.

LADY BRACKNELL:
That is satisfactory. What between the duties expected of one
during one's lifetime, and the duties exacted from one after one's
death, land has ceased to be either a profit or a pleasure. It gives   65
one position, and prevents one from keeping it up. That's all that
can be said about land.

JACK:
I have a country house with some land, of course, attached to
it, about fifteen hundred acres, I believe; but I don't depend on   70
that for my real income. In fact, as far as I can make out, the
poachers are the only people who make anything out of it.

LADY BRACKNELL:
A country house! How many bedrooms? Well, that point can be
cleared up afterwards. You have a town house, I hope? A girl   75
with a simple, unspoiled nature, like Gwendolen, could hardly be
expected to reside in the country.

JACK:
Well, I own a house in Belgrave Square, but it is let by the year
to Lady Bloxham. Of course, I can get it back whenever I like,   80
at six months' notice.

LADY BRACKNELL:
Lady Bloxham? I don't know her.

JACK:
Oh, she goes about very little. She is a lady considerably advanced 85
in years.

LADY BRACKNELL:
Ah, nowadays that is no guarantee of respectability of character.
What number in Belgrave Square?

JACK: 90
149.

LADY BRACKNELL:
[*Shaking her head*.] The unfashionable side. I thought there was
something. However, that could easily be altered.

JACK: 95
Do you mean the fashion, or the side?

LADY BRACKNELL:
[*Sternly*.] Both, if necessary, I presume. What are your polities?

JACK:
Well, I am afraid I really have none. I am a Liberal Unionist.   100

LADY BRACKNELL:
Oh, they count as Tories. They dine with us. Or come in the
evening, at any rate. Now to minor matters. Are your parents living?

JACK:
I have lost both my parents.   105

LADY BRACKNELL:
To lose one parent, Mr. Worthing, may be regarded as a
misfortune; to lose both looks like carelessness. Who was your
father? He was evidently a man of some wealth. Was he born in
what the Radical papers call the purple of commerce, or did he   110
rise from the ranks of the aristocracy?

JACK:
I am afraid I really don't know. The fact is, Lady Bracknell, I
said I had lost my parents. It would be nearer the truth to say
that my parents seem to have lost me … I don't actually know   115
who I am by birth. I was … well, I was found.

LADY BRACKNELL:
Found!

JACK:
The late Mr Thomas Cardew, an old gentleman of a very   120
charitable and kindly disposition, found me, and gave me the
name of Worthing, because he happened to have a first-class
ticket for Worthing in his pocket at the time. Worthing is a
place in Sussex. It is a seaside resort.

LADY BRACKNELL: 125
Where did the charitable gentleman who had a first-class ticket
for this seaside resort find you?

JACK:
[Gravely.] In a hand-bag.

LADY BRACKNELL: 130
A hand-bag?

JACK:
[Very seriously.] Yes, Lady Bracknell. I was in a hand-bag – a
somewhat large, black leather hand-bag, with handles to it – an
ordinary hand-bag in fact.   135

Reading

1. Why is Lady Bracknell interviewing Jack?

2. What can Jack offer his new wife in terms of material comfort?

3. Do you think scenes such as this really happened in the past?
   Explain your reasons for why you believe they probably did or
   did not happen.

4. In your opinion, should a man demonstrate that he can afford
   to provide for his wife before he proposes matrimony? Give
   your reasons.

Writing

In this unit you have read various passages about money and luxury goods, precious metals and gems. Write an article for a student blog or magazine about one of these items. Choose one of the titles and write your article in one of the writing styles below. Write between 500 and 800 words.

Titles

- Gold!
- Diamonds are forever
- Dirt, sweat and money
- Showing off

Writing styles

- Discursive
- Persuasive
- Argumentative
- Informative

Unit 6: Self-assessment

In this unit we have read an extract from a novel, a feature article, a blog, press releases, a scene from a play and some poems.

Three key skills we have looked at are: writing a letter of complaint, writing a report; and writing a persuasive speech.

Explain in your own words what you remember about the writing styles for:

- writing to complain
- writing a press release
- writing a business report
- writing a persuasive speech.

Write down three useful things to remember about giving a speech.

Make notes about Unit 6

Consider the work you have done in this unit. Then copy and complete the chart.

Two texts I remember in Unit 6 are:
Two new skills I learned are:
Two things I'm not sure about are:
I enjoyed doing:
Something I would like to do again is:
I would like to do this again because:

Unit 6: Literature extension

When you read poetry, you often need to make inferences or read between the lines. Each of these poems refers to precious objects, but what are they actually about? Choose one poem and try to explain what the poet is saying.

An emerald is as green as grass

An emerald is as green as grass;
  A ruby red as blood;
A sapphire shines as blue as heaven;
  A flint lies in the mud.

A diamond is a brilliant stone,   5
  To catch the world's desire;
An opal holds a fiery spark;
  But a flint holds fire.

              By Christina Rossetti (1872)

Gold

Gold! Gold! Gold! Gold!
Bright and yellow, hard and cold
Molten, graven, hammered and rolled,
Heavy to get and light to hold,
Hoarded, bartered, bought and sold,   5
Stolen, borrowed, squandered, doled,
Spurned by young, but hung by old
To the verge of a church yard mold;
Price of many a crime untold.
Gold! Gold! Gold! Gold!   10
Good or bad a thousand fold!
How widely it agencies vary,
To save – to ruin – to curse – to bless –
As even its minted coins express:
Now stamped with the image of Queen Bess,   15
And now of a bloody Mary.

              By Thomas Hood (1799–1845)

7 "Believe it or not"

In this unit you will:

→ **Visit** the Congo, England, Haiti, the Himalayas, Iceland, Mexico, Scotland, unknown and fictional places

→ **Read** blogs, fantasy fiction, magazine articles, news reports and poetry

→ **Write** to describe, explore, inform and entertain.

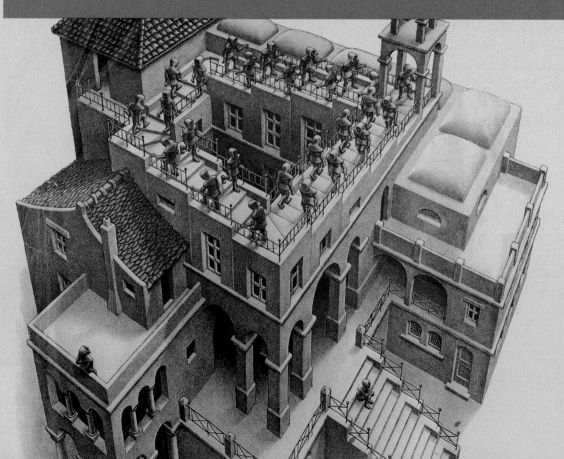

Talking point

In what ways can truth be said to be stranger than fiction?

Believe it or not.

The title of a newspaper column by Robert Leroy Ripley, American cartoonist and amateur anthropologist (1890–1949)

Truth is "stranger than fiction"

'Tis strange – but true; for truth is always strange;
Stranger than fiction; if it could be told,
How much would novels gain by the exchange!
How differently the world would men behold!
How oft would vice and virtue places change!
The new world would be nothing to the old,
If some Columbus of the moral seas
Would show mankind their souls' antipodes.

From *Don Juan*, by Lord Byron (1788–1824)

REMINDER – playing the devil's advocate

To play the devil's advocate is to oppose an argument with ideas you do not necessarily believe in to establish the validity of an argument. In a debate, it is to present a view or proposition you do not hold or believe in as a means of testing your opponent's debating skills.

It is an old maxim of mine that when you have excluded the impossible, whatever remains, however improbable, must be the truth.

Sherlock Holmes in *The Beryl Coronet*, by Sir Arthur Conan Doyle (1892)

Speaking and listening

Discussing "truth"

1. Working on your own, write down one or two things that you believe to be true, but other people doubt.

2. In pairs, take turns trying to convince your partner that what you believe is true. If necessary play the "devil's advocate" to make your partner explain his/her theories in full.

News reports and articles

Journalists, sometimes called reporters, are people who write for newspapers. Their job is to report newsworthy events. The way in which journalists write their reports or articles depends largely on the paper they write for. Some newspapers appeal more to educated professional people who want to know what is happening in the world; some papers have a more populist approach and appeal to people who just want to know what is happening in their own country or local area as a form of light entertainment.

The language used for serious national and international news is usually more academic and objective, whereas popular, tabloid newspapers use a form of journalese. Journalese is a way of condensing information using modern colloquial expressions and clichés.

Read this online news report and look at the writer's use of language.

Euronews

Mexico takes stock after major quake

Mexico is counting the cost of a major earthquake that damaged buildings and infrastructure but did not cause any fatalities. Eleven people were injured.

The 7.4 magnitude tremor rocked the capital, Mexico City, for more than one minute sending thousands panicking onto the streets.   5

The quake hit hardest in the southwestern state of Guerrero, where around 800 houses were damaged, officials said.

The tremor was one of the strongest to hit the country since the devastating 8.1-magnitude earthquake of 1985, which killed   10
thousands in Mexico City.

Mexico's interior ministry said the country would remain on high alert after 18 aftershocks to the quake were registered.

From www.euronews.com
(21 March 2012)

The writer's craft

1. Explain the headline "Mexico takes stock after major quake" in your own words. What do we mean by to "take stock" of a situation?

2. Why do you think the reporter has used such short paragraphs?

3. What does the reporter mean by saying "the country would remain on high alert"?

4. Rewrite in your own words: "Mexico is counting the cost".

5. Reduce the article to the list of details in the reporter's notebook. Include only facts and figures.

    Start like this:

    *   *Mexico earthquake - 7.4 (Richter scale).*

Human interest in news reports

Whether a journalist is writing for an informative daily newspaper or a popular tabloid, they often try to make reports more personal in order to arouse readers' anger or sympathy, or to make a dramatic event more understandable. The objective is to engage readers emotionally in what they are reading. To do this a report on a natural disaster, for instance, will include interviews with victims or rescue workers. A news article on a financial scandal might include comments made by people who have lost all their money. This is called human interest.

Some newspapers devote more columns to human interest stories about people's private lives than they do to reporting national or international news.

Here is another report on the Mexico earthquake. Note how the reporter has condensed information into one- and two-sentence paragraphs.

BANGKOK POST 21 MARCH 2012

Powerful quake shakes southern Mexico, capital

A powerful 7.4-magnitude earthquake struck southwest Mexico Tuesday, damaging hundreds of houses and sending people into the streets of the capital. But there were no immediate reports of casualties.

A powerful 7.4-magnitude earthquake struck southwest Mexico Tuesday, causing residents in the capital several hundred miles away to rush out onto the streets but no immediate reports of serious damage.   5

The quake struck south of the Pacific resort of Acapulco, between the states of Guerrero and Oaxaca, and was followed by a nearby aftershock of 5.1, the US Geological Survey said. Initially it had estimated the magnitude at 7.9.

"There are no reports of serious damage by the quake," President Felipe Calderon wrote on his Twitter account.   10

said Kristina Schake, spokeswoman for First Lady Michelle Obama. 30

The Pacific Tsunami Warning Center said a destructive, widespread tsunami had not been generated but warned of possible "local tsunami effects." 35

In Mexico City, buildings swayed, telephone and power lines were cut off and traffic lights stopped working as office workers rushed onto the streets.

"I stood up when I saw the lights moving," said Ana Fernandez, an office worker in the central 40 Roma district.

"Our boss told us to get out and we followed instructions not to shout, run or push. I was really scared but I made myself stay calm."

German tourist Gernot Nahrung said he was in the city's 45 Chapultepec park and did not feel the long swaying movement of the quake, which lasted several minutes. "My mum told me, 'It's shaking, it's shaking,'" he said.

Mexico City Mayor Marcelo Ebrand said no serious damage was visible during a helicopter survey. 50

The mayor's Twitter account said the water system and other "strategic services" were not experiencing problems.

Some windows broke at the city's international airport and the monorail between the two terminals 55 was stopped temporarily.

Local radio Formato 21 reported one person injured by the collapse of a pedestrian bridge on a bus which was not carrying passengers, in the north of the city.

It was one of the strongest quakes to shake Mexico 60 City since 1985, when an 8.1 quake left between 6,000 and 30,000 dead, according officials and rescue organizations respectively.

"We were told to evacuate around 50 people," said office worker Francisco Bernal. "The earthquake 65 was strong but now we're prepared, unlike in 1985," he added.

The quake's epicenter was inland at a depth of 12.4 miles (20 kilometers), 100 miles (162 kilometers) from the tourist city of Oaxaca, 70 according to the USGS.

From www.bangkokpost.com (21 March 2012)

Humberto Calvo, from Guerrero state civil protection services, said Acapulco was free of damage but he warned: "The problem could be in some areas between Guerrero and Oaxaca (states). We're checking." 15

Guerrero state governor Angel Aguirre told Milenio television two hours after the quake that more than 500 homes were damaged or destroyed in southern Mexico.

"We don't have human losses in the states of 20 Guerrero and Oaxaca," Aguirre said, adding that authorities were checking the state of schools and public buildings near Ometepec, the town nearest the epicenter.

The White House said President Barack Obama's 25 13-year-old daughter Malia, who is on vacation in Mexico on spring break, was safe.

"In light of today's earthquake, we can confirm that Malia Obama is safe and was never in danger,"

The writer's craft

1. Explain how the two reports on the 2012 Mexico earthquake on pages 162–4 differ.

2. In your opinion why has the reporter of the second article included information about President Obama's daughter?

3. Explain how and why the second article includes direct speech and human interest.

Writing a newspaper report

Using the information in the two reports on the Mexico earthquake, write a human interest story (report) for a popular daily newspaper. Include:

- headline and subheading
- details about the earth tremors
- human interest stories.

Write between 350 and 450 words.

Use the Writing skills box below to help you.

Writing skills
Writing a news report for the popular press

Eye-catching headline: a key fact announced in dramatic and/or emotive language that appeals to your type of readers. Use a pun or play on words unless the event involves something horrific (in which case a pun is in very poor taste).

Hook: a brief comment to make readers want to know more.

Byline: journalist's name.

Subheading with a brief paragraph introducing other details in the news item.

First paragraph written in the present tense, relating what is happening now.

- Establish the tone of your article through well-chosen words.
- Make dramatic statements using emotive language.

The **body of the report** should:

- focus on what has just happened
- write in present perfect and past tenses
- include direct speech for statements made by witnesses
- include reported speech for comments made by experts (scientists, doctors, etc.)
- mention events that may have led up to or influenced the current situation
- mention major natural disasters or scandals in the past (if relevant).

The **final paragraph** should:

- conclude the information given
- speculate on events or suggest actions that might be taken in the near future.

Before you read a feature article about Haiti, look at the different ways news reports and articles can be written.

Reading skills
News reports and articles

Journalists and reporters can influence the way that we read their news reports and articles by what they choose to include or exclude, and the type of language they employ.

Here are some of the ways journalists and reporters try to influence readers.

1. **Headlines and subheadings**
   Look at a headline to see if it contains hard facts.

   - How much of the headline is speculation?

   - Does the headline use emotive or sensational language?

2. **The structure of the report or article**
   Look at how the journalist has organised information in paragraphs.

   - What information is given first?

   - How are facts presented?

   - How much of the article is factual? How much is comment?

   - Where and how are witness statements used?

3. **The language used to tell the story**
   Look at the word choices made by the journalist.

   - Are words easy to understand or more academic?

   - Is the language used sensational and dramatic or serious and objective?

   - What tone does the journalist create: indignant, outraged, reflective, interested, nostalgic, respectful, playful … ?

   - What type of reader is the journalist writing for?

4. **The way photographs and online video footage are used**
   Do the pictures have captions that tell the readers what to think or that supply more information about the subject of the article?

   - Does the photograph look airbrushed?

   - Is it a clear image? If not, why not?

   - Is the image emotive? Does it evoke fear, pity or sadness, for example?

5. Finally, consider how much space is given to the writer's opinion. Is he/she trying to influence what, or the way, you think? If so, why?

Read about Kiki, a victim of the terrible earthquake in Haiti in 2010.
Then answer the reading questions that follow.

Mail Online

Kiki, the icon of hope in the rubble

No Hollywood director could have improved on the scene that was splashed across the pages of this and just about every other newspaper 24 hours ago.

No reader could have turned the page without 5
pausing, smiling, perhaps even shedding a tear.

That one photograph summed up the horror and – yes – the hope of what has befallen Haiti.

The crushed masonry that formed the backdrop illustrated the power that created this tragedy. 10

The determination of the rescuers who have laboured so mightily for so long was there too: sweat creasing the dust that lined their faces after their heroic efforts to find another survivor. 15

At the centre of the picture: a little boy called Kiki.

He is seven years old and he is beaming, his crooked tooth exposed in a smile as wide as his outstretched arms. 20

His huge brown eyes sunk deep into his face tell of the suffering he must have endured since his world came crashing down on him eight days earlier, but the smile overshadows everything.

It is directed at a stick thin woman reaching out 25
to him. His mother.

We cannot see her face, but we can see the faces of Kiki's rescuers – well-fed Americans who have left their comfortable homes in the world's richest country to dig for survivors of an 30
earthquake in one of the world's poorest.

Mostly they find only bodies. But not this time. And some of them, too, have their arms outstretched like Kiki.

Others applaud. Some appear stunned by what 35
they have done. As well they might be.

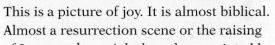

This is a picture of joy. It is almost biblical. Almost a resurrection scene or the raising of Lazarus that might have been painted by Caravaggio or Rembrandt. 40

If there is one image that stays in our minds when the world's attention has moved on from Haiti it will surely be this one. But why?

Why should it not be the picture of another Haitian child who also survived the earthquake? 45

Her name is Wideline. There is no mother stretching out her arms to her – she died in the earthquake and so did her father and their home was utterly destroyed.

Wideline's only possession is the red tartan dress 50
she wears. When she was asked how she was feeling she whispered only two words: 'hungry' and 'scared'.

Wideline is infinitely more representative of what happened to Haiti than little Kiki. 55

There are tens of thousands of children like her facing a bleak future and they will need our help for a very long time to come.

But her picture will recede along with countless others like it. 60

If not Wideline, why should the enduring image of the earthquake not be the doctors working against impossible odds to save the thousands who were so dreadfully injured?

Paul McMaster, a British surgeon working with that heroic organisation Medicins Sans Frontieres, described how one of the most urgent tasks facing him and his colleagues was finding somewhere to buy a new hacksaw. 65

They needed to replace the one they had been using to amputate the crushed limbs of people who would otherwise die from gangrene. They had used it so often it was no longer sharp enough. 70

A picture of good, selfless men and women dedicated to relieving pain in the worst possible conditions should certainly live on, but it will not. 75

Just as Wideline and the surgeons will surely fade from our collective memories, so will the other images of the earthquake: the mass graves and bodies in the streets; the buildings crushed and the looters being shot. 80

But Kiki and his rescue will remain and that, from one perspective, is wrong.

The enduring image of the Vietnam War was also a small child: nine year-old Kim Phuc fleeing naked from her village after a napalm attack, screaming in agony from the burns to her skin. 85

It will remind us for ever of the horror of warfare waged with such vile weapons and of the suffering of the innocent. And we need to be reminded. 90

It represents, at the deepest level, a victory over death

But Kiki was the exception in Haiti. Only a tiny handful have been rescued compared with the vast numbers who died under the rubble. 95

Why should we focus so much attention on him at the risk of distorting in our memories the real picture? 100

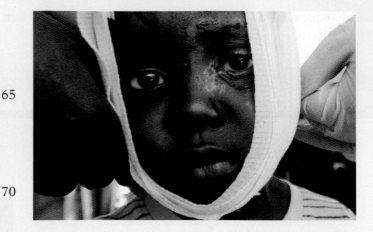

I think it's because it answers a deep need in every one of us to believe in the nobility of humanity.

It operates on so many different levels. On one level we feel awe and humility at the love of a mother who simply refuses to abandon hope. 105

Kiki's mother, Ena, was told there was no chance that her son and his sister Sabina, who was buried with him, could have survived.

It is rare for even strong adults to last for more than three or four days without a drop of water and, even if they had not had the life crushed out of them, it was virtually inconceivable that they could still be alive eight days later. 110

But Ena refused to accept the verdict of the experts and she would not leave the ruin of her home. 115

Her reward was, in one sense, a reward for everyone who saw that photograph.

And that is the essence of the photograph of Kiki's rescue. 120

That's why it has such a powerful resonance. It represents, at the deepest level, a victory over death.

There is another way of putting it. It gives us hope. 125

By John Humphrys, www.dailymail.co.uk
(23 January 2010)

Reading

1. The article on pages 167–8 is about a natural disaster and how rescue workers are trying to save people in appalling conditions. Why, in your opinion, has the journalist started with a reference to Hollywood?

2. According to the journalist, the picture of "good, selfless men and women dedicated to relieving pain ... should certainly live on, but it will not" (lines 75–7). Why do you think he says this?

The writer's craft – emotive language

1. Select a word, phrase or sentence from John Humphrys' article and discuss how and why the journalist has used it to evoke pity or sympathy.

2. Look at the rhetorical questions in lines 43–5. Explain how and why the writer has used these questions to introduce information about the little girl called Wideline.

Below is the opening of an article about Kiki written a year and a half after John Humphrys' article for the *Daily Mail*. Think about the journalist's style.

1. Is it similar or different to that of John Humphrys?

2. What effect does the writer achieve through her choice of words in this introduction? How does she want her readers to react?

REMINDER – puns in headlines

A pun is a play on words where a word is substituted with a homonym for effect.

When puns are used in newspaper headlines they refer to what is being reported.

Example:

Heartless shoemaker has no soul

A Birmingham shoe manufacturer has dismissed his workshop manager after he lost his right hand in a work-related accident. Widower, Ed Boyle, father of four under-tens, lost his right hand while …

In this example the word *soul* is a homonym of *sole* which is related to the profession of shoemaking.

Homonym (n): each of two or more words having the same spelling or pronunciation but different meanings and origins.

(*Oxford English Dictionary*)

The Sun

School is a three-smile walk for Kiki

MIRACLE boy Kiki Joachin beams with joy as he reads aloud at the front of the class – excitedly showing Sun readers that he is now back at school.

The brave seven-year-old – whose smile lit up the darkness of Haiti's earthquake hell when he was rescued from his rubble tomb after nearly eight days – couldn't stop grinning in his lessons …

By Virginia Wheeler, *The Sun* (25 May 2011)

Talking points

- Do you believe that creatures such as the Loch Ness Monster really exist?

- Is there a legendary monster in the area in which you live?

Legendary monsters

In the next few pages you are going to read about the sighting of various monsters, or cryptids, in different countries. Decide for yourself whether these sightings are genuine – or not.

The Loch Ness Monster

Loch Ness is a vast lake in the North of Scotland. The loch is one of a series of interlinked lakes running along the Great Glen, a geological fault zone which creates a distinctive incision across Scotland.

Many people believe there is a dinosaur-like creature living in Loch Ness. There is no actual proof of its existence, but sightings go back to the time of the Celtic monk St Columba in the 6th century. Since the invention of photography people have tried to catch the monster on film and many men and women swear they have seen a plesiosaur-like dinosaur swimming in the loch. Photographs suggest the creature has a humped back and a long neck. Recent technological investigation using radar and sonar equipment, however, has not revealed any evidence for the existence of a Loch Ness Monster. This, some people say, may be due to the sheer size and depth of the loch (21 square miles and almost 800 feet deep), meaning there are probably hundreds of underwater caves that "Nessie" can hide in.

12:43 PM　　　　　99% 🔋

Discovery News

LOCH NESS MONSTER-LIKE ANIMAL FILMED IN ALASKA?

THE GIST

- Video footage shot shows a mysterious Loch Ness monster-like creature.

- People who study undescribed creatures believe it is a sea serpent with a long neck.

- Sightings of the creature have been reported for years, though none have been captured.

The alleged sea serpent has a long neck, a horse-like head, large eyes and back bumps that stick out of the water ...

By Jennifer Viegas, http://news.discovery.com (18 July 2011)

Daily Mail

Is this Iceland's Loch Ness monster? Giant serpent-like sea creature caught on camera swimming in glacial river

Footage becomes a monster hit on the internet as it goes viral.

... The notorious "snake-like" creature is said to live in the Lagarfljót lake, which is 25 miles long and 367 feet deep – and it has been the subject of many a supposed sighting since reports of it first emerged in 1345 ...

By Kerry McQueeney, *Daily Mail* (8 February 2012)

The Sun

Scientists close in on Yeti

SCIENTISTS could be putting a Bigfoot in their mouths by claiming that the Abominable Snowman is alive and well.

Experts at an international Yeti conference in Russia this week insisted they are only months away from proving the beast really exists.

Igor Burtsev, head of The International Center Of Hominology, said at the meeting in Tashtagol: "We are on the brink of finding the Yeti at long last."

By Vince Soodin, *The Sun* (11 October 2011)

Daily Mail

Is this finally proof the Yeti exists? Abominable Snowman "close to being caught" after coarse hair is found in remote Russian cave.

- Villagers say 7ft-tall beast has been stealing livestock.
- More than a dozen eyewitness accounts of seeing Yeti.

They have long been thought to be merely the stuff of legend.

But Russian officials say they have found "indisputable evidence" that yetis exist – and are living in Siberia ...

By Rick Dewsbury, *Daily Mail* (11 October 2011)

The writer's craft – content, style and diction

These newspaper headlines all relate to sightings and topical news of legendary monsters.

Copy the table and then fill in details to show what the news reports on cryptids have in common and how they differ.

Look closely at the content, style and diction of each report before you start writing.

Style and diction – *how* they are written	Content – *what* is in the articles

Read this online news article about the sighting of a monster in Iceland and answer the reading questions that follow.

Daily Mail

Is this Iceland's Loch Ness Monster? Amateur footage shows "giant serpent" slinking its way through lake.

Iceland's equivalent to the Loch Ness monster has apparently been pictured on footage taken by an amateur cameraman. 5

The video, taken by Hjörtur Kjerúlf at the glacial river Jökulsá í Fljótsdal, east Iceland, appears to show the serpent-like monster known as Lagarfljótsormurinn, or Lagarfljót's Worm. 10

Belief in the existence of the worm, which is said to reside in the lake Lagarfljót, can be sourced back to at least 1345. Sightings of the beast are considered a bad omen.

Legends say the monster began life as a tiny worm 15 which a girl placed on a ring of gold to make it grow, according to Iceland Review Online.

But when the owner of the ring returned she found that instead of making the gold grow, the worm had grown into a giant snake. 20

In her terror, she flung both into Lake Lagarfljót, where the worm continued to grow and eventually became a fearsome dragon.

Lagarfljót, is a freshwater, below-sea-level, glacial-fed lake which has very poor visibility as a 25 result of siltation.

The worm is believed to be at least 91m (300ft) long, with many humps. It has sometimes been reported outside the water, lying coiled up or slithering into the trees. 30

Sometimes it is said to be as long as the lake itself, 30km (19 miles).

Kjerúlf's video was first shown by the Icelandic national broadcaster, RÚV. Sceptics say it could show a torn fishing net which blew into the river 35 and froze.

As the ice thawed, it is thought, the net may have come loose and the 'worm' wound its way through the water.

By Damian Gayle, www.dailymail.co.uk
(8 February 2012)

Reading

Imagine you are doing a project on cryptids. Read the news report above on a possible sighting of the legendary Iceland "worm" and write a short chapter for your project. Include:

a. the history of the Icelandic "worm"

b. the likelihood of this being a genuine sighting.

The following two passages are about a giant cryptid said to be living in the Congo Basin, Africa. Read both passages and then do the writing question that follows.

National Geographic TV blog

Mokele-Mbembe: Swamp monster of the Congo

The name *Mokele-Mbembe* means "one who stops the flow of rivers". That gives an indication of the traditional awe and dread that people of the Congo Basin have held for Africa's version of the Loch Ness Monster. In legends, it sometimes is described as having a gray-brown elephant-like body, with a long neck and small head.

According to Roy P. Mackal's 1987 book *A Living Dinosaur? In search of Mokele-Membe*, the earliest account by an outsider of Mokele-Mbembe was published in 1776 by a French priest, the Rev. Abbe Levain Bonaventure Proyart, who reported that missionaries in the Congo had happened upon the tracks of an enormous animal whose feet were a yard in circumference. The animal apparently had claws, which elephants and rhinos do not. Mackal also cites the reports of a German explorer, Freiherr von Stein zu Lasnitz, who visited the region just before the outbreak of World War I. Lasnitz wrote that he was told by natives of an immense semi-aquatic animal with a long neck and a muscular, alligator-like tail.

The gigantic herbivore cryptid has been hunted repeatedly over the past century by expeditions of explorers and researchers, including Mackal himself. Some claim to have come tantalizingly close. Loren Coleman and Jerome Clark's 1999 book *Cryptology A to Z* recounts the testimony of Congolese biologist Marcellin Agnagna, who in 1983 reportedly caught a glimpse of a Mokele-Mbembe wading into Lake Tele. He described it as having a long-necked form, but he was unable to see the legs or tail. Agnagna attempted to film the creature with his movie camera, but in his excitement failed to notice that he had not removed the lens cap. In 1992, a Japanese film crew, while shooting panoramic footage for a documentary, caught a 15-second shot of what appears to be a large object with a protruberance that could be a long neck, swimming briefly on the lake surface before diving.

Part of outsiders' enduring fascination for Mokele-Mbeme stems from the belief that it might be an extant dinosaur, one that somehow survived the Cretaceous-Tertiary Extinction Event 65 million years ago, which scientists believe was triggered by an immense asteroid striking a spot under what is now the Yucutan peninsula of Mexico. Some descriptions of the creature do evoke the actual long-necked dinosaurs who roamed the region tens of millions of years ago. Those creatures, who weighed upwards of 50 tons, may have been the largest land animals in the history of the planet. Their huge size and long necks may have been an evolutionary adaptation that allowed them to reach vegetation that was too high for less imposing creatures. Sauropod teeth have been found in the Koum basin in neighboring Cameroon.

If Mokele Mbeme was found and turned out actually to be a living example of a *sauropod*, it might rewrite natural history […] Cryptozoologists continue to search, in the belief that if dinosaurs do still exist in some wild, unexplored area, the Congo might be a likely spot.

From http://tvblogs.nationalgeographic.com
(9 March 2012)

▲ Are Mokele-Mbembe lurking in this swamp?

Was a Mokele-mbembe killed at Lake Tele?

Around 1960, the forest dwelling pygmies of the Lake Tele region (the Bangombe tribe), fished daily in the lake near the Molibos, or water channels situated at the north end of the lake. These channels merge with the swamps, and were used by Mokele-mbembes to enter the lake where they would browse on the vegetation. This daily excursion into the lake by the animals disrupted the pygmies' fishing activities. Eventually, the pygmies decided to erect a stake barrier across the molibo in order to prevent the animals from entering the lake.

When two of the animals were observed attempting to break through the barrier, the pygmies speared one of the animals to death and later cut it into pieces. This task apparently took several days due to the size of the animal, which was described as being bigger than a forest elephant with a long neck, a small snake-like or lizard-like head, which was decorated with a comb-like frill. The pygmy spearmen also described a long, flexible tail, a smooth, reddish-brown skin and four stubby, but powerful legs with clawed toes. Pastor Thomas also mentioned that the two pygmies mimicked the cry of the animal as it was being attacked and speared.

During my first expedition in 1985, we met with several eyewitnesses who have observed Mokele-mbembes in the Sangha and Likouala aux Herbes Rivers. Our pygmy informants also mentioned that there were at least two Mokele-mbembes still living in the Lake Tele vicinity, but they were simply too afraid to take us to a precise location where we could actually film and observe a specimen of Mokele-mbembe, due to their superstitious beliefs surrounding the animals.

During our two visits to the Congo, my colleagues and I were unable to locate a single one of the "dozens" of witnesses that allegedly observed Mokele-mbembes with the aforementioned explorers. Marcellin Agagna changed his story several times, and is now thought (by Roy Mackal) to have observed the giant African freshwater turtle, *Trionyx triunguis*. Herman Regusters and his wife Kia are the only individuals on his expedition to have observed a "long-necked member" travelling across Lake Tele, in spite of the fact that 28 other people were with them from the village of Boha. Rory Nugent's alleged Mokele-mbembe photos could be anything, although he may have seen "something" in the distance.

But Jose Bourges, the Congolese wildlife official who accompanied the 1988 Japanese expedition to the lake, reported that the entire expedition observed a large humped back of an animal, slowly moving

---

REMINDER – rhetorical questions

A rhetorical question is not a genuine question; it is for effect and does not require an answer.

Rhetorical questions have no place in serious writing and should be avoided in essays.

Take care not to end a speech with a question that could result in an undesirable answer.

The Bangombe tribe claim to have seen Mokele-mbembes.

along, as if foraging on the bottom of the 65
lake, which is three meters deep at most. So
the animals are still there, and I still want to
find one!

By William Gibbons

Bill Gibbons has conducted two major
expeditions to the Congo, in 1985–6 and in
1992, in search of the Mokele-mbembe. He
conducted two other field investigations
on the island of Mauritius in the southern
Indian Ocean in 1990 and 1997, after two
European visitors claimed dodo sightings.
Operation Congo III and Project Dodo III are
currently under development. He is currently
pursuing a PhD in Cultural Anthropology
with Warnborough College, Oxford.

Writing an article

You have been on an expedition to find Mokele-Mbembe.

Write an article on what you saw for a popular daily newspaper in
your country.

Use the information about writing news reports and articles in this
unit to help you.

Write between 350 and 450 words.

Passage 1

After crossing the torrent of Bhote Khosi, the track then zigzagged up a cliff and we had our first view of Everest to the east. Streams of snow were blowing off the summit. On ahead was Khumbu Ylha, the Sacred Mountain of the Sherpas, rearing its triangular peak above a throne of puffy white clouds… 5

Passage 2

All along the track to Thome there were clumps of blue iris and gentians the size of sapphire studs. Soon we came to a lovely wood of birch trees leafless as yet, with peeling orange bark and 10 beards of jade green lichen festooned from their branches. We passed through stands of pale pink rhododendrons and, as we ambled along, I asked Sangye Dorje whether he believed in the Yeti.

"I do," he said, and went on to explain how there 15 were two kinds of Yeti: the *mih-teh* which killed people, and the *dzu-teh* which killed only animals.

"But Yeti," he added sombrely, "is also some kind of God."

He promised that when we got to his own 20 village, Chumming, he would introduce me to a woman who was actually attacked by the beast. Usually, he said, a person who looked into Yeti's eyes was doomed to die: but she had been the exception.

Passage 3

Later, in the village of Thome (which means "Way 25 up") we ran in with some novice monks coming back from the market. They were all singing at the tops of their voices. The smallest was walloping out the rhythm on an oil-can, and a wizened old monk followed wearing purple rags and a sou'wester. 30

"Ask him," I said to Sangye, "whether he has ever seen the Yeti."

"Not I," the old man smiled. "But my aunts did." His two aunts had been pasturing their sheep when the whole flock suddenly poured off the 35 mountain with the Yeti in pursuit.

"How did it look?" I asked.

"Bigger than a man," the monk said, "with terrible yellow eyes, arms almost touching the ground, red hair growing upwards from the waist, and a white 40 crest on top … "

Passage 4

We walked until mid-afternoon and had reached the outskirts of Khumjung when Sangye called out, "Bruce! You remember about the Yeti lady? There she is!" 45

We shinned over the wall and greeted Lakpa Doma, a handsome woman in her thirties with polished red cheeks and a dazzling smile. She wore heavy gold earrings, a striped Sherpa woman's apron, and was mattocking her field while her old 50 mother cut potato slips for planting.

This was Sangye's version of her story:

One day in 1974 she was tending her family's yaks in a summer pasture near Macchermo when the Yeti sprung on her from behind a rock, dragged her to the 55 stream, but then dumped her and went on to slaughter three of the yaks simply by twisting their horns. The beast had the same yellow eyes, big brow-ridges and hollow temples. Some policemen came up from Namche to examine the yak carcasses and stated, 60 categorically, that the killer had never been a man.

"I suppose it was a *dzu-teh*?" I said.

"It was," said Sangye Dorje…

176

Passage 5

"I don't know," I said to Sangye, not sure what to say. For what, indeed, could one say? What did I, or any other Westerner, really know about the Yeti? 65

I knew, for example, that Yetis or similar species had been knocking about European literature since the Elder Pliny (Natural History VII, 9) described a race of "wild men" who lived in 70 the Mountains of Imaeus (the Eastern Himalaya), moved with astonishing speed, and had huge feet turned back-to-front. I knew that the Sherpas, too, believed that Yeti had his feet turned back. I knew that several tough-minded mountaineers, such 75 as Eric Shipton or Sir John Hunt, had not only photographed Yeti footprints in the snow, but had heard the Yeti shrieking. I also knew that Hillary's "scientific" expedition had failed to find the least trace of the creature [...] and had suggested that 80 the "tracks" were those of the snow-leopard or Tibetan blue bear, enlarged by the melting sun.

Passage 6

Of course, I reflected, it was *just* conceivable that some giant orang-outang-like ape had survived in the High Himalaya: but I, for one, was sceptical. I 85 believed, rather, that Yeti was (for want of a better term) a creature of the Collective Unconscious. Man, after all, is the inventor of his own monsters. Babies "see" monsters long before they are shown them in picture books [...] and only a few weeks 90 earlier I had watched, in a school near Alice Springs, some Aboriginal children drawing an ape-like ogre from their mythology – in a continent that never saw an ape until the coming of the whites.

I believed, too, that the people most 95 likely to "see" Yetis were either simpletons or schizophrenics; religious ascetics or the very poor (both liable to protein deficiency); or those at high altitude with a diminished supply of oxygen to the brain. Perhaps Yeti was a mountain hallucination. 100

Passage 7

We then climbed up alongside the Ngozumpa Glacier and came out into a blinding bright landscape of snow and naked rock and green lakes half-frozen over. On a patch of open water a ruddy shelldrake was nibbling at some weed. Elizabeth was 105 watching him through binoculars when I happened to turn round – and blinked.

"Look!" I blurted out. "Yeti tracks."

"Oh yeah?" drawled Elizabeth, and went on watching the shelldrake. 110

"Look at them!"

On the north-facing slope behind us there was a line of very strange footprints. They were each about fifteen inches long, wider at the toe than the heel, and on some you saw – or thought you saw – 115 the imprint of a giant big toe. They approached the base of an almost vertical bank, stopped, continued on the slope higher up, and finally petered out along a rocky ridge. I reckoned that the creature had jumped at least eight feet into the air and twelve 120 along. The tracks were perhaps a day old and had melted a little: even so, I could see that they hadn't

been made by any of the usual contenders – yak, blue bear, snowleopard, langur monkey, human or human hoaxer. No hoaxer could have jumped that   125 high, yet the Sherpas say that Yeti habitually jumps his own height and more. The strange thing was that its foot had scuffed the snow on the way up – unless it really was a Yeti-with-the-feet turned-back, in which case the jumper had been jumping down.   130

I was sure there must be some logical explanation and called Sangye over.

"Did you ever," I asked, "on any of your tasks, see anything like them?"

"Never," he said, darkly. "They were not made   135 by men."

"Then who made them?"

"Same as Yeti."

Passage 8

I still have no idea what these "Yeti tracks" were. My whole life has been a search for the   140 miraculous: yet at the first faint flavour of the uncanny, I tend to turn rational and scientific. After this excitement, the whole party was infected with Yeti-fever and kept "seeing things" on every mountain. On Cho Oyu we thought we saw   145 Reinhold Messner manoeuvring across an ice-fall. He was on the mountain that day, but not where we could see him, and the "thing" we did see turned out to be a pinnacle of rock, doubling and tripling as our eyes watered in the wind.   150

From *What Am I Doing Here?*,
by Bruce Chatwin (1983)

Sangye Dorje (n.): the author's Sherpa mountain guide.

Mattocking (v.): loosening the soil with an agricultural tool called a mattock.

Shelldrake (n.): waterbird.

Hillary (n.): Sir Edmund Hillary – New Zealand-born explorer who reached the summit of Mount Everest in 1953.

Reinhold Messner (n.): Italian mountaineer and explorer.

REMINDER – juxtaposition

Juxtaposition is placing one item next to another for a particular effect or purpose.

Chatwin creates a tranquil mood through the description of "puffy white clouds" and mentions trees and plants familiar to British readers, then, as juxtaposition, relates what his guide says about two types of yetis and a shocking report of how a woman was attacked.

Reading – Core

1. Answer the following questions about the passages from "On Yeti Tracks".

   a. Re-read passage 2. Chatwin's guide tells him that there are two types of yeti. What are the two types called and how do they differ?

   b. Why do the police say the killer of the yaks could never have been a man?

   c. Explain how and why Chatwin uses two rhetorical questions in passage 5.

   d. What makes yeti tracks identifiable in the snow?

   e. Re-read Passage 6. Explain in your own words why (at this point) Chatwin believes the yeti sightings are not genuine. Say why he does not think people have seen a real yeti. Include the following:

   - why the yeti might be an invented monster
   - why he thinks yeti sightings are "mountain hallucinations"
   - what might cause people to "see" yeti.

   f. When Chatwin eventually sees what he thinks are yeti tracks, how does he react?

   g. Why do you think Chatwin includes what his wife was doing in passage 7?

   h. Explain, using your own words, "My whole life has been a search for the miraculous: yet at the first faint flavour of the uncanny, I tend to turn rational and scientific." (lines 140–2)

2. You are with Chatwin in the Himalayas. Write a letter to your friend Kim telling him/her what happened when Chatwin saw what he thought were yeti tracks. Give your thoughts and opinions on the possibility or probability that it was a real yeti.

   Begin your letter *Dear Kim,* and include:

   - what Chatwin saw
   - what yetis are said to look like
   - why it could have been dangerous
   - whether you think it was, or was not, a real yeti.

   Write between 200 and 300 words.

Reading – Extended

1. You are a scientist on Chatwin's expedition to verify the existence of the yeti in the Himalayas. Write your journal for the day Chatwin thinks he sees yeti tracks. Comment on whether you think he is right or not. Give your reasons for believing there are, or there are not, yeti in the mountains. Use evidence from the passages to justify your views but do not copy from it.

   Write between 250 and 350 words.

2. Re-read passages 1 and 2 on page 176 and explain the following:

   a. how Chatwin creates a sense of distance and grandeur in passage 1

   b. how and why Chatwin decribes the flowers, shrubs and trees that he sees

   c. how Chatwin introduces information about the two types of yeti.

Narrative prose

In this section we are going to look at the fiction genre of fantasy.

Before you read passages from fantasy novels, however, read how fiction authors use narrators and the narrative voice to tell their stories.

The narrative voice

In Unit 3 and other units we have looked at point of view and how to identify the speaker in a poem or the narrative voice in a story. Here is a quick reminder of what we have looked at so far.

In a first-person narrative, we read the story from the narrator's point of view; we know whether the person telling the story is male or female, we may know his/her age, nationality and other details that might influence how that person sees the world or experiences events.

In a third-person narrative we do not know who is telling the story. It may be the author, or the author may have adopted a persona to tell the story.

The author may use an omniscient narrator who knows everything that is happening in the plot and what characters are thinking. This type of narrator describes scenes and what is happening without making judgmental comments or voicing opinions.

The omniscient narrator

An omniscient third-person narrator usually tells a story using two major techniques: show and tell.

- The narrator shows us people's characters through what they say, how they speak and how they react to one another. We can also learn about the past and the future from what characters say.

- The narrator tells us about the characters through description and setting. We learn what characters look like, where the characters are and what is happening to them through what the narrator tells us.

An omniscient narrator also knows what characters are thinking. These thoughts are conveyed to the reader using both the show and tell techniques.

- The narrator shows what a character is thinking through a kind of inner speech called free indirect thought. For example: *Is it over yet*?

Or

- The narrator tells what a character is thinking through direct thought. For example: *Is it over yet, he wondered*.

Now read two passages (on pages 181 and 182) from a well-known fantasy novel and look at the way the author makes the events and characters believable.

Showing and telling

The first book in J.R.R. Tolkien's trilogy *The Lord of the Rings* is *The Fellowship of the Ring*. The novel begins at a party for the famous hobbit Bilbo Baggins' 111th birthday. Bilbo reluctantly gives his heir, Frodo Baggins, a ring with strange and dangerous properties – it is the One Ring of legend. Frodo is told that the ring must be taken away from the Shire, where the hobbits live, because it holds an evil power. Frodo is warned that he must never put it on.

Frodo leaves the safety of the Shire with his small hobbit friends, Sam, Merry and Pippin, but he is soon pursued by the nine Ringwraiths, who take the form of terrifying Black Riders.

Frodo hesitated for a second: curiosity or some other feeling was struggling with his desire to hide. The sound of hoofs drew nearer. Just in time he threw himself down in a patch of long grass behind a tree that over-shadowed the road. Then he lifted his head and peered cautiously above one of the great roots.   5

Round the corner came a black horse, no hobbit-pony but a full-sized horse; and on it sat a large man, who seemed to crouch in the saddle, wrapped in a great black cloak and hood, so that only his boots in the high stirrups showed below; his face was shadowed and invisible.   10

When it reached the tree and was level with Frodo the horse stopped. The riding figure sat quite still with its head bowed, as if listening. From inside the hood came a noise as of someone sniffing to catch an elusive scent; the head turned from side to side of the road.   15

A sudden unreasoning fear of discovery laid hold of Frodo, and he thought of his Ring. He hardly dared to breathe, and yet the desire to get it out of his pocket became so strong that he began slowly to move his hand. He felt that he had only to slip it on, and then he would be safe.   20

From *The Lord of the Rings*, by J.R.R. Tolkien (1954)

The writer's craft – showing and telling

Is Tolkein showing the reader what is happening or telling, or both? Find two examples from the passage to justify your opinion.

In the next part of the story, the Hobbits wait until the Black Rider has disappeared and continue their journey, but later that evening they hear another horse.

"Hush," said Frodo. "I think I hear hoofs again."

They stopped suddenly and stood as silent as tree-shadows, listening. There was a sound of hoofs in the lane, some way behind, but coming slow and clear from the wind. Quickly and quietly they slipped off the path, and ran into the deeper shade under the oak-trees. 5

"Don't let us go too far!" said Frodo. "I don't want to be seen, but I want to see if it is another Black Rider."

"Very well!" said Pippin. "But don't forget the sniffing."

The hoofs drew nearer. They had no time to find any hiding-place better than the general darkness of the trees; Sam and Pippin crouched behind a large tree-bole, while Frodo crept back a few yards towards the lane. It showed grey and pale, a line of fading light through the wood. Above it the stars were thick in the dim sky, but there was no moon. 10

The sound of hoofs stopped. As Frodo watched he saw something dark pass across the lighter space between two trees, and then halt. It looked like the black shade of a horse led by a smaller shadow. The black shadow stood close to the point where they had left the path, and it swayed from side to side. Frodo thought he heard the sound of snuffling. The shadow bent to the ground, and then began to crawl towards him. 20

From *The Lord of the Rings*, by J.R.R. Tolkien (1954)

Writing narrative

Rewrite this excerpt from the *Lord of the Rings* in the first person. You can be Frodo, Pippin or Sam. Try to create a sense of fear or menace.

Write between 350 and 450 words.

All fiction requires a reader to suspend disbelief. A good fiction author makes his/her story believable. How does this author make his characters and setting seem real?

Shadowmancer

In the gloom of the forest her eyes began to make strange shapes out of everything she looked at. A tree appeared to change into a giant's head, a cloud looked like a swan fixed against a star, and a small tuft of grass took on the shape of a hedgehog that seemed to crawl through the wood. Kate stared into the night. Then froze. The night was staring back at her!

There in the glade, just several feet away from her, five pairs of bright eyes were gazing towards the holly bush. Kate felt the palms of her hand begin to sweat as sudden panic gripped her tightly. She dared not move for fear that they would see her. She dared not swallow for fear that they would hear her. Even at such close a distance, she could not make out any shape of the creatures, just red staring eyes. If they were smugglers, then this was the best disguise she had ever seen. She had certainly not heard their arrival; they had simply appeared.

As she looked on, Kate saw a silver outline begin to appear around each figure, like millions of tiny sparks jumping in a fire. Brighter and brighter they glowed. Then all the sparks began to draw closer together. They rolled around each other as if propelled by some unseen wind blasting the embers of a fire. As they burnt brighter they changed from silver, to red, to green, to blue. Finally, as quickly as they appeared, they vanished. Kate stared fearfully into the night. Her gaze was transfixed by what was before her.

There, standing in the glade were five tall figures dressed from head to foot in metal armour. Each wore a burnished helmet in the shape of a snake's head, with glistening eyes that shone like diamonds. Two large ivory fangs stabbed down to the front of each helmet like the sabre teeth of some long extinct creature.

The breastplates of the armour outlined every muscle, a long metal spine ran to the elbow of each arm where it was joined to a thick leather gauntlet. In between each piece of metal, Kate could see the skin of the creatures. Dark green and lifeless, it had an eerie glow that almost merged with the night. Around each waist hung a thick black leather belt, on to which was strapped what looked like a short sword with a black leather grip. The smallest of the creatures carried a round shield studded with silver, inset with glowing red jewels.

From her hiding place she could not make out the features of their faces. She could see only the bright red eyes still staring towards her. Kate aimed the pistol directly at the head of the largest creature. She took in a slow and silent breath. She was terrified. A voice inside her head screamed, *Pull the trigger*! She was unable to move, rigid with fear, petrified as a statue.

The voice screamed at her again. *Pull the trigger*!

Again she could not move. The weight of the gun began to tug against her hand as if it was being pulled from her grip. All Kate wanted to do was run and scream. She knew she would get only five paces before being caught. She knew that if she moved her hand or lowered the pistol the creatures would hear her. Kate summoned every ounce of strength to hold the pistol in front of her. She could feel the muscles in her arm begin to ache, the pain reaching from the tips of her fingers to the shoulders. She wanted to cry, she wanted to go home. Again the voice cried in her head.

Pull the trigger ... Pull the trigger.

Now trembling with fear, Kate tried to squeeze the trigger, but her finger wouldn't move. A numbing coldness began to claw its way up her arm, as if she was being slowly turned to stone.

From *Shadowmancer*, by G.P. Taylor (2003)

Writing narrative
Write another exciting scene for the story above. Continue from the words:

"A numbing coldness began to claw its way up her arm, as if she was being slowly turned to stone."

Write between 350 and 450 words.

Unit 7: Self-assessment

In this unit we have read different types of news media, blog articles and fantasy.

Two key skills we have looked at are how writers show and tell. What is the difference?

What do you remember about how journalists use emotive language in news articles?

How do they use human interest to make stories more personal?

Make notes about Unit 7

Consider the work you have done in this unit. Then copy and complete the chart.

Two texts (media, non-media or fiction) I remember in Unit 7 are:
Two new skills I learned are:
Two things I'm not sure about are:
I enjoyed doing:
Something I would like to do again is:
I would like to do this again because:

Unit 7 Literature extension

The Great Frost

From "Orlando" by Virginia Woolf (1928)

THE Great Frost was, historians tell us, the most severe that has ever visited these islands. Birds froze in mid-air and fell like stones to the ground. At Norwich a young countrywoman started to cross the road in her usual robust health and was seen by the onlookers to turn visibly to powder and be blown in a puff of dust over the roofs as the icy blast struck her at the street corner. The mortality among sheep and cattle was enormous. Corpses froze and could not be drawn from the sheets. It was no uncommon sight to come upon a whole herd frozen immovable upon the road. The fields were full of shepherds, ploughmen, teams of horses, and little bird-scaring boys all struck stark in the act of the moment, one with his hand to his nose, another with the bottle to his lips, a third with a stone raised to throw at the raven who sat, as if stuffed, upon the hedge within a yard of him. The severity of the frost was so extra-ordinary that a kind of petrifaction sometimes ensued; and it was commonly supposed that the great increase of rocks in some parts of Derbyshire was due to no eruption, for there was none, but to the solidification of unfortunate wayfarers who had been turned literally to stone where they stood. The Church could give little help in the matter, and though some landowners had these relics blessed, the most part preferred to use them either as landmarks, scratching-posts for sheep, or, when the form of the stone allowed, drinking troughs for cattle, which purposes they serve, admirably for the most part, to this day.

But while country people suffered the extremity of want, and the trade of the country was at a standstill, London enjoyed a carnival of the utmost brilliancy. The Court was at Greenwich, and the new King seized the opportunity that his coronation gave him to curry favour with the citizens. He directed that the river, which was frozen to a depth of twenty feet and more for about six or seven miles on either side, should be swept, decorated and given all the semblance of a park or pleasure ground with arbours, mazes, alleys and drinking booths etc. at his expense.

The Great Frost

Between 1560 and 1660 there was a period now known as "The Little Ice Age" that particularly affected northern Europe. Read the following passage about the effect of weather conditions in England in the early 17th century. Decide whether you think it is fiction or literary non-fiction.

1. Identify words and phrases that suggest this is an informative account for non-fiction.

2. Identify words and phrases that suggest this is descriptive writing for fiction.

3. Read the passage again and decide whether it is fiction or non-fiction. Write a paragraph to explain your views. Remember to quote from the passage to support your ideas

185

8 World famous

In this unit you will:

→ **Visit** Africa, Ancient Greece, England, France, Rhodes, Scotland, Sweden, various famous tourist sites and fictional places

→ **Read** news articles, a press release, advertising material, autobiography, biography, fiction and poetry

→ **Write** to describe, inform and entertain.

To you, o Sun, the people of Dorian Rhodes set up this bronze statue reaching to Olympus, when they had pacified the waves of war and crowned their city with the spoils taken from the enemy.

Not only over the seas but also on land did they kindle the lovely torch of freedom and independence.

For to the descendants of Herakles belongs dominion over sea and land.

Inscription on the huge statue straddling the harbour in Rhodes

Talking point

The Colossus of Rhodes (right) was one of the wonders of the ancient world.

- It was built between 292 and 280 BC to celebrate a victory.
- It was 30 metres high.
- What happened to it?
- Does it remind you of any other statue?

Celebrity (n): 1 a well-known person. 2 fame, being famous.

(*Oxford Study Dictionary*)

The talent of success is nothing more than doing what you can do well and doing well whatever you do without thought of fame. If it comes at all it will come because it is deserved, not because it is sought after.

Henry Wadsworth Longfellow (1807–82), American poet

Of all the possessions of this life fame is the noblest; when the body has sunk into the dust the great name still lives.

Friedrich Schiller (1759–1805), German poet, dramatist and philosopher

You have to remember that when you are a performer you become a celebrity, but you are not saving lives. It's not that important.

Victoria Beckham (1974–), British singer and designer

Being a celebrity is probably the closest to being a beautiful woman as you can get.

Kevin Costner (1955–), American actor and film director

Talking points

- Do the words *fame, celebrity, success* and *greatness* all mean the same thing?
- How do they differ?

Speaking and listening

Work in small groups of no more than four people.

Each member of the group should choose one quotation from those above and explain what they think the person is saying about the concept of fame or being a celebrity.

Famous people and places

Shakespeare's play *Twelfth Night* is a comedy and Malvolio's words (below) are not meant to be taken seriously in the context of the scene. But do his words ring true? Are some people born great and do some people have greatness thrust upon them? Do the activities on fame and success.

> Be not afraid of greatness: some are born great, some achieve greatness and some have greatness thrust upon 'em.

Malvolio, *Twelfth Night*, by William Shakespeare (1564–1616), British poet and dramatist

Success

Marie Curie

Christopher Columbus

Alexander Fleming

Wolfgang Amadeus Mozart

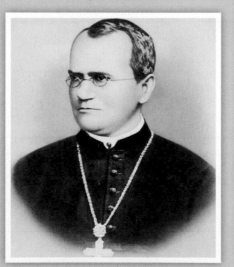
Gregor Mendel

Leonardo da Vinci

Fame

1. Make a list of 12 famous people that you know about.

2. Divide these famous people into three categories: those who were born great; those who have achieved greatness; those who have had greatness thrust upon them.

   You can name people from the past and the present. You may find that there are more people in one category than another.

   Here are a few suggestions to get you started:

   - Mahatma Gandhi
   - Charlie Chaplin
   - Nelson Mandela
   - Edwin Hubble
   - Albert Schweitzer
   - Martin Luther King
   - Maria Montessori
   - Walt Disney
   - Bill Gates
   - Steve Jobs
   - Mother Teresa
   - Amelia Earhart

A. B. C.

D. E. F.

Who did what and could we live without it?

1. Match the pictures of famous people to what they created or discovered.

2. Decide whether you think the world would be the same without their discoveries or achievements.

The Olympic Games

Historical records demonstrate the first Olympic Games were held in 776 BC. The games were dedicated to the Olympian gods and took place on the plains of Olympia in Greece, where they continued for nearly 12 centuries until Emperor 5 Theodosius declared they were a "pagan cult" and banned them.

The Olympic Games were linked to the religious festivals for Zeus, but were not part of religious ritual. The purpose was to show the physical 10 qualities and abilities of young people and to bring together as many people as possible from different city states and islands to foster friendship and good relations. Nevertheless, some specialists argue the Olympic Games owed 15 their "purity and importance" to religion.

A winner received an award immediately after each competition. Following the announcement of his name, he was given a palm branch while the spectators cheered and threw flowers. Red 20 ribbons were tied on each winner's head and hands as a symbol of triumph.

Olympic athletes

Through the 12 centuries of the Olympic Games, many wonderful athletes competed in 25 the stadium and the hippodrome of ancient Olympia's sacred area, moving the crowds with their great achievements. Although mortal, their Olympic victories immortalised them. Of the best athletes who left their mark on the sacred 30 valley of Olympia, some surpassed all limits and became legends by winning in successive Olympic Games and remaining at the forefront of their sport for more than a decade. It is worth mentioning some of their extraordinary 35 achievements, which, even by today's standards, would be the envy of athletes such as Nurmi, Zatopek or Lewis.

Participants

All free male Greek citizens were entitled to 40 participate in the ancient Olympic Games, regardless of their social status. Orsippos, a general from Megara; Polymnistor, a shepherd; Diagoras, a member of a royal family from Rhodes; Alexander I, son of Amyndas and King 45 of Macedonia; and Democritus, a philosopher, were all participants in the Games.

Married women were not allowed to participate in, or to watch, the ancient Olympic Games. However, unmarried women could attend the 50 competition and the priestess of Demeter, goddess of fertility, was given a privileged position next to the stadium altar.

Astylos of Croton

Astylos of Croton in southern Italy won a total of 55 six victory olive wreaths in three Olympiads (488–480 BC) in the stade race and the diaulos race (twice the stade) events. In the first Olympiad, he ran for Croton and his compatriots honoured and glorified him. In the two 60 successive Olympiads, however, he took part as a citizen of Syracuse. The people of Croton punished him by demolishing his statue in their city and converting his house into a prison.

Milon of Croton 65

Milon, a pupil of the philosopher Pythagoras, was one of the most famous athletes in Antiquity. He came from the Greek city of Croton in southern Italy. He was six times Olympic wrestling champion. He first won in 70 540 BC, in the youth wrestling event and then five times in men's wrestling. This is a unique achievement even in today's competition context. He also won seven times in the Pythian Games, nine times in the Nemean Games, ten 75 times in the Isthmian Games and innumerable times in small competitions. In the 67th Olympiad (512 BC), in his seventh attempt for the championship, he lost to a younger athlete, Timasitheus. There are many accounts of his achievements. 80

Leonidas of Rhodes

Leonidas of Rhodes was one of the most famous runners in Antiquity. His was a unique achievement, even by today's standards. For 85 four consecutive Olympiads (164–152 BC), he won three races – the stade race, the diaulos race and the armour race. He won a total of 12 Olympic victory wreaths. He was acclaimed as a hero by his compatriots. 90

Melankomas of Caria

Melankomas of Caria was crowned Olympic boxing champion in 49 BC and was a winner in many other events. He went down in history for the way in which he fought. His movements 95 were light, simple and fascinating. He would defeat his opponents without ever being hit himself or ever dealing a blow. He was reputed to fight for two days holding his arms out without ever lowering them. He attained his 100 excellent competitive form through continuous and strenuous exercise.

Kyniska of Sparta

Kyniska, daughter of King Archidamos of Sparta, was the first woman to be listed as an 105 Olympic victor in Antiquity. Her chariot won in the four-horse chariot race in the 96th and 97th Olympiads (396 BC and 392 BC respectively). In the Olympic Games, it was forbidden for women to be present and Kyniska 110 broke with tradition, since, in the equestrian events, the victory wreath or *kotinos*, was won by the owner, not the rider, of the horse.

From www.olympic.org

Writing

Using the information about participants in the early Olympic Games, write an informative article for a sports magazine on sportsmen and women in Antiquity. Include:

a. the participants and their sports

b. why they became famous

c. interesting details about their lives.

Write between 250 and 350 words.

Read two passages about Madame Tussaud's wax models and do either the Core or the Extended questions that follow each passage.

What makes Madame Tussauds' wax work?

It's been pulling in visitors since 1835, but why does Madame Tussauds remain so popular, even in the CGI [Common Gateway Interface] age? Patrick Barkham joined the crowds – plus Brad, Jacko, the Queen and all – to find out. 5

Johnny Depp is getting a peck on the cheek. A Kuwait scarf is draped around Bollywood star Aishwarya Rai. "Where is Tony Blair?" asks a tourist from Afghanistan […]

In an era of virtual reality, interactive Wiis 10 and 3D TVs, it is difficult to imagine a more anachronistic attraction than a crowded, dark room peopled with static wax models. But Madame Tussauds is more popular than ever. After the venerable London attraction's 15 busiest ever year, next month sees the opening of a new Madame Tussauds in Blackpool. Another, the 12th Madame Tussauds in the world, will be added in Vienna. Almost every month, a new celebrity is added to the waxen 20 line-up. Gok Wan is set for Blackpool, while the much-requested Justin Bieber will arrive in London, New York and Amsterdam next month. Tussauds' owners, Merlin Entertainments, is the world's second largest 25 leisure group after Disney […] Last year it reported visitor numbers up by 10% across its attractions with a 16% jump in profits to £239m.

Born in Strasbourg in 1761, Marie Tussaud 30 studied model-making under Dr Philippe Curtius, a doctor who became highly skilled at making anatomical models from wax. They moved to Paris and she created figures for a waxwork exhibition, narrowly escaped the 35 guillotine in the French Revolution and ended up making face masks of guillotine victims. Tussaud inherited Curtius's models and her travelling exhibition of waxworks became the touring newspaper of the day, providing vivid 40 impressions of contemporary events, particularly the revolution, in a time before photographs. When she settled in Britain and opened a museum in Baker Street in 1835, her most popular exhibit was the "chamber of 45 horrors" featuring murderers and criminals. This tradition of what academics call "dark tourism" endures today. […]

"Madame Tussaud believed she provided entertainment, artistic enlightenment, 50 historical education and a place of pilgrimage," writes Pamela Pilbeam, author of *Madame Tussaud and the History of Waxworks*. This presentation of news as entertainment continued under Tussaud's sons and grandsons, 55 who placed famous figures in dramatic historical dioramas. But Tussauds (which has

now dropped the apostrophe) never quite enjoyed the credibility of a museum and tended to be sneered at by historians. […] Pilbeam has argued that Tussauds presents an "intimately corporeal biographical history". Academics may mock, but "for most people history is biography and the story of famous people and Tussaud's always excelled in portraying them". 60 65

Perhaps there is only so much CGI and 3D TV you can take, because the youth of today seem weirdly bewitched by these figures, which still really are fashioned from wax. Each model is painstakingly crafted using modelling techniques 70 pioneered by Marie Tussaud and featuring chicken wire, newspapers and clay. The figures take four months to make and typically cost £150,000. The hair, for instance, is not a wig: each strand of real hair is individually inserted 75 into the artificial scalp.

The ubiquity of Madame Tussauds, found everywhere from Bangkok to Berlin, may reflect the globalisation of Hollywood but each city gets the waxworks it deserves. Washington DC is 80 the only Tussauds to feature a gallery of all 44 US presidents […] Madame Tussauds in London is the nearest thing to a British Walk of Fame. Unlike Hollywood's, however, here a star can disappear. The comings and goings of 85 celebrity waxworks deliciously mirror the fickle wax and wane of fame. […] Now there are 12 Tussauds around the world, many models are sent on tour: a pop star may be down the dumper in Britain but still big in Berlin. 90

The success of Madame Tussauds across three centuries is part of a long tradition of the tourism of replicas, simulations and spectacle. Its more recent blossoming may reflect a society increasingly obsessed with celebrity but 95 it is also because, as its visitors soon realise, the division between static wax and interactive virtual reality is a false one. The exhibition has moved with the times, introducing Bollywood stars, who are a big draw and interactive 100

exhibits. Most crucially, it has ripped away the ropes and the "do not touch" strictures. Tussauds has always been 3D and its waxworks are now thoroughly, irreverently interactive.

Ann Wootton from Walsall admits her 105 grandchildren wondered what she was on about when she suggested a visit to the waxworks. Now they are enthralled. "I'm absolutely amazed how you can have photos and touch the models, which you couldn't do in previous years," says 110 Wootton. "It's lovely." […]

By Patrick Barkham, *The Guardian* (26 February 2011)

Diorama (n.): a three-dimensional miniature scene using models and a painted background.

Reading – Core

1. a. In your own words, explain how Madame Tussaud first began making models out of wax. Read just lines 1–57.

    b. Describe how waxwork models are made nowadays.

    c. Explain in your own words how Madame Tussaud's first wax figures became a "touring newspaper" (line 40).

    d. "Madame Tussaud believed she provided entertainment, artistic enlightenment, historical education and a place of pilgrimage" (lines 49–51).

        Using information from the article, explain how modern Tussauds' exhibitions provide:

        •   historical education   •   a place of pilgrimage.

    e. In what ways is Madame Tussauds an "anachronistic attraction" (line 12) for today?

2. You are one of Ann Wootton's grandchildren. Write a letter to your parents telling them about your visit to Madame Tussauds in London. Include:

    a. how the wax figures are displayed to the public

    b. why you enjoyed your visit.

    Write between 200 and 300 words.

Reading – Extended

1. You are going to London on a school trip. Write a letter to the Head of your school proposing a visit to the Madame Tussauds exhibition. Say why you think it will be entertaining and educational. Use the information on pages 192–3. Include:

    a. how the models are made and presented

    b. how Madame Tussauds has always been an exhibition of modern history and contemporary events.

    Write between 250 and 350 words.

2. a. Explain what the author means by "it is difficult to imagine a more anachronistic attraction" in lines 11–12.

    b. Explain how Madame Tussaud's exhibition was originally seen as a "touring newspaper" (line 40).

    c. In what ways does Madame Tussauds today offer "an intimately corporeal biographical history" (lines 61–2)?

    d. How does Madame Tussauds reflect the "globalisation of Hollywood" (line 79)?

    e. In your opinion, how and in what ways do the "comings and goings of celebrity waxworks deliciously mirror the fickle wax and wane of fame" (lines 85–7)?

Madame Tussauds

From France to Britain

The attraction's history is a rich and fascinating one, with roots dating back to the Paris of 1770. It was here that Madame Tussaud learnt to model wax likenesses under the tutelage of her mentor, Dr Philippe Curtius. At the age of 17, she became art tutor to King Louis XVI's sister at the Palace Of Versailles and then, during the French Revolution, was hastily forced to prove her allegiance to the feudalistic nobles by making the face masks of executed aristocrats. Madame Tussaud came to Britain in the early 19th century alongside a travelling exhibition of revolutionary relics and effigies of public heroes and rogues.

At a time when news was communicated largely by word of mouth, Madame Tussauds exhibition was a kind of travelling newspaper, providing insight into global events and bringing the ordinary public face-to-face with the people in the headlines. Priceless artefacts from the French Revolution and Napoleonic Wars brought to life vividly events in Europe which had a direct bearing on everyday lives. Figures of leading statesmen and, in the Chamber of Horrors, notorious villains put faces to the names on everyone's lips and captured the public imagination. In 1835, Madame Tussauds exhibition established a permanent base in London as the Baker Street Bazaar – visitors paid "sixpence" for the chance to meet the biggest names of the day. The attraction moved to its present site in Marylebone Road in 1884.

From www.madametussauds.com/London

Effigies (n.): models or sculptures of people.

Artefacts (n.): man-made objects.

Summary

Writing a summary – Core

1. Using information from the passage on page 192 only, make notes on how Madame Tussauds exhibition of wax works gained popularity in the 19th century and why it seems surprising that it is still popular today.

2. Summarise your notes on the history and continuing popularity of Madame Tussauds. Write between 100 and 150 words.

Summary

Writing a summary – Extended

1. Using information from the passage on pages 192–3, make notes on why people wanted to see Madame Tussauds first travelling exhibition and how the exhibition has reflected social history and stayed relevant to people's lives since then.

2. Summarise your notes on how Madame Tussaud's exhibitions reflect social history and their modern relevance in no more than 250 words.

CORONATION – MADAME TUSSAUD and SONS invite their Patrons to VIEW their NEW GROUP, got up in the first style of splendour in honour of the occasion, consisting of Likenesses (in full Coronation Dresses of British manufacture) of her Majesty in her Robes of State, the Duchess of Kent, Dukes of Sussex and Cambridge, Earls Grey, Melbourne, and Normandy, Lord Lyndhurst, and Martin Luther.

Bazaar, Baker Street. Open from Eleven till Dusk, and from Seven till Ten at Night.

Brilliantly Illuminated at Eight, Admittance: 1 shilling.

Famous places

A.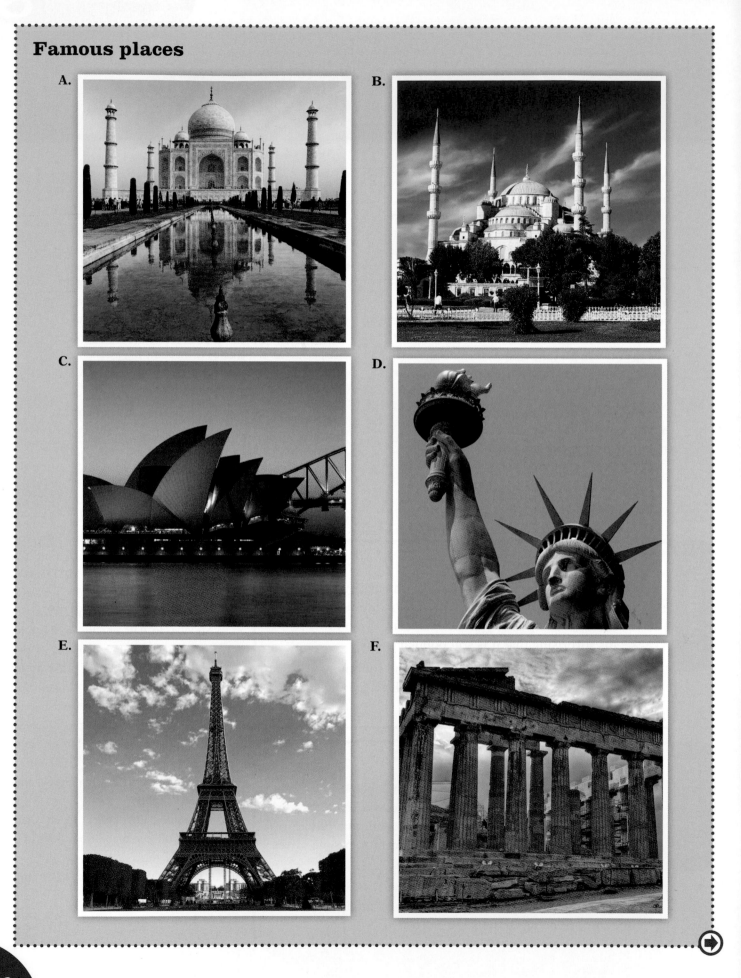

B.

C.

D.

E.

F.

G.

H.

I.

J.

1. Name these famous tourist attractions if you can.

2. How do you know about these places?

Speaking and listening

Discussing places

Working with a partner, choose one of the landmarks or buildings. Write brief notes on where it is located, when it was built and why it is famous.

When you have finished your notes, go around the classroom and find out about other sites. You need the following information for each place:

a. where it is

b. why it was built

c. why it is famous.

Biography

Be a coursework examiner

You are going to take the role of a coursework examiner and mark a short biography of Dr David Livingstone by a student (opposite).

1. Start by examining the content of the essay. It should include the following:

   - the name of the subject
   - their early life and family
   - their personality or temperament
   - their achievement/discovery/invention
   - when the person died
   - why this person is remembered
   - how this person's work benefited others.

2. Decide whether the content of the essay is presented in a meaningful order. Do the paragraphs lead to a clear conclusion?

3. Once you have examined the content of the essay, look at the student's writing style, vocabulary, spelling and grammar.

   Using a pencil, mark the essay, paying close attention to:

   - word choice (Does the student use a wide vocabulary?)
   - syntax (Have a variety of sentence structures been employed: simple, compound, complex?)
   - punctuation (Has the student used a range of punctuation accurately? Are *wh-* clauses preceded by commas?)
   - paragraphing (Are paragraphs indented? Do they each contain a topic sentence?).

"Dr Livingstone, I presume."

David Livingstone was born in Lanarkshire Scotland in 1813. His family was very poor and they all worked in a cotton mill. David Livingstone started at the cotton mill when he was ten years old. It was hard, boring work. He continued with his school lessons after his long working day. He was an avid reader and after reading many books about religion and philosophy he decided he could do good in the world by studying medicine. Working in the mill until he was 26 taught him endurance and persistence and helped him to empathise with people who had no choice in life but to live and work in the worst of conditions. Qualities that helped him in his travels in Africa. In 1836 he began studying medicine and theology on Glasgow and then joined the London Missionary Society. He wanted to go to China. But in 1841 he was posted to the edge of the Kalahari Desert in Africa instead. In 1822 Livingstone married Mary Moffatt. They had six children, but Livingstone rarely saw his family because he was travelling all the time. In the last year of her life his wife joined Livingstone on his travels but she died of malaria in 1862. This saddened him and he always regretted not seeing more of his children who had to grow up without him.

Dr Livingstone was appalled by the slave trade that still flourished in Africa. In 1856 he returned to England to publish his books, intending to show slavery was cruel and immoral. The British had stopped their involvement in slavery, but an illegal trade continued and America was still importing slave labour for her plantations.

"Missionary Travels in South Africa" was published in 1857. It caused a sensation, forcing British readers to examine their ideas about the African continent. Up until then, central Africa was thought to be a dry, mountainous region. Livingstone's book demonstrated it was in fact fertile grassland supporting a very wide range of animal life. Readers learned for the first time about great rivers such as the Zambesi and the people living in different regions, who like any native group in the world, were sometimes suspicious, but could be welcoming to outsiders.

Livingstone had a remarkable life but Livingstone wrote about his travels modestly without exaggeration. He walked from Cape Town, South Africa through the Kalahari Desert to the coastal town of Loanda which is now called Luanda in Angola then followed the Zambesi to the east coast of Mozambique, accompanied only by members of the Makololo tribe, with whom he was friends. He met a wide variety of people during his travels, including nomadic Bushmen and Bakalahari herdsmen and describes people, scenery and animal life accurately without romanticizing them. Livingstone died in Chitambo, Zambia in 1873. His body was returned to England and he was buried in Westminster Abbey. Unfortunately, the books Livingstone wrote about his travels with the intention of enlightening the British about real life in Africa encouraged people to go to Africa to exploit its natural resources.

The famous words, "Dr Livingstone, I presume" were spoken by Henry Morton Stanley, a young, ambitious American journalist. Stanley set out to find Dr Livingstone for the New York Herald newspaper. Other expeditions had already been sent to Africa to find Dr Livingstone for the same reason – to either find Livingstone alive or find evidence of his death. Stanley picked up Livingstone's trail at Lake Tanganyika and the two men finally met on 10th November 1871 in Ujiji present-day Tanzania. According to the story, Stanley's first words on approaching the only other white man in this part of Africa, was, "Dr. Livingstone, I presume?"

From very humble beginnings Dr David Livingstone became world famous.

(624 words)

Writing a biography

Write a very short biography of a person whose travels, achievements and/or discoveries changed people's lives.

Include the following information:

- place of birth and family
- education
- profession
- how and why this person became famous
- how people have benefited from this person's discovery, achievement or invention.

Write between 500 and 800 words.

Speaking and listening

A balloon debate

Five students take the roles of different famous people. (The rest of the class is the audience.)

These five famous people are in a hot air balloon. The balloon is losing height. Each famous person has a chance to argue why he/she should be saved.

One by one, in four rounds, the audience votes on who they think should jump out. After each vote, the remaining passengers in the balloon get another chance to argue for their survival until only the most valuable person to humanity remains in the balloon.

The student who is saved wins!

Here is a list of potential passengers; you may choose anyone else you think is important enough to save!

- Albert Einstein
- Marie Curie
- Abraham Lincoln
- William Shakespeare
- Mozart
- One of the Beatles
- J.K. Rowling
- Stephen Spielberg
- Ronaldiño

Making a presentation

Knowing how to make an effective presentation is a very useful skill. You may be asked to give a presentation in any of your school subjects and there will be occasions when you are required to give a presentation in your future studies and employment. Read these guidelines on how to present yourself and influence an audience. Then do the activity below.

Speaking skills
Giving a presentation and influencing an audience

- Look smart and tidy. Everyone judges by appearances (even if they say they don't!).

- Smile and try to look relaxed (even if you aren't!).

- Greet your audience politely and smile at them. (They should instinctively smile back – a positive response before you even begin.)

- Speak clearly and confidently. (This makes it sound as though you know exactly what you are talking about.) Find a spot at the back of the room, just above people's heads and start by addressing that spot to be sure that everyone can hear you.

- Pause between significant points to let the audience think about what you are saying.

- If you see that people are distracted (or nodding off), stop and ask them if they can hear you.

- Vary the pace and pitch of your voice. Never speak in a monotone or talk to your feet.

- Don't be afraid to use silence; only nervous speakers gabble. Silence, used wisely, can be very influential.

- Make eye contact with your audience and try to actively involve them in what you are saying.

If you are using rhetorical questions or asking direct questions, look at different people around you, not just at the person in front of you.

- Take off your watch before you start and put it somewhere you can see it (without it looking as if you can't wait to get to the end of your presentation!).

- Relax and enjoy what you are doing.

- Remember this one point – you know more about your subject than your audience!

- And finally, if you do make a mistake, remember that research at Cornell University in the USA has found that people who feel embarrassed are convinced their mistakes are far more noticeable than they really are. Apparently, almost everyone focuses on their own behaviour more than other people's. In this way we tend to overestimate the impact of a silly mistake. It's called the "spotlight effect".

If you do make a mistake (and everyone does at some time), don't apologise too much, just acknowledge the error, correct it if necessary and carry on.

Speaking and listening

Prepare a 3–5 minute presentation to say why a person or place that is not famous deserves to be better known. Choose one of the following topics:

a. an unsung hero

b. a wonderful place.

Autobiography

As we have seen already in this book, authors and poets try to create pictures in words so readers can visualise the scene, people or events they are writing about. To do this, creative writers use imagery that involves the five senses to give a vivid sense of what is happening on the page. But does this apply to all writing?

Read the following passage from David Livingstone's autobiographical account of his travels in Africa and decide what tone he is using in his description of this exciting but frightening event.

A FIGHT WITH A LION

The Bakatla of the village of Mabotsa were much troubled by lions, which leaped into the cattle-pens by night and destroyed their cows. They even attacked the herds in open day. This was so unusual an occurrence that the people believed that they were bewitched – "given," as they said, "into the power of the lions by a neighbouring tribe". They went once to attack the animals, but, being rather a cowardly people compared to Bechuanas in general on such occasions, they returned without killing any.

5

10

It is well known that if one in a troop of lions is killed the others take the hint and leave that part of the country. So the next time the herds were attacked, I went with the people, in order to encourage them to rid themselves of the annoyance by destroying one of the marauders. We found the lions on a small hill about a quarter of a mile in length and covered with trees.

15

A circle of men was formed round it and they gradually closed up, ascending pretty near to each other. Being down below on the plain with a native schoolmaster, named Mebalwe, a most excellent man, I saw one of the lions sitting on a piece of rock within the now closed circle of men. Mebalwe fired at him before I could and the ball struck the rock on which the animal was sitting. He bit at the spot struck, as a dog does at a stick or stone thrown at him; then leaping away, broke through the opening circle and escaped unhurt. The men were afraid to attack him, perhaps on account of their belief in witchcraft.

20

25

30

When the circle was re-formed, we saw two other lions in it; but we were afraid to fire lest we should strike the men and they allowed the beasts to burst through also. If the Bakatla had acted according to the custom of the country, they would have speared

35

202

The writer's craft – descriptive writing

In this incident the writer sets his description of an event into a story frame with a beginning, a middle and an end.

How would you describe the tone of Livingstone's "story": exciting or matter-of-fact?

Find two examples to justify your opinion.

the lions in their attempt to get out. Seeing we could not get them to kill one of the lions, we bent our footsteps towards the village; in going round 40 the end of the hill, however, I saw one of the beasts sitting on a piece of rock as before, but this time he had a little bush in front. Being about thirty yards off, I took a good aim at his body through the bush, and fired both barrels into it. The men then called 45 out, "He is shot, he is shot!" Others cried, "He has been shot by another man too; let us go to him!" I did not see anyone else shoot at him, but I saw the lion's tail erected in anger behind the bush and, turning to the people, said, "Stop a little till I load 50 again." When in the act of ramming down the bullets I heard a shout. Starting and looking half round, I saw the lion just in the act of springing upon me. I was upon a little height; he caught my shoulder as he sprang and we both came to the 55 ground together. Growling horribly close to my ear, he shook me as a terrier dog does a rat. The shock produced a stupor similar to that which seems to be felt by a mouse after the first shake of the cat. It caused a sort of dreaminess, in which there was no 60 sense of pain, nor feeling of terror, though quite conscious of all that was happening. It was like what patients partially under the influence of chloroform describe, who see all the operation, but feel not the knife. This singular condition was not 65

the result of any mental process. The shake annihilated fear and allowed no sense of horror in looking round at the beast. This peculiar state is probably produced in all animals killed by the carnivore; and if so, is a merciful provision by our 70 benevolent Creator for lessening the pain of death.

Turning round to relieve myself of the weight, as he had one paw on the back of my head, I saw his eyes directed to Mebalwe, who was trying to shoot him at a distance of ten or fifteen yards. His gun, a 75 flint one, missed fire in both barrels; the lion immediately left me and, attacking Mebalwe, bit his thigh. Another man, whose life I had saved before, after he had been tossed by a buffalo, attempted to spear the lion while he was biting 80 Mebalwe. He left Mebalwe and caught this man by the shoulder, but at that moment the bullets he had received took effect and he fell down dead. The whole was the work of a few moments and must have been his paroxysm of dying rage. In order to 85 take out the charm from him, the Bakatla on the following day made a huge bonfire over the carcase, which was declared to be that of the largest lion they had ever seen.

From *Missionary Travels in South Africa*, by Dr David Livingstone

Fiction

The passage below is from *The Earthsea Trilogy* by Ursula Le Guin, first published in the 1960s. The trilogy tells the story of Ged, a young magician who goes on to become the great Archmage Sparrowhawk and rides the mighty dragon Kalessin back from the dead. In this passage from the first part of the story, when he is still very young, Ged is in a small boat being attacked by dragons.

The Dragon of Pendor

Two dragons like the first rose up from the base of the highest tower. Even as the first one they came driving straight at Ged and even so he caught both, hurled both down and drowned them; and he had not yet lifted up   5
his wizard's staff.

Now after a little time there came three against him from the island. One of those was much greater and fire spewed curling from its jaws. Two came flying at him rattling their   10
wings, but the big one came circling from behind, very swift, to burn him and his boat with its breath of fire. No binding spell would catch all three, because two came from north and one from south. In the instant that he saw   15
this, Ged worked a spell of Changing and between one breath and the next flew up from his boat in dragon-form.

Spreading broad wings and reaching talons out, he met the two head on, withering them   20
with fire and then turned to the third, who was larger than he and armed also with fire. On the wind over the grey waves they doubled, snapped, swooped, lunged, till smoke roiled about them red-lit by the glare of their fiery   25
mouths. Ged flew suddenly upward and the other pursued, below him. In midflight the dragon-Ged raised wings, stopped and stooped as the hawk stoops, talons outstretched downwards, striking and bearing the other   30
down by neck and flank. The black wings flurried and black dragon-blood dropped in thick drops into the sea. The Pendor dragon tore free and flew low and lamely to the island, where it hid, crawling into some well or cavern   35
in the ruined town.

At once Ged took his form and place again on the boat, for it was most perilous to keep that dragon-shape longer than need demanded. His hands were black with the scalding 40 wormblood and he was scorched about the head with fire, but this was no matter now. He waited only till he had his breath back and then called, "Six I have seen, five slain, nine are told of: come out, worms!" 45

No creature moved nor voice spoke for a long while on the island, but only the waves beat loudly on the shore. Then Ged was aware that the highest tower slowly changed its shape, bulging out on one side as if it grew an 50 arm. He feared dragon-magic, for old dragons are very powerful and guileful in a sorcery like and unlike the sorcery of men: but a moment more and he saw this was no trick of the dragon, but of his own eyes. What he had taken 55 for a part of the tower was the shoulder of the Dragon Pendor as he uncurled his bulk and lifted himself slowly up.

From *The Earthsea Trilogy*,
by Ursula Le Guin (1968)

The writer's craft – description in fiction

1. Explain how the tone of Ursula Le Guin's description of being attacked by dragons differs from Livingstone's description (on pages 202–3) of being attacked by a lion. Use examples to justify your views.

2. In fantasy fiction the author has to describe what nobody has ever seen.

   Using information in the first three paragraphs of "The Dragon of Pendor", describe in your own words how you see:

   - the setting (where Ged is)

   - the dragons.

3. Ursula Le Guin has created a battle in the air. Find five verbs that help to create the sense of action and danger.

4. Find two different ways that Ursula Le Guin uses sound or the absence of sound (aural imagery).

5. When and why does Ursula Le Guin use the sense of touch (tactile imagery)?

Writing description

Write between 350 and 450 words on one of the following.

- Descriptive writing in a fictional narrative

  Write an episode from a novel or short story in which the main character faces a dangerous and powerful enemy.

  Start like this: *A minute went by and then another* …

- Descriptive writing for literary non-fiction

  Write a description of a landmark, a house or a park for a book on places to visit in your country. Use interesting and varied imagery and say why the place is worth visiting.

Auld Lang Syne

At the stroke of midnight on New Year's Eve, thousands and thousands of people around the world sing *Auld Lang Syne*, an old Scottish song. Most people know that the words are about friendship and parting, but how many really understand what the words mean?

Talking points

- Do you think the song "Auld Lang Syne" is too old-fashioned for the modern world?

- Should we create a better version or a different song for New Year's Eve?

Auld Lang Syne

By Robert Burns (1788)

Should auld acquaintance be forgot,
And never brought to mind?
Should auld acquaintance be forgot,
And auld lang syne!

Chorus: 5
For auld lang syne, my dear,
For auld lang syne.
We'll tak a cup o' kindness yet,
For auld lang syne.

We twa hae run about the braes   10
And pu'd the gowans fine;
But we've wander'd mony a weary foot
Sin auld lang syne.

Chorus

We twa hae paidl'd i' the burn,   15
Frae mornin' sun till dine;
But seas between us braid hae roar'd
Sin auld lang syne.

1. Working with a partner, write the first verse and a chorus for a new New Year's Eve song.

2. Read your verse and chorus to the class and elect a new song for your next New Year's Eve.

Robert Burns

Robert Burns was born in Ayrshire, Scotland during the terrible winter storms of 1759. His father was a hardworking tenant farmer, who came from a very poor family and was determined to provide a better home and education for his family in the hope they would escape the poverty cycle.

Despite being a delicate child, Robert Burns was a clever student with a temperament that matched the weather he was born in. His mother, who worked all day in the farmhouse and dairy, sang traditional ballads to lighten the drudgery of her days. In the evenings, she told stories while she patched her children's clothes. Robbie and his younger brothers and sisters grew up accustomed to words and song from their earliest days.

Like all children of farming families, Robbie Burns and his brother Gilbert worked alongside their father on their rented land from an early age. After his father died in 1784, however, it became evident Robbie would never make a living out of the soil; his passion was for words – stories, poems and songs – and anything that would charm a lass. Robbie always had an eye for the girls.

Robert Burns' first volume of poetry, *Poems Chiefly in Scottish Dialect*, was published in 1786: it brought him immediate fame. A second edition was published in 1787. Burns died from heart disease at the age

of 37. More than 10,000 people attended the funeral of the man known in Scotland as the "Heaven-taught ploughman".

> Man's inhumanity to man, Makes countless thousands mourn!

Robert Burns (1759–96)

The writer's craft

Read the article "Should auld acquaintance (and sources) be forgot" on the next two pages. Then, using your own words as far as possible, suggest alternative ways to say the following within the context of the article.

1. "one song ushered in 2012" (line 5).

2. "many people do not understand all the words, but that has done nothing to diminish the song's appeal" (lines 7–9).

3. "a global anthem of remembrance and fraternity" (lines 11–12).

4. "It has travelled and embedded itself in cultures across the globe" (lines 18–19).

5. "It's a malleable song" (line 20).

6. "On that point, there is consensus" (line 24).

7. "Like its lyrics, the tune of *Auld Lang Syne* has a convoluted history" (lines 47–8).

8. "Burns became very popular and very collectable in New York high society" (lines 59–61).

9. "American industrialists were into Burns because they saw him as a self-made man" (lines 68–70).

10. "*Auld Lang Syne*" (line 74).

Washington Post

SHOULD AULD ACQUAINTANCE (AND SOURCES) BE FORGOT

We might know the words to this popular New Year's Eve anthem but do we know their origin, asks Claire Prentice.

AS THE clock struck midnight on New Year's Eve, one song ushered in 2012 in time zones around the world: Robert Burns' *Auld Lang Syne*. Even in Burns' native Scotland, many people do not understand all the words, but that has done nothing to diminish the song's appeal.

Although it is most often associated with the new year, *Auld Lang Syne* is a global anthem of remembrance and fraternity. Type the title into YouTube and more than 32,000 versions come up, sung by everyone from Aretha Franklin to Alvin and the Chipmunks. The song is sung throughout the English-speaking world and has been translated into more than 40 languages.

"It has travelled and embedded itself in cultures across the globe," says Burns biographer, Robert Crawford. "It's a malleable song; it's quite unspecific about the nature of friendship, so it lends itself to many different occasions."

Its title translates as "old long since", "for old time's sake". On that point, there is consensus. But more than two centuries after Burns' death, opinion is divided on the source of the song. The poet and author denied *Auld Lang Syne* was his. Rather, he said: "I took it down from an old man."

Burns was deeply connected with rural life. He travelled the country, collecting traditional songs for posterity. He also enjoyed remaking the songs or "mending" them, as he called it. "Burns denied he wrote it because he didn't," says literary historian Murray Pittock. "He edited it, though how much we don't know."

Most experts think *Auld Lang Syne* was created by Burns in 1788 using a variety of source materials. These could date as far back as the 16th century and include works by the Scottish poets Allan Ramsay, Robert Aytoun and James Watson. "It's impossible to say how many texts and tunes *Auld Lang Syne* is derived from," Professor Pittock says.

Describing the effect *Auld Lang Syne* had on him, Burns wrote in a letter to his friend Frances Dunlop in 1788 that it "thrilled thro' my soul".

Like its lyrics, the tune of *Auld Lang Syne* has a convoluted history. The version commonly sung today is not the tune Burns set it to but the suggestion of his publisher, George Thomson. 50

Gerard Carruthers, co-director of the Centre for Robert Burns Studies in Glasgow, says Burns would have approved of this mix-and-match approach – "Burns was not a purist."

Although the poet was a proud man of the 55 people, his popularity in North America owes a lot to New York's most privileged citizens, according to Dr Carruthers, who is researching the connection for a book. "Burns became very popular and very collectable in New York high 60 society in the 1880s through to the time of the Great Depression," he says. "You had these

dances and people gathering in Times Square to welcome in the new year that were attended by people like William Randolph Hearst and Henry 65 Ford. They were the people collecting Burns' manuscripts because they realised what a good investment they were. The American industrialists were into Burns because they saw him as a self-made man." 70

The full story of the most-performed song in the world after *Happy Birthday* may never be known, but one thing is certain: If Burns was alive today, the profits from *Auld Lang Syne* would have made him a billionaire many times over. 75

By Claire Prentice, *Washington Post*
(31 December 2011)

Nobel Prize for Literature

The writer's craft – formal English

Very official documents use a style of formal language that includes words and phrases not commonly used in everyday speech.

Read the information on Alfred Nobel's will and make a list of the words and phrases you are not familiar with.

a. Use a dictionary to find their meaning.

b. Then use a thesaurus to find a more commonly used synonym or a more colloquial way to say the same thing.

Alfred Nobel and the Nobel Prizes

On 27th November, 1895, the Swedish manufacturer Alfred Nobel signed his last will and testament in Paris. When it was opened and read after his death, the will caused a major controversy in his native Sweden: Nobel had left most of his vast wealth to establishing a prize! It took five years to resolve the issue. Eventually the first Nobel Prize was awarded in 1901. Here is an extract from Nobel's will. 5

Nobel's will

[…] The whole of my remaining realizable estate shall be dealt with in the following way: the capital, invested in safe securities 10 by my executors, shall constitute a fund, the interest on which shall be annually distributed in the form of prizes to those who, during the preceding year, shall have conferred the greatest benefit to mankind. The said interest shall be divided into five equal parts, which shall be apportioned as follows: one part to 15 the person who shall have made the most important discovery or invention within the field of physics; one part to the person who shall have made the most important chemical discovery or improvement; one part to the person who shall have made the most important discovery within the domain of physiology or 20 medicine; one part to the person who shall have produced in the field of literature the most outstanding work in an ideal direction; and one part to the person who shall have done the most or the best work for fraternity between nations, for the abolition or reduction of standing armies and for the holding and promotion 25 of peace congresses. The prizes for physics and chemistry shall be awarded by the Swedish Academy of Sciences; that for physiological or medical work by the Caroline Institute in Stockholm; that for literature by the Academy in Stockholm and that for champions of peace by a committee of five persons to be 30 elected by the Norwegian Storting. It is my express wish that in awarding the prizes no consideration whatever shall be given to the nationality of the candidates, but that the most worthy shall receive the prize, whether he be a Scandinavian or not.

From www.nobelprize.org

Opposite is a passage from the Swedish Academy's press release announcing the 1983 Nobel Prize for Literature.

The Nobel Prize in Literature 1983
William Golding

Swedish Academy *The Permanent Secretary*
Press Release October 1983

William Golding's first novel, *Lord of the Flies*, 1954,
rapidly became a world success and has so remained.
It has reached readers who can be numbered in tens
of millions. In other words, the book was a bestseller*,
in a way that is usually granted only to adventure   5
stories, light reading and children's books. The same
goes for several of his later novels, including *Rites of
Passage*, 1980.

[...] William Golding can be said to be a writer of
myths. It is the pattern of myth* that we find in his   10
manner of writing.

A very few basic experiences and basic conflicts of
a deeply general nature underlie all his work as motive
power*. In one of his essays he describes how, as a
young man, he took an optimistic view of existence.   15
He believed that man would be able to perfect himself
by improving society and eventually doing away
with all social evil. His optimism was akin to that of
other utopians*, for instance, H.G. Wells.

The Second World War changed his outlook. He   20
discovered what one human being is really able to do
to another. And it was not a question of head-hunters* in
New Guinea or primitive tribes in the Amazon region.
They were atrocities committed with cold professional
skill by well-educated and cultured people – doctors,   25
lawyers and those with a long tradition of high
civilization behind them. They carried out their
crimes against their own equals. He writes:

"I must say that anyone who moved through those
years without understanding that man produces   30
evil as a bee produces honey, must have been blind
or wrong in the head."

Golding inveighs against* those who think that it is the
political or other systems that create evil. Evil springs
from the depths of man himself – it is the wickedness   35
in human beings that creates the evil systems or, that
changes what, from the beginning, is, or could be,
good into something iniquitous* and destructive. [...]

In *Lord of the Flies*, a group of young boys are isolated
on a desert island. Soon a kind of primitive society   40
takes shape and is split into warring factions, one
marked by decency and willingness to cooperate, the
other by worship of force, lust for power and violence.

From www.nobelprize.org

Unlike many other bestsellers of its time, this
novel contains serious themes and more literary
language. Golding uses "the pattern of myth" (line
10) for plot and to talk about human behaviour.
Many myths contain similar themes to those in the
novel. In *Lord of the Flies* the boys are in danger
but *they* also create danger. The "motive power"
(line 13) is a power motive: one boy's desire for
control and other boys' desire to be on the winning
side. The novel uses a typical plot from Victorian
adventure stories – young British boys escape
from dangerous tribes in remote locations. But
here the boys themselves become the iniquitous
(unjust) tribe. Golding shows how "the wickedness
in human beings" (line 35) causes evil - even small
boys are capable of cruelty.

utopians: (line 19) Utopians are idealists who
believe it is possible to reform society and live in
constant harmony.

inveighs against: (line 33) verbally attacks or
protests.

Lord of the Flies

William Golding's famous novel *Lord of the Flies* was written five years after the Second World War. In the story, a plane carrying British schoolboys has crashed on a tropical island. Survivor 12-year-old Ralph meets a plump boy wearing spectacles called Piggy and together they find a large conch shell. Ralph blows the conch like a trumpet and numerous small boys emerge from amongst the island's rich vegetation. A school choir, led by Jack Merridew, comes along the beach to join them. The boys soon realise they need some sort of order, so it is decided that holding the conch will be like "hands up" at school. Whoever holds the conch has the right to speak uninterrupted.

Read three passages taken from the beginning, middle and end of Golding's novel and do the activities that follow each passage. The first passage is from the first chapter: the boys are having a meeting. Look at the way each boy speaks. Their use of English is typical of post-war England. Each boy's vocabulary and grammar reflects his background and upbringing.

The Sound of the Shell

Ralph lifted the conch again and his good humour came back as he thought of what he had to say next.

"Now we come to the most important thing. I've been thinking. I was thinking while we were climbing the mountain." He flashed a conspiratorial grin at the other two. "And on the beach just now. This is what I thought. We want to have fun. And we want to be rescued." 5

The passionate noise of agreement from the assembly hit him like a wave and he lost his thread. He thought again. 10

"We want to be rescued; and of course we shall be rescued."

Voices babbled. The simple statement, unbacked by any proof but the weight of Ralph's new authority, brought light and happiness. He had to wave the conch before he could make them hear him. 15

"My father's in the Navy. He said there aren't any unknown islands left. He says the Queen has a big room full of maps and all the islands in the world are drawn there. So the Queen's got a picture of this island." 20

Again came the sounds of cheerfulness and better heart.

"And sooner or later a ship will put in here. It might even be Daddy's ship. So you see, sooner or later, we shall be rescued." 25

He paused, with the point made. The assembly was lifted toward safety by his words. They liked and now respected him. Spontaneously they began to clap and presently the platform was loud with applause. Ralph flushed, looking sideways at Piggy's open admiration and then the other way at Jack who was smirking and showing that he too knew how to clap. 30 35

Ralph waved the conch.

The writer's craft

Look at how Golding shows the reader something of the personality or temperament of the main characters in this passage through what they say.

Find an example for each of the following characters. Quote what that character says and explain what this shows the reader.

a. Ralph   **b.** Piggy   **c.** Jack

REMINDER – irony

Irony is created when there is a difference between what is said and what is meant; what is said and what is done; what is expected or intended and what happens.

Irony is not the same as sarcasm; sarcasm is designed to hurt, ridicule or belittle.

REMINDER – writing dialogue

When you write dialogue in a narrative, you must start a new line for each person speaking.

Indent each first line of dialogue like a paragraph.

"Shut up! Wait! Listen!"

He went on in the silence, borne on his triumph.

"There's another thing. We can help them to find us. If a ship comes near the island they may not 40 notice us. So we must make smoke on top of the mountain. We must make a fire."

"A fire! Make a fire!"

At once half the boys were on their feet. Jack clamoured among them, the conch forgotten. 45

"Come on! Follow me!"

The space under the palm trees was full of noise and movement. Ralph was on his feet too, shouting for quiet, but no one heard him. All at once the crowd swayed toward the island and was gone – 50 following Jack. Even the tiny children went and did their best among the leaves and broken branches. Ralph was left, holding the conch, with no one but Piggy.

Piggy's breathing was quite restored. 55

"Like kids!" he said scornfully. "Acting like a crowd of kids!"

Ralph looked at him doubtfully and laid the conch on the tree trunk.

"I bet it's gone tea-time," said Piggy. "What do 60 they think they're going to do on that mountain?"

He caressed the shell respectfully, then stopped and looked up.

"Ralph! Hey! Where you going?"

Ralph was already clambering over the first 65 smashed swathes of the scar. A long way ahead of him was crashing and laughter.

Piggy watched him in disgust.

"Like a crowd of kids –"

He sighed, bent and laced up his shoes. The 70 noise of the errant assembly faded up the mountain. Then, with the martyred expression of a parent who has to keep up with the senseless ebullience of the children, he picked up the conch, turned toward the forest, and began to pick his way 75 over the tumbled scar.

From *Lord of the Flies*, by William Golding

213

As you read the following passage, look at the ways Jack is challenging Ralph's leadership. A small boy is talking about a monster – "a beastie, a snake-thing". Ralph tries to calm him by saying such a thing couldn't exist on their island; then loses his patience, stating, "there isn't a beastie!" Nevertheless the younger boy is very afraid and his fear is contagious. The older boys eventually decide to find out what it is this boy thinks he has seen. Now do the activities opposite.

Gift for the darkness

Piggy looked up miserably from the dawn-pale beach to the dark mountain.

"Are you sure? Really sure, I mean?"

I told you a dozen times now," said Ralph, "we saw it." 5

"D'you think we're safe down here?"

"How [...] should I know?"

Ralph jerked away from him and walked a few paces along the beach. Jack was kneeling and drawing a circular pattern in the sand with his 10 forefinger. Piggy's voice came to them, hushed.

"Are you sure? Really?"

"Go up and see," said Jack contemptuously, "and good riddance."

"No fear." 15

"The beast had teeth," said Ralph, "and big black eyes."

He shuddered violently. Piggy took off his one round of glass and polished the surface.

"What we going to do?" 20

Ralph turned toward the platform. The conch glimmered among the trees, a white blob against the place where the sun would rise. He pushed back his mop.

"I don't know." 25

He remembered the panic flight down the mountainside. "I don't think we'd ever fight a thing that size, honestly, you know. We'd talk but we wouldn't fight a tiger. We'd hide. Even Jack 'ud hide." 30

Jack still looked at the sand.

"What about my hunters?"

Simon came stealing out of the shadows by the shelters. Ralph ignored Jack's question. He pointed to the touch of yellow above the sea. 35

"As long as there's light we're brave enough. But then? And now that thing squats by the fire as though it didn't want us to be rescued–"

He was twisting his hands now, unconsciously. His voice rose. 40

"So we can't have a signal fire ... We're beaten."

A point of gold appeared above the sea and at once all the sky lightened.

"What about my hunters?"

"Boys armed with sticks." 45

Jack got to his feet. His face was red as he marched away. Piggy put on his one glass and looked at Ralph.

"Now you done it. You been rude about his hunters." 50

"Oh shut up!"

The sound of the inexpertly blown conch interrupted them. As though he were serenading the rising sun, Jack went on blowing till the shelters were astir and the hunters crept 55 to the platform and the littluns whimpered as now they so frequently did. Ralph rose obediently and Piggy and they went to the platform.

"Talk," said Ralph bitterly, "talk, talk, talk." 60

He took the conch from Jack.

"This meeting–"

Jack interrupted him.

"I called it."

"If you hadn't called it I should have. You just 65 blew the conch."

"Well, isn't that calling it?"

"Oh, take it! Go on – talk!"

Ralph thrust the conch into Jack's arms and sat down on the trunk. 70

"I've called an assembly," said Jack, "because of a lot of things. First, you know now, we've seen the beast. We crawled up. We were only a few feet away. The beast sat up and looked at us. I don't know what it does. We don't even know what it is–" 75

"The beast comes out of the sea–"

"Out of the dark–"

"Trees–"

"Quiet!" shouted Jack. "You, listen. The beast is sitting up there, whatever it is–" 80

"Perhaps it's waiting–"

"Hunting–"

"Yes, hunting."

"Hunting," said Jack. He remembered his age-old tremors in the forest. "Yes. The beast is a 85

hunter. Only – shut up! The next thing is that we couldn't kill it. And the next is that Ralph said my hunters are no good."

"I never said that!"

"I've got the conch. Ralph thinks you're cowards, 90 running away from the boar and the beast. And that's not all."

There was a kind of sigh on the platform as if everyone knew what was coming. Jack's voice went up, tremulous yet determined, pushing against the 95 unco-operative silence.

"He's like Piggy. He says things like Piggy. He isn't a proper chief."

From *Lord of the Flies*, by William Golding

The writer's craft

1. In this passage Golding uses ellipsis points and the dash to indicate unfinished sentences or words not spoken. What effect does this have on the dialogue?

2. Give an example of how Golding makes the dialogue sound natural.

3. What atmosphere or mood does Golding create in this passage through the use of dialogue?

4. Explain how Golding is developing his characters through dialogue. Give an example of something said by each of the following characters and what this tells you about that person and their relationship with the other boys:

   • Ralph

   • Jack

   • Piggy.

As a child, Golding would have read Victorian adventure novels and comics, many of which featured exciting, dangerous incidents involving "painted savages". He has used this image here, but in a particularly alarming manner because Jack's "tribe" of young boys has become savage in every way.

This passage comes towards the end of the novel. Jack has established his own "tribe" and they are living on a high promontory overlooking the sea known as Castle Rock. Jack has stolen what remains of Piggy's glasses.

Castle Rock

"Grab them!"

No one moved. Jack shouted angrily.

"I said 'grab them'!"

The painted group moved round Samneric nervously and unhandily. Once more the silvery laughter scattered. 5

Samneric protested out of the heart of civilisation.

"Oh, I say!"

"– honestly!" 10

Their spears were taken from them.

"Tie them up!"

Ralph cried out hopelessly against the black and green mask.

"Jack!" 15

"Go on. Tie them."

Now the painted group felt the otherness of Samneric, felt the power in their own hands. They felled the twins clumsily and excitedly. Jack was inspired. He knew that Ralph would attempt a 20 rescue. He struck in a humming circle behind him and Ralph only just parried the blow. Beyond them the tribe and the twins were a loud and writhing heap. Piggy crouched again. Then the twins lay, astonished, and the tribe stood round them. Jack 25 turned to Ralph and spoke between his teeth.

"See? They do what I want."

There was silence again. The twins lay, inexpertly tied up and the tribe watched Ralph to see what he would do. He numbered them through 30 his fringe, glimpsed the ineffectual smoke.

His temper broke. He screamed at Jack.

"You're a beast and a swine and a [...] thief!"

He charged. 35

Jack, knowing this was the crisis, charged too. They met with a jolt and bounced apart. Jack swung with his fist at Ralph and caught him on the ear. Ralph hit Jack in the stomach and made him grunt. Then they were facing each 40 other again, panting and furious, but unnerved by each other's ferocity. They became aware of the noise that was the background to this fight, the steady shrill cheering of the tribe behind them. 45

Piggy's voice penetrated to Ralph.

"Let me speak."

He was standing in the dust of the fight and as the tribe saw his intention the shrill cheer changed to a steady booing. 50

Piggy held up the conch and the booing sagged a little, then came up again to strength.

"I got the conch!"

He shouted.

"I tell you, I got the conch!" 55

Surprisingly, there was silence now; the tribe were curious to hear what amusing thing he might have to say.

Silence and pause; but in the silence a curious air-noise, close by Ralph's head. He gave it half his 60 attention – and there it was again; a faint "Zup!" Someone was throwing stones: Roger was dropping them, his one hand still on the lever. Below him, Ralph was a shock of hair and Piggy a bag of fat. 65

Ralph and Piggy are walking to Castle Rock to explain to Jack why it is so important to keep a beacon fire burning. They are accompanied by the twins Sam and Eric, who are known as Samneric. Roger is up on Castle Rock standing next to a huge boulder with a lever wedged under it. Jack and his tribe are returning from a successful hunt. Read the passage below and then do the activities on page 218.

"I got this to say. You're acting like a crowd of kids." The booing rose and died again as Piggy lifted the white, magic shell.

"Which is better – to be a pack of painted Indians like you are or to be sensible like Ralph is?" 70

A great clamour rose among the savages. Piggy shouted again.

"Which is better – to have rules and agree or to hunt and kill?" 75

Again the clamour and again – "Zup!"

Ralph shouted against the noise.

"Which is better, law and rescue or hunting and breaking things up?"

Now Jack was yelling too and Ralph could no 80 longer make himself heard. Jack had backed right against the tribe and they were a solid mass of menace that bristled with spears. The intention of a charge was forming among them; they were working up to it and the neck would be swept 85 clear. Ralph stood facing them, a little to one side, his spear ready. By him stood Piggy still holding out the talisman, the fragile, shining beauty of the shell. The storm of sound beat at them, an incantation of hatred. High overhead, Roger, with 90 a sense of delirious abandonment, leaned all his weight on the lever.

Ralph heard the great rock before he saw it. He was aware of a jolt in the earth that came to him through the soles of his feet and the breaking 95 sound of stones at the top of the cliff. Then the monstrous red thing bounded across the neck and he flung himself flat while the tribe shrieked.

The rock struck Piggy a glancing blow from chin to knee; the conch exploded into a thousand white 100 fragments and ceased to exist.

From *Lord of the Flies*, by William Golding

Reading – Core

1. Read the passage on pages 216–17.

   a. Give an example of how the author tells the reader the schoolboys are now "savages".

   b. How does the author establish Jack's power at the beginning of this passage?

   c. What is Piggy trying to do when he holds up the conch to speak?

   d. When Jack backs up against his tribe, it becomes a "solid mass of menace that bristled with spears" (lines 82–3). What does this suggest about Jack's tribe?

2. Imagine you were with Ralph, Piggy, Sam and Eric. You have now been rescued from the island. Write a short account of what happened on the day you all went to Castle Rock for your autobiography. Include:

   • what happened to the conch

   • your thoughts and feelings about Jack and his tribe.

Reading – Extended

1. You are Ralph. You have been rescued from the island. Write an account to explain what happened on the day you went to Castle Rock to reason with Jack. Include:

   • your thoughts and feelings about Piggy and what he was trying to do

   • your thoughts and feelings about Jack and his tribe.

2. a. Explain the effect Golding's words create in "a solid mass of menace that bristled with spears" in lines 82–3.

   b. Discuss how Golding juxtaposes the image of a spear with the conch. Talk about his description of the conch in lines 86–9: "Ralph stood facing them ... shining beauty of the shell".

Unit 8: Self-assessment

In this unit we have read:

• different types of information texts: news articles and a press release

• non-fiction, biography and autobiography

• fiction.

What do you remember about the speaking skills needed for:

• giving a presentation?

• leading a debate?

How do writers use show and tell techniques to convey information?

Make notes about Unit 8

Consider the work you have done in this unit. Then copy and complete the chart.

Two texts (fiction or non-fiction) I remember in Unit 8 are:
Two new skills I learned are:
Two things I'm not sure about are:
I enjoyed doing:
Something I would like to do again is:
I would like to do this again because:

Unit 8: Literature extension

Pride and Prejudice

The opening lines of *Pride and Prejudice* are famous. The novel was written by Jane Austen, a quiet, single woman, who lived in her father's rectory in rural England during the early years of the 19th century. The novel was published in 1813.

Look at how Jane Austen establishes Mr and Mrs Bennet's different characters through dialogue at the beginning of Chapter 1. Then do the reading activity that follows.

Chaise and four (n.): an open carriage pulled by four horses.

Michaelmas (n.): a festival at the end of September.

It is a truth universally acknowledged, that a single man in possession of a good fortune, must be in want of a wife.

However little known the feelings or views of such a man may be on his first entering a neighbourhood, this truth is so well fixed in the minds of the surrounding families, that he is considered as the rightful property of some one or other of their daughters.

"My dear Mr. Bennet," said his lady to him one day, "have you heard that Netherfield Park is let at last?" 10

Mr. Bennet replied that he had not.

"But it is," returned she; "for Mrs. Long has just been here and she told me all about it." 15

Mr. Bennet made no answer.

"Do you not want to know who has taken it?" cried his wife impatiently.

"YOU want to tell me and I have no objection to hearing it." 20

This was invitation enough.

"Why, my dear, you must know, Mrs. Long says that Netherfield is taken by a young man of large fortune from the north of England; that he came down on Monday in a chaise and four to see the 25 place and was so much delighted with it, that he agreed with Mr. Morris immediately; that he is to take possession before Michaelmas and some of

his servants are to be in the house by the end of next week." 30

"What is his name?"

"Bingley."

"Is he married or single?"

"Oh! Single, my dear, to be sure! A single man of large fortune; four or five thousand a year. 35 What a fine thing for our girls!"

"How so? How can it affect them?"

"My dear Mr. Bennet," replied his wife, "how can you be so tiresome! You must know that I am thinking of his marrying one of them." 40

"Is that his design in settling here?"

"Design! Nonsense, how can you talk so! But it is very likely that he *may* fall in love with one of them and therefore you must visit him as soon as he comes." 45

"I see no occasion for that. You and the girls may go or you may send them by themselves, which perhaps will be still better, for as you are as handsome as any of them, Mr. Bingley might like you the best of the party." 50

"My dear, you flatter me. I certainly *have* had my share of beauty, but I do not pretend to be anything extraordinary now. When a woman has five grown-up daughters, she ought to give over thinking of her own beauty." 55

"In such cases, a woman has not often much beauty to think of."

"But, my dear, you must indeed go and see Mr. Bingley when he comes into the neighbourhood."

"It is more than I engage for, I assure you." 60

"But consider your daughters. Only think what an establishment it would be for one of them. Sir William and Lady Lucas are determined to go, merely on that account, for in general, you know, they visit no newcomers. Indeed you must go, for it will 65 be impossible for us to visit him if you do not."

From *Pride and Prejudice*, by Jane Austen

Reading

Make brief notes on the following aspects of the opening of the novel:

a. your first impression of Mrs Bennet from what she says

b. your first impression of Mr Bennet from the way he responds to what his wife says.

The writer's craft – show and tell

The title of the novel refers to Mr Darcy's pride and Miss Elizabeth Bennet's prejudice. Discuss how Jane Austen uses description and dialogue in the passage from Chapter 3 opposite.

a. Explain how Austen uses the setting and description to establish how Mr Bingley and Mr Darcy differ.

b. Explain how Austen uses dialogue to establish Mr Darcy's character.

Now read part of Chapter 3 where Mrs Bennet's daughters meet Mr Bingley and his friend Mr Darcy for the first time at a ball.

Mr. Bingley was good-looking and gentlemanlike; he had a pleasant countenance and easy, unaffected manners. His sisters were fine women, with an air of decided fashion. His brother-in-law, Mr. Hurst, merely looked the gentleman; but his friend Mr. Darcy soon drew the attention of the room by his fine, tall person, handsome features, noble mien and the report which was in general circulation within five minutes after his entrance, of his having ten thousand a year. The gentlemen pronounced him to be a fine figure of a man, the ladies declared he was much handsomer than Mr. Bingley and he was looked at with great admiration for about half the evening, till his manners gave a disgust which turned the tide of his popularity; for he was discovered to be proud; to be above his company and above being pleased; and not all his large estate in Derbyshire could then save him from having a most forbidding, disagreeable countenance and being unworthy to be compared with his friend.

Mr. Bingley had soon made himself acquainted with all the principal people in the room; he was lively and unreserved, danced every dance, was angry that the ball closed so early and talked of giving one himself at Netherfield. Such amiable qualities must speak for themselves. What a contrast between him and his friend! Mr. Darcy danced only once with Mrs. Hurst and once with Miss Bingley, declined being introduced to any other lady and spent the rest of the evening in walking about the room, speaking occasionally to one of his own party. His character was decided. He was the proudest, most disagreeable man in the world and everybody hoped that he would never come there again. Amongst the most violent against him was Mrs. Bennet, whose dislike of his general behaviour was sharpened into particular resentment by his having slighted one of her daughters.

Elizabeth Bennet had been obliged, by the scarcity of gentlemen, to sit down for two dances; and during part of that time, Mr. Darcy had been standing near enough for her to hear a conversation between him and Mr. Bingley, who came from the dance for a few minutes, to press his friend to join it.

"Come, Darcy," said he, "I must have you dance. I hate to see you standing about by yourself in this stupid manner. You had much better dance."

"I certainly shall not. You know how I detest it, unless I am particularly acquainted with my partner. At such an assembly as this it would be insupportable. Your sisters are engaged and there is not another woman in the room whom it would not be a punishment to me to stand up with."

"I would not be so fastidious as you are," cried Mr. Bingley, "for a kingdom! Upon my honour, I never met with so many pleasant girls in my life as I have this evening; and there are several of them you see uncommonly pretty."

"*You* are dancing with the only handsome girl in the room," said Mr. Darcy, looking at the eldest Miss Bennet.

"Oh! She is the most beautiful creature I ever beheld! But there is one of her sisters sitting down just behind you, who is very pretty and I dare say very agreeable. Do let me ask my partner to introduce you."

"Which do you mean?" and turning round he looked for a moment at Elizabeth, till catching her eye, he withdrew his own and coldly said: "She is tolerable, but not handsome enough to tempt me; I am in no humour at present to give consequence to young ladies who are slighted by other men. You had better return to your partner and enjoy her smiles, for you are wasting your time with me."

Mr. Bingley followed his advice. Mr. Darcy walked off; and Elizabeth remained with no very cordial feelings toward him. She told the story, however, with great spirit among her friends; for she had a lively, playful disposition, which delighted in anything ridiculous.

From *Pride and Prejudice*, by Jane Austen

9 Endings

In this unit you will:

→ **Visit** Ancient Greece, England, Scotland, Turkey, the USA, unknown and fictional places

→ **Read** poetry, prose, drama and exam-style reading passages

→ **Write** to describe, entertain and answer summary questions.

Many cultures have myths that describe the end of the world. In Norse mythology, it is Ragnarok: a fearful time that will follow great wars, strife and hatred. There will be a period of bitter cold when a terrible, ferocious wolf devours the sun. Mountains will tumble, the earth will shake and the sea will rise up to engulf the land …

But it is also said this is *not* the end of the world. The Earth will rise again, more fertile, green and beautiful than before – cleansed and regenerated. And two people will walk this new land – a man and a woman.

What stories do you know about the end of the world? Do you take them seriously?

Read "Fire and Ice", a famous poem about the end of the world. What is the poet saying about the power of fire and ice?

Fire and Ice

Some say the world will end in fire,
Some say in ice.
From what I've tasted of desire
I hold with those who favor fire.
But if it had to perish twice,   5
I think I know enough of hate
To say that for destruction ice
Is also great
And would suffice.

By Robert Frost (1920)

The writer's craft – abstract nouns

1. Identify the abstract nouns in this poem.

2. In your own words, try to explain how the poet relates fire and ice to these abstract nouns.

Now read what a dramatist, a poet and a fiction author say about books and how to end them. Then discuss the Talking points.

MISS PRISM:
Do not speak slightingly of the three-volume novel, Cecily. I wrote one myself in earlier days.
CECILY:
Did you really, Miss Prism? How wonderfully clever you are! I hope it did not end happily? I don't like novels that end happily. They depress me so much.
MISS PRISM:
The good ended happily, and the bad unhappily. That is what Fiction means.

From *The Importance of Being Earnest*, by Oscar Wilde

… a beginning, a muddle, and an end.

A comment made on modern novels by the British poet, Philip Larkin (1922–85)

Reading a book is like re-writing it for yourself. You bring to a novel, anything you read, all your experience of the world. You bring your history and you read it in your own terms.

Angela Carter, British author (1940–92)

Talking points

1. Try to think of a novel that does not follow Larkin's definition of fiction.

2. Do you agree or disagree with Miss Prism's definition of what constitutes fiction?

3. To what extent do you agree with Angela Carter's claim that we all bring something different to the reading of a book?

4. How might two readers interpret the ending of a novel or short story differently?

Fiction (n.): 1. a product of the imagination. 2. an invented story. 3. a class of literature consisting of books containing such stories. (From Latin *fictio* = pretending)

A story about endings

Read this famous story by Ray Bradbury which was first published in the 1950s. Then do the activity that follows on page 227.

August 2026: There Will Come Soft Rains

In the living room the voice-clock sang, *Tick-tock, seven o'clock, time to get up, time to get up, seven o'clock!* As if it were afraid that nobody would. The morning house lay empty. The clock ticked on, repeating and repeating its sounds into the emptiness. *Seven-nine, breakfast time, seven-nine.*

In the kitchen the breakfast stove gave a [...] sigh and ejected from its warm interior eight pieces of perfectly browned toast, eight eggs sunny side up, [...] two coffees and two cool glasses of milk.

"*Today is August 4, 2026,*" said a second voice from the kitchen ceiling, "*in the city of Allendale, California.*" It repeated the date three times for memory's sake. "*Today is Mr. Featherstone's birthday. Today is the anniversary of Tilita's marriage. Insurance is payable, as are the water, gas, and light bills.*"

Somewhere in the walls, relays clicked, memory tapes glided under electric eyes.

Eight-one, tick-tock, eight-one o'clock, off to school, off to work, run, run, eight-one! But no doors slammed, no carpets took the soft tread of rubber heels. It was raining outside. The weather box on the front door sang quietly: "*Rain, rain, go away; rubbers, raincoats for today ...*" And the rain tapped on the empty house, echoing.

Outside, the garage chimed and lifted its door to reveal the waiting car. After a long wait the door swung down again.

At eight-thirty the eggs shriveled and the toast was like stone. An aluminum wedge scraped them into the sink, where hot water whirled them down a metal throat which digested and flushed them away to the distant sea. The dirty dishes were dropped into a hot washer and emerged twinkling dry.

Nine-fifteen, sang the clock, *time to clean.*

Out of warrens in the wall, tiny robot mice darted. The rooms were a crawl with the small cleaning animals, all rubber and metal. They thudded against chairs, whirling their mustached runner, kneading the rug nap, sucking gently at hidden dust. Then like mysterious invaders, they popped into their burrows. Their pink electric eyes faded. The house was clean.

Ten o'clock. The sun came out from behind the rain. The house stood alone in a city of rubble and ashes. This was the one house left standing. At night the ruined city gave off a radioactive glow which could be seen for miles.

Ten-fifteen. The garden sprinklers whirled up in golden founts, filling the soft morning air with scatterings of brightness. The water pelted windowpanes, running down the charred west side where the house had been burned evenly free of its white paint. The entire west face of the house was black, save for five places. Here the silhouette in paint of a man mowing a lawn. Here, as in a photograph, a woman bent to pick up flowers. Still farther over, their images burned on wood in one titanic instant, a small boy, hands flung into the air, higher up, the image of a thrown ball, and opposite him, a girl, hands raised to catch a ball which never came down.

The five spots of paint – the man, the woman, the children, the ball – remained. The rest was a thin charcoaled layer.

The gentle sprinkler rain filled the garden with falling light.

Until this day, how well the house had kept its peace. How carefully it had inquired, "*Who goes there? What's the password?*" and, getting no answer from lonely foxes and whining cats, it had shut up its windows and drawn shades in an old-maidenly preoccupation with self – protection which bordered on mechanical paranoia.

It quivered at each sound, the house did. If a sparrow brushed a window the shade snapped up.

Baal (n.): an ancient god.

Bridge (n.): a card game.

The bird, startled, flew off! No, not even a bird must touch the house!

The house was an altar with ten thousand attendants, big, small, servicing, attending, in choirs. But the gods had gone away, and the ritual of the religion continued senselessly, uselessly. 80

Twelve noon.
A dog whined, shivering, on the front porch.

The front door recognized the dog voice and opened. The dog, once huge and fleshy, but now gone to bone and covered with sores, moved in and through the house, tracking mud. Behind it whirred angry mice, angry at having to pick up mud, angry at inconvenience. 85 90

For not a leaf fragment blew under the door but what the wall flipped open and the copper scrap rats flashed swiftly out. The offending dust, hair, or paper, seized in miniature steel jaws, was raced back to the burrow. There, down the tubes which fed into the cellar, it was dropped into the sighing vent of an incinerator which sat like evil Baal in a dark corner. 95

The dog ran upstairs, hysterically yelping to each door, at last realizing, as the house realized, that only silence was there. 100

It sniffed the air and scratched the kitchen door. Behind the door the stove was making pancakes which filled the house with a rich baked odor and the scent of maple syrup. 105

The dog frothed at the mouth, lying at the door, sniffing, its eyes turned to fire. It ran wildly in circles, biting at its tail, spun in a frenzy, and died. It lay in the parlor for an hour.

Two o'clock sang a voice. 110
Delicately sensing decay at last, the regiments of mice hummed out as softly as blown gray leaves in an electrical wind.

Two-fifteen.
The dog was gone. 115

In the cellar, the incinerator glowed suddenly and a whirl of sparks leaped up the chimney.

Two thirty-five.

Bridge tables sprouted from patio walls. Playing cards fluttered onto pads in a shower of pips. [...] Music played. But the tables were silent and the cards untouched. At four o'clock the tables folded like butterflies back though the paneled walls. 120

Four-thirty. 125
The nursery walls glowed.

Animals took shape: yellow giraffes, blue lions, pink antelopes, lilac panthers cavorting in crystal substance. The walls were glass. They looked upon color and fantasy. Hidden films docked though well-oiled sprockets, and the walls lived. The nursery floor was woven to resemble a crisp, cereal meadow. Over this ran aluminum roaches and iron crickets, and in the hot still air butterflies of delicate red tissue wavered among the sharp aroma of animal spoors! There was the sound like a great matted yellow hive of bees within a dark bellows, the lazy bumble of a purring lion. And there was the patter of okapi feet and the murmur of a fresh jungle rain, like other hoofs, falling upon the summer-starched grass. Now the walls dissolved into distances of parched weed, mile on mile, and the warm endless sky. The animals drew away into thorn brakes and water holes. 130 135 140

It was the children's hour. 145

Five o'clock.
The bath filled with clear hot water.

Six, seven, eight o'clock. The dinner dishes manipulated like magic tricks, and in the study a click. In the metal stand opposite the hearth where a fire now blazed up warmly, a cigar popped out, half an inch of soft gray ash on it, smoking, waiting. 150

Nine o'clock. A voice spoke from the study ceiling: "Mrs. McClellan, which poem would you like this evening?" The house was silent. The voice said at last, "Since you express no preference, I shall select a poem at random." Quiet music rose to back the voice. "Sara Teasdale. As I recall, your favorite. ... " 155

There will come soft rains and the smell of
the ground, 160

And swallows circling with their shimmering
sound;

And frogs in the pools singing at night,
And wild plum trees in tremulous white; 165

Robins will wear their feathery fire,
Whistling their whims on a low fence-wire;

And not one will know of the war, not one
Will care at last when it is done.

Not one would mind, neither bird nor tree, 170
If mankind perished utterly;

And Spring herself, when she woke at dawn
Would scarcely know that we were gone.

The fire burned on the stone hearth and the
cigar fell away into a mound of quiet ash in its 175
tray. The empty chairs faced each other between
the silent walls, and the music played.

At ten o'clock the house began to die.

The wind blew. A falling tree bough crashed
through the kitchen window. Cleaning solvent, 180
bottled, shattered over the stove. The room was
ablaze in an instant!

"Fire!" screamed a voice. The house lights
flashed, water pumps shot water from the ceilings.
But the solvent spread on the linoleum, licking, 185
eating, under the kitchen door while the voices
took it up in chorus: "Fire, fire, fire!"

The house tried to save itself. Doors sprang
tightly shut, but the windows were broken by
the heat and the wind blew and sucked upon 190
the fire. The house gave ground as the fire in
ten billion angry sparks moved with flaming ease
from room to room and then up the stairs. While
scurrying water rats squeaked from the walls,
pistoled their water, and ran for more. And the 195
wall sprays let down showers of mechanical rain.

But too late. Somewhere, sighing, a pump
shrugged to a stop. The quenching rain ceased.

The reserve water supply which had filled baths
and washed dishes for many quiet days was gone. 200

The fire crackled up the stairs. It fed upon
Picassos and Matisses in the upper halls like
delicacies, baking off the oily flesh, tenderly
crisping the canvases into black shavings.

Now the fire lay in beds, stood in windows, 205
changed the colors of drapes!

And then, reinforcements. From attic
trapdoors, blind robot faces peered down with
faucet mouths gushing green chemical.

The fire backed off, as even an elephant must 210
at the sight of a dead snake.

Now there were twenty snakes whipping over
the floor, killing the fire with a clear cold venom
of green froth.

But the fire was clever. It had sent flame 215
outside the house, up through the attic to the
pumps there. An explosion! The attic brain
which directed the pumps was shattered into
bronze shrapnel on the beams.

The fire rushed back into every closet and felt 220
the clothes hung there.

The house shuddered, oak bone on bone, its
bared skeleton cringing from the heat, its wire,
its nerves revealed as if a surgeon had torn
the skin off to let the red veins and capillaries 225
quiver in the scalded air. Help, help! Fire! Run,
run! Heat snapped mirrors like the first brittle
winter ice. And the voices wailed. Fire, fire,
run, run, like a tragic nursery rhyme, a dozen
voices, high, low, like children dying in a forest, 230
alone, alone. And the voices fading as the wires
popped their sheathings like hot chestnuts. One,
two, three, four, five voices died.

In the nursery the jungle burned. Blue lions
roared, purple giraffes bounded off. The panthers 235
ran in circles, changing color, and ten million
animals, running before the fire, vanished off
toward a distant steaming river. ...

Ten more voices died. In the last instant under
the fire avalanche, other choruses, oblivious, 240
could be heard announcing the time, cutting

the lawn by remote-control mower, or setting
an umbrella frantically out and in, the slamming
and opening front door, a thousand things
happening, like a clock shop when each clock   245
strikes the hour insanely before or after the other,
a scene of maniac confusion, yet unity; singing,
screaming, a few last cleaning mice darting
bravely out to carry the horrid ashes away! And
one voice, with sublime disregard for the situation,   250
read poetry aloud in the fiery study, until all the
film spools burned, until all the wires withered
and the circuits cracked.

The fire burst the house and let it slam flat
down, puffing out skirts of spark and smoke.   255

In the kitchen, an instant before the rain of
fire and timber, the stove could be seen making
breakfasts at a psychopathic rate, ten dozen eggs,
six loaves of toast, [...]

which, eaten by fire, started the stove working   260
again, hysterically hissing!

The crash. The attic smashing into kitchen
and parlor. The parlor into cellar, cellar into
sub-cellar. Deep freeze, armchair, film tapes,
circuits, beds, and all like skeletons thrown in a   265
cluttered mound deep under.

Smoke and silence. A great quantity of smoke.

Dawn showed faintly in the east. Among the
ruins, one wall stood alone. Within the wall, a
last voice said, over and over again and again,   270
even as the sun rose to shine upon the heaped
rubble and steam:

"Today is August 5, 2026, today is
August 5, 2026, today is ... "

From *The Martian Chronicles*, by Ray Bradbury
(including a poem by Sara Teasdale) (1951)

REMINDER – implicit meaning and reading between the lines

The implicit meaning of a story is what an author, poet or playwright suggests or
implies, but may not actually state in words. To understand implicit meaning we
infer or deduce through reasoning what the author wants to convey. The reader
has to read between the lines, using clues or the language in the text, to work
out the meaning of a story, play or poem.

REMINDER – explicit meaning

The explicit meaning of a text is the
clear, obvious and literal meaning
of what a writer says in words.

Linoleum (n.): a type of floor
covering.

Reading

1. This story begins with a "smart house" preparing
    for a new day, not recognising that no one lives
    there anymore. Give two examples of how
    Bradbury uses personification to create a sense
    of emptiness in the house.

2. Re-read lines 201–21 ("The fire crackled ...
    clothes hung there"). Select three verbs used
    by the author to personify fire and explain how
    they have been used.

3. In this story, which was written and published
    in the 1950s in the USA, we are told that

the house is now alone in the ashes of what
used to be a city and this city now gives
off a "radioactive glow" (line 47). Can this
story be read as a warning? If so, do you
think this was Bradbury's intention? Explain
your thoughts.

4. Why do you think Bradbury included the
    poem "There Will Come Soft Rains" in this
    story? What does the poem contribute to your
    understanding of the story itself?

REMINDER – storyline

The skeleton of the story – what happens; the plot.

Talking points

- Do you think the ending "makes" a story?
- Should we judge a story or novel, play or film by its ending?

Famous last words

Here is a selection of endings from stories of different genres, written in different times. How many of these endings are positive or what you could describe as a happy ending? Which endings suggest a new beginning?

Ending A

So we beat on, boats against the current, drawn back ceaselessly into the past.

From *The Great Gatsby*,
by F. Scott Fitzgerald

Ending B

And he went on, and there was a yellow light, and fire within; and the evening meal was ready, and he was expected. And Rose drew him in, and set him in his chair, and put little Elanor upon his lap.

He drew a deep breath. "Well, I'm back," he said.

Sam Gamgee's final words at the end of
The Lord of the Rings trilogy, by J.R.R. Tolkien

Ending C

I took her hand in mine, and we went out of the ruined place; and, as the morning mists had risen long ago when I first left the forge, so, the evening mists were rising now, and in all the broad expanse of tranquil light they showed to me, I saw no shadow of another parting from her.

From *Great Expectations*, by Charles Dickens

Ending D

And, like he suspected, there is a moment, when ascension has stopped, but before the drop, where everything pauses. Neither falling nor flying. An instant where time is frozen. It doesn't last as long as in the cartoons. It could be less than a second. But it's long enough to consider, with arms outstretched and bare feet together, if it might be better not to struggle anymore.

From *Boy A*, by Jonathan Trigell

Ending E

So they went off together. But wherever they go, and whatever happens to them on the way, in that enchanted place on the top of the Forest a little boy and his Bear will always be playing.

From *The House At Pooh Corner*, by A.A. Milne

Ending F

I lingered round them, under that benign sky: watched the moths fluttering among the heath and hare-bells; listened to the soft wind breathing through the grass; and wondered how anyone could ever imagine unquiet slumbers for the sleepers in that quiet earth.

From *Wuthering Heights*, by Emily Brontë

Ending G

And you who have followed me through my up-and-down life, I leave you with one last question: The grace of the world, taken or given back, is there any accounting for it.

"Maya," I whisper, "Maya thank you."

The jewel eyes blink their acceptance. The sun struggles through a rent in the smoke and they are gone.

But not gone inside my heart.

"Come on," I say to Raven, and hand in hand we walk toward the car.

From *The Mistress of Spices*, by Chitra Banerjee Divakaruni

Ending H

"After all, tomorrow is another day!"

From *Gone With the Wind*, by Margaret Mitchell

Ending I

Happiness was but the occasional episode in a general drama of pain.

From *The Mayor of Casterbridge*, by Thomas Hardy

How to end a story

Here is some advice for would-be authors on how to end a novel by Laura J. College, an American writing coach and professional ghost-writer.

CREATIVE WRITING: HOW TO END YOUR NOVEL

Have you ever read a book with an unsatisfying ending? Annoying, isn't it? You've just read this exciting, emotionally draining and captivating novel, then arrived at the end only to be left hanging on the edge of a precipice. What happened to the characters? Were all of the problems resolved? The ending to a novel is almost as important as the beginning.

How to End Your Novel with Dialogue

Some of the most wonderful novels have ended with dialogue. The main character says something witty or funny, and you close the book feeling like all has ended well. Dialogue can be a powerful way to end your novel as long as you do it creatively.

The best type of dialogue with which to end a novel is closure; the last phrase gives both the reader and the characters a sense of finality, which signals that the story is over. You'll see this done fairly often in movies, and it can be just as attractive at the end of a novel.

Just make sure, if you end your novel with dialogue, that you haven't left any questions unanswered, and that the previous prose brought the story to a close. Personally, ending a novel with a question seems cheap, as though you are cheating the reader.

How to End Your Novel with Prose

This is the most popular way to end a novel because it allows the author to say everything that needs to be said. For example, you can end your novel with an Epilogue that explains what happened after the final scene in your novel. It can project days, months or years in the future, which is especially helpful in a romance novel.

If, however, your novel does not require an epilogue, you can simply bring it to a close in the present. The characters have solved the mystery or thwarted the great evil, which means that there isn't anything left to say. It's better to end your novel with a bang than to drone on with meaningless and senseless words that only serve to leave your reader with a bad taste in his or her mouth.

How to End Your Novel with a Cliffhanger

There is only one instance in which this is acceptable, and that is when you have planned a sequel to your novel. Often, trilogies will end the first two novels with a cliffhanger, which ensures that your readers will purchase the next installment.

You have to be careful not to anger your readers, however, because if they are frustrated at the end of the novel, they'll simply give up on you as a writer. My best advice is to tie up all of the loose ends – save one – and leave the reader wanting more. A novel – even one with a sequel – that doesn't answer any of the reader's questions will be frustrating, and you might lose their interest.

By Laura J. College,
http://EzineArticles.com/314489

Reading

1. How many different ways of ending a novel does Laura College mention?

2. Describe a cliffhanger ending.

3. When, according to Laura College, should an author use a cliffhanger ending?

4. Why might ending with dialogue not be satisfactory?

5. Discuss how Laura College uses rhetorical questions in this article.

6. Do you think ending a story (novel or short story) with a question is a good idea? Give your reasons.

7. Do you think authors should attend courses or do online training before they start writing novels or short stories for other people to read? Give your reasons.

8. Think about the novels or short stories you have read at school or at home. In your opinion, which story has the best ending? Explain why.

Drama
The structure of a five-act play

In 1863, the German playwright and novelist Gustav Freytag created a model for studying Greek theatre known as Freytag's Pyramid. This model can be applied to most five-act tragedies or comedies.

As explained in Unit 4 (page 87):

- a tragedy opens in calm and proceeds through chaos and misery to a sad ending

- a comedy opens with chaos or confusion and proceeds through greater confusion to a resolution and a happy ending.

Tragedy

Act 1 – Exposition and introduction: The audience meet the characters (*dramatis personae*) and the setting is established. We learn about what has happened before the play begins and our attention is directed towards a potential conflict.

Act 2 – Rising action and complications: Action becomes more complicated. There may be a clash of interests or an intrigue. Events occur that create tension; momentum builds up.

A fundamental conflict is complicated by the introduction of secondary or related conflicts; this may include an obstacle preventing the main character achieving his/her goal.

Act 3 – Climax: Conflict reaches a high point, a turning point or a point of no return. The third act marks a change for the worse in the protagonist's affairs. A situation goes from bad to worse. The protagonist may make a fatal decision through his/her own weakness or have no choice but to continue as started.

Act 4 – Falling action: Reversals. The momentum slows but tension is heightened by the possibility of a happy ending. The audience hopes the protagonist will save him/herself and do the right thing, but fears he/she will not. During the falling action, the principal conflict between the protagonist and the antagonist comes to a crisis. The falling action often contains an element of suspense, keeping the final outcome in doubt.

Act 5 – Catastrophe: The conflict is resolved through a definitive catastrophe and normality is re-established.

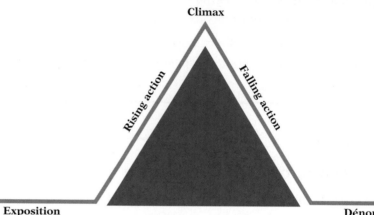

Comedy

In a comedy Act 1 opens with an element of confusion whereby the characters tie themselves in knots trying to achieve a happy ending that appears to elude them. The plot leads them through chaos towards a *dénouement* or an untying of the knots.

A comedy ends with a conclusion in which the protagonist is better off than at the beginning of the action. The protagonist is worse off than at the beginning of the action, but there is a sense of a new beginning.

Dénouement (n.): the clearing up, at the end of a play or story, of the complications of the plot. (French = unravelling).

(Oxford Study Dictionary)

Analysing plots

In pairs or a small group, draw a diagram to represent the plot of a film, television programme or play you have seen recently. Once you have a rough draft, produce a clearly labelled diagram or an explanatory timeline to show the class.

Read this scene from the end of Shakespeare's tragedy *Macbeth*, when Macbeth knows his castle is about to be attacked. Think about Macbeth's mood at the beginning and end of the scene, and try to find the turning point where his mood changes.

Macbeth, Act 5 scene 5

By William Shakespeare

MACBETH:
Hang out our banners on the outward walls;
The cry is still, "They come": Our castle's strength
Will laugh a siege to scorn. Here let them lie
Till famine and the ague eat them up.   5
Were they not forced with those that
          should be ours,
We might have met them dareful, beard to beard,
And beat them backward home.

A cry within of women.

                                 What is that noise?
SEYTON: 10
It is the cry of women, my good lord. *(Exits.)*

MACBETH:
I have almost forgot the taste of fears:
The time has been, my senses would have cool'd
To hear a night-shriek, and my fell of hair   15
Would at a dismal treatise rouse and stir
As life were in't: I have supp'd full
          with horrors;
Direness, familiar to my slaughterous thoughts,
Cannot once start me.

Enter Seyton.

                    Wherefore was that cry?

SEYTON: 20
The Queen, my lord, is dead.

MACBETH:
She should have died hereafter;
There would have been a time for such a word.
Tomorrow, and tomorrow, and tomorrow   25
Creeps in this petty pace from day to day
To the last syllable of recorded time;
And all our yesterdays have lighted fools
The way to dusty death. Out, out, brief candle!
Life's but a walking shadow, a poor player   30
That struts and frets his hour upon the stage
And then is heard no more. It is a tale
Told by an idiot, full of sound and fury,
Signifying nothing.

Reading

1. How and why does Macbeth's mood change in this scene?

2. What is his final analysis of life?

Remember to support your views with examples (dialogue and/or stage directions). Use the SQuEE technique (see page 6).

The Importance of Being Earnest

LADY BRACKNELL: [*Starting.*]
Miss Prism! Did I hear you mention a Miss Prism?

CHASUBLE:
Yes, Lady Bracknell. I am on my way to join her.

LADY BRACKNELL:
Pray allow me to detain you for a moment. This
matter may prove to be one of vital importance
to Lord Bracknell and myself. Is this Miss Prism
a female of repellent aspect, remotely connected
with education?   10

CHASUBLE: [*Somewhat indignantly.*]
She is the most cultivated of ladies, and the very
picture of respectability.

LADY BRACKNELL:
It is obviously the same person. May I ask what   15
position she holds in your household?

CHASUBLE: [*Severely.*]
I am a celibate, madam.

JACK: [*Interposing.*]
Miss Prism, Lady Bracknell, has been for   20
the last three years Miss Cardew's esteemed
governess and valued companion.

LADY BRACKNELL:
In spite of what I hear of her, I must see her at
once. Let her be sent for.   25

CHASUBLE: [*Looking off.*]
She approaches; she is nigh.

[*Enter MISS PRISM hurriedly.*]

MISS PRISM:
I was told you expected me in the vestry, dear   30
Canon. I have been waiting for you there for
an hour and three-quarters. [*Catches sight of
LADY BRACKNELL, who has fixed her with a stony
glare. MISS PRISM grows pale and quails. She looks
anxiously round as if desirous to escape.*]   35

LADY BRACKNELL:
[*In a severe, judicial voice.*] Prism! [*MISS PRISM
bows her head in shame.*] Come here, Prism!

[*MISS PRISM approaches in a humble
manner.*] Prism! Where is that baby? [*General*   40
*consternation. The Canon starts back in horror.
ALGERNON and JACK pretend to be anxious to
shield CECILY and GWENDOLEN from hearing the
details of a terrible public scandal.*]

Twenty-eight years ago, Prism, you left Lord Bracknell's   45
house, Number 104, Upper Grosvenor Street, in charge
of a perambulator that contained a baby of the male
sex. You never returned. A few weeks later, through the
elaborate investigations of the Metropolitan police, the
perambulator was discovered at midnight, standing   50
by itself in a remote corner of Bayswater. It contained
the manuscript of a three-volume novel of more than
usually revolting sentimentality. [*MISS PRISM starts
in involuntary indignation*]. But the baby was not
there! [*Everyone looks at MISS PRISM.*] Prism! Where   55
is that baby? [*A pause.*]

MISS PRISM:
Lady Bracknell, I admit with shame that I do not
know. I only wish I did. The plain facts of the case
are these. On the morning of the day you mention,   60
a day that is forever branded on my memory,
I prepared as usual to take the baby out in its
perambulator. I had also with me a somewhat old,
but capacious hand-bag in which I had intended
to place the manuscript of a work of fiction that I   65
had written during my few unoccupied hours. In a
moment of mental abstraction, for which I never
can forgive myself, I deposited the manuscript in
the basinette, and placed the baby in the hand-bag.

JACK: [*Who has been listening attentively.*]   70
But where did you deposit the hand-bag?

Perambulator (n.): a baby's pram.

Basinette (n.): a baby's bed (she is
referring to the pram).

MISS PRISM:
Do not ask me, Mr. Worthing.

JACK:
Miss Prism, this is a matter of no small importance 75
to me. I insist on knowing where you deposited
the hand-bag that contained that infant.

MISS PRISM:
I left it in the cloak-room of one of the larger
railway stations in London. 80

JACK:
What railway station?

MISS PRISM: [*Quite crushed.*]
Victoria. The Brighton line. [*Sinks into a chair.*]

JACK: 85
I must retire to my room for a moment.
Gwendolen, wait here for me.

GWENDOLEN:
If you are not too long, I will wait here for you all
my life. 90

[*Exit JACK in great excitement.*]

CHASUBLE:
What do you think this means, Lady Bracknell?

LADY BRACKNELL:
I dare not even suspect, Dr. Chasuble. I need hardly 95
tell you that in families of high position strange
coincidences are not supposed to occur. They are
hardly considered the thing. [*Noises heard overhead
as if some one was throwing trunks about. Every
one looks up.*] 100

CECILY:
Uncle Jack seems strangely agitated.

CHASUBLE:
Your guardian has a very emotional nature.

LADY BRACKNELL: 105
This noise is extremely unpleasant. It sounds as
if he was having an argument. I dislike arguments
of any kind. They are always vulgar, and often
convincing.

CHASUBLE: [*Looking up.*] 110
It has stopped now. [*The noise is redoubled.*]

LADY BRACKNELL:
I wish he would arrive at some conclusion.

GWENDOLEN: This suspense is terrible. I hope
it will last. 115

[*Enter JACK with a hand-bag of black leather in
his hand.*]

JACK: [*Rushing over to MISS PRISM.*]
Is this the hand-bag, Miss Prism? Examine it
carefully before you speak. The happiness of more 120
than one life depends on your answer.

MISS PRISM:
[*Calmly.*] It seems to be mine. Yes, here is the
injury it received through the upsetting of a
Gower Street omnibus in younger and happier 125
days. Here is the stain on the lining caused by the
explosion of a temperance beverage, an incident
that occurred at Leamington. And here, on the lock,
are my initials. I had forgotten that in an extravagant
mood I had had them placed there. The bag is 130
undoubtedly mine. I am delighted to have it so
unexpectedly restored to me. It has been a great
inconvenience being without it all these years.

JACK: [*In a pathetic voice.*]
Miss Prism, more is restored to you than this 135
hand-bag. I was the baby you placed in it.

> **Temperance beverage (n.):** a soft
> drink.

MISS PRISM: [*Amazed.*]
You?

JACK: [*Embracing her.*]
Yes ... mother! 140

MISS PRISM: [*Recoiling in indignant astonishment.*]
Mr. Worthing! I am unmarried!

JACK:
Unmarried! I do not deny that is a serious blow.
But after all, who has the right to cast a stone 145
against one who has suffered? Cannot repentance
wipe out an act of folly? Why should there be one
law for men, and another for women? Mother, I
forgive you. [*Tries to embrace her again.*]

MISS PRISM: [*Still more indignant.*] 150
Mr. Worthing, there is some error. [*Pointing to
LADY BRACKNELL.*] There is the lady who can
tell you who you really are.

JACK: [*After a pause.*]
Lady Bracknell, I hate to seem inquisitive, but 155
would you kindly inform me who I am?

LADY BRACKNELL:
I am afraid that the news I have to give you
will not altogether please you. You are the
son of my poor sister, Mrs. Moncrieff, and 160
consequently Algernon's elder brother.

JACK:
Algy's elder brother! Then I have a brother after
all. I knew I had a brother! I always said I had
a brother! Cecily, – how could you have ever 165
doubted that I had a brother? [*Seizes hold of
ALGERNON.*] Dr. Chasuble, my unfortunate
brother. Miss Prism, my unfortunate brother.
Gwendolen, my unfortunate brother. Algy, you
young scoundrel, you will have to treat me with 170
more respect in the future. You have never
behaved to me like a brother in all your life.

ALGERNON:
Well, not till to-day, old boy, I admit. I did
my best, however, though I was out of 175
practice. [*Shakes hands.*]

GWENDOLEN: [*To JACK*]
My own! But what own are you? What is your
Christian name, now that you have become some
one else? 180

JACK:
Good heavens! ... I had quite forgotten that
point. Your decision on the subject of my name
is irrevocable, I suppose?

GWENDOLEN: 185
I never change, except in my affections.

CECILY:
What a noble nature you have, Gwendolen!

JACK:
Then the question had better be cleared up 190
at once.
[...]

JACK:
The Army Lists of the last forty years are here.
These delightful records should have been my
constant study. [*Rushes to bookcase and tears the* 195
books out.] M. Generals ... Mallam, Maxbohm,
Magley, what ghastly names they have – Markby,
Migsby, Mobbs, Moncrieff! Lieutenant 1840,
Captain, Lieutenant-Colonel, Colonel, General 1869,
Christian names, Ernest John. [*Puts book very* 200
quietly down and speaks quite calmly.] I always
told you, Gwendolen, my name was Ernest,
didn't I? Well, it is Ernest after all. I mean it
naturally is Ernest.

LADY BRACKNELL: 205
Yes, I remember now that the General was
called Ernest. I knew I had some particular
reason for disliking the name.

GWENDOLEN:

Ernest! My own Ernest! I felt from the first that you could have no other name!

JACK:

Gwendolen, it is a terrible thing for a man to find out suddenly that all his life he has been speaking nothing but the truth. Can you forgive me? 215

GWENDOLEN:

I can. For I feel that you are sure to change.

JACK:

My own one! 210

CHASUBLE: [*To MISS PRISM.*] 220

Lætitia! [*Embraces her*]

MISS PRISM: [*Enthusiastically.*]

Frederick! At last!

ALGERNON:

Cecily! [*Embraces her.*] At last! 225

JACK:

Gwendolen! [*Embraces her.*] At last!

LADY BRACKNELL:

My nephew, you seem to be displaying signs of triviality. 230

JACK:

On the contrary, Aunt Augusta, I've now realised for the first time in my life the vital Importance of Being Earnest.

From *The Importance of Being Earnest*, by Oscar Wilde

Coursework idea

Literature texts can be used for the Directed Writing assignment in Component 4 Coursework Portfolio. If you choose this option, discuss your chosen text with your teacher. Then select a passage that is about two sides of A4 long. Adopt a persona and write in a particular style, such as a letter or a diary entry. You need to respond to the facts, opinions and arguments contained in your chosen text. You do not need to discuss the author's choice of words or literary features of the text. Write between 500 and 800 words.

Writing

You are one of the characters in this scene. Choose your character and write in the first person. Describe how Jack's real identity was finally established.

Write between 350 and 450 words.

Preparing for Reading Passages

You need to understand how to approach Reading Passages questions. On the following pages there are two exam-style Reading Passages. One is for Core level, the other is for Extended level. Make sure you know which one you should do.

Follow the instructions carefully and time yourself.

Reading Passages – Core

Time: 1 hour 45 minutes

PART 1

Read Passage A carefully and then answer **Questions 1** and **2**.

Passage A: Istanbul

The American author Bill Bryson is visiting Istanbul in Turkey.

It is the noisiest, dirtiest, busiest city I've ever seen. Everywhere there is noise – car horns tooting, sirens shrilling, people shouting, muezzins wailing, ferries on the Bosphorus sounding their booming horns. Everywhere, too, there is ceaseless activity – people pushing carts, carrying trays of food or coffee, humping huge and ungainly loads (I saw one guy with a sofa on his back), people every five feet selling something: lottery tickets, wristwatches, cigarettes, replica perfumes.   5

Every few paces people come up to you wanting to shine your shoes, sell you postcards or guidebooks, lead you to their brother's carpet shop or otherwise induce you to part with some trifling sum of money. Along the Galata Bridge, swarming with pedestrians, beggars and load bearers, amateur fishermen stood pulling the most poisoned-looking fish I ever hope to see from the oily waters below. At the end of the bridge two guys were crossing the street to Sirkeci Station, threading their way through the traffic leading brown bears on leashes. No one gave them a second glance. Istanbul is, in short, one of those great and exhilarating cities where almost anything seems possible.   10   15   20

I wandered around for a couple of hours, impressed by the tumult, amazed that in one place there could be so much activity. I walked past the Blue Mosque and Aya Sofia, peeling postcard salesmen from my sleeve as I went, and tried to go to Topkapi, but it was closed. I headed instead for what I thought was the national archaeological museum, but I somehow missed it and found myself presently at the entrance to a large, inviting and miraculously tranquil park, the Gülhane. It was full of cool shade and happy families. There was a free zoo, evidently much loved   25 by children, and somewhere a café playing Turkish torture music, but softly enough to be tolerable. 30

   At the bottom of a gently sloping central avenue, the park ended in a sudden and stunning view of the Bosphorus, glittery and blue. I took a seat at an open-air taverna, ordered a Coke and gazed across the water to the white houses gleaming on the 35 brown hillside of Üsküdar two miles across the strait. Distant cars glinted in the hot sunshine and ferries plied doggedly back and forth across the Bosphorus and on out to the distant Princes' Islands, adrift in a bluish haze. It was beautiful and a perfect place to stop. 40

Question 1

a. Give four examples of why Bryson thinks Istanbul is a noisy city. **(4)**

b. Explain why the Galata Bridge seemed crowded. **(2)**

c. Why does Bryson say Istanbul is "one of those great and exhilarating cities where almost anything seems possible"? **(2)**

d. Explain in your own words: "I walked past the Blue Mosque and Aya Sofia, peeling postcard salesmen from my sleeve as I went". **(2)**

e. Describe in your own words why Bryson found the Gülhane Park "inviting and miraculously tranquil". **(4)**

f. Describe in your own words what Bryson sees when he takes a seat in an open-air taverna in the final paragraph. **(6)**

Total: 20 marks

Question 2

Imagine you are a journalist travelling with Bill Bryson during his visit to Istanbul. Using details from the whole passage, write an article about your day with Bryson for a popular newspaper.

Include what Bryson thought and felt about:

- the city
- the people
- the atmosphere.

You should base your ideas on what you have read in the passage, but do not copy from it.

Write between 200 and 300 words.

Total: 15 marks

PART 2

Question 3 is based on **Passage B**.

Read Passage B carefully.

Passage B: A Visitor's Guide to Istanbul

This passage is taken from a tourist guide to Istanbul in Turkey.

Asia and Europe come together in this wonderful city. Home to
16 million people, Istanbul is defined by Eastern and Western
influences. Founded in the 7th century BCE and once known
as Constantinople, Istanbul was the most important city of the   5
Byzantine and Ottoman empires. There are spectacular historical
sites to be seen, full of monuments built during these two great
empires. Fortunately, most are in the Old City, Sultanahmet, a
UNESCO World Heritage Site.

Begin with Aya Sofya, considered to be one of the world's   10
greatest architectural achievements. Aya Sofia was the cathedral
of Constantinople, until the city was conquered in 1453 by the
Ottoman Turks, when it was converted into a mosque. Today it is a
museum. Within walking distance of Aya Sofya is the Hippodrome.
This was where crowds of up to 100,000 went to see chariot races,   15
athletic events, victory celebrations and executions. Today the site
is a public garden named At Meydani, the Square of the Horses.

The Great Palace is also in Sultanahmet. The extensive complex
of royal apartments, staterooms, gardens and courtyards reached
down to the shores of the Sea of Marmara. Built by Constantine   20
in the 4th century, the palace was expanded by subsequent
emperors and had no equal in Europe. Also in the Old City are
the Topkapi Palace, the Blue Mosque, the Archaeological Museum
and the Grand Bazaar.

The Topkapi Palace was built between 1459 and 1465 by Sultan 25
Mehmet II, who used it as his principal residence, as did the
Ottoman Sultans who followed him. Spectacular views of Istanbul
and the Marmara Sea can be enjoyed from the palace balconies.

The Archaeological Museum houses a collection of antiquities
dating back over 5,000 years. Both the museum and its gardens   30
are filled with magnificent statues. Not to be missed is the
Sarcophagus of Alexander the Great.

The Grand Bazaar is a labyrinth of 65 streets lined with 4,000
shops arranged according to their products, which include just
about everything: gold, silver, carpets, leather goods, jewellery,   35
pottery, clothing, furniture, antiques and books, to name but a
few. It is one of the world's largest covered markets.

No trip to Istanbul is complete without crossing the Galata
Bridge on the Golden Horn, a flooded river valley and a natural
harbour flowing into the Bosphorus. Lovely parks and gardens   40
line its shores.

Question 3

a. Make notes on the tourist attractions and interesting sights of Istanbul as described in **Passage B**. Include:

- what there is to see in the Old City
- what makes it an interesting place to visit.

10 marks are available for the content of your notes.

b. Use your notes to write a summary of what **Passage B** tells you there is to see in Istanbul's Old City and why it is an interesting place for tourists to visit.

You must use continuous writing (not note form) and use your own words as far as possible.

Write between 100 and 150 words.

Up to 5 marks are available for the quality of your writing in the summary.

Total: 15 marks

Reading Passages – Extended

Time: 2 hours

PART 1

Read Passage A carefully and then answer **Questions 1** and **2**.

Passage A: Dr Zinc

This is a description of a most peculiar public speaker and the ways in which he attempts to influence his audience.

My friends had advised me, if I was at a loose end and required entertainment, to wander down to the public gardens to see Dr Zinc in action. When I got there I saw a bizarre, cadaverous   5 figure, gesticulating wildly at a small audience that had gathered around him. He behaved in a theatrical manner, intoning some well-prepared soliloquy and throwing himself around like a tree in a gale. He wore a melancholy expression and his straggly hair hung down untidily. I joined the crowd to hear what this eccentric 10 fellow had to say.

'Be sure, that at half past three on some day in the near future, the world will come to a sorry end. The sun will burn us up and behold, at this very moment, oh, horrible to relate, a fiery asteroid is bearing down upon us. In the great continents 15 there will be interminable droughts, and the people will perish for lack of water. We can do nothing, for this process has already started.'

At this point, Dr Zinc paused and gasped noisily, before gulping down some of the earth's last water supply. When he   20 started again, he seemed to have lost his thread as well as his voice as, with some hoarseness, he described the deadly illnesses that would cover the earth, and he treated his audience to lurid descriptions of new and peculiar diseases. He shed several tears to communicate his great love for the animals which were the origin of these frightening diseases, and which would, no doubt, be experimented upon and tortured by scientists in white coats. 25

"But worst of all, oh terrible, terrible," he resumed, "will be the wars that will consume us all with nuclear destruction. In the hands of evil people, whole nations will be eradicated and the lands rendered infertile and inhospitable." 30

I was beginning to find this man the very opposite of entertaining, and certainly his audience was not laughing. I suddenly realised that they believed what he said. Most of them were deathly pale and some clasped their hands together. The woman next to me twitched uncontrollably. So this was the magic of rhetoric, and I saw how easily one person could influence a group of gullible citizens. As he continued to describe the activities of unspeakable criminals, his audience appeared to lean towards him as if he might be their protector. Every now and again they moaned and sobbed like pet dogs left at home too long by their owners. It seemed that their predicament might be eased by making a handsome contribution to Dr Zinc's funds. Cheerful givers were always loved by those who controlled things like the rainstorms and thunderbolts which, he observed, were likely to happen over the public gardens later that afternoon. At this point, some untidy and threatening individuals appeared with plastic buckets and started to demand donations. 35 40 45 50

"Friends," he continued, "it is with a heavy heart that I make these predictions. I am a lover of green fields and the happy, innocent families that pass through them." Here he paused to shed more tears and to mumble something incomprehensible about the subversive evils of the media that poisoned all honest minds. His picture of ultimate destruction was, as he had hoped, too much for the audience who wailed and lifted their hands to the not-so-blue skies. Some clasped their cell phones to their ears and made final calls to their loved ones. An elderly woman in the crowd suddenly jumped up in anger and shouted at the top of her voice, "Rubbish, you are talking absolute nonsense!" But it was a waste of breath. In the panic that ensued, no one could hear a word she said. 55 60

Question 1

Your school or college has a group for older students, which debates matters of general interest and current affairs. Imagine that you are a member of this group and have been asked to attend Dr Zinc's talk in the public gardens.

Write a report to the committee that organises the group. In your report give your reasons as to whether or not Dr Zinc should be invited to speak at one of the debates.

Use ideas and details from the passage to support your views.
Write between 250 and 350 words.

Up to 15 marks will be available for the content of your answer and up to 5 marks for the quality of your writing.

Total: 20 marks

Question 2

Re-read the descriptions of:

a. Dr Zinc in paragraph 1

b. his audience in paragraphs 5 and 6.

Explain the effects the writer creates by using these descriptions. Support your answer by selecting words and phrases from these paragraphs.

Write between 200 and 300 words.

Total: 10 marks

Questions adapted from Cambridge IGCSE English - First Language
0500/02 May/June 2007

PART 2

Question 3 is based on **Passage B**.

Read Passage B carefully.

Passage B: Doom and Gloom

In this short essay, the writer argues against always thinking that the worst will happen.

It has always been fashionable to predict doom and gloom. After all, it attracts more attention than good news. Many have feared the wrath to come from anything from angry deities to asteroids. 5
While some of these predictions may have come true, many of the world's problems have actually been solved by human ingenuity. The trouble is that dangers suddenly emerge without warning and fill the media with news that spreads unease.

At the present time, many of these dangers occur because our 10
world appears to have grown much smaller. Yet it is precisely because of this that so many good things have happened. Take transport, for example. Nowadays it takes so little time to visit relatives in another country, and, for many people, it is comparatively cheap. Students can spend time in new places, 15
learning to live with new friends all over the globe. They can share each other's cultures and benefit from education and the undertaking of important projects.

On a larger scale, politicians are beginning to face their responsibilities towards the world as a whole. No longer can they turn their backs on poverty wherever it may occur. They are slowly realising that one country's pollution is another's poison and that emissions of greenhouse gas are linked to their economies and affect all of us. This process of facing up to reality may be frustratingly slow, but it marks a small step forward in human progress. 20

25

We also hear daily of new cures for diseases. Yes, it is true that as we find easy ways of controlling diseases like polio, new viruses and bacteria break out, but with our rapidly increasing knowledge of medical science, exciting forms of treatment are just around the corner. In a generation's time, we can look forward to cures for cancer and diabetes. 30

So we muddle our way towards some sort of progress. We are a vast anthill of tribes all struggling to live on a tiny planet. We have marvellous inventions such as television to help us share our knowledge of each other, and to prevent the isolation that builds barriers between us. The Internet allows us to communicate quickly and efficiently with each other. It provides us with a vast encyclopaedia of knowledge and the means to buy and sell goods in an electronic market. International sport reaches more countries whose people share the pride of competition and victory. Think how many people now have the opportunity to 'attend' concerts where before they were too isolated ever to have heard and seen a live performance. 35

40

With all these good things to help us, the best news is that it lies within all of us to further solutions to the world's problems and to cooperate in making life acceptable for everyone. With increasing knowledge and education we can, if we have the will, oblige our leaders to move forward, not to stagnate in a world of pessimism and fear. 45

50

Question 3

a. Make notes on the encouraging aspects of life in the 21st century, according to the writer of **Passage B**.

b. Now use your notes to write a summary on the positive and encouraging aspects of life in the 21st century.

You must use **continuous writing, not note form and use your own words as far as possible.**

Write between 200 and 250 words.

Up to 15 marks are available for the content of your answer and up to 5 marks are available for the quality of your writing.

Total: 20 marks

Question adapted from Cambridge IGCSE English - First Language
0500/02 May/June 2007

Figurative language

You have already seen that most authors and poets use figurative language and imagery to convey ideas and to create a mood or a specific tone.

On the next few pages you are going to read two famous war poems that talk about death in different ways. Before you read them, explore how poets use aural imagery to create sound effects that add tone, mood and atmosphere to their poetry.

What sounds do you hear when you read these words from "Anthem for Doomed Youth"?

"Only the stuttering rifles' rapid rattle
Can patter out their hasty orisons"

Poets use various techniques to create aural imagery: alliteration, assonance, consonance, sibilance.

Alliteration is the repetition of the same consonant sound at the beginning of each word, as in:

- "**f**ell with their **f**aces to the **f**oe"

- "**g**limmers of **g**oodbyes"

- "**r**ifles **r**apid **r**attle".

Assonance is the repetition of vowel sounds, as in the *ar* sound in these lines:

"st**ar**s that are st**arr**y in the time of our d**ar**kness".

Consonance is the repetition of consonant sounds in adjacent words where the vowels are different, as in the harsh, staccato *st* and *tt* sounds in these lines:

"Only the mon**st**rous anger of the guns.
Only the **st**uttering rifles' rapid ra**tt**le
Can pa**tt**er out their ha**st**y orisons."

Sibilance is the repetition of the *s, z* and *sh* sounds (in English this can include the letter *c* – as in *lettuce*) in adjacent words, as in: "the bree**z**e in it**s** li**s**tle**ss**ne**ss**".

This well-known poem was written early in the First World War and published as an ode of remembrance in *The Times* newspaper. Make notes on how the poet uses metaphors and different types of imagery. Then do the activity below.

The writer's craft – mood or tone

Work with a partner or in a small group. Start by reading the poem aloud.

One person should read the poem while listeners write down words that convey a mood or tone, such as the adjective "solemn" (line 5) or the abstract noun "glory" (line 8).

Now:

- discuss the subject of this poem
- discuss the theme of the poem
- choose one or two lines as examples and discuss the words that create the tone or mood of the poem.

For the Fallen

With proud thanksgiving, a mother for her children,
England mourns for her dead across the sea.
Flesh of her flesh they were, spirit of her spirit,
Fallen in the cause of the free.

Solemn the drums thrill; Death august and royal   5
Sings sorrow up into immortal spheres,
There is music in the midst of desolation
And a glory that shines upon our tears.

They went with songs to the battle, they were young,
Straight of limb, true of eye, steady and aglow.   10
They were staunch to the end against odds uncounted;
They fell with their faces to the foe.

They shall grow not old, as we that are left grow old:
Age shall not weary them, nor the years condemn.
At the going down of the sun and in the morning   15
We will remember them.

They mingle not with their laughing comrades again;
They sit no more at familiar tables of home;
They have no lot in our labour of the day-time;
They sleep beyond England's foam.   20

But where our desires are and our hopes profound,
Felt as a well-spring that is hidden from sight,
To the innermost heart of their own land they are known
As the stars are known to the Night;

As the stars that shall be bright when we are dust,   25
Moving in marches upon the heavenly plain;
As the stars that are starry in the time of our darkness,
To the end, to the end, they remain.

By Laurence Binyon (1869–1943), *The Times*
(21 September 1914)

This poem was written three years after "For the Fallen". How does the tone and mood differ from that of the previous poem?

Anthem for Doomed Youth

What passing-bells for these who die as cattle?
  Only the monstrous anger of the guns.
  Only the stuttering rifles' rapid rattle
Can patter out their hasty orisons.
No mockeries for them; no prayers nor bells,   5
  Nor any voice of mourning save the choirs, –
The shrill, demented choirs of wailing shells;
  And bugles calling for them from sad shires.

What candles may be held to speed them all?
  Not in the hands of boys, but in their eyes   10
Shall shine the holy glimmers of goodbyes.
  The pallor of girls' brows shall be their pall;
Their flowers the tenderness of patient minds,
And each slow dusk a drawing-down of blinds.

By Wilfred Owen (1917)

Characteristics and abilities of super-beings and their enemies

- super strength
- the ability to fly
- telepathy
- shape-shifter
- hyper-intelligent
- fearless
- tender-hearted
- unerring sense of justice
- unquestioning belief in doing what he/she believes is right
- unquestioning belief that what he/she is doing is necessary
- special gadgets
- special weapons
- hard-hearted
- ugly beyond words
- extremely good looking
- charismatic
- super-fast (self-propelled or in a super-vehicle)

Writing narrative

Super-hero saves the world

Children nowadays are familiar with images of super-heroes with special powers: Superman, Spiderman, Batman and the like. This is nothing new. A long narrative poem was written in Old English during the 10th century about the deeds of brave, super-human Beowulf, who first defeated the evil swamp monster Grendel, then destroyed the monster's fiendish mother and 50 years later, when he was an old man, mortally wounded a marauding dragon.

Whether the hero is a normal person or a fictional super-being such as Superman, his/her greatness and bravery is dependent on the horror and malice of the enemy: the greater the power of the enemy, the greater the valour of the hero.

Listed in the box on the left are defining characteristics that can be applied to super-beings and their mortal enemies. Invent a super-being of your own, male or female, and devise a wicked enemy who is intent on destroying our world. Then create a world-threatening, life-threatening situation in which your super-hero has to save humankind from the powers of evil.

Write an exciting episode to end a story in which a super-hero either does or does not save the world.

Write between 350 and 450 words.

Unit 9: Self-assessment

In this unit we have read:

- a science-fiction story
- war poems
- part of the final act of a tragedy
- the dénouement of a famous comedy.

We have also practised doing exam-style questions.

Make notes about Unit 9

Two texts (poetry, prose or drama) I remember in Unit 9 are:
Two new skills I learned are:
Two things I'm not sure about are:
I enjoyed doing:
Something I would like to do again is:
I would like to to this again because:

Unit 9: Literature extension

Read the following poem by Thomas Hardy and think about the different ways he conveys his sense of loss, and the way he uses setting and the weather to create atmosphere.

Mead (n.): the Old English word for a meadow or field.

Falter (v.): to stumble or move haltingly.

The Voice

Woman much missed, how you call to me, call to me,
Saying that now you are not as you were
When you had changed from the one who was all to me,
But as at first, when our day was fair.

Can it be you that I hear? Let me view you, then,   5
Standing as when I drew near to the town
Where you would wait for me: yes, as I knew you then,
Even to the original air-blue gown!

Or is it only the breeze in its listlessness
Travelling across the wet mead to me here,   10
You being ever dissolved to wan wistlessness,
Heard no more again far or near?

Thus I; faltering forward,
Leaves around me falling,
Wind oozing thin through the thorn from norward,   15
And the woman calling.

By Thomas Hardy (1840–1928)

Writing narrative

Rewrite Hardy's poem in prose as an episode at the beginning or ending of a story.

Write about 350 words.

The writer's craft – a poet's choice of words

Listless as an adjective means lacking in energy or lethargic. What do you think Hardy means by "the breeze in its listlessness" (line 9)?

"Wistlessness" is a word Hardy invented for this poem. What real word could be used to replace it? It does not have to rhyme with "listlessness".

10 Exam practice

In this unit you will:

→ **Visit** Africa, Alaska, England, France, Gibraltar, India, Libya, Spain and the USA

→ **Improve** your exam skills and strategies

→ **Practise** responding to exam-style questions.

This unit contains exam-style questions similar to those you will find in Reading Passages, Directed Writing and Composition. Make sure you know whether you are going to do the Reading Paper 1 (Core) or Reading Paper 2 (Extended).

There are two sets of exam-style questions to give you practice in responding to each of the above assessments. The first set in each pair gives you help with answering the questions. The notes in the margin will help you to answer each question, but you will have to add your own notes to each passage too. The second set is for you to do without any help.

When you practise answering exam-style questions, remember to time yourself. Write down the time that you start and calculate when you have to finish. Do not go over the time limit.

Reading Passages (Core)

Read carefully **Passage A, A Trading Post In Alaska** and then answer **Questions 1** and **2**. You must answer all the questions and have 1 hour and 45 minutes to complete all your answers. Dictionaries are not permitted.

The notes in the margin will help you answer some of the questions, but you will also have to annotate each passage yourself.

Passage A: A Trading Post in Alaska

It is 1890. Máire McNair a young woman from Belfast in Northern Ireland has travelled to Alaska in North America to be a school teacher at a trading post. Máire has grown up hearing stories about Selkie Folk, people who take on the appearance of humans but are really seals and belong to the sea.

A babble of shouts and riotous colour drew her attention from the view above to the shore in front. Unfamiliar words and sounds accosted her ears, as did pungent odours of smoke and fish. Women dressed in bright calico colours, bare feet visible from beneath their skirts, and scarves atop their heads, shuffled small   5
children out of the way in readiness for their landing.

 Nearby, turbaned men with hair cut rough below their ears began to wade into the water, their dun-coloured trousers rolled to their knees. It wasn't all wild colour and excitement; among these rainbow clothes a few stood out in their darker browns and blacks of   10
merino wool and thick cotton trousers, and the lighter whites and beiges of linen shirts.

 Just before the boat could go no further a man from the group moved towards them, parting the fish that thronged the water. He wore none of the bright cottons or dark wools. His chest was   15
bare and he glided through the water with a rhythm so graceful Máire wondered what the water might conceal beneath his hips. He was truly a creature of the sea with his dark tilted eyes and

Suggests indistinct words (noise/sound).

Suggests a jumble of bright colours (sight).

Evokes the smell.

These are different to what Máire is used to.

Everything seems very bright.

There are plain colours too.

Daniel does not look like the other men.

He looks as if he "belongs" to the sea, like one of the Selkie Folk she's heard about.

coal-black hair that hung long and loose about his shoulders, and a body that moved through the current like liquid. 20

He arrived at the boat and reached up for her. Wolf tattoos rippled on the back of his hands as he gestured her to come. Máire gasped at the sight of such primal markings. The Indian noted her reaction but made no remark, only raised his brow a fraction and gestured once again for her to come. 25

"Daniel." Mrs Paxson addressed this black-haired man with some surprise. "We don't usually see you at the mission." She nodded to a short wiry man wading through the water in Daniel's wake. "Oh good, George, you're here. You can take me ashore. Daniel is taking Miss McNair, the schoolteacher." 30

[…] Daniel deposited Máire on the bank and, without a word, headed to the forest above that quickly swallowed him whole. Where was his home, if not here by the sea? How much claim on him had that forest that absorbed him so completely it was as though he were part of it? What was he, 35 if not of the sea?

"Don't just stand there gawking, girl," said Mrs Paxson. "Get yourself up to the trading post and help Mr Paxson unpack the stores. I'll be along in a short while." She turned back to the men surrounding her and continued to issue orders about 40 the cargo.

Suppressing her annoyance Máire nodded, groped for her skirts and made her way towards the cluster of vertically planked buildings. When she reached the building most likely to be the trading post, she realized she had acquired a group of 45 followers who now crowded behind her. Máire turned around and smiled feebly at them. Faces, very young and very old, male and female, stared expectantly at her. A young girl dressed in bright red calico pressed forward.

"Are you the school teacher?" 50

"Yes, yes." Máire nodded vigorously. "I am the school teacher." She said it slowly and loudly, hoping they would understand her words. "School teacher," she repeated, pointing to her chest. "Miss McNair."

They all giggled. Had she said something wrong? Just 55 as she desperately searched their faces for a clue to the misunderstanding, a door opened behind her.

"I thought I heard voices," said Mr Paxson. He stepped down beside Máire, facing the group. "I see you've found yourself a welcoming committee." He spoke to the group using another 60 language, a language full of air and sea. Their language.

From *Selkie Dreams*,
by Kristin Gleeson (2012)

This might surprise or frighten Máire because she gasps at the sight of them.

Indian: Native American or First Nations Tlingit Indian of Alaska.

Mrs Paxson appears to be in charge: she tells people what to do, which wasn't normal in those times.

She would wear a long skirt – it's 1890.

Why do they smile "expectantly"? How does this make Máire feel?

Máire is not familiar with the sounds of this language.

Question 1

a. How do Máire and Mrs Paxson get to dry land? **(2)**

b. Read paragraph 1 again. Give three words or phrases the writer uses to describe how Máire sees the people she is going to live among before she is taken to the shore. **(3)**

c. Give two examples of words or phrases that describe what Máire hears at the trading post and explain how they are used. **(2)**

d. Apart from what she can hear and see, what else does Máire notice before she is taken ashore? **(2)**

e. In what ways is Daniel different to the other people on the shore? **(2)**

f. What do we learn about Mrs Paxson from what she says in paragraphs 3 and 4? **(3)**

g. Re-read paragraph 5. Explain in your own words why you think Máire had "acquired a group of followers". **(6)**

Total: 20 marks

Question 2

You are Máire McNair. The next day you wake up in Mrs Paxson's small house at the trading post. Write an entry in your private journal about your first impressions of the trading post.

In your journal you should:

- give your impressions of the people you are going to be living with
- explain your thoughts on how things are different to what you are used to
- express your concerns about working as a teacher at the trading post.

Base your ideas on what you have read in the passage but do not copy from it.

Begin your journal entry: "Well here I am at last, but it's all so strange ..."

Write about 200 to 300 words.

Up to 10 marks are available for the content of your answer and up to 5 for the quality of your writing.

Total: 15 marks

Be careful with easy-looking questions like this; there may be more involved. Máire and Mrs Paxson arrive in a boat, but how do they get from the boat to the shore?

This asks you to think about the description in the passage from Máire's point of view.

Find examples, quote and explain the effect or meaning.

Think about how you write description using the five senses.

Note the plural s in "ways".

This is how the writer shows the reader what a character is like through dialogue.

This type of question asks you to think about what you have read and to write from the main character's point of view, not your own.

Think about where Máire comes from and why everything around her might seem strange. Imagine how she feels and explore ideas about what she sees, hears and feels.

Read carefully **Passage B, An American in India** and then answer **Question 3a** and **3b**.

Passage B: An American in India

American student Brian Gallagher went to India on an exchange programme. Here he writes about his experience and what he found so different from his life in America.

It would be difficult to underestimate the value of spending time in a foreign country, especially a country that is so particularly foreign to one's own – as India is to mine. Typically mundane experiences, such as walking down a nondescript and common street, become the most incredible adventures. Surrounded by 5
novelty, the world is suddenly alive and fascinating. I remember very clearly my first impressions of India, and how enamored I was with everything that I saw around me. Nothing could bore me, because everything was colored with the culture of my surroundings – and what a different color it was! I was mystified 10
by the cryptic languages I saw on billboards and the towers of Hindu temples along the roadsides. I was entirely bemused by the animals in the streets, as well as all the rickshaws and the old British-style taxis that I saw everywhere. I was pleasantly amused by Indian courtesy and impressed by Indian attitudes 15
towards marriage and the family. Everything, everywhere, jumped out at my senses and engaged my mind like it could never have at home.

It was these small and everyday things that made India such a wildly different place. The extraordinary things, of course, 20
were impressive; but they were impressive because they were extraordinary. It was far more remarkable to find the merely common things that seemed extraordinary. Each one revealed either something truly singular about India, or something in my own conception of the world that had been clouded by 25
my relatively sheltered life. And recognizing either one was incredibly mind-opening. It was by getting in touch with these common differences that I was able to understand India, at least in a limited sense. By dealing one-on-one with the students and faculty at Manipal, I gained an insight into Indian character and 30
by speaking with friends about their futures, I learned a little about Indian values and aspirations. These tiny and individual experiences eventually add up to the whole that is Indian culture and while I would never pretend to comprehend that whole in its fullness, I am incredibly grateful to have come to understand a 35
portion of it.

By Brian Gallagher, www.iaeste.org

Different

Different and interesting

Interesting

Different

Interesting

IAESTE: The International Association for the Exchange of Students for Technical Experience.

Question 3

Answer the questions in the order set.

a. Notes

Brian Gallagher leaves America to study in India and see 'everyday things' in a new way in a new environment. **Make notes on what Brian Gallagher finds different and interesting about his new environment.**

Write your answers using short **notes**.

You do **not** need to use your own words.

Up to **10 marks** are available for the content of your answer.

> This means there are at least 10 points to find to answer the question.

Total: 10 marks

b. Summary

Now use your notes to write a summary of what Brian Gallagher finds different and interesting in India as described in Passage B.

You must use **continuous writing** (not note form) and use your own words as far as possible.

> Remember not to quote, copy word for word or 'lift' from the passages.

Your summary should include all ten points from Question 3a.

Write between 100 and 150 words.

Up to 5 marks are available for the quality of your writing.

Total: 5 marks

Here are more exam-style questions for you to practise on your own.

Read carefully **Passage A, Escape from Málaga** and then answer **Questions 1** and **2**. You must answer all the questions and have 1 hour and 45 minutes to complete all your answers. Dictionaries are not permitted.

Passage A: **Escape from Málaga**

It is 1936, the beginning of the Spanish Civil War. Elizabeth, Alex and Juan are trying to get from the city of Málaga to Almeria in Southern Spain.

As far as she could see, in both directions, there were people, hundreds of people walking in the same direction: wounded men, women, children, old people, goats, donkeys, even some chickens in a crate. The entire city seemed to be on the move. An immense silence hung over them, broken only by the plaintive cries of the   5
children begging for food and the curses and moans of the elderly, who struggled to keep up. There was no need for them to speak; there was nothing to say. They all knew that they had to walk as fast as they could to avoid the danger. If they dawdled they would die; this was a race for their lives and even the youngest among   10
them seemed to know it. They urged their crying children on and when someone's grandmother gave up and sat by the roadside, too exhausted to continue, they walked on without her. They had to reach Almeria and safety at all costs.

"*Que desbandá*," Juan murmured, visibly moved to see so   15
many homeless people.

Elizabeth wondered how far these people had come; some were wrapped in coats and blankets, others had nothing more than a single garment to wear; some were barefoot, their feet tom and bleeding. One old woman sat by the roadside, weeping,   20
her legs swollen with ulcers, the blood running down into her sandals. There were so many children, dozens and dozens of children, most of them under ten years old. Some were lucky and sat in baskets astride rheumatic-looking donkeys, others rode on their fathers' backs or lay in their mothers' arms, but   25
many more ran behind, their tiny legs trying to keep up with their families, terrified they would get lost, and all of them crying for food.

"Exactly how far is it to Almeria?" asked Elizabeth.

"Well it's a hundred miles from Málaga; so we're looking at   30
another three days and three nights, if we can keep up the pace," answered Alex.

Elizabeth groaned; she did not want to tell them, but already she felt unable to walk any further. Her feet were sore and she was frightened to remove her shoes in case she could not put them on   35
again; her back hurt and she was still desperately hungry.

"Keep an eye out for a lorry. Maybe we'll be lucky and be able to get a lift," Juan said, but with little conviction.

The fishing village of Torre del Mar lay before them, in the estuary of the river Vélez. The mountains had receded inland, 40 bare granite outlines on the horizon, leaving at their feet a wide flat valley, a fertile plain of orange trees and avocados. She saw a moving column of black shapes was snaking its way along the valley floor, a second stream of refugees arriving to join the exodus.

"Look at all those people; where are they coming from?" she 45 asked.

"I don't know," Juan answered. "From the *pueblos,* I suppose."

He stopped a woman who was pushing an old pram, laden with bedding. Her face was the colour of a walnut and just as wrinkled; her eyes peered out at him, suspiciously, from beneath a 50 wide straw hat.

"*Señora,* where are all these people coming from?" he asked.

She stared at him, amazed at his ignorance.

"They're running away from the soldiers, of course" she said.

"The *fascistas* have taken Zafarraya and broken through the pass; 55 they'll be in Vélez any day."

Then, not waiting for him to reply, called her children to her and hurried on her way, disappearing quickly into the crowd.

"So Málaga will soon be surrounded," he said.

"What's this?" Alex asked. 60

A huge cloud of white dust was being thrown from the dirt road by a convoy of lorries that was heading towards them. The drivers drove fast, honking their horns continuously with the expectation that everyone would jump aside in deference. They cut a swathe through the exhausted pilgrims, who stumbled and 65 fell to avoid being mown down. As the first lorry reached them Alex and Juan leapt to one side, pulling Elizabeth with them.

From *Between the Sierra and the Sea,*
by Joan Fallon (2011)

Question 1

a. How are people leaving Málaga? **(2)**

b. How long will it take Elizabeth, Alex and Juan to get to Almeria? **(1)**

c. Explain in your own words "The entire city seemed to be on the move" in line 4. **(2)**

d. Re-read the first paragraph of the passage, starting, "As far as she could see … ".
Explain in your own words how the writer creates a sense of urgency and danger? **(4)**

e. State three things the writer tells you about people's appearance. **(3)**

f. Re-read paragraph 8 of the passage, starting, "The fishing village of Torre del Mar ... ". Describe in your own words as far as possible where the people are and what is happening. **(4)**

g. Choose two phrases the writer uses to evoke pity for the people leaving Málaga. Explain the effect of these phrases. **(4)**

20 marks

Question 2

You are Alex. You have arrived in Almeria. Write a letter to your parents telling them about the journey from Málaga to Almeria with Elizabeth and Juan.

In your letter you should:

- explain how you have got to Almeria
- give your impressions of the people walking from Málaga to Almeria
- express any concerns you may have about what is happening.

Base your letter on what you have read in Passage A, but do not copy from it.

Be careful to use your own words. Address each of the three bullet points.

Begin your letter,

Dear Parents,

I've finally managed to reach Almeria ...

Write about 200 to 300 words.

Up to 10 marks are available for the content of your answer and up to five marks for the quality of your writing.

Total: 15 marks

Read **Passage B, Escape to Gibraltar** carefully and then answer **Question 3a** and **3b**.

> **Isthmus (n.):** a narrow strip of land connecting two areas of land that would otherwise be separated by the sea.
>
> **Gibraltar:** a British island colony across a narrow isthmus from Spain.

Passage B: Escape to Gibraltar

It is 1936, the beginning of the Spanish Civil War. Hubert Caetano lives with his parents in La Linea, a town on the coast across the narrow isthmus from Gibraltar in southern Spain. Hubert's father is a worker's union representative in the hospital where he works.

At dawn there was a violent banging on the door and when my mother tentatively opened it, it was torn aside by rough soldiers who burst into their bedroom and unceremoniously dragged my father out with them, hitting him as they went and calling him a Red traitor. [...] We were unable to find out what was happening to him, 5 not even where he was being kept. There was chaos everywhere. Then, two days later, just as suddenly as he had been taken, he was back. Bald, battered and bruised from many beatings. [...]

As the days went by the situation became more dangerous, but what finally convinced my father that we should try to leave 10 was the presence of the dreaded Moorish troops. Now though, it was impossible to get across the isthmus into Gibraltar, the obvious place to flee to. Desperately he searched for ways to get us all away from the anarchy in the country, but to no avail, no one wanted to risk the wrath of the merciless Nationalist soldiers and their followers by helping suspects to escape. He had practically given up hope when, very late one night, there was a knock on our door. We froze, but it was only a frightened old fisherman who had spent a long time critically ill at the hospital and was grateful for my father's care of him. He just came in to say that the following night he would leave his oars inside his boat on the beach and was quickly gone.

And so it was that on that moonless night we carefully made our way on to the beach. Down by the fence we could just make out the lights of Nationalist soldiers patrolling the frontier. With difficulty we managed to launch the boat that had fortunately been left near the waters edge and, as noiselessly as possible, rowed out into the darkness. It was just a short distance really though our great fear made it seem an interminable journey. Even in the darkness we could make out the imposing north face of the Rock rising vertically into the black sky. What a welcome sound that muffled crunch was as the boat's keel dug into the soft beach sand.

From *Gibraltar: Rock of Ages*,
by Hubert Caetano (2003)

15

20

25

30

Question 3

Answer the questions in the order set.

a. Notes

What do you learn about why some ordinary people were afraid at the beginning of the Spanish Civil War **and** why did the author's family have difficulty trying to get to safety according to **Passage B**?

Write your answer in short **notes**.

You do **not** need to use your own words.

Up to 10 marks are available for the content of your answer.

Total: 10 marks

b. Summary

Now use your notes to write a summary of what **Passage B** tells you about why ordinary people were afraid at the beginning of the Civil War in Spain **and** the difficulties the author's family faced trying to get to safety.

You must use **continuous writing** (not note form) and **use your own words as far as possible**.

Your summary should include all ten points from Question 3a.

Write between 100 and 150 words.

Up to 5 marks are available for the quality of your writing.

Total: 5 marks

Reading Passages (Extended)

Read carefully **Passage A, A Street March** and then answer **Questions 1** and **2**. You must answer all the questions and have 2 hours to complete all your answers. Dictionaries are not permitted.

The notes in the margin will help you answer some of the questions, but you will also have to annotate each passage yourself.

This information tells you who and what you are reading about.	**Passage A: A Street March** *It is 1936. Bill Maguire, a British journalist, is in London to report on a fascist demonstration.*
Ominous sounding words: "darker" and "mass".	On the left, towards Tower Bridge, Bill could make out the darker, more orderly mass of the fascist troops, and hear the thud of a
Indicates a heavy, ominous sound.	band in the middle distance. The stretch of road separating the two factions was no more than a quarter of a mile long, but was occupied
You do not have a dictionary. Does it matter if you do not know what this word means? Can you guess its meaning from the context or ignore it?	by a veritable army of police over 6,000 overall had been drafted into 5 the area for the day – both on foot and on horseback. It was raining slightly and a faint, acrid smell rose from the damp rubber capes of the men and the steaming coats of the horses. The officers on foot carried batons at the ready. All the men wore that look of phlegmatic
Bill is an experienced journalist, not young, impressionable or easily frightened.	preparedness that Bill had seen on the faces of police everywhere. 10 The anti-fascist crowd seemed to be increasing both in size and confidence by the minute, the narrow line of police delegated to hold
The crowd is angry and there aren't enough police to hold them back.	them back bulged and leaned dangerously, strained to near breaking point by the explosive pressure of so many angry bodies. Bill turned right, his intention first to speak to the police, and then get into the 15
Bill wants to report both points of view.	crowd behind the cordon for the point of view of the protesters. A few intrepid commercial vehicles – baker's and newsagent's delivery vans, and a horse-drawn milk float – had entered Royal Mint Street
There are three sets of people involved: two political groups and the police.	from the north side, and belligerent drivers, determined not to be cowed by the situation, bellowed abuse at the police and both 20 political factions. Blaring horns, revving engines and the panicky
The author is building tension by increasing the noise.	whinnying of horses combined with the mounting clamour on both sides to create a deafening din.
A new paragraph starts for a new action.	Suddenly, a boy darted from the crowd in Cable Street, ducking beneath the linked arms of the police, and hurled 25 something into the middle of the road. The firecracker skittered and fizzled for about thirty yards before exploding in a series
It sounds like gunfire.	of sharp reports and a plume of sulphurous yellow smoke. The reports, so like gunfire, galvanized the police. The boy was overwhelmed in a moment, the firecracker kicked aside, but not 30
It seems like a bomb or gunfire.	before the horse pulling the milk float had shied violently, its hooves clattering and skidding on the wet road. The float lurched, and a crate tipped off the far side, sending shards of glass, borne on a widening river of milk, flowing across the road towards the gutter. Unsettled, one of the police horses reared and then 35 side-stepped rapidly, mounting the pavement opposite Bill, its head, wild-eyed, snapping up and down, its massive hindquarters bunched beneath it.

Bill flattened himself against the wall of the warehouse, but
still it kept coming until its enormous flank buffeted him, winding   40
him, and the flailing boot of its rider grazed his cheek as he
fell. As the officer regained proper control, his shout of apology
caused the horse to kick out one last time with its hind leg, as if in
retaliation, catching Bill a painful blow on the point of the elbow.
For a moment he was nauseous with pain, and sat slumped against   45
the wall with his head bent forward. He was shocked, the sense of
freedom and exhilaration that had been his only a minute ago had
been completely knocked out of him, along with his breath. To his
right, opposite the warehouse doorway, there was no kerb, and a
river of milk, now grey with dirt, washed around him.   50

He began to struggle up, his head still swimming. Hands grabbed
his arms and hauled him, a voice shouted in his ear: "Not a good
place to be, sir, if I may say so, why don't you cut along home?"

There were policemen on either side of him, anxious to
remove him as soon as possible. Bill ran his hands through his   55
hair and felt in his breast pocket for his press card.

"Thanks. Sorry I'm in your way. I'm press." The big sergeant
gave his card a cursory and disparaging glance.

"We've got our work cut out here, sir."

He moved off towards Cable Street, but as he did so the crowd   60
suddenly and violently broke through the police cordon, with
an effect like a dam bursting. The street was filled with a torrent
of yelling men, some brandishing their placards like spears,
others clutching an assortment of missiles ranging from stones
to tin cans and coins. Oblivious once more to everything but the   65
excitement, Bill turned and keeping level with them ran back the
fifty yards or so to the top of Thomas More Street.

From *A Flower That's Free*,
by Sarah Harrison (1984)

> **Milk float (n.):** a horse-drawn wagon containing pint bottles of milk.
>
> **Crate (n.):** a metal crate of glass milk bottles.

> Uses effective imagery.

> "Torrent" suggests out of control.

> Suggests a sense of aggression.

> It's the excitement of danger.

Question 1

You are the newspaper reporter, Bill Maguire. Write your news report on
the demonstration.

> Write in the first person.

Your newspaper report should comment on:

- what happened during the demonstration
- your impressions of the people involved
- your thoughts and feelings about crowd behaviour.

> You need to infer what Bill thinks and feels from what is written in the passage.

Base your newspaper report on what you have read in Passage A. but be
careful to use your own words. Address each of the bullet points.

Begin your newspaper report: *Despite the presence of 6,000 police officers trouble started near Tower Bridge yesterday …*

Write about 250–350 words.

Up to 15 marks are available for the content of your answer and up to five marks for the quality of your writing.

20 marks

Question 2

Re-read the descriptions of:

a. what the anti-fascist crowd is doing, and what the police are trying to do in paragraph 2, beginning "The anti-fascist crowd seemed to be …"

b. the effect of the firecracker in paragraph 3, beginning "The firecracker skittered and fizzled …".

Select **four** powerful words or phrases **from each paragraph**. Your choices should include imagery. Explain how each word or phrase selected is used effectively in the context.

Write about 200–300 words.

Up to 10 marks are available for the content of your answer.

10 marks

REMINDER–keywording

Identifying and marking key words in the question that tell you *how* you need to answer it. (See page 7)

Writing skills
Strategy for Extended responses

- Keyword the question before you start to answer it.

- Annotate the text according to the question. Some notes have already been made on this passage to help you.

- For question 1 you need to infer and annotate. (Make notes in the margin of the text.)

- Number the relevant points in the order you want to make them.

- Remember you do not have time to make a rough draft, so link these numbered points together

- Check what style of writing you need to use in the answer (letter, diary entry, news report or article, etc.).

- Use your own words as far as possible.

Writing skills
Strategy for Language questions

- Find and annotate the lines given in each part of the question.

- Think about the writer's choice of words.

- Quote from the passage and comment on the effect of the writer's words.

Read carefully **Passage B, Crowd Behaviour during the French Revolution, 1789** and then answer Questions **3a** and **3b**.

Passage B: Crowd Behaviour during the French Revolution, 1789

This is an examination of how people in the street behaved during the French Revolution.

[...] A man looks down the street to see what is occurring. He sees an army of women marching through the streets, followed closely behind by an equally large legion of their men folk. [...] He hears thunderous shouts. These voices ring in his ears. They sound like a unison chant from a demonic horde. Not a vocalized   5
unison, but more of a unison of purpose, of emotion. His desire to escape has been to no avail. Just as he feels he has made it to freedom, he hears a familiar voice among the crowd. It cries out, "Long live the Third Estate". The voice he recognizes as his own. It has found a feverish pitch, matching the crowd's, and   10
chants the slogans that are being strewn all around. Softly at first, but with each repetition it grows louder and more animalistic in demonstration. Feverishly he roars, "Death to the *calottins*" [a type of clergy]. Falling into line with the others who are flooding the streets, he is carried away by the crowd. Carried to a   15
destination he does not know, he finds himself where he desires to be. Years of frustration and hatred toward a government in which he has no voice finally find an outlet. He marches to depose a dictator and establish a life of liberty.

This is the scene that many people think of when asked about   20
the French Revolution. This subject brings to mind pictures of men standing near the guillotine holding aloft a freshly severed head. This period is probably one of the bloodiest periods in the history of France. Is this, however, all there is to it? Is the French Revolution nothing more than a horde of blood-thirsty   25
savages running around looking to kill someone? For many the answer would be yes. This, however, is not the case. The French Revolution has another side, an often unexplored side. This is the side of the Revolution that brings a level of humanity to the chaos. It shows that the people were not originally out for blood. The crowds   30
that formed in Paris at this time were merely trying to survive. During the period of 1787–1789, the crowd formed of necessity, not of savagery. They formed, as did any other pre-industrial crowd, in order to combat the rising food prices. Their wages had been stagnant for years, but the price of bread had taken a dramatic upsurge. In an   35
attempt to survive, the peoples of Paris took on the role of the crowd.

Indeed the grain shortage became so bad in 1789 that Mayor Bailly recorded in his journal,

The nearer 14 July came, the greater became the shortage of food. The crowd, besieging every baker's shop, received a   40
parsimonious distribution of bread, always with warnings about

possible shortages the next day. Fears were redoubled by the complaints of people who had spent the whole day waiting at the baker's door without receiving anything.

There was frequent bloodshed; food was snatched from   45
the hand as people came to blows; workshops were deserted;
workmen and craftsmen wasted their time in quarreling, in
trying to get hold of even small amounts of food and, by losing
working time in queuing, found themselves unable to pay the next
day's supply.   50

The bread, moreover, seized with such effort, was far from
being of good quality: it was generally blackish, earthy and
sour. Swallowing it scratched the throat, and digesting it caused
stomach pains.

He also revealed that [...] while the bread the peasants   55
could obtain was mouldy and rotten, the king and his ministers
were fed with fresh bread of the finest quality. All of this worked
together to fuel the anger of the crowd.

From The Heart of the Crowd: A Study of the Motives of the
Peasant Class in the French Revolution,
by Nathan Kinser (1999)

Question 3

Answer the questions in the order set.

a. Notes

> There are two aspects to this question: why people were marching in the street and what influenced or affected their behaviour.

What, according to the writer of **Passage B**, caused ordinary men and women to march in the streets and turn into a rioting crowd or mob during the French Revolution?

Write your answer using short **notes**.

Your do not need to use your own words.

> This means you need to find at least 15 relevant points in the passage.

Up to 15 marks are available for the content of your answer.

Total: 15 marks

b. Summary

> Rewrite your notes as the summary in your own words as a far as possible. Do not 'lift' from the texts and do not quote.

Now use your notes to write a summary of what **Passage B** tells you about the why people marched in the streets and became an angry crowd or mob during the French Revolution.

> Use compound and complex sentences to combine information concisely so you do not go over the word limit.

You must use continuous writing (not note form) and **use your own words** as far as possible.

Your summary should include all 15 points in **Question 3a** and must be 200–250 words.

Up to 5 marks are available for the quality of your writing.

Total: 5 marks

Summary skills
Strategy for Summary questions

- Identify the relevant information.
- Rewrite these words and phrases in your own words in the margin of Question 3b.
- For part **a.** remember to make notes that are clear enough for another person to read.
- For part **b.** you need to organise your notes according to the question.
- Remember to use your own words as far as possible.
- If you only write less than 200 words, you have left something out.
- If you go over 250 words, you have not used an appropriate summary style.

Here are some more exam-style questions for you to practise on your own.

Read carefully **Passage A, Travelling in the Desert** and then answer **Questions 1** and **2**. You must answer all the questions and have 2 hours to complete all your answers. Dictionaries are not permitted.

The notes in the margin will help you answer some of the questions, but you will also have to annotate each passage yourself.

Passage A: Travelling in the Desert

In this passage a British journalist describes a visit to the Libyan desert in North Africa.

The plateau, the high dunes, the dry wadi beds and the verdant oases of the South Western desert are a veritable open air museum. The "Fezzan" is littered with millions of pre-historic 5 spear heads; arrow heads; crushing and cutting tools; shards of pottery; and even the eggshells of ostriches from pre-history. On my very first day, lunching in the shade of an acacia tree, I picked up a Stone Age cutting tool that was literally lying at my feet.

Twelve thousand years of civilization can be charted through 10 the engravings and delicate rock paintings demonstrating the slow march of climate change - the shift from hunting to pastoral pursuits; tribal differences; mysterious religious ceremonies; the introduction of the horse; and finally, as the desert encroached, the camel. 15

The talented artists who engraved their observations in the rocky cliffs above the winding river beds had a purity of line of which Picasso would have been envious. I saw the gentle movements of giraffes, the lumbering bulk of rhino, the last moments of a dying elephant and the lassooing of a group of ostriches 20

As we wandered the desert we saw a camel giving birth; we ambled through wadis accompanied by chirping mulla mulla birds; we came across cracked, salt lakes where strange, bulbous trees live and die; snowy white patches of gypsum; swathes of green plants with pale purple flowers, (a consequence of only three days rain two months before); we raced in 4x4's our Tuareg drivers vying with each other to get there first (wherever "there" was) and we leapt over impossible, impassable dunes whipped into geometric knife-edges by the ever-present desert wind; and unforgettably lazed beside the great blue-green slashes of still water, fringed with succulent date palms and stands of pampas grass that comprise the beautiful oases where turtle doves flutter through the air, tiny pink shrimps swirl in the water and, on one occasion, a solitary white camel was tethered on the shady bank.

White camels are highly prized and our driver told me that his family had won races across the Arab world with his fifteen-strong herd. When I explained that England has no desert, he exclaimed sadly "then there is no yellow". The Tuareg are not of Libya, Algeria, Niger, or Mali, they are the people of the Sahara. Proud, honest and exceedingly generous, they are a joy to be around. They acted as our drivers, guides and cooks, regaling us with traditional songs, dispensing chilled water from goat skin bags, and on one occasion picking herbs from a desert bush to alleviate constipation! Every day after lunch they brewed Tuareg champagne - strong green tea boiled over a driftwood fire, poured from a height to make cappuccino-like foam, then reheated and poured into small glasses with plenty of sugar. They seemed to genuinely enjoy showing us their territory. But they have had to adapt, choose a nationality, settle in villages and learn Arabic, French, Italian and English.

The Tuareg were a thorn in the side of ancient Rome, plundering the trade routes from Africa to the port of Leptis Magna (one hour east of Tripoli). Eventually the Romans were forced to make peace. To safeguard the vital shipments of ivory, slaves, and the thirty-five thousand wild animals that were sent to Rome for gladiatorial displays graphically shown in Ridley Scott's box office smash Gladiator. The decadent Emperor Commodus made Leptis Magna rich and one of its citizens, Septimus Severius, became Emperor of Rome. The remains of the city, with its theatre, temples, courts of justice, market, saunas, latrines, hunting baths, and lighthouse were intact before the war.

The historical monuments, the pre-historic rock paintings, and the camaraderie of the fiercely loyal, intelligent and resourceful Tuareg people combined to make this my most highly prized journey throughout the world. Not to mention the romance of the desert.

By Angela Clarence, *The Observer* (21 May 2000)

Question 1

Imagine you are the writer of Passage A. Write a diary entry in which you explore your thoughts and feelings about your trip so far. You are using these diary entries for your travel blog.

In your entry, include:

- the impact of the scenery and landscape
- your reactions to people and places.

You should write between 250 and 350 words.

Up to 15 marks are available for the content of your answer and up to 5 marks for the quality of your writing.

Total: 20 marks

Question 2

Re-read the descriptions of:

a. wandering in the desert in paragraph 4 (beginning, "As we wandered the desert ... ")

b. the Tuareg in paragraph 5 (beginning, "White camels ... ").

Select four powerful words or phrases from each paragraph. Explain how each word or phrase is used to make these descriptions effective.

Write between 200 and 300 words.

Up to 10 marks are available for the content of your answer.

Total: 10 marks

Read carefully **Passage B, Travelling in the Desert in the 15th Century** and then answer **Question 3a** and **3b**.

Passage B: Travelling in the Desert in the 15th Century

This is a passage from a novel set during the 15th century. Nicholas, a Flemish merchant, and his friend Umar from Timbuktu are part of a camel caravan transporting goods from Timbuktu to the North African coast across the Sahara Desert, via the oasis settlement of Arawan.

There are few wells in the Sahara, and the journey between them   5
depends on navigations as exact and as strict as that employed by
a captain at sea, venturing out of sight of his port, and into waters
unknown. In time of clear skies, the Sahara caravan makes its way
as the birds do, and the captains: by the sun and the stars, and by
whatever landmarks the sand may have left. But the winds blow,   10
and dunes shift, and the marks left by one caravan are obliterated
before the next comes. And so men will wander, and perish.

    The guide Umar had chosen for Nicholas was a Mesufa
Tuareg, and blind. For two days, walking or riding, he turned
the white jelly of his sightless eyes to the light and the wind, and   15
opened his palpitating black nostrils to the report of the dead,
scentless sand, which was neither scentless nor dead, but by some
finesse of aroma proclaimed its composition and place. At each

mile's end, he filled his hands with the stuff and, rubbing, passed it through his brown fingers. Then he smiled, and said, "Arawan".   20

"Umar," Nicholas said. "I hope you know what you're doing."

To begin with, they spoke very little. With the rest, they walked through the first night and part of the day, halting rarely. Sleep was brief, and taken by day. During the worst of the heat, they lay with the camels under the white, shimmering sky, and ate,   25
and rested.

Their drovers made tents of their mantles, but Umar's hands erected the light, makeshift awning that sheltered Nicholas and himself, and arranged the cloths, coated by Zuhra with mercuric paste, which they wore against the sting and bite of the pests of   30
the desert. Then, mounting while the sun still glared upon them, they rode until dark, each man his own tent, alone under his own cone of shelter. The chanting, the chatter stopped then, and even the goats became silent.

The nights were marginally cooler. Then the riders revived,   35
and dismounted, and unlashed the bullock-skins of warm water, and drank, and filled the leather bags at their sides. And the camels had their one meal of the day, from the fodder they carried themselves.

The company was congenial enough, and consisted of men   40
and women and children, for there were families going to Arawan. As the heat became less, they grew lively. Every hour, the ropes on the loads needed adjusting: a camel would kick and bite and, roaring, disrupt the procession; the goats would stray; a dispute would break out over some trifle. At such times, the caravan   45
carried its own clamour with it, like a long, narrow household perpetually singing, arguing, quarrelling, cackling. They hardly stopped for food, except during the enforced sleep through the heat, but passed between them gourds of maize and sour milk or rough bread. The fresh food had spoiled by the second day.   50

On the second day, the blind man came to them both and said, [...] Many horsemen have passed this way to Arawan recently. Not today. Perhaps three days ago."

Nicholas said, "Someone told you?" The pale, shining sands were everywhere pristine.   55

"My nose," said the man. "The manure has been covered while fresh. It is unusual."

"It's Akil," said Umar, when they were alone. [...]

Nicholas said, "Would Akil's men dare to attack us?" [...]

"We could avoid Arawan," Urnar said. [...] "Two or three   60
hundred camels are rather few against troops of armed Berbers."

"Six would move quickly," [...]

"Until the nomads observe them," said Umar. "And it means only six camels to carry food, fodder and water, our belongings

and us, if we tire. It leaves no margin for sandstorms or straying   65
or accidents. And lastly, if we don't get to the water at Arawan,
there are exactly two hundred miles between the first well after
that and the next one."

From *Scales of Gold*, by Dorothy Dunnett (1991)

Question 3

Answer the questions in the order set.

a. Notes

What, according to the writer of **Passage B**, were some of the difficulties
and dangers of travelling in the desert in the past?

Write your answer using short **notes**.

Your do not need to use your own words.

Up to 15 marks are available for the content of your answer.

Total: 15 marks

b. Summary

Now use your notes to write a summary of what **Passage B** tells you
about the difficulties and dangers of travelling in the desert in the past.

You must use **continuous writing** (not note form) and **use your own
words** as far as possible.

Your summary should include all 15 points in Question 3a and must
be 200–250 words.

Up to 5 marks are available for the quality of your writing.

Total: 5 marks

Directed Writing and Composition (Core and Extended)

In Paper 3 you have to answer two writing questions. You have 2 hours to
complete both your answers. Dictionaries are not permitted.

Section 1 is compulsory. Read the information carefully and then answer
the question in the appropriate writing style.

In **Section 2** there is a choice of questions: only answer **one** question.
Choose the question that is best for *you* and write a descriptive or
narrative composition in the appropriate style.

Here are some exam-style questions. Some of the information in the text
for Question 1 has been annotated for you, but you will have to finish
making notes on the texts yourself to answer correctly.

Section 1: Directed Writing

Question 1

You are about to start your long school vacation. You would like to go
abroad but your parents cannot take time off from their jobs for a holiday.

Writing skills
Strategy for Directed Writing

- Keyword the question.
- Identify the relevant information in the texts provided as you would for a summary.
- Make notes in the margin according to the question.
- Remember to write your answer in the appropriate style and register (formal, neutral or informal).
- Quote information to support your argument.
- Add interesting details of your own that are relevant to the question.
- Remember this question is examining your writing skills: leave yourself time to edit and make corrections.
- Check the word limit and do not write more than necessary.

You have enough money saved to cover the cost of a trip abroad on your own, but your parents do not want you to travel alone.

You see the advertisement (at the bottom of this page) for *Not Alone Tours* in a magazine and print off the online brochure.

Write a letter to your grandparents, asking them to help you persuade your parents to let you go on holiday alone.

In your letter you should:

- say why you think you are old enough and responsible enough to travel alone
- give the reasons you believe *Not Alone Tours* is a good choice for your proposed trip
- ask your grandparents to convince your parents that they would not need to worry about your safety.

Base your letter on the information in the advertisement and on-line information. Include details and personal opinions to help your argument.

Begin as follows: *Dear Grandparents, ...*

Write between 250 to 350 words.

Up to 10 marks will be given for the content of your answer and up to 15 marks for the quality of your writing.

Total: 25 marks

Not Alone Tours

You want to see the highlights of America's Grand Canyon – the ancient capitals of Europe – the cities and culture of North Africa – the Great Wall of China …

You want to travel and experience real adventure!

But you know setting off on a journey of discovery all by yourself,   5
or even with a friend, can be complicated, and sometimes even dangerous.

Not Alone Tours is the answer.

With **Not Alone Tours** you can see the sights and enjoy a real holiday without nasty surprises on the way. Visit towns you've only 10 ever heard about and stay in safe, comfortable hotels. Get to know a region properly with experienced, English-speaking local guides. Let **Not Alone Tours** take care of your accommodation and transport, and relax. Our friendly and experienced Tour Managers take care of the details of your trip, as well as being a mine of   15 information on the history and culture of the places you visit.

Join like-minded singles for a safe, totally enjoyable touring holiday with

Not Alone Tours

Home Holidays City breaks Cruise Florida Ski Worldwide UK Adventure

amsterdam barcelona dublin krakow new york paris venice

Not Alone Tours

Taking your first vacation on your own is a big step. But remember, with **Not Alone Tours you're not alone!** This is why we're the number one choice for singles holidays.

Not Alone Tours guarantees you years of experience and expertise in tours for single travellers.   5

> There are experienced guides.

Accommodation
On our tours, the price you see is based on a single room. You'll never have to share. You'll also have the time to read or relax as you choose, if you want to be by yourself for a while.

Tour leaders
Your holiday will be arranged and led by one of our friendly, professional tour leaders. He/she will tell you everything you want   10 to know about your destination, culture and currency. Our tour guides are fluent in the local language.

Destinations
We offer famous, interesting and secret destinations in more than 20 countries around the world. Whether you want an exciting coach tour through the Rockies, an informative tour of Edinburgh or a   15 hike along the Great Wall of China, we've got something for you.

In good company
You won't be the only one feeling nervous and excited! Before your trip, you can use the **Not Alone Tours** website to network with fellow travellers and ask for advice from people who've already made your trip. After your trip, you can keep in touch with new friends and   20 share your photos, memories and useful tips.

At the airport
Airports are stressful places. But we make sure you're met by your tour leader, who will help you check in and answer any last minute questions.

Emergency 24-hour service
It's unlikely you'll have problems while you are away, but if you do,   25 help is one phone call away – an emergency phone line 24-7. You can be sure we won't let you down.

> There's an emergency phone line.

Call us on 011 99 7301110 or email us: info@notalonetours.com

Section 2: Composition

Questions 2 and 3

Write about 350 to 450 words on **one** of the following:

Descriptive Writing

Describe the relevant part of the holiday – don't tell a story.

2. a. Describe a holiday that went disastrously wrong.

OR

2. b. Children often keep a box of special things. Describe the contents of such a box.

Narrative Writing

Be sure to use these words.

3. a. *The door slammed with a thud behind them* … Write an episode from a story where the main characters realise they are trapped.

OR

3. b. Write a short story in which the main character realises he/she has made a big mistake.

> **Up to 10 marks will be given for the content of your answer and up to 15 marks for the quality of your writing.**

Total: 25 marks

Writing skills
Strategy for Descriptive and Narrative Writing

- Choose the question that best suits your writing skills.
- Keyword the question carefully.
- If you are doing the narrative option, check to see whether you have to write a full story or just an episode.
- If you are writing a narrative episode, check to see whether it is at the beginning, middle or end of the story.
- If the narrative option begins or ends with certain words, be sure to use them *exactly* as you are told. Don't forget them!
- Remember to write your answer in the appropriate style.
- If you are doing the descriptive option, *do not* write a story.
- Try to use a wide vocabulary, but do not go to silly extremes.
- Remember this question is examining your writing skills: leave yourself time to edit and make corrections.
- Double-check your grammar and punctuation.
- Check the word limit and do not write more than necessary.

REMINDER

- Always leave time to edit and correct.
- Never sit in an exam doing nothing.
- Proofread what you have written.
- Double-check your spelling and grammar in *all* your exams, not just English.
- Check your answers until the last minute of the exam.

Here are some more exam-style questions for you to practise on your own.

In Paper 3 you have to answer two writing questions. You have 2 hours to complete both your answers. Dictionaries are not permitted.

Section 1 is compulsory. Read the information carefully and then answer the question in the appropriate writing style.

In Section 2 there is a choice of questions: only answer one question. Choose the question that is best for you and write a descriptive or narrative composition in the appropriate style.

Question 1

There are plans to build a large hotel with a golf course on Tanuca Island, a small island of outstanding natural beauty.

You live on the island and you are a wildlife conservationist. You have read the news article "Opportunity or Disaster" about the sale of the land on Tanuca to Maurice Compton, owner of Compton Hotel Resorts. Write a letter to the Tanuca Island council urging them not to permit the sale of the land for the new hotel resort.

In your letter you should:

- explain how the resort will affect the natural environment
- express your thoughts on the employment prospects for local people
- persuade the council that the island is not a suitable place for such a big resort.

Base your letter on the information in the newspaper article, but be careful to use your own words. Include details and personal opinions to help your argument.

Begin your letter:

Dear Members of Tanuca Council,

I have read about the plans to build a large hotel and golf course on Tanuca Island …

Write about 250 to 350 words.

Up to 10 marks will be given for the content of your answer and up to 15 marks for the quality of your writing.

Total: 25 marks

Opportunity or Disaster?

By Alexis Bruni on Tanuca Island,
27 September 2012

Tiny Tanuca to have huge new hotel resort and golf course

Prior to actual purchase, Compton Hotel Resorts have submitted
a planning proposal to Tanuca Council for a new luxury holiday
resort complex on Tanuca Island. Compton's newest and, they
say, largest resort is to be built among the hills of the idyllic
little island of Tanuca, overlooking Tabeira Cove with its   5
crystal clear waters and multi-coloured fish. The London-based
Compton group has also announced that a large area of natural,
undeveloped land will be transformed into a golf course on the
north side of the island. This, they tell me, will require extensive
landscaping as hills will have to be "smoothed down" and natural   10
sand dunes on the coast converted into "sand-bunkers".

Building plans

The proposed Tanacu Island Hotel Resort will be accessible by a
new ferry service from the mainland. The 300-bed luxury hotel
resort will include bungalows for employees brought in from the
mainland; the golf course will have a time-share apartment   15
complex. There are also plans to construct a "floating lounge
restaurant" in beautiful Tabeira Cove.

Conference facilities for business people in the hotel itself consist
of over 3,000 square metres of function space spread over three
floors to host meetings and private functions such as weddings.   20
The health spa and gym will have seven treatment rooms,
an outdoor Olympic-size swimming pool and three outdoor
tennis courts.

Employment and infrastructure

The current owner of the land, Maria Gracia Lanetti, says she
has been assured that all buildings will be integrated into the   25
environment. She is delighted that the Hotel Resort will offer
employment opportunities for the local community and people
from the mainland. At present there are no plans to build a school
or medical facilities on Tanuca, but Compton does not rule out the
need for these in the future.   30

Tanuca's inhabitants

Tanuca, a hitherto tranquil and unspoilt island, is home to just
400 inhabitants. Its idyllic natural beauty is the last safe haven for
wildlife and birds in the Mediterranean. But Tanuca is all set to be
transformed into a vacation paradise for the wealthy. Ecologists,
conservationists and animal lovers are concerned that the native   35
birds and mammals, which include the very rare Spindling
Warbler and the minute Tanuca Shrew, will be disrupted, if not

destroyed. Natural habitats will be razed for the resort complex. Watering the golf course alone means re-routing the only two streams on the island, where there is very little annual rainfall.   40

Fishing and the sea

Fishermen say the constant movement of ferries and boats travelling to and from Tabeira Cove will ruin the fishing; they fear the waters will be permanently polluted. The local seal and sea lion populations, which use north coast of Tanacu for their breeding grounds, are already in decline from oil spills and   45
mercury poisoning; this will end *their* stay on Tanuca forever.

We at *The Island News* say there has already been far too much development on the other islands around Tanuca. It's time the government stepped in to prevent foreign companies such as Compton destroying our islands. Tanuca Island Council needs to   50
consider how so-called progress and employment opportunities might lead to the end of our natural Island life.

Section 2: Composition

Questions 2 and 3

Write about 350 to 450 words on **one** of the following:

Descriptive Writing

2. **a.**   Describe a market scene or busy street you know.

   OR

2. **b.**   You discover an old photograph album that has been hidden away for many years. Describe the album and what you find in it.

Narrative Writing

3. **a.**   *The clock chimed the hour and I knew …* Write the opening of a story where the main character has to make a decision.

   OR

3. **b.**   Write a story or an episode of suspense in which a character is being followed.

   Up to 10 marks will be given for the content of your answer and up to 15 marks for the quality of your writing.

   Total: 25 marks

Language reference

In this section, you will find lots of useful information on the parts of speech, syntax and punctuation, and how we use them. You can use it for quick reference or work through the information and activities as a revision aid.

Colour-coding parts of speech

An easy way to understand syntax is to colour-code the different parts of speech. That will also help you understand how writers choose words and use language to achieve specific effects.

Use different colours to code nouns, verbs, adjectives and adverbs. Here are some suggestions and ways to remember the colours:

Nouns in red. Everything we see, feel, taste, touch or hear is a noun.

Verbs in blue. Verbs "move" just like water, which is blue.

Adjectives in yellow. Adjectives describe, changing the way we see or understand things. Similarly, yellow paint changes other colours.

Adverbs in green. Adverbs describe (yellow) verbs (blue). Mixing yellow and blue paint makes green.

Now test out your colour-coding, as well as your knowledge of the parts of speech.

Copy this grid. Decide which word in each sentence is the noun, verb, adjective and adverb. Colour the words according to the colour code above.

Sharp	knives	cut	smoothly.
Careful	students	write	neatly.
Monkeys	climb	trees	rapidly.
Interesting	lessons	go	quickly.

REMINDER – syntax

Syntax is the study of how words are organised in a sentence.

Parts of speech

Verb	Noun	Pronoun	Adjective	Adverb	Preposition	Conjunction	Exclamation
run	race	she	quick	quickly	against	and	Stop!
walk	walk	he	slow	slowly	with	but	Hi!
read	book	it	interesting	interestingly	for	because	Wow!

Nouns

Nouns are the words for people, places and things. Proper nouns name a particular person, place or things and always start with a capital letter, for example:

- The Taj Mahal, Charing Cross, Cleopatra, Hercules and Peter Rabbit are red-letter names.

All other nouns are called common nouns, as in:

- A **clown**'s **nose** is red. **Fingernails** and **poppies** are red.

We can see most of the things represented by nouns, but not all. The names of some things like emotions and qualities are called abstract nouns, such as:

- **Love**, **hate** and **anger** are red.

Write one or two sentences about where you are now. Colour-code all the nouns red.

Start like this: *I am sitting in a room with …*

Compound nouns

When two nouns are used together, they form a compound noun. The first noun usually functions like an adjective (see Adjectives on page 284), for example:

- pop music, class teacher, reading book.

Some compound nouns are spelled as one word, for example:

- foot+ball, tea+pot, fire+man.

Some are hyphenated, for example:

- taxi-driver, can-opener, mouse-trap.

Some are two separate words, for example:

- jewel thief, door knob, horror film.

Forming the plural for compound nouns can be awkward. The plural of a common (single word) noun is usually made by adding an -s or -es; changing a y to an i and adding -es or changing an f to a v and adding -es, For example:

- toy – toy**s**, box – box**es**, baby – babi**es**, hoof – hoo**ves**

1. What are the plurals for the following?
    a. toy box
    b. baby-sitter
    c. rooftop
2. Make the following compound nouns into plurals.
    a. jewel thief
    b. book shelf
    c. bus driver
    d. film actress
    e. grand piano

The plural of some nouns involves changing vowels or adding a syllable:
foot – f**ee**t, goose – g**ee**se, tooth – t**ee**th, man – m**e**n, child – child**ren**.

1. Turn the following compound nouns into plurals.

   a. coral reef

   b. baby tooth

   c. field mouse

   d. ox cart

   e. wolf cub

2. What would the plurals of the following compound nouns be?

   a. brother-in-law

   b. mouse-trap

   c. child protégé

   d. passer-by

   e. onlooker

   f. step-child

   g. housewife

   h. Member of Parliament

   i. police-constable

   j. carving knife

   k. dessert spoonful

   l. dove-cot

Noun phrases

A noun phrase is a group of words placed around a single-word noun (common, proper or abstract) or around a compound noun or pronoun (see Pronouns on page 279).

Whereas a noun tells us what something or someone is called, a noun phrase gives more information about "who" or "what". To make a noun phrase, we start with a noun (compound or proper) and add information.

- Hannah (proper noun); my **best friend** Hannah (noun phrase)

- My **best friend** Hannah became an **award-winning** actress.

- teacher (noun); **English** teacher (compound noun); **Our** English teacher (noun phrase)

- **Our** English teacher is the **best** teacher in the school.

A noun phrase often starts with a determiner or definite article such as: *that*, *those*, *a*, *an* or *the*.

- That red exercise book is mine.

- The most comfortable chair in the house.

- The worst train journey I've ever had was last summer.

Make sentences with noun phrases using the following words.

a. double-decker red buses London I saw lots of in

b. blue pick-up is truck mine that

c. Oscar-winning actress an now she is film

d. purple-winged rare in of the this part country are these butterflies

A noun phrase can form the subject, object or complement (see Complement on page 291) of a clause or sentence.

> Identify the noun phrases in the following sentences.
>
> My youngest cousin Susan goes to a private elementary school. Her class teacher is a bossy woman called Ms Clothilde Cardigan. Ms Cardigan wears the same baggy green jumper every day and lots of shiny cheap jewellery; my cousin says she looks like a Christmas tree.

Pronouns

Pronouns are used instead of nouns, often to avoid repetition. For example:

- When Claudia had finished reading the book, Claudia put the book down.
- When Claudia had finished reading the book, **she** put **it** down.

or

- Lucas gave me the answer. Lucas said that working out the answer was easy.
- Lucas gave me the answer. **He** said **it** was easy.

There are different types of pronoun.

Subject/ personal pronouns	Object/ personal pronouns	Possessive pronouns	Possessive adjectives	Reflexive pronouns
I	me	mine	my	myself
you	you	yours	your	yourself
he	him	his	his	himself
she	her	hers	her	herself
it	it	its	its	itself
we	us	ours	our	ourselves
you	you	yours	your	yourselves
they	them	theirs	their	themselves

Subject pronouns act as the subject of a sentence: *I, you, he, she, it, we, you* and *they*. They are also classed as personal pronouns because they refer to ourselves and other people.

- **I** live in New York. **They** live in Delhi.

> Identify the subject pronouns in these sentences.
>
> **a.** Have you ever been skating?
>
> **b.** She won't come with us.
>
> **c.** I used to live there.
>
> **d.** We are looking at nouns and pronouns.
>
> **e.** They are going to New York next week.

Object pronouns are used as the object of a sentence: *me, you, him, her, it, us, you* and *them*. They are also classed as personal pronouns.

- Maya moved to sit next to **them**.

Identify the object pronouns in these sentences.

a. Give me the bag.

b. He asked her to help.

c. We met them at the airport.

d. The instructions tell you how to do it.

e. He said you should come round tonight.

Possessive pronouns show that something belongs to someone: *mine, yours, his, hers, its, ours, yours* and *theirs*.

Possessive pronouns are similar to possessive adjectives (*my, his, her*). The difference is that the object follows the possessive adjective but does not follow the possessive pronoun, for example:

- That pen is mine. (possessive pronoun)

- That is **my** pen. (possessive adjective)

Identify the possessive pronouns in these sentences.

a. That book is mine.

b. Is this yours?

c. No, I'm sorry, that's his.

d. The toys in the garden are theirs.

e. The problem looked difficult but we discovered its answer was obvious.

Demonstrative pronouns refer to things: *this, that, these* and *those*.

- **That** is Taro's favourite song.

Identify the demonstrative pronouns in these sentences.

a. This is the answer.

b. No, that is the answer.

c. These are my friends.

d. Those are beautiful flowers. Where did you get them?

Verbs

A verb is a word that shows what a person or thing is doing.

Copy the grid and colour the verb in each sentence blue.

The	dog	growled	angrily.
Her	cat	eats	mice.
Athletes	train	every	day.
The	crowd	shouted	excitedly.

Copy the grid and complete the verb forms in blue.

Infinitive	Past tense	Past participle (+ has)
To growl	*The dog*	*The dog has growled.*
To eat	*The cat ate.*	*The cat* ....
To train	*The athlete*	*The athlete* ....
To forget	*I*	*I* ....
To know	*We*	*We* ....

Past perfect

We use the past perfect tense to emphasise that an action in the past finished before another action in the past started. To remind yourself how the past perfect is used in historical accounts, go back to page 114 in Unit 5.

We also use the past perfect in reported speech.

- I **had finished** my homework before I went out with my friends.
- We **had done** grammar before, but we soon saw this was easier to understand.
- "I've had my lunch," he said. He said he **had had** his lunch.

In conversation we often leave out the past perfect tense. For example we say:

- "I did my homework before I went out with my mates, who were waiting for me."

Rather than:

- "After I had finished my homework I went out with my friends, who had been waiting for me."

This is because *after* and *before* tell the listener which action happened first and make the conversation more informal.

However, it is better to use the past perfect in written English, especially in formal reports, letters and accounts where the information given needs to be clear and a colloquial register is inappropriate.

"I had had enough so I stopped."

Change the following dialogue into reported speech:

"We've been doing grammar lessons all week. I've found them really useful," said Lee.

Lee said ...

Active and passive voice

Remember, verbs are active when the subject of the sentence (the agent) does the action.

- The shark **swallowed** the fish.

Verbs are passive when the subject of the sentence has the action done to it.

- The fish **was swallowed** by the shark.

Sometimes, turning an active sentence to passive, or vice versa, simply means moving the agent:

- The shark (agent and subject) + verb = active
- The fish (object) + verb = passive

---

1. Rearrange these sentences and change the verbs from active to passive.

   a. Poets write poetry.

   b. Journalists write newspaper reports.

   c. Playwrights write plays.

2. Now change the following more complicated passive sentences to active.

   a. Diamonds were accidently discovered by coal miners.

   b. The Earth was hit by a giant meteorite.

   c. My eyes were blinded by thousands of brilliant tiny stars.

Modal verbs

Expressing possibility, obligation and deduction

We use the modal verbs *could, should, might* and *must + have* when we make deductions.

One of the sentences below is incorrect. Say which and why.

> We all went down to Paul's house, but he wasn't there. Joan said Paul must of gone to the cinema. Abel agreed; he said Paul could have gone to the cinema. I thought he might not have heard us; he could have been listening to music and didn't hear us knock. He should have been doing his homework anyway.

We use *could, should, ought to, must* and *have to* to express obligation.

Organise the following expressions according to their level of obligation.

a. We have to speak to the principal about this problem.

b. We could speak to the principal about this problem.

c. We should speak to the principal about this problem.

d. We ought to speak to the principal about this problem.

e. We must speak to the principal about this problem.

Must, have to **and** *have got to*

These three forms of saying that something has to be done are usually interchangeable but there are some differences.

Have to and *have got to* can refer to external authority, as in:

- You **have got to** wear a car seat belt in this country.
- Even if you sit in the back of the car, you **have to** wear a seat belt.

(In this country wearing seat belts in a car is a legal obligation.)

> Working with a partner, decide which of the following statements represents a personal decision and which is a legal or external obligation.
>
> **a.** I've got toothache; I must see the dentist.
>
> **b.** I can't come out; I've got to do my homework.
>
> **c.** We have to pay 17% tax on luxury goods.
>
> **d.** I've got to fill in a job application form.
>
> **e.** You must come and see us!
>
> **f.** This is difficult to remember; I must work harder in lessons.
>
> **g.** I've got to work harder if I'm going to pass.
>
> **h.** All children under 16 have to go to school.

Phrasal verbs and idiomatic expressions

We often use phrasal verbs instead of their one-word equivalent in informal speech.

- *Come in* – instead of *enter*
- *Bring up* – instead of *raise* or *vomit*
- *Put out* – instead of *extinguish* or *upset*
- *Do up* – instead of *fasten* or *decorate*
- *Run into* – instead of *meet* or *crash*

> **1.** What do the following idiomatic expressions really mean?
>
> **a.** She broke down when she heard the news.
>
> **b.** The echo died away.
>
> **c.** Horace turned up at the party.
>
> **2.** How many phrasal verbs can you make from the verb *put*? For example:
>
> - *put out = extinguish*
>
> **3.** Make phrasal verbs with *get* and write the formal equivalents. For example:
>
> - *get along (with someone) = to be friendly/to have a good relationship*

Adjectives

Adjectives are words that describe a noun or add to its meaning. They also follow verbs to describe feelings. For example:

- A **cold** drink can make us feel **cooler**.
- A **dangerous** animal can make us feel **frightened**.
- A **boring** book usually makes us feel **bored**.

> Copy these sentences. Colour the adjectives yellow.
>
> a. Hot weather makes me feel lazy.
> b. Funny jokes make me laugh.
> c. Sad stories make me unhappy.

Opposites

> Copy the grid and put in the missing words.
>
> | happy | *sad* |
> |---|---|
> | wealthy | |
> | tidy | |
> | intelligent | |
> | cool | |

Comparatives

We make comparisons by adding letters to the end of an adjective or by using other words with the adjective.

When an adjective has only one syllable, add *-er* to make the comparison, for example:

- I was sad. You were sadd**er** than me.

When an adjective has two syllables and ends with a *y*, change the *y* to an *i* and add *-er*, for example:

- That's a pretty flower. This one is much prett**ier** than that one.

When an adjective has two syllables but does not end in a *y*, use the words *more + than*, for example:

- Your puzzle's very complicated, but mine is **more** complicated **than** yours.

> Copy and complete the grid by filling in the missing adjectives and comparatives. Two have been done for you.
>
> | Adjective | Comparative (+ *than*) |
> |---|---|
> | *glad* | *gladder* |
> | | *funnier* |
> | *obvious* | *more obvious* |
> | *safe* | |
> | | *crazier* |
> | *inconvenient* | |

Superlatives

We usually make the superlative form of an adjective by adding *-est* to short words or preceding a multi-syllabic word with *the most*. For example:

- This is the short**est** explanation.
- This is **the most** comprehensive explanation.

Irregular comparisons and superlatives are formed like this:

good	better	best
bad	worse	worst
little	less	least
many	more	most
some	more	most
much	more	most

Copy and complete the grid by filling in the missing comparatives and superlatives.

Adjective	Comparative (+ *than*)	Superlative (*the* + ...)
sad	... *than*	*the ...*
ugly	... *than*	*the ...*
fashionable	... *than*	*the ...*

Absolute terms

Not all adjectives have a comparative (*-er/more + than*) or a superlative (*-est/the most*), or even an irregular form. The word *perfect*, for example, functions as an absolute term. We cannot say something is *more* perfect or *the most* perfect; it is either perfect or not.

Look at the ten words below. Decide which adjectives function as absolute terms and cannot be used to make comparisons. Explain why. Use a dictionary to help you.

The first one has been done for you.

a. unique

Unique. Something cannot be more unique or the most unique because unique means one of a kind; there is no other like it.

b. dead

c. impossible

d. infinite

e. priceless

f. solitary

g. supreme

h. empty

i. impeccable

j. blind

How much or how many

Some adjectives tell us how many: *hundreds, seven, two, both*.

They describe number or quantity.

This quantity can be:

- **definite:** *four, fourth, twenty-two, twenty-second*
- **indefinite:** *all, several, some, much, many, any, none*.

1. Copy the sentences below. Colour the adjectives yellow.

    a. The tall man wore a hat with two feathers in it.

    b. Jonas came second in the race. His friend came first.

    c. The weather was freezing; we both caught bad colds.

    d. She didn't get many cards for her twenty-first birthday.

2. Make two sentences of your own using the different kinds of adjective: one definite and one indefinite.

Adverbs

Adverbs describe verbs. They give us more information about when, where or how something happens, for example:

- We shout **loudly** or **angrily** or **enthusiastically**.
- We can come to school **happily** or **reluctantly**.
- Some people run **fast**; other people run **slowly**.

Many adverbs (but not all) are formed by adding *-ly* to an adjective: *smooth-ly, rough-ly, bad-ly, calm-ly, quick-ly, clear-ly*.

1. Copy these sentences and add an adverb in green. The first one has been done for you.

    a. The teacher took the register ...

       The teacher took the register rapidly.

    b. The students finished their work ...

    c. The children were playing ...

    d. He was driving ...

    e. We ran round the pitch ...

Adverbial phrases

Adverbs give us more information about verbs by telling us when or how or where something happens.

- I told you this yesterday. (when)
- Crabs walk sideways. (how)
- He ran downstairs. (where)

The part of a sentence that tells the reader when, where or how something happens is called an adverbial clause.

- I'm going to the dentist **tomorrow morning**. (when)

- The teacher spoke to us **as if he was in a bad mood**. (how)

- Sam ran **all the way home**. (where)

These adverbials are called adverbials of time, manner and place.

1. Copy the following sentences and colour the adverbial phrases green. Explain what extra information each adverbial clause is providing. The first one is done for you.

   a. I was extremely tired all day.
      I was extremely tired all day. (extremely = how; all day = when)

   b. Last week they had a party in their garden.

   c. We were shown how to do this earlier this morning.

   d. We answered the questions carefully before the end of the lesson.

   e. My cat usually sleeps peacefully on my bed throughout the day.

   f. We will all be going home soon.

   g. I'm going directly home and as soon as I get there I'm going to do my homework quickly.

2. Make three simple sentences of your own (with only one verb in each sentence) including adverbials to give the reader more information as to where, when or how.

   Write the adverbs and adverbial phrases in green. Use the subject/verb/adverbial structure. For example:

   - Sloths live in trees. (subject + verb + adverbial)

   - Sloths eat all day.

   - Sloths move slowly.

3. Make sentences with subject + verb + object + adverbial. For example:

   - I (subject) + put (verb) + my books (object) + on the shelf (the adverbial).

4. Rearrange the following words to make one long sentence with different adverbials.

   A SINGING I MY THIS BLUE MORNING GARDEN HEARD PRETTY BIRD IN

Prefixes

Letters that are added to the beginning of a word are called a prefix. They change or add to the meaning of the original word. Prefixes include: *dis-, un-, im-, in-, il-, ir-*.

The following prefixes change a word to its opposite or antonym.

- dis + appear = disappear (note that there is only one *s*)
- un + usual = unusual
- im + moral = immoral (notice that you need double *m* here)
- in + capable = incapable
- il + legal = illegal (double *l* needed here)
- ir + responsible = irresponsible

1. Add a prefix to the following adjectives to form opposites.

   a. educated
   b. embark
   c. efficient
   d. equal
   e. expert

2. Choose an *im-, in-, ir-,* or *il-* prefix for the following:

   a. audible
   b. convenient
   c. legible
   d. mortal
   e. regular
   f. resolute
   g. passive
   h. essential
   i. sane
   j. reverent

Suffixes

Letters added to the end of a word are called a suffix. They make a different word. Suffixes include: *-ible, -able, -ful, -less*.

- responsible, miserable, skilful, careless

1. Choose an *-ible* or *-able* ending and change the following nouns into adjectives.

   a. capability
   b. suitability
   c. credibility
   d. sensibility
   e. durability

2. Choose an *-ence* or *-ance* to change the following verbs into nouns.

   a. to attend
   b. to depend
   c. to observe
   d. to repent
   e. to exist

Jabberwocky

Twas brillig, and the slithy toves
   Did gyre and gimble in the wabe;
All mimsy were the borogoves,
   And the mome raths outgrabe.

"Beware the Jabberwock, my son   5
   The jaws that bite, the claws that catch!
Beware the Jubjub bird, and shun
   The frumious Bandersnatch!"

He took his vorpal sword in hand;
   Long time the manxome foe he sought –   10
So rested he by the Tumtum tree,
   And stood awhile in thought.

And, as in uffish thought he stood,
   The Jabberwock, with eyes of flame,
Came whiffling through the tulgey wood,   15
   And burbled as it came!

One, two! One, two! And through and through
   The vorpal blade went snicker-snack!
He left it dead, and with its head
   He went galumphing back.   20

"And hast thou slain the Jabberwock?
   Come to my arms, my beamish boy!
O frabjous day! Callooh! Callay!"
   He chortled in his joy.

Twas brillig, and the slithy toves   25
   Did gyre and gimble in the wabe;
All mimsy were the borogoves,
   And the mome raths outgrabe.

By Lewis Carroll (1832–98)

Talking point – nonsense rhymes

"Jabberwocky" is a famous nonsense rhyme or nonsense poem, but is it really nonsense?

- Read it aloud. Does it make any sense?

- Does the poem tell a story? If so, what is the story?

- Think about how you interpret the meaning of Lewis Carroll's made-up words.

Invented words

Work with a partner.

1. Find five invented words in the "Jabberwocky".

2. Look at the following words and the context in which each has been used. Decide whether the word is a verb, noun, adjective or adverb and find an alternative real word to replace it.

   a. frumious (line 8)

   b. whiffling (line 15)

   c. vorpal (line 18)

   d. galumphing (line 20)

   e. frabjous (line 23)

The suffix *logy* forms a noun to indicate an area of study, as in *biology*. It comes from the Greek *logia* meaning study.

1. Read the following list of areas of study and write down what you think they are.
   - Biology – *bio* = life + *logy* = the study of life forms
   - Archaeology –
   - Geology –
   - Palaeontology –
   - Criminology –
   - Pathology –
   - Zoology –
   - Crypto-zoology –
   - Graphology –
   - Psychology –
   - Genealogy –
   - Astrology –
   - Sociology –
   - Ophthalmology –
   - Cardiology –

2. Choose one subject from the list above and make notes on why you would like to study that subject.

3. Choose a subject you would never want to do and make notes on why.

4. In pairs, take turns explaining what you would like to study and why.

5. Take turns saying which subject you wouldn't want to do and explain why.

Syntax

Sentence structure

The basic elements needed to make a complete sentence are a subject and a verb. So a simple sentence can be made up of two words, for example:

- Fire burns. (noun + verb; Fire = subject + burns = verb)

However, we cannot make two-word sentences with every verb.

What is wrong with these subject/verb combinations?

- Fire causes
- Fire provides

There is obviously a word missing to explain what fire causes or what fire provides. This word is called the object.

- Fire causes **damage**.
- Fire provides **warmth**.

We can make sentences with three words composed of a subject + verb + object.

- Fire makes smoke. (noun + verb + noun; Fire = subject + makes = verb + smoke = object)

Look at the next example.

- Clouds carry rain. (subject + verb + object)

> Make a subject + verb + object sentence about the sun.
>
> *The sun* ...

Sometimes we use compound nouns and phrasal verbs in simple sentences.

- Rainwater causes **flash flooding**.
- Melt water **fills up** mountain streams.

> Make some more simple sentences using one verb and two nouns.
>
> You may use compound nouns and phrasal verbs, but do not use adjectives or adverbs.
>
> Write about the seasons where you live: spring, summer, autumn, winter.

Complements

Here is another type of short sentence:

- Rain is water.

The word *water* is a noun but it is not referring to something different to the rain. It is giving information about it.

- Rain is wet.

The word *wet* is an adjective that gives information about the subject, rain.

In both cases the word that comes after the verb is complementing or completing information about the subject.

Here we have subject + verb + complement.

A complement can be a noun or a noun phrase.

- You are **students**.
- You are **IGCSE English students**.

A complement can be an adjective or an adjectival phrase.

- These students are **studious**.
- These students are **responsible** and **hardworking**.

A complement can be a pronoun.

- That's **him**!
- The fountain pen was **mine**.

Imperatives

As you can see, it is possible to make a simple sentence with one verb in many different ways.

We can also make the shortest type of sentence using just one word – an imperative verb, for example:

- Go!

This sentence is a command so we know that the subject is *You*.

Simple, compound and complex sentences

As well as simple sentences, there are two other main types of sentence: compound and complex.

A **simple sentence** has a subject and a verb. For example:

- I **read** the question.

A **compound sentence** has two clauses of equal importance joined by conjunction words such as *and, but, or, nor, then,* and *so*. For example:

- I understood the question, **but** I didn't know the answer.

A **complex sentence** has one main clause and one or more subordinate clauses. For example:

- I ate toast with jam before I went to the local market to buy fruit.

Minor sentences

There is also a special type of sentence, which is not really a sentence at all – the minor sentence. Minor sentences are used in modern fiction, usually for dramatic effect. Look at this example from Kate Grenville's *The Secret River*.

"**And always cold**. There was a kind of desperation to it, a fury to be warm ..."

The minor sentence makes a statement that the following sentence uses for effect.

Working with different types of sentence

1. Working with a partner, identify the simple, compound and complex sentences in this paragraph.

> Pip opened the door. The room was dark, but there was moonlight coming through the window. The old lady opened her eyes and looked at him. Pip tried not to feel scared. He walked into the room, went up to the old lady's chair and sat down next to her.

2. Join each pair of simple sentences below to make one compound sentence. Use *and, but* or *so*. Do not use a comma. For example:

   - The team played badly. They lost the match.
   - The team played badly **so/and** they lost the match.

     a. They work hard in lessons. They should do well in their exams.

     b. The tourist climbed to the top of the hill. It was too foggy to take photographs.

     c. The children heard a loud rumble of thunder. They ran for shelter.

3. Join each pair of simple sentences to make one complex sentence. Do not use *and, but* or *so*, or any other conjunctions or connectives. You may rearrange or add words. For example:

   - The manager made the team train hard. They only lost one match that season.
   - As the manager made them train hard they only lost one match that season.

     a. The students worked hard in lessons. They did well in their exams.

     b. The tourist climbed the top of the hill. He took prize-winning photographs.

     c. I was running along a stony path. I fell down and cut my hands and knees.

4. Change the following compound or complex sentences into two or more simple sentences without changing the meaning.

     a. Due to having a hole in his pocket and being careless the boy lost his ticket.

     b. I found an unusual gold ring in the grass that looked valuable, which meant I knew I shouldn't keep it so I took it to the police station.

5. Now combine the subjects below in different ways to make simple, compound and complex sentences:

   - rain
   - snow
   - rivers.

Sentences for different purposes

We can use different types of sentence to achieve certain effects. Look at the different purposes sentences can have.

Declarative

Used for suggestions and statements.

- Let's go for a picnic.
- I haven't got time to go on a picnic.

Interrogative

Used for questions, rhetorical questions, requests and queries.

- Would you like to join us for a picnic?
- So what purpose does the old-fashioned picnic serve in social life today?
- Could you help me do the shopping, please?
- Is this the price of the green apples or the red?

Exclamatory

Used for showing one's feelings or making a point.

- I hate picnics!
- What a pity.

Imperative

Used for giving instructions, orders or commands.

- Check the plug is in the wall socket.
- Open your books at page 21.
- Do as I tell you.

Conditional

Used to express what one would do or what might happen under certain conditions.

- Ice will melt in a warm room.
- If it rains we can't have our picnic.
- If you learn all this your English will improve.
- If they had worked harder at school, they would have passed all their exams.

Write a sentence of your own for each purpose:

a. declarative
b. interrogative
c. exclamatory
d. imperative
e. conditional.

Using sentence skills

Here are some examples of different writing styles: descriptive writing from the novel *The Impressionist*; informative writing from *Starting Out in Journalism*; narrative writing from *The Hound of the Baskervilles*; and informative writing from the feature article "Ice Cold in Alaska".

Read each passage carefully and then do the activity that goes with it.

The Impressionist

So, the rain.

It falls first over the mountains, an unimaginable shock of water. Caught in the open, herdsmen and woodcutters pull their shawls over their heads and run for shelter. Then in a chain reaction, cloud speaking to cloud, the rain rolls over the foothills, dousing fires, battering on roofs, bringing smiles to the faces of the people who run outside to greet it, the water for which they have been waiting so long.

By Kari Kunzru (2002)

1. Find a minor sentence (one with no verb).
2. Find the longest sentence and count the clauses in it.

Starting Out in Journalism

The second big advantage (to being a freelance journalist) is that the freelance can work for anyone at any time in any capacity they choose. The world is their oyster. If you are living in, say, Cardiff or Newcastle, you may well be able to write an article for an Australian magazine. Somebody living in South America or the subcontinent of India can just as easily contribute to UK papers. [...]

So what sort of people become freelance journalists? The answer is that almost anyone who can write reasonably grammatical English can be trained to produce saleable articles and reports.

From the London School of Journalism

1. Find a declarative statement.
2. Find a rhetorical question.
3. Find a simple sentence.

The Hound of the Baskervilles

By Sir Arthur Conan Doyle (1902)

"Hist!" cried Holmes, and I heard the sharp click of a cocking pistol. "Look out! It's coming!"

There was a thin, crisp, continuous patter from somewhere in the heart of that crawling bank. The cloud was within fifty yards of where we lay, and we glared at it, all three, uncertain what horror was about to break from the heart of it. I was at Holmes's elbow, and I glanced for an instant at his face. It was pale and exultant, his eyes shining brightly in the moonlight. But suddenly they started forward in a rigid, fixed stare, and his lips parted in amazement. At the same instant Lestrade gave a yell of terror and threw himself face downwards upon the ground. I sprang to my feet, my inert hand grasping my pistol, my mind paralysed by the dreadful shape which had sprung out upon us from the shadows of the fog. A hound it was, an enormous coal-black hound, but not such a hound as mortal eyes have ever seen. Fire burst from its open mouth, its eyes glowed with a smouldering glare, its muzzle and hackles and dewlap were outlined in flickering flame. Never in the delirious dream of a disordered brain could anything more savage, more appalling, more hellish be conceived than that dark form and savage face which broke upon us out of the wall of fog.

(line numbers: 5, 10, 15, 20)

1. Find a compound sentence with two clauses of equal importance.

2. Find an exclamatory sentence.

3. Find an imperative statement.

How many different types of sentence are used in this passage?

Ice Cold In Alaska

Our adventure is winding to an end. But in the dark of night we are startled awake by a splitting boom, like dynamite being detonated. We sit up in our sleeping bags. Miles Glacier is calving, great chunks of ice falling from its side and crashing into the lake. Again, and again – all through the night. We can't sleep, not just because of the noise, but because of what it might mean.

When we stick our heads out of the tent the next morning, our fears are confirmed. The passageway across the lake is filled with house-sized chunks of glacier ice. "Maybe we can make it through there," I say, pointing. Just then the huge shards of ice grind and shift, and what looked like a small berg overturns with a deep "sploosh", revealing its blue underside that now towers 20ft into the air. "We could get crushed in that," Sam says. We decide to wait another night to see if the ice floats away, but in the meantime, the glacier continues to calve.

By Eowyn Ivey, *Observer* (29 January 2012)

Punctuation

Read the passage and then do the following activities to test your knowledge of punctuation.

It was a hot afternoon, and the railway carriage was correspondingly sultry, and the next stop was at Templecombe, nearly an hour ahead. The occupants of the carriage were a small girl, and a smaller girl, and a small boy. An aunt belonging to the children occupied one corner seat, and the further corner seat on the opposite side was occupied by a bachelor who was a stranger to their party,   5
but the small girls and the small boy emphatically occupied the compartment. Both the aunt and the children were conversational in a limited, persistent way, reminding one of the attentions of a housefly that refuses to be discouraged. Most of the aunt's remarks seemed to begin with "Don't" and nearly all of the children's remarks began with "Why?" The bachelor said nothing out loud.   10
"Don't, Cyril, don't," exclaimed the aunt, as the small boy began smacking the cushions of the seat, producing a cloud of dust at each blow.

  "Come and look out of the window," she added.

  The child moved reluctantly to the window. "Why are those sheep being driven out of that field?" he asked.   15

  "I expect they are being driven to another field where there is more grass," said the aunt weakly.

  "But there is lots of grass in that field," protested the boy; "there's nothing else but grass there. Aunt, there's lots of grass in that field."

  "Perhaps the grass in the other field is better," suggested the aunt.   20

  "Why is it better?" came the swift, inevitable question.

  "Oh, look at those cows!" exclaimed the aunt. Nearly every field along the line had contained cows or bullocks, but she spoke as though she were drawing attention to a rarity.

  "Why is the grass in the other field better?" persisted Cyril.   25

  From *The Story-Teller*, by Saki (H.H. Munroe, 1870–1916)

Punctuation marks

1. Working with a partner, name at least five different punctuation marks in the passage.

Commas

2. How and why has the author used commas in this sentence?

   "It was a hot afternoon, and the railway carriage was correspondingly sultry, and the next stop was at Templecombe, nearly an hour ahead." (lines 1–2)

3. We do not generally use a comma before a conjunction word such as *and*, but the author has broken the rules here:

   "The occupants of the carriage were a small girl, and a smaller girl, and a small boy." (lines 2–3)

   a. What is the effect of putting a comma before "and" twice in this sentence?

   b. Rewrite the sentence with only one conjunction word.

Complex and simple sentences

4. The author uses the simple sentence below without commas in the middle of a paragraph that contains complex and compound sentences (line 10).

   "The bachelor said nothing out loud."

   What effect does he achieve by using this simple sentence here?

Paragraphs

5. Re-read the beginning of the passage from "It was a hot afternoon …" to "producing a cloud of dust at each blow" (lines 1–12).

   a. What does the text look like? Is it cramped and full, or is it neatly separated like the dialogue that follows?

   b. Does the form of the paragraph (the way it has been written) reflect its content (the atmosphere in the carriage)?

Question marks

6. Find two different uses for the question mark in the passage.

Exclamation marks

7. What is the purpose of the exclamation mark here?

   "'Oh, look at those cows!' exclaimed the aunt."

Apostrophes

8. a. Why has the author the used apostrophe *s* ('s) twice in the sentence below?

   b. There is another apostrophe in the word "Don't". What is its function?

   "Most of the aunt's remarks seemed to begin with 'Don't' and nearly all of the children's remarks began with 'Why?'" (lines 9–10)

Speech marks

9. Look at the way the author has set out dialogue.

   a. Would the content of the passage be any different if the narrator told us what the aunt and the children say as reported speech?

   b. What does the direct speech show us about the aunt and Cyril?

Quotation marks

10. **a.** Why has the author used quotation marks around "Don't" and "Why?" in the sentence below?

    b. Would it make any difference if there were no quotation marks?

    > "Most of the aunt's remarks seemed to begin with Don't and nearly all of the children's remarks began with Why?"
    > (lines 9–10)

Commas

Commas are used to separate clauses in a sentence.

Commas are always placed after an adverbial clause.

Full stops

Full stops mark the end of a sentence.

Full stops are also used to mark an abbreviated word or phrase: for example, Prof., p.m.

Question marks

A question mark replaces a full stop after questions in dialogue or direct speech.

A question mark is used to end interrogative sentences.

Exclamation marks

The exclamation mark replaces a full stop after an exclamation: for example, "Oh, no!"

The exclamation mark ends exclamatory sentences: for example, "Oh, look at those cows!"

The exclamation mark is also used to end imperative commands: for example, "Stop, now!"

Speech marks

Speech marks are placed around what people say to separate dialogue from narrative.

Indent the first line of dialogue like starting a new paragraph.

Close speech marks *after* a comma, full stop, question or exclamation mark in dialogue, for example:

- "No! Do it like this!" she exclaimed.

Quotation marks

Quotation marks are used to identify what someone has said, for example:

- The children's remarks began with "Why?".

We use quotation marks to show that words belong to someone else and that we have not spoken or written them ourselves. Notice that there is a full stop after the words that have been quoted above because the quotation comes into a reporting sentence; it is not dialogue.

Apostrophe *'s*

The apostrophe *s* (*'s*) – also called the Saxon genitive – indicates possession or ownership:

- the aunt's remarks = the remarks made by the aunt.

When the owner is singular, the apostrophe goes before the *s* as in *aunt***'s**.

When the owners are plural, the apostrophe goes after the *s* as in:

- the girl**s'** faces = the faces of the two girls
- the adult**s'** stories = the stories of the two adults.

However, when a plural is made without an *s*, such as *children*, we put the apostrophe before the *s* to make:

- the children**'s** remarks
- the women**'s** bags
- the men**'s** jackets.

Never use an apostrophe *s* (*'s*) to make a plural.

Unfortunately, the use of apostrophe *s* is complicated by numerous irregular plurals in English and names that end in *s*. Look at the following correct sentences.

- Charles' brother Thomas was always called Tommy. But no one ever called Charles 'Charlie'.

The name Charles ends with an *s*, so to show that Tommy 'belongs' to his brother Charles we put an apostrophe after the *s* on Charles. However, nowadays it is also acceptable to add the *'s* after the original *s* for example, *Dickens's novels* or *Keats's poems*.

Look at how the apostrophe is used in this sentence:

* The children's aunt had no sense of humour.

We are talking about the aunt 'belonging' to the children, but *children* is an irregular plural and has no *s*, so we put the apostrophe before the *s*.

The following sentences are all correct:

* The girls' hands were clean, but the boys' hands were filthy. (There is more than one girl and more than one boy.)
* The women's shawls were made of silk, the same as the men's ties.
* The babies' hats were pink or blue, but Mary's baby sister's was white.

Apostrophes in dates and epochs

You do not need to use an apostrophe before an *s* when you are talking about epochs such as the 1920s or the 1800s. These sentences are correct:

* There were many pop groups in Liverpool during the 1960s.
* There were many scientific advances and discoveries during the 1600s.

Apostrophes for omission

An apostrophe is used to abbreviate words, combine words or shorten longer words, for example:

* don't = do not
* shan't = shall not
* won't = will not
* 'cept = except
* 'cause = because.

We've been using apostrophes to shorten words for a long time. Some words have become permanently abbreviated like *Halloween* (All Hallows' Eve), *phone* (telephone) and *bus* (autobus).

The tricky thing about using the apostrophe for omission is not *when* to use it, but when *not* to use it! Avoid *don't, won't, can't,* etc. in any type of formal writing.

Strictly speaking, you should only abbreviate words in direct speech.

Never use colloquial English in reports or letters of complaint.

And remember, the word *can't* in full is *cannot*, and *cannot* is all one word.

It's and its

Many people forget that we only use an apostrophe in *it's* to abbreviate *it is* or *it has*, for example:

- *It's raining.* (It is raining.)
- *It's been raining.* (It has been raining).

Its (without an apostrophe) is a possessive pronoun, as in *his/hers/its*, for example:

- The cat licked its paws.

The troublesome apostrophe *s* (*'s* and *s'*)

1. Some of the sentences below contain some common apostrophe *s* mistakes. Write out the incorrect sentences correctly.

   a. There was a sign at the side of the road that said 'Strawberry's for sale'.

   b. Cherry's first name is really Cheri, but we call her Cherry.

   c. The baby's in the nursery were all crying.

   d. The horse's hooves made a clip-clop noise as it trotted home.

   e. The horse's hooves made a clip-clop noise as they trotted home.

2. Copy out and punctuate the following sentences. Be careful – some sentences may need more than one apostrophe or none at all.

   a. Marcos plays for his schools football team.

   b. Marcos teams mascot is a goat called Gladys.

   c. Gladyss owner takes her to every school match but Marcos doesn't like goats very much.

   d. Most schools these days have sports teams for girls and boys; they play matches at weekends.

   e. Sylvias present was a puppy; its paws were all white so she called it Socks.

   f. During the 1920s in New York, young people danced together at afternoon tea dances.

   g. In the 1920s womens dresses were short with fancy frills and the men always wore hats.

   h. Thousands of childrens lives were ruined during the 1800s because they worked in factories.

   i. Australias rugby team beat New Zealands then went on to play Wales.

   j. Welsh rugby players are often good singers as well.

Abbreviation with apostrophes

1. Write out this dialogue using apostrophes so that it makes sense.

   "I cant do that, it aint right. You mustn't do it either or ill tell my dad, and my dadll tell yours."

2. Shakespeare used apostrophes to skip syllables in blank verse and keep the lines iambic (10 syllables per line). Identify how he shortens words in this exchange:

ROSS:

        By th' clock 'tis day,
And yet dark night strangles the travelling lamp.
Is't night's predominance or the day's shame
That darkness does the face of Earth entomb
When living light should kiss it?

OLD MAN:

        'Tis unnatural,
Even like the deed that's done. On Tuesday last,
A falcon, tow'ring in her pride of place,
Was by a mousing owl hawk'd at and kill'd.

From Macbeth, Act 2 scene 4, by William Shakespeare

3. Write out the complete form of each of the following:

a. 'twas
b. 'gainst
c. whate'er
d. ne'er
e. murd'rous
f. whisp'ring
g. whosoe'er
h. he'd

Dashes (–)

We use the dash (–) for a number of purposes:

- in informal communication such as emails to replace commas, the colon, the semi-colon or brackets
- to indicate interrupted statements or incomplete utterances.

Avoid using dashes in formal writing.

Read the following passage from the novel *Lord of the Flies*, which is about a group of British schoolboys who are marooned on a desert island. In this passage, Jack has called a meeting to discuss what is to be done about a "beast" and challenge Ralph, the boys' elected leader.

Look at how the author uses dashes in the dialogue. What purpose do they serve?

"Talk," said Ralph bitterly, "talk, talk, talk."

He took the conch from Jack.

"This meeting –"

Jack interrupted him.

"I called it."   5

"If you hadn't called it I should have. You just blew the conch."

"Well, isn't that calling it?"

"Oh, take it! Go on – talk!"

Ralph thrust the conch into Jack's arms and sat down on
the trunk.   10

"I've called an assembly," said Jack, "because of a lot of
things. First, you know now, we've seen the beast. We crawled up.
We were only a few feet away. The beast sat up and looked at us.
I don't know what it does. We don't even know what it is –"

"The beast comes out of the sea –"   15

"Out of the dark –"

"Trees –"

"Quiet!" shouted Jack. "You, listen. The beast is sitting up
there, whatever it is –"

"Perhaps it's waiting –"   20

"Hunting –"

From *Lord of the Flies*, by William Golding

Ellipsis points (...)

Ellipsis is the word given to the omission of words or phrases: it is
indicated by three dots (...).

1. Read the passage on page 314 from *The Chosen Man*. It is 1637.
   Mistress Hawkins is telling the main character, Ludo, about a
   Cornishman called Robert. The scene is told from Ludo's point
   of view: he is only half listening to what is being said.

2. Look at how the author uses dashes and ellipsis points.

   a. What purpose do the ellipsis points serve here?

   b. Explain why the author has also used the dash.

Mistress Hawkins was full of it so Ludo let her gabble on unhindered.

"... Robert was drugged or knocked on the head and taken onto a Navy ship – you know, we hear about such things but I never did rightly credit it till now ... They was in the Middle Sea, alongside merchantmen, cargo ships, you know – to keep them   5 from the pirates – oh, my, what a danger. A Falmouth ship carrying tin was taken right in front of his eyes! Imagine! And they on board, the captain and like, couldn't do nothing, and him thinking they was going to be taken as well and he'd never see his son or Molly again ..." Her voice rose an octave with each aspect   10 of the drama. "'course pirates don't dare go for Navy ships, least ways that's what they say, so he was safe, but he wasn't to know that, was he?

From *The Chosen Man*, by J.G. Harlond

Semi-colons (;)

We use the semi-colon to link clauses that could each form a complete sentence on their own. We also use semi-colons to separate items in a list or description.

1. Working with a partner, identify all the semi-colons in the passage opposite from the opening of Dickens' *Great Expectations*. It forms part of the exposition of the novel and explains why Pip (the narrator) is living with his older sister and where they live.

2. Look at how Dickens crowds the long sentence from "At such a time ..." to "was Pip." (lines 5–16) with details, each separated by a semi-colon.

   a. Why do you think Dickens used the semi-colon instead of making shorter sentences?

   b. Rewrite the second part of the sentence beginning "... and that the dark flat wilderness ..." (line 10) without using semi-colons. Start like this:

      I also discovered that the dark, flat wilderness ...

Ours was the marsh country, down by the river, within, as the river wound, twenty miles of the sea. My first most vivid and broad impression of the identity of things, seems to me to have been gained on a memorable raw afternoon towards evening. At such a time I found out for certain, that this bleak place overgrown with nettles was the churchyard; and that Philip Pirrip, late of this parish, and also Georgiana wife of the above, were dead and buried; and that Alexander, Bartholomew, Abraham, Tobias, and Roger, infant children of the aforesaid, were also dead and buried; and that the dark flat wilderness beyond the churchyard, intersected with dykes and mounds and gates, with scattered cattle feeding on it, was the marshes; and that the low leaden line beyond, was the river; and that the distant savage lair from which the wind was rushing was the sea; and that the small bundle of shivers growing afraid of it all and beginning to cry, was Pip.

"Hold your noise!" cried a terrible voice, as a man started up from among the graves at the side of the church porch. "Keep still, you little devil, or I'll cut your throat!"

A fearful man, all in coarse grey, with a great iron on his leg. A man with no hat, and with broken shoes, and with an old rag tied round his head. A man who had been soaked in water, and smothered in mud, and lamed by stones, and cut by flints, and stung by nettles, and torn by briars; who limped, and shivered, and glared and growled; and whose teeth chattered in his head as he seized me by the chin.

"O! Don't cut my throat, sir," I pleaded in terror. "Pray don't do it, sir."

From *Great Expectations*, by Charles Dickens

Colons (:)

1. Read the following passage from *The Secret River*. It is the beginning of the 19th century; William Thornhill has recently arrived in Australia on a convict ship.

2. Work with a partner.

   a. Identify all the colons.

   b. Choose one sentence with a colon and explain its function and how it has been used.

   c. Why do you think the author uses the colon instead of making shorter sentences?

When he got up and stepped out through the doorway there was
no cry, no guard: only the huge living night. The air moved around
him, full of rich dank smells. Trees stood tall over him. A breeze
shivered through the leaves, then died, and left only the vast fact
of the forest.   5

He was nothing more than a flea on the side of some enormous
quiet creature.

Down the hill the settlement was hidden by the darkness.
A dog barked in a tired way and stopped. From the bay where
the *Alexander* was anchored there was a sense of restless water   10
shifting in its bed of land and swelling up against the shore.

Above him in the sky was a thin moon and a scatter of stars as
meaningless as spilt rice. There was no Pole Star, a friend to guide
him on the Thames, no Bear that he had known all his life: only
this foreign blaze, unreadable, indifferent.   15

All the many months in the *Alexander*, lying in the hammock
which was all the territory he could claim in the world, listening
to the sea slap against the side of the ship and trying to hear the
voices of his own wife, his own children, in the noise from the
women's quarters, he had been comforted by telling over the   20
bends of his own Thames. The Isle of Dogs, the deep eddying pool
of Rotherhithe, the sudden twist of the sky as the river swung
around the corner to Lambeth: they were all as intimate to him
as breathing. Daniel Ellison grunted in his hammock beside him,
fighting even in his sleep, the women were silent beyond their   25
bulkhead, and still in the eye of his mind he rounded bend after
bend of that river.

Now, standing in the great sighing lung of this other place and
feeling the dirt chill under his feet, he knew that life was gone.
He might as well have swung at the end of the rope they had   30
measured for him. This was a place, like death, from which men
did not return. It was a sharp stab like a splinter under a nail: the
pain of loss. He would die here under these alien stars, his bones
rot in this cold earth.

He had not cried, not for thirty years, not since he was a   35
hungry child too young to know that crying did not fill your belly.
But now his throat was thickening, a press of despair behind his
eyes forcing warm tears down his cheeks.

There were things worse than dying: life had taught him that.
Being here in New South Wales might be one of them.   40

From *The Secret River*, by Kate Grenville

The colon can be used for various different purposes. Look at the following examples.

It can lead from an introduction to a theme:

> "When he got up and stepped out through the doorway there was no cry, no guard: only the huge living night." (lines 1–2)

We use the colon to develop a thought or point made in an opening clause, for example:

> "There were things worse than dying: life had taught him that." (lines 39–40)

The colon can be used to lead from a statement into an example or explanation, for example:

> "It was a sharp stab like a splinter under a nail: the pain of loss." (lines 32–3)

We also use colons to introduce a list of items in formal writing, for example:

> To do this exercise, you will need:
>
> * coloured pencils
>
> * paper
>
> * scissors.

Test your punctuation skills

1. Punctuate this passage from *The Chosen Man*. You need most forms of punctuation.

> The stone wall was warm to the touch marcos alonso almendro just eighteen blond and bright as a new doubloon stood in what had once been the doorway of a shepherds hut impatiently studying the road below the two men staying in his mothers hostel would have to pass this way but so far only two farm carts and an elderly peasant leading donkeys with laden panniers had passed by no foreigners in carriages nothing for what seemed hours time had passed he now needed to shade his eyes the view from the low hilltop was good it would be impossible for anyone to get by without him knowing

2. In pairs, compare how you have punctuated the passage. Where there are differences, take turns to explain your choice of punctuation marks.

Glossary

Abstract noun
Something we cannot see or touch but exists as an idea or an emotion: e.g. confidence, fear, anger.

Active verbs
In an active sentence the subject or 'agent' performs the action: e.g. **The big shark ate** the little fish.

Adaptation
A work that has been rewritten in a different genre or medium: e.g. a novel rewritten as a radio play.

Adjective
A word that describes something: e.g. expensive, useful, pretty, dangerous.

Adverbials
Words that say where, when or how something happened: e.g. on the roof, last week, silently.

Allegory
A story that represents something else, sometimes as an extended metaphor for an important historical and/or political event as in *Animal Farm* (a story about animals but on a deeper level an allegory of the Russian Revolution and Communism).

Alliteration
The repetition of the same consonant sound at the beginning of words: e.g. "Five **m**iles **m**eandering with **m**azy **m**otion" (*from* "Kubla Khan", S.T. Coleridge).

Allusion
Reference to a person, event, place or literary work that the writer assumes the reader will recognise. Allusions are used to make a point in poetry, prose or drama. Many pre-20th-century British writers use allusions to the Christian Bible and Greek/Roman mythology because their readers attended church regularly and studied the Classics at school. Allusions that are clear to readers in one era may require footnotes for later readers.

Ambiguity
When something is ambiguous (adj.) there is more than one possible meaning.

Anachronism
Referring to an event, person or object in a time when that event, person or object did not exist: e.g. the clock in Shakespeare's play *Julius Caesar*.

Anagram
A word made by rearranging the letters of another word or phrase: e.g. cheat/teach, study/dusty.

Anecdote
A short, interesting, sometimes amusing story about a real person or event.

Antagonist
The counterpart to the main character or **protagonist** in a work of fiction: the antagonist opposes the protagonist and/or may be a source of conflict in the plot.

Anthropomorphism
Where animals or objects are given human characteristics; often called **personification**. Anthropomorphism is used in animal stories and fantasy such as *Alice's Adventures in Wonderland*, where animals and playing cards speak and are given human qualities.

Anticlimax (sometimes called bathos)
Sudden drop from a dignified tone or dramatic build up to something very ordinary or trivial, which often causes laughter.

Anti–hero
A protagonist who lacks conventional heroic qualities.

Articles
Sometimes called determiners: e.g. a, an, the, this, some.

Assonance
The repetition of vowel sounds: e.g. "Overnight, very/ Whitely, discreetly, / Very quietly …" (*from* "Mushrooms", Silvia Plath).

Audience
The readers of a text and/or the people for whom the author is writing; the term can also apply to those who watch a film or to television viewers.

Autobiography
A written account of the author's life.

Biography
A written account of someone's life (not written by the subject of the book).

Blank verse
Poetry written in **iambic pentameter** (ten-syllable line with five stresses or iambs); when spoken aloud blank verse is close to the rhythm of normal English speech.

Caesura (cæsura or cesura)
A pause that breaks the rhythm or pace in a line of poetry: caesura can be created by a comma, semi-colon, a full stop or a dash.

Character(s)
The people in any story or play who can be discussed in a number of ways:
- the protagonist is the main character
- the antagonist is the opponent
- a **foil** is a secondary character who contrasts with a major character.

Characters may be classified as 'complex', having both strengths and weaknesses, or 'flat' – fulfilling a role in the text without having a real personality.

Characterisation
How an author portrays or conveys a character's personality.

Chronological writing
Writing where the sequence of events corresponds to the order in which they happened. Non-chronological writing may begin with or contain a flashback or details of a later event.

Cliché
An expression, idiom or phrase that has been repeated so often it has lost its significance.

Climax
The turning point in a story, often when the end result becomes inevitable; usually, but not always, a very dramatic moment.

Colloquial language
Informal, everyday speech as used in conversation; it may include slang expressions. Not appropriate in written reports, essays or exams.

Coming-of-age story
A short story or novel where a young character undergoes an experience that changes his/her world view.

Conflict
A struggle between opposing forces, often the driving force of a story: conflicts can exist between individual characters, groups of characters or between a character and society (what the main character wants and what society expects). The conflict between the Montagues and Capulets in *Romeo and Juliet* causes the main characters to behave unwisely. In *Lord of the Flies* Jack's priorities are in direct conflict to those of Ralph and Piggy. Man-versus-nature is an important conflict in many sci-fi stories.

Connotation
Associations or ideas attached to words such as *duty, honour, responsibility*.

Consonance
Repetition of consonants in lines of poetry such as the *bl/c/k* in "Thistles sp**ik**e the summer air/Or **crack**le open under **bl**ue-**black** pressure" (from "Thistles", Ted Hughes).

Couplet
A verse form of two consecutive rhyming lines: e.g. "I'm a poet/And didn't know it." Shakespeare often ended important scenes with a couplet so the audience would remember a key point.

Dénouement
Literally, the "untying of the knots": the events that follow the climax of a drama or narrative when conflicts are resolved and all is revealed (and characters can live happily ever after).

Dialogue
Words spoken by characters in prose or drama.

Diction
A writer's choice of words: another term for lexis or vocabulary.

Direct speech
Writing exactly what a person says (**dialogue**), as opposed to indirect speech or reported speech where the writer rephrases (reports) what someone has said:

- "Do you understand this, Sam?" said the teacher. (direct speech)

- The teacher asked Sam if he understood. (indirect or reported speech).

Dramatic irony
When the audience or reader knows something the characters in the story, play or film do not. In *Macbeth*, King Duncan thanks and praises Lady Macbeth for her kindness and comments on the gentle, tranquil atmosphere of Macbeth's castle: the audience knows Lady Macbeth is planning to murder him that night while he sleeps in the castle.

Dystopia
A vision of a society that is the opposite of utopia (the book *Utopia*, written by Sir Thomas More and published in 1516, is about a fictional morally good and perfect place). In a dystopian society the conditions of life are miserable and can also seem morally wrong by modern readers' standards; there may be oppression and violence as in Huxley's *Brave New World* or Orwell's *1984*.

Elegy
A poem of mourning from the Greek *elegeia*, a reflection on the death of someone or on sorrow generally: a form of lyric poetry.

Ellipsis
Deliberate omission of a word or words that are implied by the use of ellipsis points .... Ellipsis points in brackets [...] show where a passage has been shortened.

Emotive language
Words and phrases used to affect the reader's emotions or attitudes.

- Emotive adjectives: e.g. poor, helpless, innocent.

- Emotive verbs: e.g. begged, pleaded, sobbed.

End-stopped line
A line of poetry that ends in a full stop or has a natural pause: a stanza in a poem that does not run on to the next is said to be end-stopped.

Enjambment
When a line of poetry flows into the next line without a pause.

Eponymous hero/heroine
Character whose name is also the title of the book/play/poem: e.g. Macbeth, Cristabel.

Euphemism
An agreeable or less offensive expression for one that may seem harsh or unpleasant: e.g. *passed away* instead of *died*.

Fiction
Novel or short story: any prose narrative that is not true.

Figurative language
Writing, or dialogue in drama, that makes what the writer wants to convey more meaningful, descriptive or memorable. Figurative language includes metaphors, similes, hyperbole, personification, onomatopoeia, verbal irony and oxymoron.

First-person narrative
A story told from the point of view of the writer or a fictional **persona** using *I*, as in autobiography and travel writing.

Foil
A character who represents characteristics, values or ideas directly opposed to those of a main character. In the play *Macbeth*, Lady Macduff, a caring wife and mother, is a foil for the childless, ambitious Lady Macbeth.

Foreshadowing
Clues suggesting the outcome of a story (but not when the outcome is deliberately revealed through the use of a narrator or flashback).

Genre
Type of literature, drama, film or play: e.g. tragedy, comedy, sci-fi, fantasy, adventure, romance, thriller, etc.

Homophones or homonyms
Words that sound the same but have different meanings: e.g. maid/made, hare/hair, bough/bow.

Hyperbole
A description which exaggerates ('hype'), using extremes or superlatives for effect: e.g. "We waited for hours!" (five minutes).

Iambic pentameter
Ten-syllable lines with five repetitions of a two-syllable pattern (iambs), where

the stress is always on the second syllable. Dramatists in Shakespeare's time wrote plays in iambic pentameter; nowadays it is used mostly in poetry.

Imagery

A picture in words, often using a metaphor or simile (**figurative language**) which describes something in detail: writers use visual, aural (auditory) or tactile imagery to convey how something looks, sounds or feels in all forms of writing, not just fiction or poetry.

Irony

The difference between what is said and what is meant; what is said and what is done; what is expected or intended and what happens. It is also saying the opposite of what you mean: e.g. "Sorry about this long explanation …".

Sarcasm is meant to be hurtful and involves malice. In *To Kill a Mocking Bird* Jem and Scout are saved by a man who had *ironically* been the object of their fear and suspicion at the beginning of the novel. The children say things about this man being dangerous (what they say), but he saves them when they are attacked (what he does). Irony should not be confused with sarcasm.

Lyric poetry

A type of poem (sonnet or ode) with a speaker who expresses his/her thoughts and feelings: in classical Greece, the lyric was a poem written to be sung accompanied by a lyre.

Metaphor

When an author says one thing *is* another (not *like* another as in a simile): e.g. *the ship ploughed the waves* (a ship is not a plough and cannot plough water).

Motif

Recurring idea or image; a motif differs from a theme in that it can be expressed as a word or phrase. A motif can have symbolic importance as with the innocence of the mocking bird in *To Kill a Mocking Bird* or the conch (a symbol of democracy) in *Lord of the Flies*.

Narrator

The person telling the story who is not necessarily the author except in autobiography.

- First-person narrators (*I*) can play a major or minor role in the story they are telling. However they must be considered unreliable because they can only reveal a personal interpretation of events. Writers invent fictitious first-person narrators to tell their stories, as in *Wuthering Heights*.

- A third-person narrator or an omniscient narrator is not a character in the story. Speaking in the third person, this narrator tells the reader what characters think, say and do – they know everything so they are called omniscient.

Noun

A word given to a person, place or thing which we can identify with our five senses.

- Common nouns are people, places, things: e.g. nurse, river, salt, insect, smoke, wind.

- Proper nouns are the names of people, places or things: e.g. Mr Smith, Toronto, Apollo.

- Abstract nouns are things we cannot touch but know: e.g. hunger, jealousy, longing.

Onomatopoeia

Where sounds are spelled out as words: e.g. whoosh, buzz, wham, clunk.

Oxymoron

A contradiction in terms or putting together opposites: e.g. bitter-sweet, living death. In *Romeo and Juliet* Romeo describes love as "cold fire" and "sick health".

Parable

A story told to illustrate a moral or spiritual truth. The word comes from the Greek *parabole* meaning comparison.

Paradox

Contradictory statement or something that conflicts with common-sense: something is paradoxical when different elements seem to cancel each other out. However, while a paradox may seem contradictory it can also illustrate a truth as in: e.g. more haste, less speed.

Paragraph/paragraphing

A group of sentences (minimum of two, except in modern fiction) linked by a single idea or subject. Each paragraph should contain a **topic sentence**. Paragraphs should be planned, linked and organised to lead up to a conclusion in most forms of writing.

Passive verbs

In a passive sentence the subject or 'agent' is mentioned after the passive verb form: e.g. The little fish **was eaten by the big shark**.

Passive verbs are used in more formal writing such as reports: e.g. An eye-witness was interviewed by the police … Results have been analysed by the sales team …

Pathos (n.)

The effect in literature or drama that provokes a sense of sadness or pity.

Persona

Many novels and poems use the **point of view** of a fictitious speaker as a narrator. The 'voice' you hear speaking in a poem may be that of a persona, not the poet.

Personification

When something non-human is given human qualities.

Plot

The sequence of events in a film, play, story or narrative poem.

Point of view

Perspective from which the story is told: how the reader experiences the story or poem.

Pronoun

A word that stands in place for a noun: *he, she, they, we, all, each, both*. For example: Boise swam in the river, **she** wasn't afraid.

Prose

Any form of writing that is not poetry or a script.

Protagonist

The main character in a film, play or story.

Register

The appropriate style and tone of language chosen for a specific purpose and/or audience.

Rhetoric

Rhetoric originally referred to the art of speaking to impress and/or persuade an audience.

- Rhetorical language is language used in speeches to sway an audience.
- Rhetorical questions are questions that do not require an answer but serve to give the speaker an excuse to explain his/her views. Rhetorical questions should be avoided in formal writing and essays.

Rhyme
Repetition of similar sounding words in poetry.
- End rhyme occurs at the end of two or more lines (as in couplets and limericks).
- Internal rhyme occurs in the middle of a line, as in "… all the **night** through fog-smoke **white**" (from "The Ancient Mariner", S.T. Coleridge).

Rhythm
Term used to describe sound patterns or 'movement' in poetry.

Rubric
Words that act as instructions: the information that tells you what to do or how to answer a question (on an exam paper or in a text book). Rubric can also refer to headings or explanatory notes. In ancient texts rubric was written in red ink.

Setting
The time and place where a story, film, play or poem occurs.

Simile
Figurative language that describes one thing as being *like* or *as* something else: e.g. they ran like the wind; as lovely as a summer rose.

Sonnet
Lyric poem consisting of 14 lines; a sonnet can be arranged in different ways.
- Petrarchan (Italian) sonnet divides content into two ideas and consists of an octave (eight lines) followed by a sestet (six lines).
- Shakespearean (English) sonnet has three quatrains (four lines each) followed by a concluding couplet (two lines).

Speaker
The *voice* of a poem, which may not be that of the poet him/herself (**persona**); the speaker in a poem is the equivalent of the narrator in prose fiction.

Structure
The way the various elements of a poem, drama story or essay are assembled: the framework of a work of literature or the organisation of any text.

Style
A writer's choice of words (including **figurative language**), syntax, point of view.

Syllable
The smallest unit of speech that produces a distinct sound within a word.
- Monosyllabic words make one sound: e.g.one, sound, dog, big, hope.
- Polysyllabic words contain more than one syllable: e.g. syll/a/ble = three syllables.

Symbol
Something that stands for something else: e.g. flags are used as symbols for national identity. In literature a symbol is usually something that has a special significance in the text. Keats starts "Ode to a Nightingale" with a real nightingale that becomes a symbol for innocence and joy.

Symbolism
The use of specific objects or images to represent abstract ideas: a **symbol** is something tangible or visible but the idea it symbolises may be abstract or universal. Piggy's glasses in *Lord of the Flies* symbolise a link to the material, civilised world and the ability to see things clearly.

Theme
The main idea or message conveyed by the writing. A theme can be represented by a **motif** (the mockingbird in Harper Lee's novel or the fire beacon in *Lord of the Flies*. Themes in *Macbeth* include the ambition, loyalty and power.

Thesis statement
The statement made at the beginning of a discursive or argumentative essay (which will be examined and discussed in the following paragraphs). For example: Attending school until the age of 16 should be compulsory for students throughout the world.

Tone
Tone refers to the way a writer creates mood or atmosphere. Tone may be playful, formal, intimate, angry, serious, tender, serene, melancholy, etc.

Topic sentence
The key sentence of a paragraph that contains the principal idea or subject being discussed.

Tragedy
A tragedy is a story that ends with a negative or unfortunate outcome that could have been avoided. The ending may be a result of a flaw in the main character's personality as with Macbeth, who brings about his own death and the death of many others because he gives in to ambition (which he knows to be wrong). Romeo and Juliet die because they are the victims of their parents' feud and act unwisely because they are in love. The adults in the play *Romeo and Juliet* could have prevented the tragedy.

Zeitgeist
A German word meaning time or spirit, it is the intellectual atmosphere of an age or period.

Index

247 Magazine 102

accounts of an incident or experience 70
Adams, Jean *Families and Children: Ancient Egyptian Marriage* 110
Adams, William Lee *Bhutan's Royal Wedding* 108
adjectives 284
    absolute terms 285
    comparatives 284
    how much or how many 286
    opposites 284
    superlatives 285
adverbs 286
    adverbial phrases 286–7
advertisements 19
air 29
alliteration 62, 245
animals
    animal adjectives 42
    animal imagery 41
    animals and people 44–7
    animals in folklore 40
    animals in holy texts 40
    moral tales and human nature 41
    Shakespeare's animal imagery 42–3
    Williams, Mike *Taming the wolf: domesticating the dog* 44–5
    Working Elephants in Thailand 46–7
annotating 6
apostrophes 298, 300–1
    abbreviation with apostrophes 302–3
    apostrophes for omission 301
    apostrophes in dates and epochs 301
    it's and its 302
Aristotle *The Poetics* 86
Arundel Manuscript 40
Asclepius and the Two Travellers 3
assonance 245
audiences 85, 90
Austen, Jane *Pride and Prejudice* 219–21
autobiography 202

Baker, Green *The Nine Parts of Speech* 68
balloon debate 200
Barkham, Patrick *What makes Madame Tussauds' wax work?* 192–3
Beckham, Victoria 187
bestiaries 40–1
Bhutan 108–9
Bible 40
Binyon, Lawrence *For the Fallen* 246, 247
biography 115, 198, 200
    Livingstone, David 199
Blake, William *A Poison Tree* 118
blog writing 152
Bowes, Gemma *Tips for Travel Writing* 12
Bradbury, Ray *The Martian Chronicles* 224–7

Brewster, Elizabeth *Where I Come From* 25
Brontë, Emily *Wuthering Heights* 229
Bryson, Bill 238–9
    A Walk in the Woods 19
Burns, Robert 207
    Auld Lang Syne 206, 208–9
Butler, Alan *Plymouth's Drum Theatre hosts moving play Ivan and the Dogs* 102
Byron, Lord *Don Juan* 161

Cabaret 135
Caetano, Hubert *Gibraltar: Rock of Ages* 258–9
Carroll, Lewis *Jabberwocky* 289
Carter, Angela 223
celebrity 187
characters 86, 87
Chatwin, Bruce *What Am I Doing Here?* 176–8, 179
Chaucer, Geoffrey 41
Christmas 57, 58
chronological order 12, 107
Clarence, Angela *Children of the Stars* 6, 7
    Travelling in the Desert 265–6
Cleopatra 112–13
clichés 162
Coleridge, Samuel Taylor *Kubla Khan* 21–2
colloquial expression 162
colons 306–8
Colossus of Rhodes 187
colour-coding parts of speech 276
Colton, Charles Caleb 107
Columbus, Christopher 188
comedy 86, 87, 232
commas 298, 299
Commedia dell'Arte 103–4, 105
consonance 245
Copper River, Alaska 36–8
Cornwall, England 10
Costner, Kevin 187
Crawford, Amy *Who Was Cleopatra?* 112–13
cryptids 170, 171
    Loch Ness Monster 170–2
    Mokele-Mbembe 173–6
    Yetis 171, 176–8
Curie, Marie 188
currency 136–7

Daily Mail 168, 171, 172
Dampier, William *A New Voyage Round the World* 9
dashes 215, 303–4
data 35
Defoe, Daniel *Robinson Crusoe* 9, 13
    Tour Thro' the Whole Island of Great Britain 9–10
Delille, Jacques 107
dénouement 232
Desai, Anita *Circus Cat, Alley Cat* 130–3
descriptive writing 6, 24, 75, 203, 205, 272
devil's advocate 161
Dewsbury, Rick *Scientists close in on Yeti* 171
dialogue 90, 123, 213

dash 215
    suspension points 215
diamonds 148–9
Dickens, Charles *Bleak House* 63, 64
    Great Expectations 228, 305, 306
diction 62, 86, 87
direct and indirect speech 165, 300
directed writing 60, 269–70
discursive essays 126, 127
Divakaruni, Chitra Banerjee *The Mistress of Spices* 229
dogs 44–5
Dopoko, Mbella Sonne *Pain* 29
Doyle, Sir Arthur Conan *The Beryl Coronet* 161
    The Hound of the Baskervilles 296
drama
    Ancient Greece 86–7
    classic British drama 94–8, 99
    comedy 232
    Commedia dell'Arte 103–4, 105
    Kabuki 84
    Kathakali 82
    making comparisons 85
    modern drama 100–1, 102, 103
    Noh theatre 83
    scripts and dialogue 90–1
    structure of a five-act play 231
    theatre language 81
    tragedy 231–2
    writing a review 99
Dunnett, Dorothy *Scales of Gold* 267–9

earth 28
Eastenders 88
Egypt, ancient 110–15
elements 28
elephants 46–7
ellipsis points 215, 304–5
empathy 87
endings 223
    Bradbury, Ray *The Martian Chronicles* 224–7
    famous last words 228–9
    Frost, Robert *Fire and Ice* 223
    how to end a story 230, 231
    Shakespeare, William *Macbeth* 233
    Wilde, Oscar *The Importance of Being Earnest* 234–7
entertaining writing 69, 115, 123
    short stories 124
Evans, Paul *The Crusade for Crusoe's Islands* 13–15
exclamation marks 298, 299
expeditions 8
explicit meaning 227
exploring writing 123

Fair Trade goods 152
    Gold: every piece tells a story 153
    The British Association of Fair Trade Shops 153
Fallon, Joan *Between the Sierra and the Sea* 256–7
fame 187
    balloon debate 200

Barkham, Patrick *What makes Madame Tussauds' wax work?* 192–3
    famous last words 228–9
    famous people 188–9
    famous places 196–7
    Olympic Games 190–1
family 109, 116, 117
    Adams, Jean *Families and Children: Ancient Egyptian Marriage* 110
    Saroyan, William *My Name is Aram* 122–3
    Saving Richard Parker 128, 129
    Tan, Amy *The Joy Luck Club* 125, 126
fantasy 180–3
feature articles 38, 166, 175
fiction 62–3, 204–5, 223
    fantasy 180–3
figurative language 245–7
fire 30
Fitzgerald, F. Scott *The Great Gatsby* 138–9, 140, 228
Fleming, Alexander 188
French Revolution 263–4
Freytag, Gustav 231
friends 107
Frost, Robert *Fire and Ice* 223
full stops 299

Gallagher, Brian 254, 255
Gandhi, Mohindar 28
Gayle, Damian *Is This Iceland's Loch Ness Monster?* 172
genre 180
Geographical 15
Gibbons, William *Was a Mokele-mbembe killed at Lake Tele?* 174–5
Gleeson, Kristin *Selkie Dreams* 251–2
gold 142–3, 146, 153
    Hood, Thomas *Gold* 159
Golding, William 211
    Lord of the Flies 212–18, 303–4
Great Frost 185
Greek mythology 30
Greek theatre 86–7
    modern soap operas 88, 89
Grenville, Kate *The Secret River* 292, 307, 308
Gross National Happiness 108, 109
Guardian, The 34, 89, 193

Haiti earthquake 167–8
Hardy, Thomas *The Mayor of Casterbridge* 229
    The Voice 249
Harlond, J.G. *The Chosen Man* 304–5, 308
Harrison, Sarah *A Flower That's Free* 260–1
Haynes, Natalie *What do soap operas have in common with Greek tragedies?* 89
Heaney, Seamus *Death of a Naturalist* 64
Heaney, Seamus *Follower* 117
Herrick, Robert *To Anthea, Who May Command Him Anything* 118
holiday brochures
    Antarctica expedition 16

Banff & Lake Louise 19
Historic Venice 18
Indonesian adventure 17
New York, New York! 18
holiday of a lifetime 16, 19
homonyms 169
Hood, Thomas *Gold* 159
Houston Chronicle 31
Hsia Yu 28
Hughes, Ted F*ull Moon and Little Frieda* 119
    Pike 52, 53
Humphrys, John *Kiki, the icon of hope in the rubble* 167–8,
    169
Hurlers 10
Huxley, Aldous *Brave New World* 228

Ice Age 8
identifying information 6
idioms 114–15, 283
imagery 53, 62
    animal imagery 41
    Shakespeare's animal imagery 42–3
implicit meaning 227
Independent, The 45
India 254
indirect and direct speech 165, 300
informative writing 47, 48, 69, 115
International Association for the Exchange of Students for
    Technical Experience (IAESTE)   255
interview scripts 61
invented words 289
irony 213
Islam 28
island endemics 13–15
Istanbul 238–41
Ivey, Eowyn *Ice Cold in Alaska* 36–8, 296

Joachin, Kiki 167–8, 169
journalism 162, 295
Juan Fernández Islands, Chile 13–15
juxtaposition 178

Kabuki 84
Kathakali 82
keywording 6, 262
Kilkelly, Daniel 'Enders reveals Greek tragedy influence 88
Kinser, Nathan *The Heart of the Crowd* 263–4
Kublai Khan 28
Kunzru, Kari *The Impressionist* 295

La Granja, Segovia, Spain 20
Lagarfljót, Iceland 172
Lamartine, Alphonse de 107
Larkin, Philip 223
Lawrence, D. H. *Snake* 50–1, 53
Lee, Laurie *As I Walked Out One Midsummer Morning* 20
LeGuin, Ursula *The Earthsea Trilogy* 204–5
Leonardo da Vinci 188

Lessing, Doris *Flight* 76–9
letters of complaint 140, 141
Li, Martin *How to Write the Perfect Travel Article* 11
Ling, Joan Gir *The Yangtze River Three Gorges Project* 33
lions 40
literature extension
    Austen, Jane *Pride and Prejudice* 219–21
    Desai, Anita *Circus Cat, Alley Cat* 130–3
    Hardy, Thomas *The Voice* 249
    Hood, Thomas *Gold* 159
    Hughes, Ted *Pike* 52, 53
    Lawrence, D. H. *Snake* 50–1, 53
    Lessing, Doris *Flight* 76–9
    Rossetti, Christina *An Emerald Is As Green As Grass* 159
    Woolf, Virginia *Orlando* 185
Livingstone, David 199
    Missionary Travels in South Africa 202–3
Loch Ness Monster 170–2
London 63, 260–1
London School of Journalism *Starting Out in Journalism* 295
Longfellow, Henry Wadsworth 187
Los Roques, Venezuela 6, 7
love 107
    different forms of love 117
    human emotions 118
    synonyms for love and hate 119

Macoushi Indians 4–5
Madame Tussaud's, London 192–5
Magliaro, Elaine *Wind Turbines* 29
Mansfield, Katherine *Her First Ball* 65–7
marriage 121
Martel, Yann *Life of Pi* 128, 129
McQueeney, Kerry *Is This Iceland's Loch Ness Monster?* 171
media releases 149
    Argyle Pink Diamonds 151
memories 55
    Obreht, Teá *The Tiger's Wife* 55–6
    Ondaatje, Michael *Running in the Family* 59, 60
    Thomas, Dylan *Quite Early One Morning* 57, 58
Mendel, Gregor 188
metaphor 53, 62
Mexico City earthquake 162, 163–4
Midas 147
    Midas and the River Pactolus 146
Milne, A.A. *The House at Pooh Corner* 229
Mishukov, Ivan 100–1, 102, 103
Mitchell, Margaret *Gone With the Wind* 229
modal verbs 111
Mokele-Mbembe 173–6
money 135
    Fitzgerald, F. Scott *The Great Gatsby* 138–9, 140
    history of money 136–7
    Wilde, Oscar *The Importance of Being Earnest* 154–7
Money Song, The 135
monsters 170
    Loch Ness Monster 170–2
    McQueeney, Kerry *Is This Iceland's Loch Ness Monster?*
    171

Mokele-Mbembe 173–6
Soodin, Vince *Scientists close in on Yeti* 171
Viegas, Jennifer *Loch Ness Monster-like Animal Filmed in Alaska?* 170
Yetis 171, 176–8
mood 62–4, 67, 246
Morris, Mervyn *Little Boy Crying* 73
Mozart, Wolfgang Amadeus 188
Mungoshi, Charles *Before the Sun* 74
myths 27, 30–1

narrative writing 49, 75, 248, 249, 272
narrative voice 180
omniscient narrator 180
showing and telling 181–2
Taylor, G.P. *Shadowmancer* 183
Tolkien, J.R.R. *The Lord of the Rings* 181–2
National Geographic *Mokele-Mbembe: Swamp monster of the Congo* 173
Native American mythology 30–1, 32
nature 27
mood and tone 62–4
Naylor, Hattie *Ivan and the Dogs* 100–1, 102, 103
Nelson, Dean *Bhutan's 'Gross National Happiness' Index* 109
New European, The 33
news reports 38, 162
direct and indirect speech 165
human interest 163
Kiki, the icon of hope in the rubble 167–8, 169
Mexico takes stock after major quake 162, 163, 165
news reports and feature articles 166, 175
Powerful quake shakes southern Mexico, capital 163–4, 165
Wheeler, Virginia School is a three-smile walk for Kiki 169
writing 165
Ngugi Wa Thiongo *Weep Not, Child* 70, 71
Nobel Prize for Literature 210
Golding, William Lord of the Flies 211–18
Nobel, Alfred 210
Noh theatre 83
Norman, Susan In Your Hands 3
Norse mythology 27, 223
note-making 45
nouns 277
compound nouns 277–8
noun phrases 278–9

Obreht, Teá *The Tiger's Wife* 55–6
Observer, The 7, 38, 265
Olympic Games 190–1
Ondaatje, Michael *Running in the Family* 59, 60
Orinoco Delta 7
Ovid *Metamorphoses* 27, 147
Owen, Wilfred *Anthem for Doomed Youth* 247
oxymoron 20

Palmstruch, John 137
Paper 1 Reading Passages 238–41, 241–3, 243–4
exam practice 251–3, 254–5, 256–8, 258–9
Paper 2 Reading Passages 260–2, 263–4, 265–6, 267–9

strategy 262, 265
Paper 3 strategy 270, 272
Writing 269–71, 272, 273–5
paradox 20
paragraphs 298
parts of speech 276, 277
adjectives 284–6
adverbs 286–7
nouns 277–9
prefixes 288
pronouns 279–80
suffixes 288
verbs 281–3
past tenses and modern idioms 114–15
pathos 81
personification 29, 62
persuasive writing 19
writing to argue and persuade 39
plot 86–7, 232
poetry 22, 63, 73
Baker, Green *The Nine Parts of Speech* 68
Binyon, Lawrence *For the Fallen* 246, 247
Blake, William *A Poison Tree* 118
Brewster, Elizabeth *Where I Come From* 25
Carroll, Lewis *Jabberwocky* 289
Coleridge, Samuel Taylor *Kubla Khan* 21–2
comparing poems 53, 57
Dopoko, Mbella Sonne *Pain* 29
Frost, Robert *Fire and Ice* 223
Hardy, Thomas *The Voice* 249
Heaney, Seamus *Death of a Naturalist* 64
Heaney, Seamus *Follower* 117
Herrick, Robert To Anthea, *Who May Command Him Anything* 118
Hood, Thomas *Gold* 159
Hughes, Ted *Full Moon and Little Frieda* 119
Hughes, Ted *Pike* 52, 53
Lawrence, D. H. *Snake* 50–1, 53
Magliaro, Elaine *Wind Turbines* 29
Morris, Mervyn *Little Boy Crying* 73
Mungoshi, Charles *Before the Sun* 74
Owen, Wilfred *Anthem for Doomed Youth* 247
Rossetti, Christina *An Emerald Is As Green As Grass* 159
Scott, Dennis *Marrysong* 121
Stevenson, Robert Louis *Travel* 23
Wordsworth, William *Composed Upon Westminster Bridge* 63, 64
points of view
poetry 73
short stories 65, 67
Polo, Marco 28
prefixes 288
Prentice, Claire *Should Auld Acquaintance Be Forgot* 208–9
presentations 201
press releases 149
Argyle Pink Diamonds 150
Priestley, J.B. *An Inspector Calls* 94–8, 99
pronouns 279
demonstrative pronouns 280

object pronouns 280
possessive pronouns 280
punctuation 198, 215, 297
apostrophes 298, 300–3
colons 306–8
commas 298, 299
dashes 303–4
ellipsis points 304–5
exclamation marks 298, 299
full stops 299
punctuation marks 298–9
question marks 298, 299
quotation marks 299, 300
semi-colons 305–6
speech marks 299
test your punctuation skills 308
puns in headlines 169

question marks 298, 299
quotation marks 299, 300

radio transcripts 60
rafting 36–8
Raleigh, Walter 7
reading skills 6, 35
register 109
religion 40
reminiscing 55
report writing 152
Revell, Jane *In Your Hands* 3
reviews 99
rhetorical questions 174
rhythm 62
Rio Tinto 149, 150, 151
Selecting a diamond 148
Ripley, Robert Leroy 161
romance 120
Rossetti, Christina *An Emerald Is As Green As Grass* 159

Saint-Exupéry, Antoine de 107
Saki (H.H. Munroe) *The Story-Teller* 297
salt 28
Saroyan, William *My Name is Aram* 122–3
scanning 6, 45
Schiller, Friedrich 187
school past and present 68–9
school in rural Africa 70–2
Scott, Dennis *Marrysong* 121
scriptwriting 61, 90–1
self-assessment
Unit 1 25
Unit 2 49
Unit 3 75
Unit 4 105
Unit 5 129
Unit 6 158
Unit 7 184
Unit 8 218
Unit 9 249

Selkirk, Alexander 13, 14, 15
semi-colons 198, 305–6
sentences 291
complements 291–2
conditional 294
declarative 294
exclamatory 294
imperative 292, 294
interrogative 294
minor sentences 292
simple, compound and complex sentences 292, 298
using complex sentences 140
using sentence skills 295
working with different types of sentence 293
Shakespeare, William 41, 90
animal imagery 42
apostrophes and abbreviation 303
As You Like It 81
influence of Commedia dell'Arte 104
King Lear 29
Macbeth 43, 92, 93, 116, 233
Twelfth Night 188
short stories 65
Lessing, Doris *Flight* 76–9
Mansfield, Katherine *Her First Ball* 65–7
writing to entertain 124
sibilance 62, 245
simile 53
skimming 6
slapstick 103
Smithsonian 143
soap operas 88, 89
song 86
Soodin, Vince *Scientists close in on Yeti* 171
Sophocles 86
Spanish Civil War 256–7, 258–9
spectacle 86, 87
speech marks 299
speech writing 144, 145
SQuEE technique 6, 56, 67
stage directions 90, 91, 99
Standard English 152
statistics 35
Steinbeck, John *The Grapes of Wrath* 62
Stevenson, Robert Louis *Travel* 23
success 188
suffixes 288
-logy 290
summaries 4, 15, 111, 195 this is actually here
using complex sentences 140 not sure about this
Sun, The 169, 171
suspension points 215
Swiston, Marie *How Coyote Gave Fire to the People* 30–1
Sydney Morning Herald 208, 209
sympathy 87
synonyms for love and hate 119
syntax 198, 276
sentence structure 291–2
sentences for different purposes 294
using sentence skills 295

talking points
    All the world's a stage... 81
    Asclepius and the two travellers 3
    Auld Lang Syne 206
    Colossus of Rhodes 187
    education in rural areas 72
    endings 228
    fame, celebrity, success and greatness 187
    fiction 223
    friends 107
    Greek theatre 87
    money 135
    monsters 170
    nature 29
    nonsense rhymes 289
    salt 30
    tourism and the environment 19
Tan, Amy *The Joy Luck Club* 125, 126
Taylor, G.P. *Shadowmancer* 183
techniques 12
Telegraph, The 109
Tennyson, Alfred *In Memoriam* 27
theatre *see* drama
Thomas, Dylan *Quite Early One Morn*ing 57, 58
thought 86
tigers 55–6
Timbuktu, Mali 28
Time 108
Times, The 246
tips 12
Tolkien, J.R.R. *The Lord of the Rings* 181–2, 228
tone 62–4, 109, 246
tourism 8
tragedy 86, 87, 88, 89
    catastrophe 232
    climax 232
    exposition and introduction 231
    falling action 232
    rising action and complications 231
travel writing 4, 9
    Bowes, Gemma *Tips for Travel Writing* 12
    Clarence, Angela *Children of the Star*s 6, 7
    Defoe, Daniel *Tour Thro' the Whole Island of Great Britain* 9–10
    Evans, Paul *The Crusade for Crusoe's Islands* 13–15
    holiday brochures 16–19
    Ivey, Eowyn *Ice Cold in Alaska* 36–8
    Li, Martin *How to Write the Perfect Travel Article* 11
    Waterton, Charles *Wanderings in South America* 4–5
Trigell, Jonathan *Boy* 229
truth 161
Tuareg 28

verbs 281–3
    active and passive voice 282
    modal verbs 282–3
    must, have to and have got to 283
    past perfect 281
    phrasal verbs and idiomatic expressions 283

Viegas, Jennifer *Loch Ness Monster-like Animal Filmed in Alaska?* 170

wampum 136, 137
Wangchuck, King Jigme Khesar 108
Wangchuck, King Jigme Singye 109
Wangchuck, Queen Jetsun Pema 108
Warao Indians 7
Waterton, Charles *Wanderings in South America* 4–5
Watts, Jonathan *China warns of "urgent problems" facing Three Gorges Dam* 34
wealth 138–9, 154–7
Webter, Donovan *The Devastating Costs of the Amazon Gold Rush* 142–3, 144
Weclome to Chiangmai *Working Elephants in Thailand* 46–7
Wheeler, Virginia *School is a three-smile walk for Kiki* 169
Wilcox, Ella Wheeler 107
Wilde, Oscar *The Importance of Being Earnest* 120, 154–7, 223, 234–7
Williams, Mike *Taming the wolf: domesticating the dog* 44–5
wolves 44–5
Woolf, Virginia *Orlando* 185
word choice 20
Wordsworth, William *Composed Upon Westminster Bridge* 63, 64
would + infinitive 111
wourali 4–5

Yangtze River, Three Gorges Project 32, 33–4, 35
Yetis 171, 176–8

zoos 55–6

William J Gibbons: 'Was a Mokele-Mbembe killed at Lake Tele?', from *Mokele-Mbembe: Mystery Beast of the Congo Basin* (Coachwhip Books. 2006), reprinted by permission of the author.

Kristin Gleeson: extract from *Selkie Dreams* (Knox Robinson, 2012), reprinted by permission of the publishers.

William Golding: extracts from *Lord of the Flies* (Faber, 1962), copyright © William Golding , 1954, 1962, © renewed 1982 by William Gerald Golding, reprinted by permission of Faber & Faber Ltd and G P Putnam's Sons, a division of Penguin Group (USA) Inc.

Kate Grenville: extract from *The Secret River* (Canongate, 2006), copyright © Kate Grenville 2005, reprinted by permission of the publishers, Canongate Books Ltd (UK), Grove/Atlantic, Inc (USA), and The Text Publishing Co Pty Ltd (Australia).

Sarah Harrison: extract from *A Flower That's Free* (Warner, 2000), copyright © Sarah Harrison 1984, reprinted by permission of The Orion Publishing Group, London.

Natalie Haynes: extract from 'What do soap operas have in common with Greek Tragedy?', *The Guardian*, 12.4.2010, copyright © Guardian News & Media Ltd 2010, reprinted by permission of GNM Ltd.

Seamus Heaney: 'Death of a Naturalist' and 'Follower' from *Death of a Naturalist* (Faber, 1966), copyright © Seamus Heaney 1966, reprinted by permission of Faber & Faber Ltd, and from *Opened Ground: Selected Poems 1966-1996*, copyright © Seamus Heaney 1998, reprinted by permission of the publishers, Farrar Straus & Giroux, LLC.

Ted Hughes: 'Pike' from *Lupercal* (Faber, 1960), copyright © Ted Hughes 1960,'Full Moon & Little Frieda' from *New Selected Poems 1957- 1994* (Faber, 1995), copyright © Ted Hughes 1995, and lines from 'Thistles' from *Wodwo* (Faber, 1967), copyright © Ted Hughes 1967, reprinted by permission of Faber & Faber Ltd, and from *Collected Poems*, copyright © 2003 by the Estate of Ted Hughes, reprinted by permission of the publishers, Farrar Straus & Giroux, LLC.

John Humphrys: extract from 'Kiki, Icon of Hope in the Rubble', *Daily Mail* online, 23.1.2010, reprinted by permission of Solo Syndication for Associated Newspapers Ltd.

Mary Innes: extract from *The Metamorphoses of Ovid* translated with an introduction by Mary M Innes (Penguin Classics, 1955), copyright © Mary M Innes, 1955, reprinted by permission of Penguin Books Ltd.

Eowyn Ivey: 'Ice Cold in Alaska', *The Observer*, 29.1.2012, copyright © Guardian News & Media Ltd 2012, reprinted by permission of GNM Ltd.

Patrick J Kiger: 'Mokele-Mbembe: Swamp Monster of the Congo' published at www.tvblogs.nationalgeographic.com, reprinted by permission of the author.

Nathan Kinser: 'Heart of the Crowd: A Study of the Motives of the Peasant Class in the French Revolution' (1999) reprinted by permission of the author and of Eric Wake, University of the Cumberlands, www.ucumberlands.edu.

Hari Kunzru: extract from *The Impressionist* (Penguin, 2003), copyright © Hari Kunzru 2003, reprinted by permission of Penguin Books Ltd.

Laurie Lee: extract from *As I Walked Out One Midsummer Morning* (Penguin, 1971), copyright © Laurie Lee 1969, reprinted by permission of Curtis Brown Ltd, London, on behalf of The Partners of the Literary Estate of Laurie Lee.

Doris Lessing: 'Flight' from *The Habit of Loving* (MacGibbon & Kee, 1957), copyright © Doris Lessing 1957, reprinted by permission of HarperCollins Publishers Ltd, and HarperCollins Publishers, USA..

Martin Li: 'How to write the perfect travel article' (abridged) from *The Insider Secrets of Freelance Travel Writing* published at www.transitionsabroad.com, reprinted by permission of the author.

Kerry McQueeney: extract from 'Is this Iceland's Loch Ness Monster? Giant 'serpent-like sea creature caught on camera', *Daily Mail*, 8.2.2012, reprinted by permission of Solo Syndication for Associated Newspapers Ltd.

Elaine Magliaro: 'Wind Turbines' haikus, published online reprinted by permission of the author.

Yann Martel: *Life of Pi* (Canongate, 2002), copyright © Yann Martel 2001, reprinted by permission of the publishers, Canongate Books Ltd, Houghton Mifflin Harcourt Publishing Company and the author c/o Westwod Creative Artists Ltd.

A A Milne: *The House at Pooh Corner* (Methuen & Co, 1928/Egmont, 2011), copyright © The Trustees of the Pooh Properties 1928, reprinted by permission of the publishers, Egmont UK Ltd.

Mervyn Morris: 'Little Boy Crying' from *The Pond* (New Beacon Books, 1973, 1979), copyright © Mervyn Morris 1973, reprinted by permission of New Beacon Books Ltd.

Hattie Naylor: extracts from *Ivan and the Dogs* (Methuen Drama, 2010), copyright © Hattie Naylor 2010, reprinted and reproduced as audio by permission of United Agents, www.unitedagents.co.uk.

Dean Nelson: extract from 'Bhutan's Gross National Happiness Index', *The Telegraph*, 2.3.2011, copyright © Telegraph Media Group Ltd 2011, reprinted by permission of TMG

Barbara Nuzum: extract from 'The Connection between Reading and Success', published on www.helium.com, 30 January 2010, copyright © Barbara Nuzum 2010, reprinted by permission of the author.

Téa Obreht: extract from *The Tiger's Wife* (Weidenfeld & Nicolson, 2011), copyright © Téa Obreht 2011, reprinted and reproduced as audio by permission of the publishers, The Orion Publishing Group, London and of The Gernert Company on behalf of the author.

Michael Ondaatje: extract from *Running in the Family* (Picador, 1984), copyright © Michael Ondaatje 1982, reprinted by permission of Bloomsbury Publishing Plc and W W Norton & Company, Inc.

Sylvia Plath: lines from 'Mushrooms' from *The Colossus and other Poems* (Faber, 1967), copyright © Sylvia Plath 1957, 1958, 1959, 1960, 1961, 1962, 1967, reprinted by permission of Faber & Faber Ltd and Alfred A Knopf, a division of Random Inc

Claire Prentice: 'Old Lang Syne': New Year's song has a convoluted history', *Washington Post*, 30 12.2011, reprinted by permission of the author.

J B Priestley: *An Inspector Calls* (Heinemann Educational 1947), reprinted by permission of United Agents on behalf of The Estate of the late J B Priestley.

Will Randall: extract from *Botswana Time* (Abacus, 2005), reproduced in digital format by permission of the Kate Hordern Literary Agency on behalf of the author.

William Saroyan: extract from 'The Summer of the Beautiful White Horse' from *My Name is Aram* (Harcourt, 1940, Penguin 1944), copyright © William Saroyan 1940, 1944, reprinted and reproduced as audio by permission of the Wm Saroyan Foundation and the Trustees of Leland Stanford Junior University.

Vikram Seth: extract from *A Suitable Boy* (Phoenix, 1993), copyright © Vikram Seth 1993, reprinted in digital format by permission of David Godwin Associates.

Paul Shoebottom: extract from 'Reading and Success' published on http://esl.fis.edu, reprinted by permission of the author.

John Steinbeck: extract from *Grapes of Wrath* (Penguin, 1976), copyright © John Steinbeck 1939 reprinted by permission of Penguin Books Ltd.

Amy Tan: extract from *The Joy-Luck Club* (Penguin, 2006), copyright © Amy Tan 1989, reprinted by permission of Abner Stein for the author, and G P Putnam's Sons, a division of Penguin Group (USA) Inc.

G P Taylor: extract from *Shadowmancer* (Faber, 2003), copyright © G P Taylor 2003, reprinted and reproduced as audio by permission of Faber & Faber Ltd and the author c/o Caroline Sheldon Literary Agency Ltd.

Ngég Wa Thiong'o: extract from *Weep Not, Child* (Penguin SA, 2009), copyright © Ngég Wa Thiong'o, 1964, reprinted by permission of Penguin Books (South Africa) (Pty) Ltd

Dylan Thomas: 'Memories of Christmas' first published in *The Listener*, 20 December 1945, from *Quite Early One Morning* (J M Dent,1954), copyright © Dylan Thomas 1945, copyright © New Directions Publishing Corp 1954, reprinted and reproduced as audio by permission of David Higham Associates and New Directions Publishing Corp.

Jonathan Trigell: extracts from *Boy A* (Serpent's Tail, 2004), copyright © Jonathan Trigell 2004, reprinted by permission of the publishers

J R R Tolkien: extracts from *The Lord of the Rings: The Fellowship of the Ring* (Allen & Unwin, 1966), copyright © George Allen & Unwin Ltd 1966, reprinted by permission of HarperCollins Publishers Ltd.

Jennifer Viegas: extract from 'Loch Ness Monster-like animal filmed in Alaska?', *Discovery News*, 18.7.2011, reprinted by permission of Discover Communications LLC.

Jonathan Watts: extract from 'China warns of 'urgent problems'' facing Three Gorges dam, *The Guardian*, 20.5.2011, copyright © Guardian News & Media Ltd 2011, reprinted by permission of GNM Ltd.

Donovan Webster: 'The devastating costs of the Amazon gold rush', *The Smithsonian Magazine*, February 2012, copyright © Donovan Webster 2012, reprinted by permission of the author.

Virginia Wheeler: extract from 'School is a three-smile walk for Kiki', *The Sun*, 26.5.2011, reprinted by permission of the Sun/News International Syndication.

Mike Williams: extract from 'Taming the Wolf: domesticating the dog', *The Independent* 27.9.2010, copyright © The Independent 2010, reprinted by permission of Independent Print Ltd.

and to the following for permission to reprint copyright material:

Agence France-Presse for 'Powerful quake shakes southern Mexico, capital', as published in *Bangkok Post*, 21.3.2012.

Banff Lake Louise Tourism for advertisement for Banff and Lake Louise.

The British Association of Fair Trade Shops (BAFTS) for information article from www.bafts.org.uk.

Euronews S A for 'Mexico takes stock after major quake', *euronews*, 21.3.2012, copyright © euronews 2012.

Exodus Travels Ltd for advertisements for holidays in Indonesia and Antarctica..

The Fairtrade Foundation for 'Gold: Every piece tells a story' from www.fairtrade.org.uk.

International Olympics Committee for extract from www.olympic.org.

London School of Journalism for 'Freelance Journalism: Starting out in Journalism'

Madame Tussauds, London for 'From France to Britain' from www.madametussauds.com/London.

Manhattan Gold & Silver, Inc for 'Midas and the River Pactolus' at www.mgsrefining.com.

The Nobel Foundation for extract from 'The Will' and the full text of Alfred Nobel's Will, www.nobelprize.org/alfred_nobel/will and from the Swedish Academy Press release, Nobel Prize for Literature 1983, William Golding, www.nobelprize.org/nobel_prizes/literature/laureates

The Chancellor, Master and Scholars of the University of Oxford for extract from the University of Oxford Student Gateway website.

Rio Tinto Diamonds for article about selecting a diamond from www.argylediamonds.com.au, copyright © Rio Tinto 2009, and extracts from Press Releases 4.11.10 and 21.2.12

Virgin Holidays Ltd for advert for New York City holiday.

***Welcome to Chiangmai and Chiangrai* Magazine** for extract from 'Elephants at Work', www.chiangai-chiangrai.com, 16.6.2010.

Although we have made every effort to trace and contact all copyright holders before publication this has not been possible in all cases. If notified, the publisher will rectify any errors or omissions at the earliest opportunity.

Any third party use of these extracts outside of this publication in any medium is prohibited, and interested parties should apply directly to the copyright holders named in each case for permission.